Word 2002

A Tutorial to Accompany

PETER NORTON'S®

Introduction to Computers

FOURTH EDITION

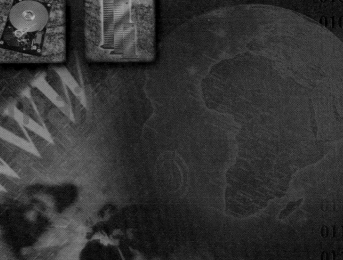

Mc Graw Hill **Glencoe McGraw-Hill**

New York, New York   Columbus, Ohio   Chicago, Illinois   Peoria, Illinois   Woodland Hills, California

Word® *2002*
A Tutorial to Accompany
Peter Norton's® *Introduction to Computers*

Glencoe/McGraw-Hill

A Division of The **McGraw·Hill** Companies

Send all inquiries to:
Glencoe/McGraw-Hill
21600 Oxnard St., Suite 500
Woodland Hills, CA 91367-4906

ISBN: 0-07-829773-7
Development: FSCreations, Inc.

Preface

Word 2002, one of the instructional tools that complements *Peter Norton's® Introduction to Computers,* covers the basic features of Word 2002. Glencoe and Peter Norton have teamed up to provide this tutorial and its ancillaries to help you become a knowledgeable, empowered end user. After you complete this tutorial, you will be able to create and modify many different types of Word documents including newsletters, business correspondence, and even Web pages.

Objectives of the *Word 2002* Tutorial

Word 2002: A Tutorial to Accompany Peter Norton's Introduction to Computers presents hands-on instruction on Word 2002. The objectives of the *Word 2002* tutorial are:

◆ To introduce the basic concepts and skills of Microsoft Office XP using Word 2002.

◆ To prepare you to become a Microsoft Office User Specialist at the Core skill level.

◆ To provide hands-on tutorial exercises and realistic applications of the new Word 2002 features.

◆ To help you develop proficiency in Word 2002 applications.

◆ To help you explore and navigate the World Wide Web, search the Internet, create a Web page, communicate via e-mail, and more.

◆ To empower you to accept responsibility for learning.

◆ To help you demonstrate the skills and knowledge you have acquired by creating a personal portfolio.

Structure and Format of the *Word 2002* Tutorial

Word 2002 covers a range of functions and techniques and provides hands-on opportunities for you to practice and apply your skills. Each lesson includes the following:

◆ **Contents, Objectives, and MOUS Skills.** The Contents and Objectives at the beginning of each lesson provide an overview of the Word features you will learn. A list of the Core level Microsoft Office User Specialist (MOUS) objectives covered in the lesson is also provided.

◆ **Explanations of Important Concepts.** Each section of each lesson begins with a brief explanation of the concept or software feature covered in that lesson. The explanations help you understand "the big picture" as you learn each new Word feature.

◆ **Word in the Workplace.** Word in the Workplace, which appears in the margin at the beginning of each lesson, presents a real-world overview on how the lesson material may be applied within an organization.

◆ **New Terms.** An important part of learning about computers is learning the terminology. Each new term in the tutorial appears in bold type and is defined in the Glossary.

◆ **Hands On Activities.** Because most of us learn best by doing, each explanation is followed by a Hands On activity that includes step-by-step instructions that you complete at the computer. Integrated in the steps are full-screen figures to guide you along the way as well as notes and warnings to help you learn more about Word.

◆ **Word Basics.** This element appears in the margin next to Hands On activities. Word Basics lists the general steps required to perform a particular task. Use the Word Basics as a reference to quickly and easily review the steps to perform a task.

◆ **Hints & Tips.** This element appears in the margin and provides tips for increasing your effectiveness while using the Word program.

◆ **Another Way.** This margin element provides alternate ways to perform a given task.

◆ **Did You Know?** Read each Did You Know?, another element that appears in the margin, to learn additional facts related to the content of the lesson or other interesting facts about computers.

◆ **Web Note.** Web Notes, also appearing in the margin, contain interesting facts and Web addresses that relate to the content of the lesson and to your exploration of the World Wide Web.

◆ **Illustrations.** Many figures are provided to point out the specific features on the screen and illustrate what your screen should look like after you complete important steps.

◆ **Using Help.** Using Help activities encourage you to access online Help to explore topics related to the lessons in more depth.

◆ **Self Check Exercises.** To check your knowledge of the concepts presented in the lesson, a Self Check exercise is provided at the end of each lesson. After completing the exercise, refer to *Appendix B: Self Check Answers* to verify your understanding of the lesson material.

◆ **On the Web.** At the end of each lesson, an On the Web section teaches you important concepts relating to the use of the World Wide Web.

◆ **Summary.** At the end of each lesson, a Summary reviews the major topics covered in the lesson. You can use the Summary as a study guide.

◆ **Concepts Review.** At the end of each lesson are four types of questions: True/False, Matching, Completion, and Short Answer; in addition, an Identification exercise provides you with an opportunity to identify screen elements relating to the lesson. Complete these objective-type exercises to review the concepts and skills that have been presented in the lesson.

◆ **Skills Review.** The Skills Review section provides guided hands-on exercises to practice each skill you learned in the lesson.

◆ **Lesson Applications.** The Lesson Applications provide additional hands-on practice. These exercises combine multiple skills learned in the lesson.

◆ **Projects.** The projects provide additional hands-on practice to apply your problem-solving and critical thinking skills. Each project allows you to apply multiple skills learned in the lesson. The Projects section contains an *On the Web* project, which reinforces the skills learned in the lesson's *On the Web* section, as well as a *Project in Progress* that builds from one lesson to the next.

◆ **Case Study.** The Case Study is a capstone activity that allows you to apply the various skills you have learned throughout the Word tutorial to plan, create, and modify Word documents.

- **Portfolio Builder, Answers to Self Check, Command Summary, and MOUS Certification Objectives.** These appendices provide a wealth of information. The Portfolio Builder gives an overview of portfolios and provides tips on creating your personal portfolio. Answers to the Self Check exercises found within each lesson are provided in Appendix B. The Command Summary (Appendix C) reviews the mouse and keyboard techniques for completing Word tasks. MOUS Certification Objectives (Appendix D) correlates the MOUS "Core-level" Word 2002 skills to this tutorial.

- **Glossary and Index.** A Glossary and an Index appear at the back of the tutorial. Use the Glossary to look up terms that you don't understand and the Index to find specific information.

- **Word Data CD.** Attached to the inside back cover of this tutorial you will find the Word Data CD. This CD contains all the files you need to complete the Hands On activities and the end-of-lesson activities in the entire tutorial. You must copy the files from the Word Data CD to a folder on your hard drive or network drive. (Instructions for copying these files from the Word Data CD are provided on pages 8–11 of this tutorial.)

New Features of Microsoft Office XP®

Below is a selective list of the new features of Microsoft Office XP:

- **Task Panes.** Using the task panes in Microsoft Office XP, you can efficiently perform varied tasks such as opening files, formatting a document, or conducting searches.

- **Speech Recognition.** You can dictate text directly into a file using speech recognition, or you can format text using voice commands.

- **Handwriting Recognition.** This feature allows you to enter handwritten text into a file using your mouse or convert your handwritten text to typed characters.

- **Ask a Question Box.** You can get immediate online help and avoid using the Office Assistant by typing your Help question directly into the Ask a Question box. (The Office Assistant is now hidden by default.)

- **Smart Tags.** The smart tags feature allows you to access contextual information directly from your file. (A smart tag typically appears embedded in your file after you complete a task such as pasting data.)

- **Microsoft Design Gallery Live.** Every Office XP user can access Clips Online and choose among thousands of images and animations available for download over the Web.

- **Document Recovery.** The Document Recovery feature removes the worry about losing your documents. If your computer should crash or a program error should occur while you are working with Office XP, the Document Recovery feature allows you to save and recover your current files.

- **Web Discussions.** Discussions about documents are now so easy. The Web Discussions feature allows you to use a Local Area Network or the Internet to discuss content of a document with other members of a team.

About Peter Norton

Acclaimed computer software entrepreneur Peter Norton is active in civic and philanthropic affairs. He serves on the boards of several scholastic and cultural institutions and currently devotes much of his time to philanthropy.

Raised in Seattle, Washington, Mr. Norton made his mark in the computer industry as a programmer and businessman. *Norton Utilities*™, *Norton AntiVirus*™, and other utility programs are installed on millions of computers worldwide. He is also a best-selling author of computer books.

Mr. Norton sold his PC-software business to Symantec Corporation in 1990 but continues to write and speak on computers, helping millions of people better understand information technology. He and his family currently reside in Santa Monica, California.

Reviewers

Many thanks are due to the following individuals who reviewed the manuscript and provided recommendations to improve this tutorial:

Kenneth Wallace
Craven Community College
New Bern, North Carolina

Rhonda Davis
Isothermal Community College
Spindale, North Carolina

Nancy Jobe
Ivy Tech State College
Evansville, Indiana

Katherine Burkhart
Star Technical Institute
Lakewood, New Jersey

Tommy Davis
Gulf Coast Community College
Panama City, Florida

Sherri Brinkley
MVC Business School
Arnold, Missouri

What Does This Logo Mean?

It means this courseware has been approved by the Microsoft® Office User Specialist Program to be among the finest available for learning *Microsoft Word 2002*. It also means that upon completion of this courseware, you may be prepared to become a Microsoft Office User Specialist.

What Is a Microsoft Office User Specialist?

A Microsoft Office User Specialist is an individual who has certified his or her skills in one or more of the Microsoft Office desktop applications of Microsoft Word, Microsoft Excel, Microsoft PowerPoint®, Microsoft Outlook® or Microsoft Access, or in Microsoft Project. The Microsoft Office User Specialist Program typically offers certification exams at the "Core" and "Expert" skill levels.* The Microsoft Office User Specialist Program is the only Microsoft approved program in the world for certifying proficiency in Microsoft Office desktop applications and Microsoft Project. This certification can be a valuable asset in any job search or career advancement.

More Information:

To learn more about becoming a Microsoft Office User Specialist, visit **www.mous.net**.

To purchase a Microsoft Office User Specialist certification exam, visit **www.DesktopIQ.com**.

To learn about other Microsoft Office User Specialist approved courseware from Glencoe/McGraw-Hill, visit **www.glencoe.com/norton**.

---

* The availability of Microsoft Office User Specialist certification exams varies by application, application version, and language. Visit **www.mous.net** for exam availability.

Microsoft, the Microsoft Office User Specialist Logo, PowerPoint, and Outlook are either registered trademarks or trademarks of Microsoft Corporation in the United States and/or other countries.

SYSTEM REQUIREMENTS FOR MICROSOFT OFFICE XP

Below is a list of the system requirements for Microsoft Office XP. For additional information, see the Microsoft Office XP Web site at **www.Microsoft.com/Office/**.

Hardware

Pentium III processor, 133-megahertz (MHz) or higher; CD-ROM drive, super VGA (800 x 600) or higher-resolution monitor with 256 colors; and compatible pointing device

Memory Requirements

◆ Windows 98 or Windows 98 Second Edition: 24 MB RAM plus 8 MB RAM for each Office program running simultaneously

◆ Windows Millennium Edition (Windows Me), or Windows NT®: 32 MB RAM plus 8 MB RAM for each Office application running simultaneously

◆ Windows 2000 Professional: 64 MB RAM plus 8 MB of RAM for each Office application running simultaneously

◆ Windows XP Professional or Windows XP Home Edition: 128 MB of RAM plus 8 MB of RAM for each Office application running simultaneously

Minimum Hard Disk Space

Note: Hard disk space requirements will vary depending upon your system configuration and custom installation choices.

Office XP Standard: 210 MB

Office XP Professional and Professional Special Edition: 245 MB

Operating System

Windows 98, Windows 98 Second Edition, Windows Millennium Edition (Windows Me), Windows NT 4.0 with Service Pac 6 (SP6) or later, Windows 2000, or Windows XP or later.

Table of Contents

Lesson 3: Advanced Document Creation 162

Publishing on the Internet

You don't need to be a mechanic in order to drive a car . . .

You can just turn the key and go! Back in the dark ages of online communication (about seven to ten years ago!), only programming experts could post information on the Internet. But now, with the right software and an Internet account, you can publish your own materials for viewing by a worldwide audience. One of the easiest and fastest ways to publish your work online is to create your own page on the World Wide Web.

The Internet isn't limited to big business—individuals, private organizations, and small companies actually publish the vast majority of materials on the Internet. The variety of online publishing opportunities is almost limitless, and people are using these opportunities to enhance their businesses, share information, entertain, and educate others.

have to be a computer whiz to create HTML documents. In fact, you don't even need to know anything about HTML! With the right tools, you can quickly create attractive, interesting pages that are ready to be published on the Web.

Do it yourself

To create a Web page, you must format a document with special tags—called Hypertext Markup Language (HTML) tags. These tags, which surround the text they affect, make the document "readable" by the Web browser, and tell it to display the text as a heading, a table, a link, normal text, and so on.

A few years ago, you would need to be (or need to hire!) a programming expert to prepare HTML tags and prepare your Web page for publication. Fortunately, now you don't

Customize your own design

Microsoft Office XP, with its suite of applications including Microsoft Word, Microsoft Excel, Microsoft Access, and Microsoft PowerPoint, can convert ordinary documents into HTML files. This feature lets you create any type of document, save it in HTML format, and then immediately open the document in a Web browser (such as Microsoft Internet Explorer). There you can see the page just as it would appear on the Internet if you published it. You can even make changes to the original documents, resave the documents in HTML format, and view your changes in your browser—without typing a single HTML tag! In addition, many desktop applications (including those in the Microsoft Office XP suite) now have tools that let you embed graphics, create hyperlinks, and add other special features to your HTML documents.

You can also create feature-rich Web pages using your Web browser. Using a browser's editing tools, you can create new pages from scratch or use predesigned templates. Here's one quick and easy way to design a Web page: Find a Web page you like, copy it to disk, and then open it in Edit mode in the browser. You then can use that page's HTML formatting as the basis for your page! Using a browser-based editor, you work directly with HTML tags only if you want to. If you prefer, Microsoft Office XP and your browser can do all the HTML formatting for you—you don't even need to "look under the hood!"

After you have created your Web pages, simply contact your Internet Service Provider (ISP). Your ISP can provide you with space on a Web server and an address where others can find your pages. Using your chosen HTML editing tools, you can update, expand, and refresh your Web site whenever you want . . . *just turn the key and go!*

Getting Started

CONTENTS

- What Is Word?
- Using the Mouse
- Starting Your Computer
- Creating Your *Word Data* Folder
- Starting the Word Program
- Exploring the Word Window
- Working With Folders and Files
- Getting Help With Word
- Exiting the Application Program and Shutting Down Your Computer
- On the Web: Getting Help on the Web

OBJECTIVES

After you complete this section, you will be able to do the following:

- ▶ Explain the purpose of the Word program.

- ▶ Use your mouse to point, click, double-click, right-click, select, and drag.

- ▶ Start and shut down your computer.

- ▶ Copy files from a CD-ROM, and change attributes of files and folders.

- ▶ Start and exit Microsoft Word.

- ▶ Name the main components of the Word window and display and hide toolbars.

- ▶ Open, scroll, name, save, close, and reopen files.

- ▶ Get help from Word's Office Assistant, ScreenTips, Ask a Question box, Answer Wizard, Contents, and Index.

- ▶ Identify buttons on the Web toolbar and get help on the Web.

- ▶ Connect to and disconnect from the Internet.

**MOUS
Objectives**
In this lesson:
W2002-4-3
See Appendix D.

So, just what is Word? Word is one of the **application programs** in the Microsoft Office suite. (Even though Word is part of the Office suite, you can purchase and use it as a stand-alone application.) Word is a powerful word processing program that enables you to create a full range of business and personal correspondence. Using Word, you can create letters, resumes, e-mail messages, and other more complex documents, such as invoices, flyers, newsletters, and Web pages. Word extends the boundaries of word processing with its ability to add graphics, charts, colors, and tables. Other Word features include step-by-step mail merge, spelling and grammar checking, and simplified table creation, to name a few.

HINTS & TIPS

Practice using the mouse until you become comfortable with it. Although keyboard alternatives exist for most mouse actions, you will be more efficient if you can use both keyboard actions and the mouse.

USING THE MOUSE

You will use the **mouse** extensively in Microsoft Word. The mouse is the key to the graphical user interface because it lets you choose and manipulate on-screen objects without having to type on the keyboard. Although the mouse is the most popular pointing device, you may also use several other pointing devices. **Trackballs** have buttons like the mouse, but instead of moving the mouse over the desktop, you spin a large ball. Laptops often employ either a small **joystick** in the middle of the keyboard or a **touch-sensitive pad** below the keyboard. Each of these devices lets you point to items on the screen and click buttons to perform actions on those items.

You can perform several actions with the mouse:

◆ An arrow on the screen pointing toward the upper left is called the **pointer** (or **mouse pointer**). Moving the mouse to position the pointer on the screen is called **pointing**.

◆ To **click** the mouse, point to an object and quickly press and release the left mouse button.

◆ To work with an object on the screen, you must usually **select** (or **choose**) the item by clicking the object—pressing and quickly releasing the mouse button.

◆ To **double-click,** point to an object and click the left mouse button twice in rapid succession without moving the pointer.

◆ To **right-click,** point to an object, press the right mouse button, and then quickly release it.

◆ To **drag** (or **drag-and-drop**), point to an object you want to move, press and hold the left mouse button, move the mouse to drag the object to a new location, and then release the mouse button.

Your mouse probably has two or three buttons. Whenever the directions in this tutorial say *click,* use the left mouse button. If you must use the right mouse button, the directions will say *right-click* or *click the right mouse button.*

STARTING YOUR COMPUTER

Microsoft Word is just one of many application programs that requires **operating system** software such as Windows 2000, Windows Millennium Edition (Windows Me), or Windows 98. The operating system software oversees every operation you perform on your computer. When you turn on your computer, the computer gives itself a complex set of instructions to start up. This start-up process is called **booting the system** or performing a **system boot,** and is derived from the expression "pulling oneself up by the bootstraps." First, a built-in program tests the computer. This **Power On Self Test (POST)** checks the memory, keyboard, display, and disk drives of the computer system. Next, files from the hard drive containing essential operating system components are loaded. Because computer systems and setups vary greatly, you may see a series of screens informing you of the progress of the startup procedure. Finally, the opening screen appears.

HANDS **on**

Booting the System

In this activity, you will start your computer and boot the operating system. All activities and figures in this tutorial were developed using the Windows 2000 operating system. If you are using a different version of Windows, the information appearing on your screen may vary slightly from the activities and figures in this tutorial.

WARNING *If Windows 2000 is not the operating system on the computer you are using, ask your instructor, computer lab assistant, or network administrator how to boot your system.*

1. Press the power button or flip the power switch to turn on the computer. If the monitor connected to the system has a separate power switch, turn on that switch as well.

2. Observe the booting process.

   a. Listen for the POST sound. A single beep means the system passed all the tests; a series of beeps indicates a hardware problem. If you hear a series of beeps, check your keyboard and monitor connections, read the message on the screen, or consult your computer manual to fix the problem. You may need technical help from the manufacturer, a lab assistant, or a technician. (Your computer may not make any sounds while booting.)

   b. Watch the screen. After a few moments, you may see a memory indicator while the system checks the random access memory. Then some information appears on the screen, followed by the Windows 2000 copyright screen. A progress indicator gives you a visual clue as to how much more of the operating system needs to be loaded into memory. The Log On to Windows screen may appear next, requesting your user name and password.

When you **log on** to a computer with Windows 2000, you inform the operating system who you are. The operating system then loads your personal settings to complete the booting process. Systems that have multiple users, such as networks, keep track of who is allowed to access the computer by assigning unique **user names** and **passwords.**

3. If you are prompted for a user name and/or password, type your user name in the User name text box and/or press ⌨Tab⌨ and type your password. If you do not know your user name and/or password, ask your instructor for help.

Asterisks appear as you type your password. This way, others who may see your log-on screen will not learn your password.

4. Click OK.

Word **BASICS**

Booting the System

1. Turn on the computer.

2. Turn on the monitor.

3. Observe the booting process.

4. Close the Getting Started with Windows 2000 window, if necessary.

NORTON

ONLINE

Visit **www.glencoe.com/norton/online/** for more information on Microsoft Word 2002.

The system completes the booting process. You may see the Getting Started with Windows 2000 window. A **window** is a rectangular on-screen frame in which you do your computing work.

> **NOTE** *When this tutorial mentions a button, a picture of the button is displayed within the text. For instance, when a step instructs you to click the Close button ▣, the button will be illustrated as shown here.*

5. If necessary, click the **Show this screen at startup check box** to clear the option to prevent the Getting Started with Windows 2000 window from appearing each time you boot your computer. Then click the **Close button ▣** in the upper-right corner of the window.

Now your screen should resemble Figure GS.1. This screen, called the Windows 2000 **desktop,** is the background for your computer work. Several **icons** (pictures) appear on the desktop. These icons represent some of the resources that are available on your system—such as programs, data files, printers, disk drives, and others. Your desktop may include a large number of icons, or just a few. The **taskbar,** the bar across the bottom of the desktop, contains **buttons** that you can click to perform various tasks.

Figure GS.1
Windows 2000 desktop

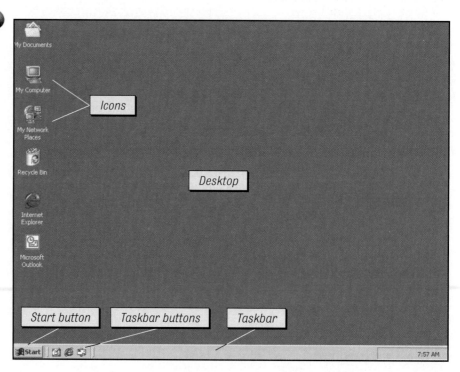

Did you know?

Windows 2000 keeps track of the date and time a file was created, the date and time a file was modified, and the date a file was last opened, as well as the file type, location, and size.

CREATING YOUR *WORD DATA* FOLDER

The data files you need to work through this tutorial are provided on the CD-ROM housed in the back of this tutorial. CD-ROMs can hold hundreds of megabytes of data; however, as their name implies *(Compact Disc-Read-Only Memory)*, you cannot modify the data they contain. Thus, before you can begin your work, you must copy the *Word Data* folder from the Data CD to a hard drive or a network drive. You'll then use the *Word Data* folder throughout the rest of the tutorial.

HANDS on

Copying Folders and Files From a CD

In this activity, you will create your *Word Data* folder by copying a folder from the Data CD (in the back of this tutorial) to a hard drive or a network drive.

> **WARNING** *Ask your instructor whether you should complete this activity. If so, confirm (1) whether to complete step 3 to change the Folder Options settings on the computer you are using and (2) the exact path and folder where you must store your* Word Data *folder.*

1. Insert the Data CD into the CD drive of your computer.

2. Click the **Start button** 🔳Start on the Windows taskbar. Then, point to **Programs**, point to **Accessories**, and click **Windows Explorer**.

The Explorer window opens and displays the name of the default location (such as My Documents) in the title bar at the top of the window. The Explorer window consists of two **panes**—the Folders pane and the Contents pane. When you click a drive icon or folder name in the Folders pane (the left pane), the **folders** (or subfolders) and files contained in that drive or folder appear in the Contents pane (the right pane).

3. If you want your Explorer window to match the activities and figures in this tutorial (and if you have permission to change the settings on the computer you are using), click **Folder Options** on the Tools menu.

   a. In the Folder Options dialog box, click the **General tab**, if it is not on top. If necessary, click the option buttons to select these settings:

   ◆ In the *Active Desktop* area, select **Use Windows classic desktop**.

   ◆ In the *Web View* area, select **Enable Web content in folders**.

   ◆ In the *Browse Folders* area, select **Open each folder in the same window**.

   ◆ In the *Click items as follows* area, select **Double-click to open an item (single-click to select)**.

   b. In the Folder Options dialog box, click the **View tab**. Click to select *only* the following options on the View tab; make sure no other options are selected on the View tab:

   ◆ Do not show hidden files and folders

   ◆ Hide file extensions for known file types

   ◆ Hide protected operating system files (Recommended)

   ◆ Show and manage the pair as a single file

   ◆ Show My Documents on the Desktop

   ◆ Show pop-up description for folder and desktop items

WORD 2002

Word BASICS

Copying Data From a CD

1. Insert the CD into the CD drive.

2. Open Windows Explorer.

3. In the Folders pane, click the CD drive icon. (If necessary, double-click the CD drive icon to expand the sublevels.)

4. In the Contents pane, click to select the folder that you want to copy.

5. Click Copy on the Edit menu.

6. In the Folders pane, click the drive/folder where you want to store the copied folders/files.

7. Click Paste on the Edit menu.

Another Way 💲

To copy the contents of one folder to another folder, select the files and/or folders to copy, and then press and hold Ctrl while you drag the files and/or folders to the desired folder.

4. Click **OK** to close the Folder Options dialog box.

5. In the Explorer window, click **List** on the View menu if it is not already selected.

6. If a plus sign (+) appears beside the My Computer icon in the Folders pane of the Explorer window, click the **plus sign** to expand the sublevels.

7. In the Folders pane, find and click the drive icon that represents your CD drive. You may need to scroll down in the Folders pane.

The contents of the Data CD, the *Word Data* folder, appear in the Contents pane, as shown in Figure GS.2.

Figure GS.2
Contents of the Data CD

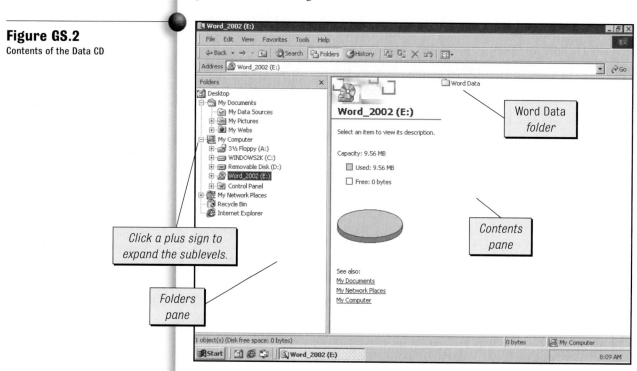

8. In the Contents pane, click the *Word Data* folder to select it.

9. Click **Copy** on the Edit menu.

10. In the Folders pane, click the appropriate drive icon (and folder, if necessary) where you want to store the *Word Data* folder.

NOTE *Check with your instructor to determine if you should create a new folder (or subfolder) in which to store the* Word Data *folder. If so, follow these steps to create a new folder: (a) Point to New on the File menu and then click Folder. (b) Type the new folder name and press* Enter⏎ *. (c) In the Contents pane, double-click the newly created folder to open it.*

11. Click **Paste** on the Edit menu.

A Copying box may appear on the screen to indicate the progress of the copying process. In a few moments, the *Word Data* folder (and all its contents) will be copied from the Data CD to the drive and/or folder you selected.

12. In the Contents pane, double-click the *Word Data* folder.

The contents of the *Word Data* folder appear, as shown in Figure GS.3. As you can see, the *Word Data* folder contains several folders and files. You'll store your work in these folders as you progress through the tutorial.

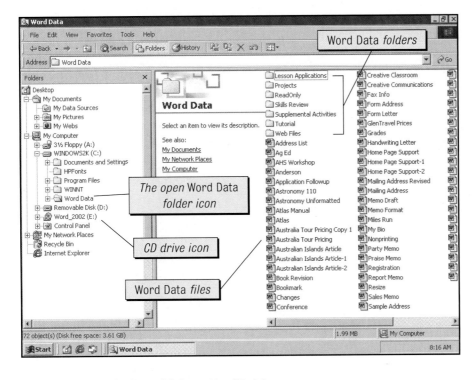

13. Remove the Data CD from the CD drive.

Setting File Attributes

An **attribute** is a property that controls the use of a file or folder. By nature of the storage medium on which they reside, CD-ROM files and folders have a *read-only* attribute, which allows you to view files, but not write to them. To actually use and save changes to the files you copied from the Data CD, you must remove the *read-only* attribute. In this activity, you will change the attributes of the files and folders in your *Word Data* folder.

NOTE *Ask your instructor if you should complete this activity.*

1. In the Folders pane of the Explorer window, right-click the *Word Data* folder.

WARNING *Carefully confirm that you have right-clicked the correct folder on your computer. You don't want to change the file and folder attributes of the wrong folder on your computer.*

Visit **www.glencoe.com/norton/online/** for more information on Microsoft Word 2002.

2. On the shortcut menu that appears, click **Properties**.

The Word Data Properties dialog box appears with the General tab on top.

3. In the *Attributes* area of the Word Data Properties dialog box, click to clear the **Read-only check box** (see Figure GS.4).

Figure GS.4
General tab of the Word Data
Properties dialog box

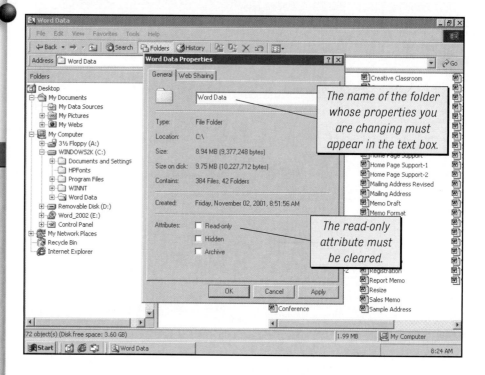

The name of the folder whose properties you are changing must appear in the text box.

The read-only attribute must be cleared.

Word BASICS

Setting File Attributes

1. Open Windows Explorer, and navigate to the folder or file whose attributes you want to change.

2. In the Folders pane of the Explorer window, right-click the selected file or folder.

3. On the shortcut menu, click Properties.

4. In the *Attributes* area of the Properties dialog box for the selected folder/file, click to clear and/or select the check boxes for the desired attributes.

5. Click Apply.

6. In the Confirm Attribute Changes dialog box, click the desired option to apply; then click OK.

7. Click OK to close the Properties dialog box.

8. Close the Explorer window.

4. Click **Apply**.

The Confirm Attribute Changes dialog box appears asking whether you want to unset (or remove) the read-only attribute and apply the changes to only the selected folder *or* whether you want to apply these changes to the selected folder, subfolders, and files.

5. Click the **Apply changes to this folder, subfolders and files option** and click **OK**.

6. Click **OK** to close the Word Data Properties dialog box.

You have successfully removed the read-only file attributes from the files and folders in your *Word Data* folder. You are now ready to begin working with the *Word* tutorial.

7. Click the **Close button** ☒ in the upper-right corner of the Explorer window.

The Explorer window closes and you return to the Windows desktop.

STARTING THE WORD PROGRAM

Before you can start Word, both Word and Windows 98 (or higher version) must be installed on the computer you are using. When Word is installed on a computer, the program is added to the Programs menu so that you can use the Start button [Start] to launch it. Therefore, to start Word, you simply click the Start button [Start], point to Programs, and click Microsoft Word. After a few moments, Word is launched and its window appears.

Using the Start Button to Launch Word

In this activity, you will start Word using the Start button [Start].

1. **Click the Start button** [Start] **on the Windows taskbar.**

2. **Point to Programs. If necessary, click the double arrow at the bottom of the menu to list all items on the Programs menu.**

The Programs menu appears; it should look similar to Figure GS.5. Depending on the applications installed on your computer, your Programs menu may be different from Figure GS.5.

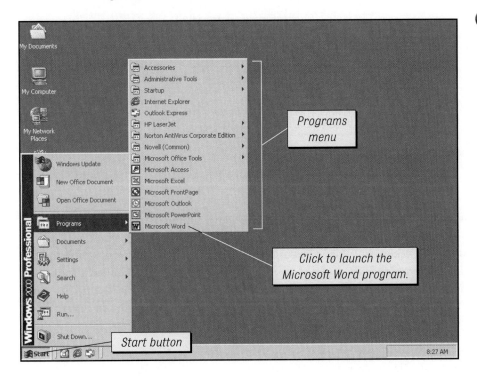

3. **Click Microsoft Word.**

The Word program starts and its window appears.

Launching Word

1. Click the Start button.

2. Point to Programs, and click Microsoft Word.

Figure GS.5
Programs menu

Another Way

You can start Word by clicking New Office Document on the Start menu. Click the General tab in the New Office Document dialog box, click Blank Document, and click OK.

WORD 2002

EXPLORING THE WORD WINDOW

The Word **application window** is shown in Figure GS.6. Your window may look slightly different, because Word allows users to **customize,** or alter, the Word window to suit individual needs. The Word window contains many standard Windows elements, including a title bar; the Minimize, Restore Down, and Close buttons; a menu bar; and one or more toolbars. These items should seem familiar if you have ever used a Windows 98, Windows 2000, or Windows Me application.

NOTE *The Language bar, which provides tools for handwriting and speech recognition, will appear in the upper-right corner of the application window if it has been installed on the computer you are using. To close the Language bar, point to the bar, right-click, and click Close the Language bar on the shortcut menu.*

Figure GS.6
Word application window

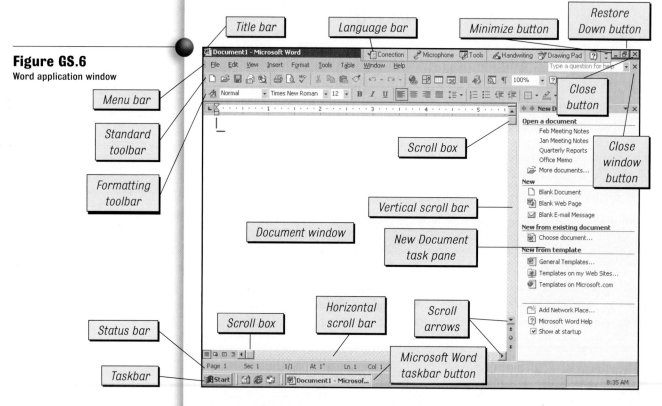

Across the bottom of the screen is the taskbar, including the Start button and other buttons for **navigating** Windows. Buttons on the taskbar show which applications are open. When the Word taskbar button is active, you know that Word is ready to use. Across the top of the screen, the **title bar** shows the name of the application and the name of the current file. Word, by **default,** gives a temporary name of *Document* followed by a unique number to each unsaved file. In Figure GS.6, the default file name is *Document1.*

Working With Menus and Commands

As shown in Figure GS.6, the Word **menu bar** appears below the title bar. The menu bar displays menu names found in most Windows applications, such as File, Edit, and Help. Word also includes menus just for word processing, such as the Table menu. Table GS.1 provides a brief description of the menus available on the Word menu bar.

Table GS.1	The Word Menu Bar
Menu	**Contains Commands That Let You . . .**
File	Control your files by opening, saving, printing, and closing them.
Edit	Locate and rearrange elements within a file by finding, copying, moving, and deleting them.
View	View files in different ways; display and hide toolbars and the task pane; and insert headers and footers.
Insert	Insert various elements into your files.
Format	Change the appearance of the elements within a file.
Tools	Use special tools, such as spelling, online collaboration, Web tools, and automatic correction features.
Table	Insert, fill-in, and format an arrangement of columns and rows as tabular information in files.
Window	Work with multiple files at once, in one or more windows.
Help	Access the online Help system, the Microsoft Office Assistance Center home page on the Web, and the Detect and Repair feature.

Menus list the **commands** available in the application. To display a menu's commands, click a menu name on the menu bar or press [Alt] on the keyboard plus the underlined letter in the menu name. The application will display a **short menu,** a list of the most basic commands, with arrows at the bottom. If you either hold the pointer on the menu name or point to the arrows at the bottom of the menu for a few seconds, or if you click the arrows, an **expanded menu** appears. This expanded menu shows all commands available on that menu. The most basic commands appear when a menu opens; when the list expands, less common commands appear also. Figure GS.7 shows both versions of Word's Tools menu—as a short menu and an expanded menu.

After you use one of the additional commands from the expanded menu, Word adds that command to the short menu. This feature enables you to **personalize** the menus; Word automatically customizes menus as you work, placing the commands that you use often on the short menu.

After you display a menu, you can choose a command by clicking the desired command or by pressing the underlined letter in the command name. An ellipsis (. . .) after a command indicates that choosing the command will display a **dialog box** in which you may specify details. Pointing to a command that has an arrow to the right of it displays another list of commands called a **submenu.**

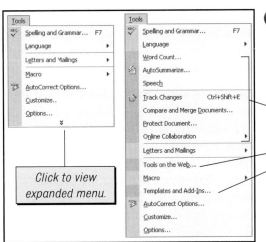

Click to view expanded menu.

Figure GS.7
Short and expanded Tools menus in Word

The expanded Tools menu shows more commands.

Working With Toolbars and Buttons

Below the menu bar are Word's Standard and Formatting toolbars, as shown in Figure GS.6 on page 14. A **toolbar** contains buttons for many of the most frequently used commands. Although you can access these commands on one of the menus, clicking a toolbar button is often more convenient. You can quickly identify any toolbar button by pointing to it and reading the name that appears below it in a small text box called a ScreenTip.

NOTE *For the activities and figures in this tutorial, the Standard and Formatting toolbars are displayed on two separate rows. If your Standard and Formatting toolbars share one row below the menu bar, you can display them as two separate rows by clicking Customize on the Tools menu. On the Options tab of the Customize dialog box, click to select the* Show Standard and Formatting toolbars on two rows *option and click Close. If you don't see a ScreenTip when you point to a toolbar button, click Customize on the Tools menu. On the Options tab of the Customize dialog box, click to select the* Show ScreenTips on toolbars *option and click Close.*

The icon on each toolbar button symbolizes the command. For example, on the Standard toolbar, the New Blank Document button 🗋 is symbolized by a piece of paper. As with the menus, you can also customize the toolbars. The most basic buttons appear on the main toolbar, while buttons used less often are accessible by clicking Toolbar Options ▪ at the end of a toolbar and navigating to the Toolbar Options list. If a button appears on the list but does not appear on the toolbar, you can open the Toolbar Options list and click the button to place a check mark beside it; Word then adds the button to the toolbar. To remove a button from the toolbar, open the Toolbar Options list and click the button to clear its check mark.

The Formatting toolbar appears directly below the Standard toolbar, as shown in Figure GS.6 on page 14. This toolbar includes commands for controlling the appearance of various elements within a file. For instance, using the Formatting toolbar, you can modify the font size and style, alignment, color, and other features that affect appearance.

In addition to the Standard and Formatting toolbars, Word includes other toolbars, such as Drawing, Task Pane, and Web, to name a few. As their names imply, each toolbar includes specific commands to serve a unique purpose; for instance, the Web toolbar includes commands that allow you to access a Web site and navigate the Web efficiently. To display or hide the various toolbars, point to Toolbars on the View menu to access the Toolbars submenu. A check mark next to a toolbar name indicates that toolbar is displayed. To hide a toolbar, click the toolbar name to clear the check mark; to display a toolbar, click the toolbar name to insert the check mark.

Another Way

To display toolbars as separate rows, click the Toolbar Options button ▪ and click Show Buttons on Two Rows.

HINTS & TIPS

- To move a toolbar left or right, point to the handle on the left end. When the four-way arrow appears, drag the toolbar.

- You can drag a toolbar handle to place a toolbar on another part of the screen. For example, you can "dock" a toolbar by attaching it to the left or right edge of the application window, or you can make the toolbar "float" by releasing it somewhere else in the application window.

WORD 2002

Working With the Status Bar and Scroll Bars

The **status bar** is the horizontal area that appears at the bottom of the application window just above the Windows taskbar. (See Figure GS.6 on page 14.) On the left side of the status bar, Word provides information about a selected command, an operation in progress, or other information about the program. The right side of the status bar contains status indicators that turn special keys or modes (Overtype, for example) on or off. These indicator buttons display darkened when turned on and dimmed when off. Just double-click the status indicator to toggle the particular key.

> **NOTE** *If the status bar or scroll bars are not visible on your screen, click Options on the Tools menu. If necessary, click the View tab in the Options dialog box. Then, in the Options dialog box (View tab), click to select Status bar, Horizontal scroll bar, and Vertical scroll bar. Click OK to close the Options dialog box.*

Oftentimes a window on your screen, such as a dialog box, a Help window, or the application window, may contain more information than you can view at one time. As you work, you can move around in a window to bring the hidden portions into view. You can perform this procedure, called **scrolling,** using the scroll bars, scroll arrows, and scroll box. (See Figure GS.6 on page 14.) Use the **vertical scroll bar** to move up and down in a window, and use the **horizontal scroll bar** to move from side to side. Clicking the **scroll arrows** at each end of the bar, dragging the **scroll box** within the bar, or clicking between the scroll box and a scroll arrow allows you to navigate within a window at varying speeds. In some dialog boxes and windows, scroll bars will automatically appear when you need them so that you can display information that is hidden from view.

Working With the Task Pane

After you launch Word, notice a task pane on the right side of the application window. A **task pane** is a window that provides quick access to commonly used commands and features while you work with your file. There are eight different task panes in Word. The New Document task pane (shown in Figure GS.8) appears by default each time you open Word. (If the task pane is not visible, right-click any toolbar and click to select Task Pane on the Toolbars submenu that appears.) Options in a task pane that appear in colored text are **hyperlinks.** When you point to a hyperlink, the text is underlined and the pointer changes to the shape of a hand. Then, when clicked, the hyperlink activates an appropriate command or feature. For instance, if you click <u>Black Document</u> in the New Document task pane, Word opens a new, blank document.

Because task pane options are also commands on menus, a task pane may open when you choose a particular menu command. For instance, clicking New on the File menu will open the New Document task pane. Clicking Office Clipboard on

HINTS & TIPS

If your mouse has a wheel, learn to use the wheel to scroll vertically.

Another Way

- To scroll in a window or dialog box, use the arrow keys on the keyboard. Pressing an arrow key moves the insertion point in the indicated direction.

- To move immediately to the beginning of a file, press `Ctrl` + `Home`.

- To move immediately to the end of a file, press `Ctrl` + `End`.

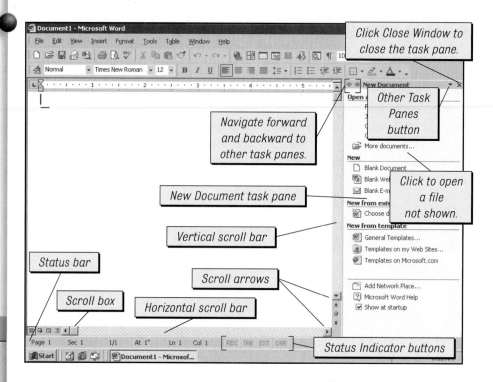

If Microsoft Word stops responding while you are working with a file, don't panic. Close and restart Microsoft Word. In the Document Recovery task pane, you can open the file, see the repairs that Word made, and compare the versions that Word recovered. Then, you can save the best version of the file and delete the other versions.

the Edit menu will open the Clipboard task pane. To display the list of available task panes, click the Other Task Panes button ▼ in the task pane. You can manually open another task pane by choosing from the task panes list. Or, during each computer session, you can also use the Back button ◄ and Forward button ► in the task pane to move to the task panes you have recently accessed.

You can easily change the width of the task pane to allow more space for your work in the application window. To resize the task pane, point to the left edge of the task pane until you see a two-headed arrow. Click and drag the task pane to the left or right to the desired width. To close the task pane, click its Close button ☒.

HANDS on

Working in the Application Window

In this activity, you will explore your application window.

1. Click View on the menu bar.

The short View menu displays.

2. Click the arrows at the bottom of the View menu.

The expanded View menu displays all the commands on the View menu.

3. Point to Toolbars on the View menu.

The Toolbars submenu lists the common toolbars. A check mark appears next to the toolbars that are currently displayed.

Another Way

To open the Toolbars submenu, right-click anywhere on the menu bar, on any visible toolbar, or on the title area of the task pane.

4. If a check mark appears before **Standard** in the Toolbars submenu, go on to step 5. If a check mark does not appear, click **Standard**.

The Toolbars submenu closes and the Standard toolbar is displayed.

5. If check marks do not appear before **Formatting** and **Task Pane** in the Toolbars submenu, click to select the two toolbar options. (You must redisplay the Toolbars submenu each time you select or clear a toolbar on the Toolbars submenu.)

6. On the Toolbars submenu, click to clear any other toolbars that are currently displayed. If necessary, click a blank area of the application window to close the Toolbars submenu and the View menu.

7. In the task pane, click the **Close button** ☒ to hide the New Document task pane.

The document area enlarges to fill the screen.

8. Verify that the Standard and Formatting toolbars are displayed as separate rows, as shown in Figure GS.8 on page 18. If the toolbars are on the same row, click **Customize** on the Tools menu, click the **Options tab** if it is not on top, and click to select **Show Standard and Formatting toolbars on two rows**. Click the **Close button** in the Customize dialog box.

9. Point to the **Microsoft Word Help button** ⍰ on the Standard toolbar, and read the ScreenTip. As your time permits, point to other buttons on the toolbars and read the ScreenTips.

10. Click **New** on the File menu.

The New Document task pane reappears.

Word **BASICS**

Exploring the Word Window

1. Point to Toolbars on the View menu.

2. On the Toolbars submenu, click to select or clear a toolbar.

3. Click Customize on the Tools menu.

4. On the Options tab of the Customize dialog box, click to select or clear *Show Standard and Formatting toolbars on two rows*. Click Close.

5. Point to toolbar buttons and read the names of the buttons.

WORKING WITH FOLDERS AND FILES

Any time you want to use a **file** that you or someone else created, you must first **open** it. Opening a file means copying that file from disk into the memory of your computer so that you can update or view it. There are several ways to open a Word file: you can click the Open button 🖿 on the Standard toolbar, click the Open command on the File menu, or click *More documents* in the New Document task pane. In each instance, the Open dialog box is displayed, where you specify the drive, folder, and file that you want to open.

HANDS on

Opening a File

In this activity, you will open the *Creative Communications* file in your *Word Data* folder.

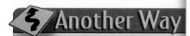

WORD 2002

Opening a File

1. Click the Open button on the Standard toolbar.

2. In the Open dialog box, click the appropriate drive/folder in the Look in box.

3. Double-click the folder, if necessary, in which the files are stored.

4. Click the desired file and click the Open button in the Open dialog box.

Figure GS.9

Open dialog box

Did u know?

You can resize the Open and Save dialog boxes. Point to a corner of the dialog box until you see a two-headed arrow. Click and drag diagonally to the desired size.

---

1. Click the **Open button** 📂 on the Standard toolbar.

The Open dialog box appears. The Look in box shows the current folder or drive.

> **WARNING** *If you're sharing a computer with one or more users in a lab or school environment, the list of files displayed in the Open dialog box may not contain the file you wish to open. Continue with steps 2 through 4 to properly navigate to your files.*

2. In the Open dialog box, verify that the *Files of type* list box is set to **All Word Documents**.

3. Click the **Look in triangle button** to display a list of the available drives.

4. In the list of drives, click the drive that contains your *Word Data* folder. In the list of folders/files that appears, click the *Word Data* folder to select it and click the **Open button** in the lower-right corner of the Open dialog box.

> **NOTE** *If your* Word Data *folder is not stored at the root level of the drive, you must navigate to it. If necessary, ask your instructor or lab assistant for assistance in locating your folders and files.*

Below the Look in box, you now see a list of the folders and files contained in the *Word Data* folder, as shown in Figure GS.9.

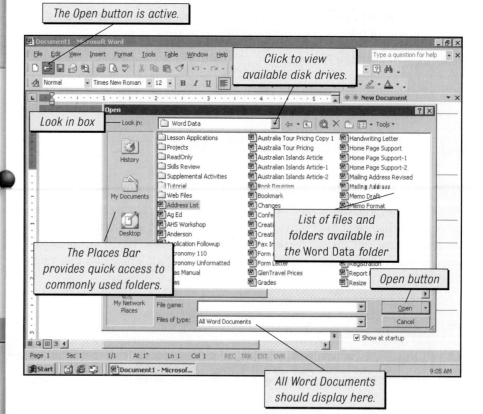

5. Click *Creative Communications* in the list of file names, and click the **Open button** in the dialog box.

The New Document task pane closes and the *Creative Communications* file opens.

6. On the vertical scroll bar, drag the scroll box to the bottom of the bar.

The information contained at the end of the file becomes visible in the application window.

7. On the horizontal scroll bar, click the left scroll arrow several times, and watch the window scroll to the left.

8. Press `Ctrl` + `Home` to jump to the beginning of the file, and press `Ctrl` + `End` to jump to the end of the file. Finally, press `Ctrl` + `Home` again to return to the beginning of the file.

Saving a File

After working with a file for a few minutes, you should **save** it. Saving a file transfers its contents from the computer's memory to disk for you to retrieve later. It's important to save your work frequently in case something goes wrong with the computer. For example, if you have not saved your file and your computer malfunctions or a power outage occurs, portions or all of your work may be lost.

As you have already learned, Word names a new, unsaved file *Document* followed by a unique number (for example, *Document1*) as the default file name. When you save a file, you should give the file a meaningful name so you can determine at a glance what information the file contains. Besides naming a file, you also must specify where to store the file (the drive and **path**). A file name, including the drive and path, can contain up to 215 characters, including spaces. The file name, however, may not include any of the following characters: \ / : * ? " < > | .

When you save a new file for the first time, the Save As dialog box appears—whether you click the Save button on the Standard toolbar or choose either the Save or the Save As commands on the File menu. However, after you've initially named and saved a file, issuing the Save command either from the File menu or by clicking the Save button automatically updates the file on disk with the version currently in memory, without redisplaying the Save As dialog box.

If you want to save a copy of the file with a different name and/or in a different place, you must click the Save As command on the File menu. When you do this, the Save As dialog box appears so that you can specify a new file name, location, or file type. Note that when you use the Save As command, you are not renaming a file. Instead, you're saving a copy of the file under a different name, in a different place, or as a different file type. The original file with the original name, location, and file type will not be deleted, moved, or renamed.

HANDS on

Naming and Saving a File

In this activity, you will save *Creative Communications* in a different location and with a different file name in your *Word Data* folder.

1. Click **Save As** on the File menu.

The Save As dialog box appears.

2. If your *Word Data* folder does not appear in the Save in box of the Save As dialog box, click the **Save in triangle button**, click the name of the drive in which your *Word Data* folder is stored from the drop-down list (and, if necessary, double-click the folder in which the *Word Data* folder is stored). Then, double-click the *Word Data* folder to open it.

3. Click the *Tutorial* folder in the window below the Save in box, and click the **Open button** in the Save As dialog box.

The *Tutorial* folder opens and appears in the Save in box.

4. In the File name box, edit the file name to be *Creative Communications-Explored* as shown in Figure GS.10. Then click the **Save button** in the Save As dialog box.

Word saves the file in a different folder with a different name. Now the newly created file is displayed in the application window, and the title bar and the taskbar button show the new file name.

Word BASICS

Naming and Saving a File

To save a file with the same name and in the same location:

- Click the Save button on the Standard toolbar.

To save a file with a new name and/or in a different location:

1. Click Save As on the File menu.

2. In the Save As dialog box, select the drive/folder in the Save in box.

3. Type a name for the file in the File name box.

4. Click the Save button in the Save As dialog box.

Figure GS.10

Saving a file in the *Tutorial* folder

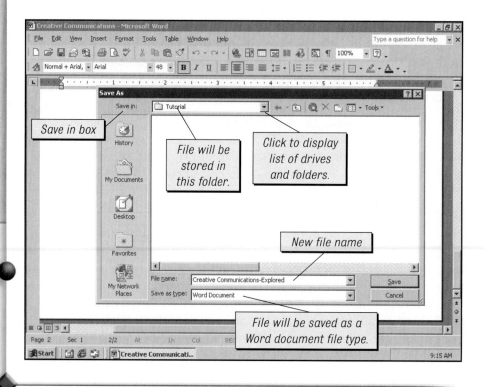

Closing and Reopening Files

When you are finished working with a file, you should **close** the file—just like you put away file folders at the office when you're finished using them. Closing a file removes it from memory, but leaves the application program running. Technically, you do not need to close one file to open another because Word lets you have several files open at once. However, to free up more memory, it's a good idea to close files that you are no longer using.

When a file is open, two Close buttons are displayed on the screen: one for the file on the *menu bar* and one for the application program on the *title bar*. When closing a file, make sure you click the correct Close button. Clicking the Close Window button ☒ on the menu bar will close the open file, whereas, clicking the Close button ☒ on the title bar will close the application program—so be careful!

NOTE *When more than one file is open, it is possible to click the title bar's Close button to close the displayed file without closing the application program, which can be confusing. However, you can add a Close button ⬚ to the Standard toolbar; using this button avoids the problem of accidentally closing the application program when you intend to only close a file. (You can add a Close button to the Standard toolbar by accessing the Customize dialog box [Commands tab] through the Tools menu.)*

If you've used a file recently, you can reopen that file by choosing the file name from the list of recently opened files that appears in the *Open a document* area of the task pane or near the bottom of the File menu. By default, Word lists the last four files you've opened.

HANDS on

Closing and Reopening a File

In this activity, you will close *Creative Communications-Explored* and then reopen the file.

1. Click the **Close Window button** ☒ at the right end of the menu bar. If you receive a message asking whether you want to save the changes, click **No**.

Word closes the file, clearing the document window completely.

2. Click **File** on the menu bar.

The name of the file you just closed appears near the bottom of the menu, and it is listed first, as shown in Figure GS.11.

3. To reopen *Creative Communications-Explored,* click its file name near the bottom of the File menu.

The file reappears in the application window.

Closing and Reopening a File

To close a file:

1. Click the Close Window button on the menu bar.

2. Respond to the Save prompt, if necessary.

To reopen a file:

Click the file name at the bottom of the File menu.

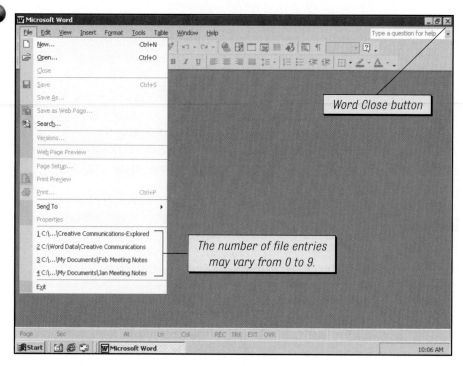

WORD 2002

To close a file, click Close on the File menu.

Did you know?

To immediately display all the information on a Help topic, click the Show All hyperlink in the Help window, if there is one.

HINTS & TIPS

You can print a Help topic by first displaying the topic and then clicking the Print button in the Help window.

Did you know?

You can turn off the Office Assistant when you likely will not need help. On the Help menu, click Hide the Office Assistant, and the Office Assistant will disappear.

GETTING HELP WITH WORD

While you are using Word, you may need to reference the extensive **online Help system**—an electronic manual that you can open with the press of a key or the click of a mouse. Word provides several different Help tools: the Office Assistant, ScreenTips, the Ask a Question box, the Answer Wizard, the Contents, and the Index.

While using the Help system, you will see many hyperlinks that provide details about a topic. When clicked, most of the hyperlinks expand to reveal explanatory text. Some hyperlinks may link to other Help frames with related topics or to Web sites. Pictures, graphic elements, and objects may also contain hyperlinks. In the Help window, you can click the hyperlink again to hide or collapse the expanded Help information.

Within a Help window, you may also see words in a sentence that are in colored text. These words are **glossary terms** and are also hyperlinks. Click the glossary term to display its definition (in green text in parentheses immediately following the term); click the term or the definition again to hide the definition.

Using the Office Assistant and ScreenTips

You can access most of the Help tools through the **Office Assistant,** an animated character that can answer specific questions, offer tips, and provide help for the program's features—sometimes even before you ask. You can activate the Office Assistant by clicking the animated character on your screen (if visible), by clicking the Microsoft Word Help button [?] on the Standard toolbar, by clicking the

Microsoft Word Help command on the Help menu, by clicking the Microsoft Word Help hyperlink in the New Document task pane, or by clicking the Show the Office Assistant command on the Help menu.

In addition to accessing the Office Assistant through the Help menu, you can also access **ScreenTips**—helpful text boxes that provide information on various program elements. When you click *What's This?* on the Help menu, the pointer changes to a question mark pointer. While the question mark pointer is displayed, you can click an element on the screen—a menu command, a toolbar button, or another element—to see its description. Click anywhere on the screen to remove the ScreenTip.

Using the Ask a Question Box

The **Ask a Question** box at the right end of the menu bar allows you to quickly access Help topics. You simply click the Ask a Question box and type a word, phrase, or question, press Enter, and select one of the Help topics that appear. You can then explore to find the answer to your question. You can revisit Help topics you've recently explored by clicking the Ask a Question triangle button and then clicking a topic in the drop-down list.

HANDS on

Asking for Help

In this activity, you will explore Help using ScreenTips, the Office Assistant, and the Ask a Question box.

1. With *Creative Communications-Explored* open, click **What's This?** on the Help menu.

The pointer changes to a question mark pointer.

2. Click the **Open button** on the Standard toolbar, and read the ScreenTip that appears.

3. Click anywhere on the screen to remove the ScreenTip. As your time permits, use *What's This?* to explore other elements of the application window.

4. If the Office Assistant is not currently displayed in the application window, click **Show the Office Assistant** on the Help menu. Then click the **Office Assistant**.

The Office Assistant asks what you would like to do.

5. In the Office Assistant balloon, type print a Help topic, as shown in Figure GS.12. Then click the **Search button**.

The Office Assistant lists the topics you could explore for your answer.

Word BASICS

Using ScreenTips

1. Click *What's This?* on the Help menu.

2. Click the screen element you wish to identify.

3. Click anywhere to remove the ScreenTip.

Another Way

- Press F1 to display the Office Assistant.

- Press Shift + F1 to access ScreenTips.

Word BASICS

Using the Office Assistant and the Ask a Question Box

To use the Office Assistant:

1. Click Show the Office Assistant on the Help menu.

2. Click the Office Assistant.

3. In the Office Assistant balloon, type a search topic.

4. Click the Search button.

5. Click the topic that best describes the help you wish to obtain.

6. Read the text in the Help window.

To use the Ask a Question box:

1. In the Ask a Question box, type a topic to describe the help you wish to obtain.

2. Press Enter↵.

3. Click the desired Help topic.

4. Read the text in the Help window.

---

6. Click the **Print a Help topic option**.

A Help window appears on your screen.

7. If the Office Assistant balloon is still visible, click the **Office Assistant character** to close the balloon.

8. In the Help window, point to the **Print the current topic** option.

As you point, the pointer changes to a hand and the words become underlined because this text is a hyperlink.

9. Click the **Print the current topic** hyperlink.

Specific information about printing a Help topic is displayed in the Help window, as shown in Figure GS.13.

10. Read the Help information.

11. Click the **Print a collection of topics** hyperlink and read the Help information that appears.

12. Click the two hyperlinks to hide the Help information on those topics.

13. Click the **Close button** 🗙 in the Help window.

14. Click the **Ask a Question box** located at the right end of the menu bar, type find a file, and press Enter↵. In the drop-down list of topics you could explore, click the **Find a file topic**.

A Help window displays information about finding files.

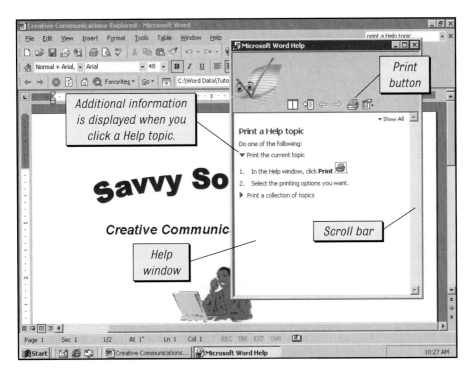

15. Click the **Show All** hyperlink at the top of the Help window.

All of the Help information for the *Find a file* topic is revealed. (Note, too, that the Show All hyperlink has now become the Hide All hyperlink.) As you scroll down the Help window, notice that the natural language searches hyperlink is a glossary term, and its definition appears in green text immediately after the term.

16. Click the glossary term or its definition to hide the definition.

17. Click the **Hide All hyperlink.** (You may need to scroll to the top of the Help window to display the Hide All hyperlink.)

HANDS on

Using the Answer Wizard, Contents, and Index

Sometimes the Help topics that appear when you use the Office Assistant or the Ask a Question box do not completely answer the questions you may have. To perform a more extensive search of the online Help system, you can use these Help tools: the Answer Wizard, Contents, and Index. The **Answer Wizard** can answer specific questions in the same manner as the Office Assistant; however, it provides many more topics from which to choose for further exploration. You can use the **Contents** to view a listing of general Help topics; this method can be useful if you don't know the name of a feature. You can search for specific words or phrases or choose from a list of keywords in the **Index.** In this activity, you will continue to explore Help using the Answer Wizard, Contents, and Index.

WEB NOTE

If the Office Assistant does not provide a topic that answers your question, click the *None of the above, search for more on the Web* option. A new Help window appears that allows you to connect to the Web to obtain further help. Or, you can click *Office on the Web* on the Help menu to go directly to the Microsoft Office Assistance Center site.

Visit **www.glencoe.com/norton/online/** for more information on Microsoft Word 2002.

1. If necessary, click the **Show button** 🔲 in the Help window.

The Help window expands, revealing the navigation pane, which contains the Contents, Answer Wizard, and Index tabs. Note, too, that the Show button changes to a Hide button 🔲.

> **NOTE** *If the navigation pane of the Help window is somewhat narrow, the Answer Wizard tab may not be visible. In this instance, click the directional arrows near the tabs until you see the Answer Wizard tab.*

2. Click the **Answer Wizard tab**, if it is not on top.

3. In the *What would you like to do?* box in the navigation pane, highlight the existing text *(Type your question here and then click Search),* if it is not already selected. (You can triple-click to quickly highlight the existing text.) Then, type team Web site and click the **Search** button.

Topics that may answer your question appear in the *Select topic to display* box. The first topic is selected and the related Help information appears in the right pane.

4. In the *Select topic to display* box, click the **Create a team Web site topic**, as shown in Figure GS.14.

5. Read the Help information.

6. Click the **Contents tab**, scroll to the top of the navigation pane, if necessary, and double-click the closed book icon in front of the Getting Started with Microsoft Office category.

The closed book icon changes to an open book icon, and the category expands to show an individual Help topic (indicated by a question mark icon) and a subcategory (indicated by another book icon). The pane on the right still shows the previous search results.

7. In the navigation pane, double-click the **Getting Help subcategory**.

8. When the subcategory expands, click the <u>**About getting help while you work**</u> topic.

The Help topic's information appears in the right pane of the Help window.

9. Click the **Back button** 🔲.

The Help information on the previous topic reappears.

Word BASICS

Using the Answer Wizard and Contents

To use the Answer Wizard:

1. Click the Show button in the Help window, if necessary.

2. Click the Answer Wizard tab in the navigation pane, if necessary.

3. In the *What would you like to do?* box, type a search topic.

4. Click the Search button.

5. In the *Select topic to display* box, click the topic you want to read.

To use the Contents tab:

1. Click the Show button in the Help window, if necessary.

2. Click the Contents tab in the navigation pane, if necessary.

3. Double-click the book in front of the Help category you wish to open.

4. Double-click a subcategory or click a topic you wish to read.

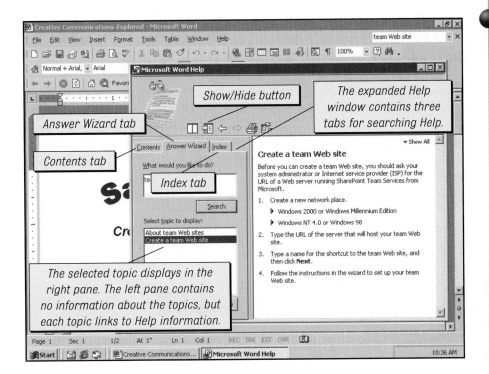

WORD 2002

Word BASICS

Using the Index Tab

1. Click the Show button in the Help window, if necessary.

2. Click the Index tab in the navigation pane, if necessary.

3. In the *Type keywords* box, type one or more keywords.

4. Click the Search button.

5. If desired, double-click an entry in the *Or choose keywords* box to narrow your search.

6. In the *Choose a topic* box, click the topic you wish to read.

10. Click the **Index tab** and type **menu** in the *Type keywords* box.

As you type each letter, the highlight within the *Or choose keywords* box jumps to the next word that contains the letter you just typed. In this instance, Help jumps to *menu*.

11. Click the **Search button**.

The results of the search are listed in the *Choose a topic* box, and the first topic is displayed in the right pane of the Help window.

12. In the *Or choose keywords* box, scroll to the word *customize* and double-click it so that both *menu* and *customize* appear in the *Type keywords* box.

The list of topics that contain both keywords appears in the *Choose a topic* box; as you can see, a two-word (or phrase) search results in fewer topics than a one-word (or phrase) search.

13. Click the **Hide button** 🔲; then click the **Close button** ✖ in the Help window.

14. Click **Hide the Office Assistant** on the Help menu.

15. Click the **Close Window button** ✖ on the menu bar to close *Creative Communications-Explored*. If a dialog box appears asking if you want to save changes to the file, click **No**.

HINTS & TIPS

In the Help window, click the Auto Tile feature to arrange or tile an open file, the task pane, and the Help window. Then, to activate any area on the screen, click the desired location. Click Untile to turn off the Auto Tile feature.

EXITING THE APPLICATION PROGRAM AND SHUTTING DOWN YOUR COMPUTER

When you are finished with an application program, you should exit the program properly. Failure to close an application can lead to problems the next time you want to start it. Exiting the program closes any open files and removes the application program from computer memory. You can exit Word by clicking the title bar's Close button ☒ or by clicking the Exit command on the File menu. After exiting Word, you may choose to shut down your computer if you have no other programs running.

WARNING *Check with your instructor or computer lab assistant for the "shut down" procedures in your lab or school environment.*

HANDS on

Exiting Word and Shutting Down

In this activity, you will exit the application program and shut down the computer you are using, following the procedures for your lab or school environment.

1. Click the Close button ☒ on the title bar.

Word disappears from the screen, and you return to the Windows desktop.

2. Follow the "shut down" procedures for your lab or school environment or continue with step 3.

NOTE *If you plan to proceed directly to the* On the Web *activity, do not shut down your computer at this time.*

3. Click the Start button ⊞ Start.

4. Click Shut Down.

The entire screen darkens a bit, and the Shut Down Windows dialog box appears.

5. Click the Shut down option in the drop-down list (if it isn't already selected) and click OK.

After a few moments, a message may appear, indicating that you may turn off your computer.

6. Turn off your computer and the monitor, if necessary.

Word BASICS

Exiting Word and Shutting Down
To exit Word:

- Click the title bar Close button or click Exit on the File menu.

To shut down your computer:

1. Click Start.

2. Click Shut Down.

3. In the Shut Down Windows dialog box, click Shut Down and click OK.

4. If a message appears, turn off your computer and monitor.

Self Check

Test your knowledge by answering the following questions. See Appendix B to check your answers.

T   F   **1.** Both toolbars and menus can be customized for individual users.

T   F   **2.** To start Word, click the Start button, point to Programs, and click Microsoft Word.

T   F   **3.** The task pane is a window that provides quick access to commonly used commands and features.

T   F   **4.** The only way to access the online Help system is through the Office Assistant.

T   F   **5.** To exit Word, click the Close Window button on the menu bar or click Close on the File menu.

NORTON
ONLINE

Visit **www.glencoe.com/norton/online/** for more information on Microsoft Word 2002.

GETTING HELP ON THE WEB

Every day, computer users around the world use the Internet for work, play, and research. The **Internet** is a worldwide network of computers that connects each Internet user's computer to all other computers in the network. Vast quantities of infinitely varied information—from simple text in the form of an e-mail message to extremely complex software—can pass through these connections. The most popular tool used to access the Internet is the **World Wide Web** (**WWW** or the **Web**). A document published on the Web is referred to as a **Web page** and is stored in a specific place on the Web called a **Web site.**

Using your Web **browser**—a software tool used to navigate the Web—you can access most Internet services and all World Wide Web pages directly from the Word window. By using hyperlinks in the online Help and using other Help commands, you can instantly jump to a Web site and search for help on the Web. In this activity, you will display the Web toolbar in the Word window, learn about Help on the Web, and then explore for help on the Web.

1. Start Word if it is not currently running.

2. Point to **Toolbars** on the View menu, and click **Web** on the Toolbars submenu, if it is not already selected. (If Web has a check mark next to it, the Web toolbar is displayed already. Click outside the menu to leave the toolbar selected and close the menu.)

   NOTE *If the Web toolbar appears on your screen as a* **floating toolbar,** *you can move it. Click the title bar of the floating Web toolbar and drag the toolbar to appear directly below the last displayed toolbar. When you release the mouse button, the toolbar will snap into place and become a* **docked toolbar.**

3. Using the *What's This?* feature, read ScreenTips to identify buttons on the Web toolbar. (Use the keyboard shortcut ⟨ ⇧ Shift ⟩ + ⟨ F1 ⟩ to quickly access the *What's This?* feature.)

4. Connect to the Internet using your Internet service provider (ISP). If necessary, type your user name and password. If you are not sure how to connect to the Internet or you do not know your user name and password, ask your instructor for assistance.

Let's explore the online Help system to learn whether Microsoft provides technical assistance for questions not answered in the online Help.

5. In the Ask a Question box, type technical assistance from Microsoft and press ⟨ Enter ⟶ ⟩. Click the **About Microsoft technical resources option**. In the Help window, click <u>Show All</u>.

   WARNING *Be sure to type in the Ask a Question box and not in the Address text box located on the Web toolbar that you just displayed.*

6. Scroll down the Help window and read the information about Microsoft's technical resources.

Now, let's explore the hyperlink to the Microsoft Office Web site.

7. In the Help information, click the **Microsoft Office Web site** link that appears in the paragraph that explains Microsoft's Office Web site.

Your Web browser connects you to the Microsoft Office Tools on the Web site.

8. If necessary, click the **Microsoft Office Tools on the Web taskbar button**, maximize the browser window, and click the **United States hyperlink** on the world map.

9. Read the Microsoft Office Tools on the Web page, scrolling as necessary to see various hyperlinks. Look for and click the **Assistance Center** link. Then, click the **Word link** for assistance with Word.

10. Read the page, noting the various links that might provide additional help for Word users.

11. Explore one article of interest.

12. Keep clicking the **Back button** [← Back ▾] until you return to the Tools on the Web page.

In some instances, even though you've explored both the online Help system and the Microsoft Office Tools on the Web site, you still may not have found an answer to your question. If you need additional assistance, you can communicate directly with Microsoft by using the Search on Web feature within the online Help system.

13. Click the **Help taskbar button** to return to the Help window, and then click the **Show button** [▣], if necessary.

The navigation pane with the Contents, Answer Wizard, and Index tabs appears.

14. Click the **Answer Wizard tab** and click the **Search on Web button** at the bottom of the navigation pane. Scan the information that appears in the Help window.

As shown in Figure GS.15, the Help window displays a form that allows you to provide specific feedback directly to Microsoft. If you have your instructor's permission and have an unanswered question, you can complete the form and click the *Send and go to the Web* button. Microsoft should then respond directly to you about the issue.

15. Click the **Close button** [✕] in the Help window. Hide the Web toolbar, and exit Word. Close any open browser windows, and disconnect from the Internet if your instructor tells you to do so. (To quickly close an open window, right-click its taskbar button and click **Close** on the shortcut menu.)

WARNING *You may proceed directly to the exercises for this section. If, however, you are finished with your computer session, follow the "shut down" procedures for your lab or school environment.*

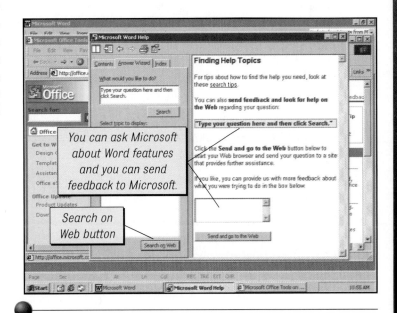

Figure GS.15
Asking Microsoft for more assistance

SUMMARY AND EXERCISES

SUMMARY

This section introduced basic computer and Windows-based application terms; explained how to start and exit Word; and explored menus, toolbars, the task pane, and other objects in the Word window. You learned to open, name, save, close, and reopen files. Also, you learned to get help with Word features from the online Help system. In addition, you learned to connect to the Internet and explore for help on the World Wide Web.

Now that you have completed this section, you should be able to do the following:

- Explain the purpose of the Word program. (page 5)
- Use your mouse to point, click, double-click, right-click, select, and drag. (page 6)
- Start your computer and boot the Windows 2000 operating system. (page 6)
- Copy files from a CD to a hard drive or a network drive. (page 9)
- Change file attributes. (page 11)
- Start Microsoft Word. (page 13)
- Explore the application window and identify common window elements. (page 14)
- Open a file. (page 19)
- Save a file with a different file name and in a different folder. (page 21)
- Close and reopen a file. (page 22)
- Display ScreenTips for various screen elements, and use the Office Assistant and the Ask a Question box to obtain help. (page 24)
- Access and use the Answer Wizard, Contents, and Index to obtain help. (page 27)
- Exit Word and shut down the computer. (page 30)
- Connect to the Internet; identify buttons on the Web toolbar; explore the Web for help; and disconnect from the Internet. (page 32)

CONCEPTS REVIEW

1 TRUE/FALSE

Circle T if the statement is true or F if the statement is false.

T   F   **1.** Items listed on menus are called commands because they tell the computer what to do.

T   F   **2.** A user may personalize toolbars and menus.

T   F   **3.** To display a list of the more common toolbars, click View on the menu bar and point to Toolbars.

T   F   **4.** A task pane can only be used when no files are open.

T   F   **5.** Word provides the following Help tools: the Office Assistant, ScreenTips, the Ask a Question box, the Answer Wizard, Contents, and Index.

T   F   **6.** To reopen a file that you recently closed, you can click the file name from the list at the bottom of the File menu.

T   F   **7.** The Office Assistant is controlled by a command on the Tools menu.

T   F   **8.** To scroll up or down in a window, use the vertical scroll bar.

T   F   **9.** The status bar includes the Start button.

T   F   **10.** To exit Microsoft Word, click the Close button on the title bar or click the Exit command on the File menu.

2 IDENTIFICATION

Label each of the elements of the Word window in Figure GS.16.

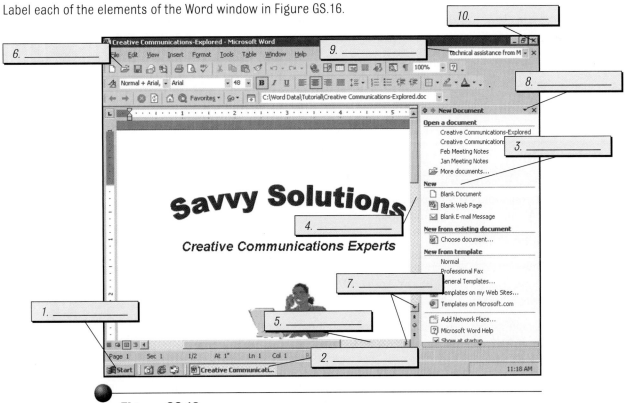

Figure GS.16

SUMMARY AND EXERCISES

SKILLS REVIEW

Complete all of the Skills Review problems in sequential order to review your skills to start Word; identify window elements; open, name, save, close, and reopen files; get Help; and exit Word.

1 Launching the Application, Opening a File, and Exploring a Window

1. Click the **Start button** [Start], point to **Programs**, and click **Microsoft Word**.

2. On the Standard toolbar, click the **Open button**.

3. In the Open dialog box, click the **Look in triangle button**. Then click the drive that contains your *Word Data* folder. (If your *Word Data* folder is not stored at the root level of the drive, navigate to the folder.) Then, double-click the *Word Data* folder.

4. Click *Home Page Support* in the list of file names, and click the **Open button** in the dialog box.

5. Point to various buttons on the Standard toolbar and read the ScreenTips.

2 Naming, Saving, Closing, and Reopening a File

1. With *Home Page Support* still open, click **Save As** on the File menu.

2. In the Save As dialog box, double-click the *Skills Review* folder to open it.

3. In the File name box, edit the name to be *Home Page Support-Explored*. Click the **Save button** in the dialog box.

4. Click the **Close Window button** [X] on the menu bar.

5. Click the **File menu**, and click *Home Page Support-Explored* in the list of files at the bottom of the File menu.

3 Using Help

1. Click the **Ask a Question box**, type **copy a file**, and press [Enter]. In the list of options that you could explore, click the **Copy a file option**. In the Help window, click **Show All** and read the information.

2. Collapse the **How?** link.

3. Click the **Show button** [ ], if necessary, to display the navigation pane. Then, in the *What would you like to do?* box on the Answer Wizard tab, type **crash recovery** and click the **Search button**.

4. In the *Select topic to display* box, click the **Recover files topic**. In the Help window, click the **Show All hyperlink** and explore all the information about document recovery.

5. Click the **Hide button** [ ], click the **Restore Down button** [ ], and click the **Close button** [X] in the Help window.

4 Closing a File and Exiting the Application

1. Click the **Close Window button** ☒ on the menu bar.

2. Click the **Close button** ☒ on the title bar.

PROJECTS

1 Two at a Time?

Can you open two files with one click of the Open button? Search Help to find out if or how it can be done. Now, simultaneously open *Atlas Manual* and *Australia Tour Pricing* in your *Word Data* folder. Save *Atlas Manual* as *Atlas Manual 1* in the *Projects* folder in your *Word Data* folder; save *Australia Tour Pricing* as *Australia Tour Pricing 2* in the *Projects* folder in your *Word Data* folder. Then close the files. Reopen *Atlas Manual 1* from the File menu. Reopen *Australia Tour Pricing 2* from the appropriate task pane. Close all open files.

2 Button, Button, Who Has the Button?

To avoid accidentally closing the application program when you only want to close a file, you decide to add a Close button to the right of the Open button on the Standard toolbar. Explore Help for information on customizing a toolbar. After you've added the Close button, test it by opening a file and then closing it with the Close button. Now remove the Close button from the toolbar. Is there more than one way to add and remove a toolbar button? When would you recommend restoring the original toolbar settings?

ON the WEB 3 Stamps or Electronic Postage?

Who isn't extremely busy? Who isn't looking for ways to be better organized? Someone recently suggested to you that you could save time by printing electronic postage instead of waiting in a line to buy postage. You decide to use your online Help system and to explore the Web for answers to your questions about electronic postage (*Hint:* First search for *electronic postage* in your online Help system, and then use the Office on the Web command on the Help menu to access the Microsoft Office Assistance Center Web site and explore the Office eServices link.) Do you need to install a program to use electronic postage? Is an electronic postage program already installed on your computer? Can you print postage directly on an envelope or a label from your computer? What does it cost to get started with an electronic postage plan? Be prepared to discuss the information you discovered on the Web with your class. Close all open browser windows and disconnect from the Internet if your instructor tells you to do so. Close the Help window and exit Word.

Word Basics

CONTENTS

- Introducing Microsoft Word
- Starting Microsoft Word
- Exploring the Word Window
- Viewing a Document
- Selecting Text
- Navigating a Document
- Editing Text and Saving a File
- Moving and Copying Text
- Managing Folders and Changing File Types
- Previewing and Printing
- Creating a Document From a Template
- Using Language and Grammar Tools
- On the Web: Inserting Hyperlinks

MOUS Objectives
In this lesson:
W2002-1-1
W2002-1-3
W2002-1-5
W2002-3-5
W2002-4-1
W2002-4-2
W2002-4-3
See Appendix D.

OBJECTIVES

After you complete this lesson, you will be able to do the following:

- ▶ Explain word processing.
- ▶ Start Microsoft Word.
- ▶ Name the main components of the Word window and display and hide toolbars.
- ▶ View a document in all four views.
- ▶ Select text and navigate a document.
- ▶ Edit text using Insert, Overtype, Undo, Redo, and Repeat.
- ▶ Rename and save a file.
- ▶ Move and copy text.
- ▶ Manage folders and change file types.
- ▶ Preview and print a document, labels, and envelopes.
- ▶ Create a document from a template.
- ▶ Use language and grammar tools including the Thesaurus tool.
- ▶ Insert text using AutoText, AutoComplete, AutoCorrect, and the Insert menu.
- ▶ Search for a file.
- ▶ Insert a hyperlink into a document.

INTRODUCING MICROSOFT WORD

Microsoft Word is a powerful **word processing** program that enables you to create all kinds of documents including letters, reports, and even complicated brochures and newsletters. Using Word, you can easily perform basic word-processing functions, such as typing, editing, printing, and saving text. In addition, many features allow you to **format** (arrange) and enhance text, making it attractive and easy to read. Word will correct typing, spelling, and grammar errors. Other Word features help you find and replace text quickly and easily. Special tools allow you to add graphics, pictures, tables, sounds, and links to any document and to the Internet. Word also offers prewritten documents that you can adapt to your needs, instead of creating them from scratch.

Word provides an extensive online Help system which is always right there to answer your questions and provide tips about tasks you want to perform. You can navigate easily through your documents no matter how long or short they are. You can manage your Word files by naming and renaming files, copying and deleting files, and saving documents as various file types. You can even ask Word to convert any document to a Web page—Word will guide you step-by-step to create a Web page you can publish on an intranet or the Internet. From the Word window, you can also navigate and search the World Wide Web. You can even create an e-mail message right in the Word window, send a Word document as an e-mail message, or attach a Word document to an e-mail message.

STARTING MICROSOFT WORD

Before you can start Microsoft Word, both Microsoft Word and Windows 98 (or higher version) must be installed on the computer you are using. The figures in this tutorial use Windows 2000; if you are using a different version of Windows, the information appearing on your screen may vary slightly.

> **WARNING** *You must create the* Word Data *folder for this tutorial from the* Data CD *located on the inside back cover of this tutorial. If you have not created the* Word Data *folder, ask your instructor for help or review* Getting Started.

HANDS on

Launching Microsoft Word

In this activity, you will start Microsoft Word.

1. Turn on your computer.

> **NOTE** *If you are prompted for a username and/or password, enter the information at this time. If you do not know your username and/or password, ask your instructor for help.*

The Windows operating system boots the computer.

2. Click the Start button 🔳 **Start** **on the Windows taskbar.**

3. Point to Programs and click Microsoft Word.

The Word program starts and a new, blank document appears.

EXPLORING THE WORD WINDOW

The Word application window is shown in Figure 1.1. Your window may look slightly different because Word allows users to customize, or alter, the Word window

---

Word
in the workplace

Organizations that install Microsoft Word aim to minimize input time and maximize output quality. Get acquainted with all the basic features of Word so that you will know which features you need in a given situation. Likewise, become familiar with varied ways to perform a task so that you will know which method(s) are most efficient.

Word **BASICS**

Launching Word

1. Click the Start button.

2. Point to Programs then click Microsoft Word.

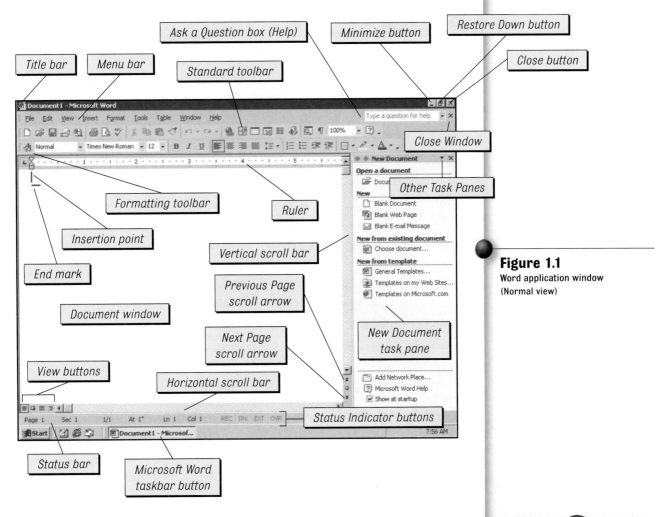

Figure 1.1
Word application window
(Normal view)

to suit individual needs. The Word window contains many standard Windows elements which you learned about in *Getting Started*. As shown in Figure 1.1, the document window displays the insertion point and the end mark. The **insertion point** (a blinking vertical bar) indicates where text will be inserted when you begin typing. The **end mark** (a short horizontal line) moves downward in your document each time you begin a new line. Word, by default, gives a temporary name to all documents. In Figure 1.1 the document is called *Document1*.

The task pane that appears at the right side of the application window provides quick access to commonly used commands and features. There are eight different task panes in Word (these eight options appear when you click the Other Task Panes triangle button). The New Document task pane in Figure 1.1 appears by default each time you open Word. The task pane disappears by default when you open a new blank or existing document; it can be reopened at any time by clicking Task Pane on the View menu.

Identifying Menus and Commands

As shown in Figure 1.1, the Word menu bar appears below the title bar. The menu bar displays menu names found in most Windows applications, such as File, Edit, and Help. Word also includes menus just for word processing, such as Format and Table.

Table 1.1 provides a brief description of the menus available on the Word menu bar.

WORD 2002

Table 1.1	The Word Menu Bar

Menu	Contains Commands That Let You . . .
File	Control your document files by opening, saving, and printing them.
Edit	Rearrange text and other elements of documents by locating, copying, moving, and deleting text.
View	View documents different ways; display and hide toolbars.
Insert	Insert various elements, such as page breaks, pictures, symbols, and hyperlinks, into your documents.
Format	Determine the appearance of text in your documents; for example, the size of characters or the alignment of a paragraph.
Tools	Use Word's special word processing tools, such as a spelling and grammar checker, thesaurus, and automatic correction features.
Table	Insert, fill-in, and format an arrangement of columns and rows as tabular information in documents.
Window	Work in multiple documents at once, in one or more windows.
Help	Access Word's online Help system and Microsoft Office on the Web for word processing assistance and support.

Identifying Toolbars, Buttons, and the Ruler

Below the menu bar is Word's Standard toolbar, as shown in Figure 1.1 on page 41. A toolbar contains a row of buttons for many of the most frequently used commands. Although you can access these commands on one of the menus, clicking a toolbar button is often more convenient. You can quickly identify any toolbar button by pointing to it and reading the name that appears in a small text box called a ScreenTip.

The Formatting toolbar appears directly below the Standard toolbar. This toolbar contains buttons that control the appearance of text.

> **NOTE** *If your Standard and Formatting toolbars share one row below the menu bar, you can display them as two separate toolbars by clicking Customize on the Tools menu. On the Options tab, select the* Show Standard and Formatting toolbars on two rows *option and click Close.*

The icon on each toolbar button symbolizes the command. For example, on Word's Standard toolbar the New Blank Document button ◻ is symbolized by a piece of paper. Table 1.2 presents each button available on the Word Standard toolbar and explains its function. The Standard toolbar, like Word's menus, is adaptive. The most common buttons appear on the main toolbar, while buttons used less often are accessible by clicking Toolbar Options ◌ at the end of the toolbar. When you click a button on the Toolbar Options list ◌ that is not displayed on the toolbar, Word adds it to the main toolbar. You can also move buttons that are not frequently used from the toolbar to the Toolbar Options list.

In addition to the Standard and Formatting toolbars, the Toolbars command on the View menu provides access to many other toolbars, each arranged for a different purpose. The **ruler** displays below the Standard and Formatting toolbars, as shown in Figure 1.1 on page 41, enabling you to judge measurements, such as paragraph indentions, on document pages. (If the ruler does not appear on your screen, click Ruler on the View menu.)

WEB NOTE

The Internet connects your computer to millions of other computers all over the world. You can exchange messages, programs, and data files with every one of them.

HINTS & TIPS

By default, the ruler displays measurements in inches. You can change to another unit of measure on the General tab of the Options dialog box (Tools menu) by using the *Measurement units* list box.

Table 1.2 **The Word Standard Toolbar**

WORD 2002

Button	Name	Action
	New Blank Document	Creates a new document.
	Open	Opens a document.
	Save	Makes a permanent copy of a document to a file on disk.
	E-mail	Opens a header to send your document as an electronic mail message.
	Search	Finds files wherever you work, such as on your computer, your local network, or your Microsoft Outlook mailbox.
	Print	Prints the entire document.
	Print Preview	Previews the document.
	Spelling and Grammar	Checks for spelling and grammar errors.
	Cut	Removes the selected item(s) from the document to the Clipboard—a temporary storage place for information that is used by all Windows applications.
	Copy	Copies the selected item(s) and places this copy on the Office Clipboard.
	Paste	Pastes the selected item(s) from the Clipboard into the current location.
	Format Painter	Copies the formatting from the selected item(s) to another item(s).
	Undo	Reverses the last command.
	Redo	Repeats the last command.
	Insert Hyperlink	Inserts a link from the current document to another part of the current document, another document, or an Internet site.
	Tables and Borders	Displays or hides the Tables and Borders toolbar.
	Insert Table	Inserts a table.
	Insert Microsoft Excel Worksheet	Inserts an Excel worksheet.
	Columns	Adjusts text to a column format.
	Drawing	Displays or hides the Drawing toolbar.
	Document Map	Turns the Document map feature on or off.
	Show/Hide ¶	Shows or hides the formatting marks.
100%	Zoom	Increases or decreases the displayed size of the document.
?	Microsoft Word Help	Displays the Office Assistant—an animated character than can answer your specific questions, offer helpful tips, and provide help for any Word feature.
X	Close	Closes the current document.

VIEWING A DOCUMENT

Word allows users to see all documents, including Web pages, in **WYSIWYG** (what you see is what you get). As shown in Figure 1.2, four view option buttons are located at the lower left in the Word window. A document might be created in Outline View and switched to other views for editing, formatting, and printing. The four views are identified in Table 1.3. (Point to a view button to easily identify it through a ScreenTip.) In addition, you can easily reduce or magnify the document area displayed on screen by changing the Zoom setting.

Table 1.3	Document Viewing Options	
Button	**View Type**	**Typical Use**
☰	Normal View	The main view used for typing, editing, and formatting text.
▣	Web Layout View	Used mostly for editing and formatting documents to be posted as Web pages.
▤	Print Layout View	Used for seeing how documents will look when printed.
▦	Outline View	Used only for organizing and developing the content of documents.

HANDS on

Viewing a Document in All Four Views

In this activity, you will see a document in all four views. Scrolling the document will help you observe differences in the views. You will also change the Zoom setting.

1. **Open the *Atlas* file in your *Word Data* folder, and click the Web Layout View button ▣ in the lower left area of the screen.**

Long lines of text and very narrow side margins characterize this view, as shown in Figure 1.2. Also, there are no horizontal lines to divide the document into separate pages.

2. **Scroll rapidly to the end of the document while watching the status bar.**

The status bar is *not* active in Web Layout View because on the Web the whole document functions as one page.

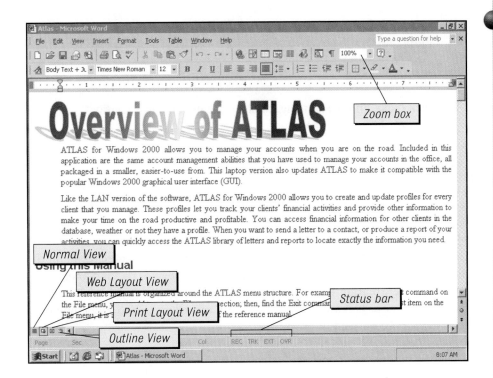

Figure 1.2
Atlas document in Web Layout View

3. Scroll to the beginning of the document then click the **Print Layout View button** ▣.

The document takes the appearance of a printed sheet.

4. Scroll gradually to the top of page 2, and notice the break between pages 1 and 2.

5. Scroll slowly to the *Using ATLAS for Windows 2000* heading at the top of page 3.

6. Click the **Outline View button** ▦.

The Outlining toolbar appears at the top of the document below the Formatting toolbar. A mark at the left of each paragraph of text indicates a separate unit of text that you can move above or below other units by selecting it and clicking the arrows in the Outlining toolbar.

7. Click the Normal View button ▤.

In Normal View, side margins are visible on the left and right side of the text, and horizontal dotted lines divide the screen into pages.

8. Click the **Zoom box triangle button** 100% ▾ on the Standard toolbar, then click the **150% option**.

The document size enlarges to 150%.

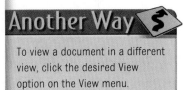

To view a document in a different view, click the desired View option on the View menu.

Visit **www.glencoe.com/norton/online/** for more information on Microsoft Word 2002.

9. Click the **Zoom box triangle button** 100% ▾ again, then click the **100% option**.

Word returns the document to its previous size.

10. Click **Close** on the File menu to close the document; click **No** if prompted to save changes.

SELECTING TEXT

Occasionally, you may need to select text in the form of words, sentences, lines, or whole paragraphs as you work with a document. You can select a word by double-clicking it. You can select a sentence by pressing Ctrl and clicking anywhere in the sentence. You can select a line of text by simply pointing to it and clicking in the **selection bar,** the invisible column between the left edge of the document window and the left margin of the page. Selecting an entire paragraph is as easy as triple-clicking anywhere in the paragraph. You can select an entire document by clicking Select All on the Edit menu.

HANDS on

Selecting Words, Sentences, Lines, and Paragraphs

In this activity, you will select a word, a sentence, a line of text, and a paragraph.

1. Open the *Home Page Support* file in your *Word Data* folder and click the Normal View button ☰, if necessary.

NOTE *Since the Normal View is the main view used for typing and editing documents, from here forward assume that all Word activities require you to be in the Normal View unless the instructions specify otherwise.*

2. Press Ctrl and click anywhere in the last sentence of the first paragraph.

The sentence is selected (highlighted).

3. Move the pointer to the selection bar and point to the second line of text in the second paragraph.

Your pointer becomes an arrow called the Normal Select pointer.

4. Click within the selection bar.

The line of text is selected, as shown in Figure 1.3.

Word BASICS

Selecting Text

- Double-click to select a word.

- Press Ctrl and click to select a sentence.

- Point to a line in the selection bar and click to select a line of text.

- Triple-click to select a paragraph.

- Click Select All on the Edit menu to select an entire document.

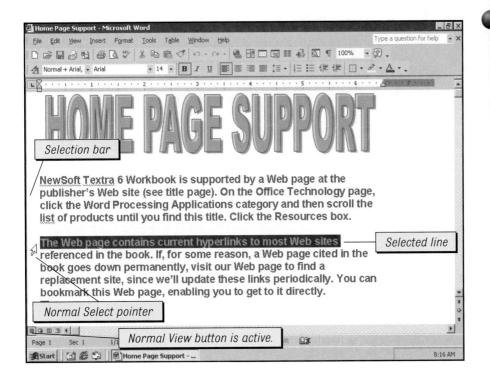

Figure 1.3
Selected line

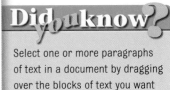

5. Double-click the word *Office* in the first paragraph.

The word *Office* is selected.

6. Triple-click anywhere in the second paragraph.

The entire paragraph is selected.

7. Click **Select All** on the Edit menu to select the entire document.

8. Click anywhere in the document window to deselect the text.

9. Click **Close Window** ☒ to close the document, and click **No** if prompted to save changes.

Did you know?

Select one or more paragraphs of text in a document by dragging over the blocks of text you want to select.

Another Way

Select one or more paragraphs by selecting a line in the selection bar and dragging the pointer down or up.

NAVIGATING A DOCUMENT

Scrolling through a document to locate a specific word or phrase can be time consuming, especially in a long document. There are better methods of locating specific text. Word has several features that allow you to navigate a document more efficiently.

The Go To feature allows you to go to a specific page, line, section, heading, and so on. On the Go To tab in the Find and Replace dialog box, you can type a page number to command Word to go directly to that page. From that location, you can direct Word to go back or forward a certain number of pages.

You can quickly locate a particular word or phrase through the Find tab of the Find and Replace dialog box. Type the text you wish to find and Word will search for it and highlight the first occurrence *following* the location of your insertion point in the document. As you continue to search the entire document, Word will highlight every occurrence of the text.

HANDS on

Finding Specific Text and Pages

In this activity, you will use the Find and Replace dialog box to find specific words and you will then use the Go To feature to locate specific pages in the *Atlas* file.

1. Open *Atlas* in your *Word Data* folder and click the **Normal View** button, if necessary.

Immediately after opening the file your insertion point will be at the beginning of the document. Word can search for specific pages and text from any point; however, if you start the search process in the middle of the document, Word will just search from that point to the end of the document. (At the end of the document, a dialog box will ask if you wish to continue the search from the document's beginning.)

2. Click the **Find button**.

The Find and Replace dialog box appears.

> **NOTE** *If the Find button is not on the Standard toolbar, click Toolbar Options, point to Add or Remove Buttons, point to Standard, then click a check mark next to the Find button to add it to your toolbar. You may also click Find on the Edit menu.*

3. On the Find tab, type administrator in the *Find what* box, as shown in Figure 1.4

Word BASICS

Navigating a Document

To find specific text:

1. Click the Find button on the Standard toolbar.

2. Type text in the *Find what* box.

3. Click Find Next.

To jump to a specific page:

1. Click the Find button then click the Go To tab.

2. Click Page in the *Go to what* box.

3. Type a page number and click Go To to jump to the page.

4. Type + or −, the number of pages, then click Go To to go forward or back.

Figure 1.4
Find and Replace dialog box

Did you know?

Click the Select Browse Object button at the bottom of the vertical scroll bar then click the Browse by Page tool. Word will advance to the next page.

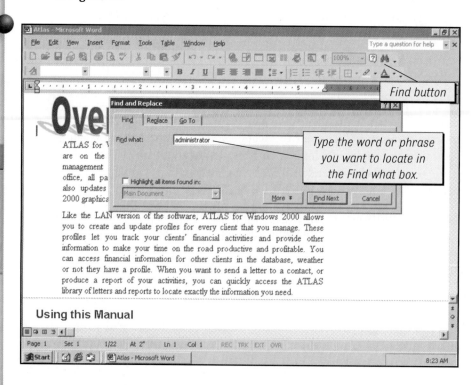

4. Click Find Next.

Word jumps to the first occurrence of the word *administrator* on page 5 of the document.

5. Click Find Next again.

A dialog box indicates Word has finished searching the document. No more occurrences of the word are found.

6. Click OK.

7. Click the Go To tab in the Find and Replace dialog box. In the *Go to what* list box, click Page, if it is not already selected. Then type 5 in the *Enter page number* box.

8. Click the Go To button.

Word jumps directly to the top of page 5, and the status bar indicates that you are now on page 5 of 22 (5/22). The insertion point is at the beginning of the page but is not blinking.

9. In the *Enter page number* box, type +4 and press Enter←┘.

Word moves forward four pages; you are now on page 9 as indicated on the status bar (9/22).

10. In the *Enter page number* box, type −6 and click the Go To button.

Word moves back six pages; you are now on page 3.

11. Click Close ☒ on the Find and Replace dialog box.

12. Click Close Window ☒ to close the *Atlas* document, and click No if prompted to save changes.

EDITING TEXT AND SAVING A FILE

The power of a word processing program becomes apparent when you want to revise your document. The ease of inserting, changing, deleting, and replacing text means that you can type a rough draft of your ideas quickly and then go back later to refine, or edit, your document.

After you have edited an existing document, you can rename and save it using the Save As dialog box. This preserves the original document so you can access it later. You can change the name of any document in the Open or Save As dialog box when the file name no longer suits the document.

Inserting Text

As you point to text in a document, the pointer becomes an **I-beam pointer.** Position the pointer where you want to type, then click. The pointer becomes a blinking vertical bar called the insertion point. When you type, text will begin at the insertion point. As you type, you can delete characters to the left of the insertion point by pressing Backspace; you can delete characters to the right of the insertion point by pressing Delete. When you type to the end of a line, the text and the insertion point

Another Way ⑤

You can use the Bookmark feature to jump immediately to a marked location in a long document, or you can use the Document Map feature to navigate to a specific heading in your document. Explore Help for more information on these features.

HINTS & TIPS

To view symbols representing locations where a hard return or character spaces have been entered in your document, click the Show/Hide button on the Standard Toolbar.

will move automatically to the next line. This basic word processing feature is called **word wrap.** When you wish to begin typing on a new line, press ⌈Enter◄┘⌉ to insert a **hard return** that moves the insertion point to the next line.

> **NOTE** *Insert a hard return only to move text or the insertion point to the next line, to insert blank lines into your document, to begin a new paragraph, or to apply certain Word commands. Otherwise, allow your copy to wrap with the* soft returns *that Word inserts automatically.*

Word involves two typing modes. When you use **Insert mode,** the text you type appears on the blank screen or is inserted into existing text, pushing the characters after it to the right. When you use **Overtype mode,** your text types over the existing text. Use Insert mode—the default typing mode—to insert new text; use Overtype mode to edit text. Always determine which mode is active before you type to avoid replacing text accidentally. When Word is in Overtype mode, the status indicator button in the status bar will display OVR in black letters. When Insert mode is active, the status indicator button will display a dimmed or gray OVR button. You can switch back and forth between the modes by double-clicking the OVR button or by pressing ⌈Insert⌉.

HANDS on

Inserting Paragraphs

In this activity, you will add two paragraphs to the *Atlas* document. You will also use the Word Count toolbar to count the number of lines in your document.

1. Point to **Toolbars** on the View menu and click **Word Count** to display the Word Count toolbar, if necessary.

> **NOTE** *If the Word Count toolbar appears to float in the document window, drag its title bar up until it docks beneath the Formatting toolbar. This toolbar allows you to count the words, characters, lines, pages, and paragraphs in a document.*

2. Open *Atlas* in your *Word Data* folder.

3. On the Word Count toolbar, click the **Word Count Statistics triangle button** ⌈<Click Recount to view>⌉ ▾ and click **Lines.**

Notice that you have 318 lines of text in the document.

4. Scroll to page 2, click after the last character in the last line of the second paragraph, and press ⌈Enter◄┘⌉.

The insertion point jumps down one line to begin a new paragraph. Now you will activate Insert mode to insert new text.

5. Point to the **OVR status indicator button** on the status bar.

The word *Overtype* appears as a ScreenTip. If OVR appears in black letters, Overtype mode is active. If OVR is gray or dimmed, Insert mode is active.

Inserting Paragraphs

1. Click to position the insertion point where you want text to appear.

2. If OVR is active, double-click it to activate the Insert mode or press ⌈Insert⌉.

3. Type the text, pressing ⌈Backspace⌉ or ⌈Delete⌉ to erase errors as you type.

To include footnotes and endnotes in your word counts, click Word Count on the Tools menu and select *Include footnotes and endnotes.*

6. If OVR is black, double-click **OVR** to activate Insert mode.

7. **Type the following text**: We have also included a small "map" in the upper-right corner of each page. This map indicates exactly where the described menu or dialog is in the program.

The insertion point moves to the right as you type and wraps to the next line when a line is full.

8. Click the **Recount button** [Recount] on the Word Count toolbar.

The Word Count toolbar shows that you now have 321 lines of text in your document.

9. Click the **Find button** [🔍].

10. In the Find and Replace dialog box, click the **Go To tab**.

11. In the *Go to what* list box, click **Page**, if it is not already selected. Then type **5** in the *Enter page number* box and click **Go To**.

Word jumps directly to the top of page 5, and the status bar indicates that you are now on page 5 of 22 (5/22). The insertion point is at the top of the page but not blinking.

12. Click the **Close button** in the Find and Replace dialog box.

The blinking insertion point appears to the left of the *Logging In* heading.

13. **Type the following paragraph**: If you are new to Windows 2000, look over this section to familiarize yourself with the Windows conventions.

The insertion point pushes the heading to the right as you type new text.

14. Press [Enter⏎].

Your document should now resemble Figure 1.5.

15. Point to **Toolbars** on the View menu and click to deselect the Word Count toolbar.

Changing a File Name and Saving a File

After making changes in an existing document, you may prefer to keep the original document intact so you can refer to it later. To preserve the original document, it is best to save your edited file under a new name. Click Save As on the File menu to access the Save As dialog box. Choose the location (drive and path) in the *Save in* box in which you want to save your file, then type a meaningful name in the *File name* text box and click the Save button.

If you decide later that the file name no longer suits the file, you can easily change it in the Open dialog box. In the *Look in* box, navigate to and open the folder in which your file is stored. Click the file, click Tools, then click Rename on the drop-down menu. When a rectangle appears around the file name, type the new name and press [Enter⏎].

HANDS on

Renaming and Saving a File

In this activity, you will save the *Atlas* file with a new file name then you will rename the file in the Open dialog box. The *Atlas* document should be open in the Word application window containing the text you typed in the previous activity.

1. **Click Save As on the File menu.**

The Save As dialog box appears.

2. **Click the Save in triangle button, and navigate to the *Word Data* folder, if necessary.**

3. **Double-click the *Tutorial* folder, type Atlas in Progress in the *File name* box, and click Save.**

4. **Close *Atlas in Progress*.**

5. **Click Open on the File menu.**

The contents of the *Tutorial* folder appear in the Open dialog box, including your new file *Atlas in Progress*.

6. **Click *Atlas in Progress*, click Tools `Tools ▾` on the dialog box toolbar, then click Rename on the drop-down list.**

A rectangle appears around the highlighted file name.

7. **Type Atlas Revised as the new file name, then press `Enter ◄──`.**

8. **Click Cancel to close the Open dialog box.**

Word BASICS

Renaming a File

Saving a file with a new name:

1. With the file open, click Save As on the File menu.

2. In the Save As dialog box, navigate to the folder in which you want to save your file.

3. Type the new file name in the *File name* text box and click Save.

Changing a file name:

1. Click Open (for the Open dialog box) or Save As (for the Save As dialog box) on the File menu.

2. Click the file, click the Tools button, then click Rename.

3. Type the new file name and close the dialog box.

Replacing and Deleting Text

You learned earlier in this lesson how to navigate a document and how to locate and select text. You can use these techniques when you need to insert a single word or a missing character within a word. As you learned this is best accomplished in Insert mode. Occasionally, you will need to replace incorrect characters with correct ones by *overtyping* them. You can replace text in Overtype mode.

While editing a rough draft, you will often need to **delete** characters, words, phrases, sentences, or even whole paragraphs. Deleting text is a two-step procedure. First you must select the text you want to delete. After you select text, press `Delete` to remove it or begin to type to replace the words. You can also replace text throughout an entire document by using the Replace feature. In the Find and Replace dialog box, type the text to find and the text to replace it. Word will jump to each occurrence, and you can choose to replace the text, skip to the next occurrence, or replace all occurrences.

HANDS on

Replacing and Deleting Letters and Words

In this activity, you will find and replace or remove incorrect letters and words in *Atlas*.

1. Open *Atlas* in your *Word Data* folder.

2. Click the **Find button** 🔍, type use from. in the *Find what* box, then click **Find Next**.

The first occurrence of these characters is highlighted within *Atlas*.

3. Click anywhere in the document, and then click before the *r* in the highlighted words.

NOTE *If the Find and Replace dialog box covers the status bar or is in the way, click its title bar and drag it to another area of the window.*

4. Activate Overtype mode, if necessary, and type or to replace the letters *r* and *o*.

5. Find the word *weather* in the document and overtype it as whether, as shown in Figure 1.5.

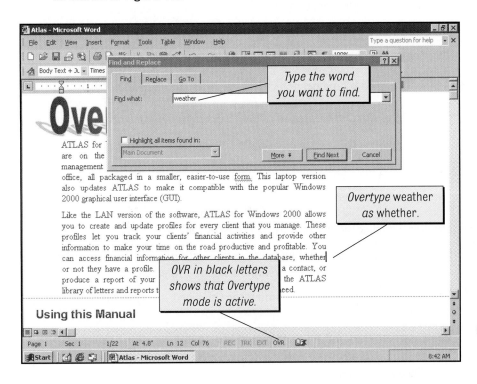

Word BASICS

Replacing Text

To overtype:

1. Click before the character you want to replace.

2. Activate Overtype mode, then type the character(s).

To insert text:

1. Click the location where you want to type.

2. Activate Insert mode and type the character(s).

To replace text:

1. Click the Find button.

2. Click the Replace tab.

3. In the *Find what* box, type the word or phrase to be replaced.

4. In the *Replace with* box, type the new text.

5. Click Find Next.

6. At each occurrence, click Replace, Replace All, or Find Next.

Figure 1.5
Word window in Overtype mode

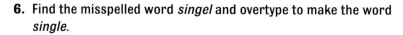

Selecting and Deleting Text

To delete a character:

1. Click before the character.

2. Press `Delete`.

To delete a word:

1. Double-click the word to select it.

2. Press `Delete`.

To delete a phrase:

1. Click before the first character.

2. Drag through the phrase to select it.

3. Press `Delete`.

6. Find the misspelled word *singel* and overtype to make the word *single*.

NOTE *A wavy red line may appear under some words (such as* singel*) to mark words or abbreviations not in the Word spelling dictionary that might be spelling errors. Similarly, a wavy green line may mark possible grammar errors. Some wavy lines will disappear as you edit the document; otherwise, ignore them for now. You will learn more about them later in this lesson.*

7. Find the phrase *than type*; overtype the *a* with e.

8. In the Find and Replace dialog box, click the **Replace tab**.

9. Type Alt in the *Find what* box. Press `Tab` and type `Alt` in the *Replace with* box. Then click the **Find Next button**.

10. At the first occurrence of *Alt*, click the **Replace button**.

Word replaces *Alt* with `Alt` and continues searching the document.

11. At the second occurrence of *Alt*, click the **Find Next button** to avoid the change.

A dialog box indicates the entire document was searched and no other occurrences were found.

12. Click **OK**.

13. Activate Insert mode. Find the words *first you* and insert the word time so the phrase reads *first time you*.

14. Click the **Find tab** and find the word *menues*.

15. Select the second *e* and press `Delete` to remove it.

The space occupied by the deleted character closes automatically.

16. Find the word *existing* and delete the *s* to make the word *exiting*.

17. Find the words *lap top* and delete the space between them.

18. Click the **Go To tab** then go to the first paragraph on page 7.

The word *the* is repeated twice in the second line.

19. Double-click the repeated word to select it and press `Delete`.

20. Go to page 10, item 2, and select and delete the words *the* and *key* to match this phrase: . . . *using* <u>backspace *to erase*</u> . . .

21. On page 12, delete the comma after the word *alerts* in the last bulleted item.

22. Close the Find and Replace dialog box, then save your document as *Atlas Edited* in the *Tutorial* folder in your *Word Data* folder. Close the document.

Visit **www.glencoe.com/norton/online/** for more information on Microsoft Word 2002.

Undoing, Redoing, and Repeating Actions

As you edit documents, you may be unsure about a particular word choice or the phrasing of a sentence. Use the **Undo** or **Redo** features if you change your mind after you've edited a part of your document. The Undo button  reverses actions (for example, deletes the text just typed). (The button's ScreenTip changes to Can't Undo if you cannot reverse the last action.) The Redo button  reverses an *undo* action. You can also use the Repeat command on the Edit menu to repeat an action.

HANDS on

Using Undo, Redo, and Repeat Features

In this activity, you will locate a specific word, select and replace it, then undo that action. After the word is restored, you will repeat the action.

1. Open *Atlas* in your *Word Data* folder.

2. Open the Find and Replace dialog box. On the Find tab, click the **More button**, then click to select the **Match case check box**.

Word will now skip occurrences of the text that do not match the capitalization used in the *Find what* box.

3. Type Important: in the *Find what* box, as shown in Figure 1.6. Then, click **Find Next**.

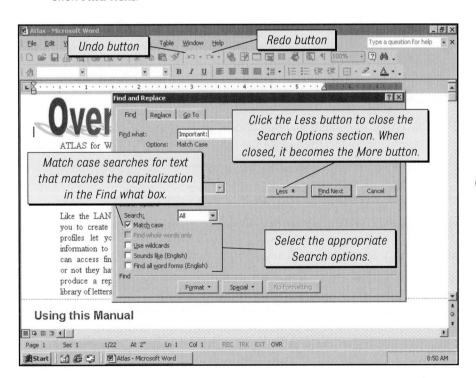

Word jumps to *Important:* which appears highlighted in the application window.

4. While the word is selected, click anywhere within the document and press Delete.

Word BASICS

Undoing, Redoing, and Repeating Actions

1. Click the Undo button to delete text just typed, or click the Undo arrow and click the action(s) you want to undo on the drop-down menu.

2. Click the Redo button to reverse an *Undo* action.

Figure 1.6
Select the Match case search option

5. Click the **Undo button** 🔙 *(Undo Clear)* to restore the word *Important:*.

The word is restored, and the Undo button's ScreenTip reads *Can't Undo*, since the action has been completed.

6. In the same sentence, select the word *checkbox* and then type button to replace it.

7. Click the **Undo button** 🔙 *(Undo Typing)* to restore the word *checkbox*. Click the **Redo button** 🔜 *(Redo Typing)* to restore the word *button*. Click the **Undo button** 🔙 *(Undo Typing)* to restore the word *checkbox*.

8. In the Find and Replace dialog box, clear the *Match case* search option, and click the **Less button** to close the Search Options section of the dialog box.

9. Find the word *TIP:*, click two times before the word to place the insertion point at that location, then type ATLAS (no space).

10. Click **Find Next** to advance to the next occurrence of *TIP:*, then click twice before the word to activate the insertion point.

11. Click **Repeat Typing** on the Edit menu.

The word *ATLAS* is inserted before *TIP:*. The Repeat Typing command has repeated the last word you typed.

12. Close the Find and Replace dialog box.

13. Save your document as *Atlas Undone* in the *Tutorial* folder in your *Word Data* folder, then close the file.

MOVING AND COPYING TEXT

The Cut, Copy, and Paste features enable you to reword sentences and paragraphs by moving or copying text from one place to another. When you **cut** text you remove it from the document then save it on the **Office Clipboard,** a temporary holding area for text and graphics. You can then **paste** this cut text into the current document; into another document; or into a different Office application, such as Microsoft Excel or Microsoft PowerPoint. Thus, cut-and-paste is a means of moving text. Another way to move text is simply to drag it from its present location and drop it in a new location. The drag-and-drop method is handy when you want to move a small amount of text a short distance within the same document.

Cutting and deleting are different procedures. Deleting text is like erasing it; you should delete text that you have no further use for in your document. Cutting is a way to move text; you should cut text that you want to move to another location.

HINTS & TIPS

When you delete, cut, or paste text, Microsoft Word can automatically adjust the spacing around the text. To activate this feature, click Options on the Tools menu and click the Edit tab. Click to select the *Smart cut and paste* check box if necessary.

In addition to moving text, you may want to **copy** text to the Clipboard from one location and place it in another location. Copying text does not remove it from the original location. Copying can save the time and effort of retyping and avoids the risk of typing errors. You can select text, press [Ctrl], and use drag-and-drop to copy it to a new location. Again, drag-and-drop works best when you want to copy only a few words and drag them within the same paragraph.

The Paste Special command on the Edit menu allows you to paste (or **embed**) items from the Office Clipboard in a different format. For example, you can cut text from a Word document and paste it as a picture into another Word document or a PowerPoint slide. Similarly, you can cut data from an Excel worksheet and paste it into a Word document.

Cutting, copying, and pasting involve the Office Clipboard. You can cut or copy a single piece of text or several blocks of text. Any text you cut or copy is stored on the Office Clipboard. You can paste each text item into a different place or you can paste all the items into one location. You can paste items from the Office Clipboard individually or all at once. Click Paste to paste only the last item you cut or copied. Click Paste All to paste all of the items stored on the Office Clipboard. To view the contents of the Clipboard, click Office Clipboard on the Edit menu to activate the Clipboard task pane.

NOTE *Remember that you can reverse all of these actions—cutting, copying, and pasting—with the Undo* ↺ *and Redo* ↻ *buttons and the Repeat command on the Edit menu.*

HANDS on

Using the Office Clipboard and the Drag-and-Drop Method

In this activity, you will move a sentence to a new location and copy and paste text from one location to another.

1. Open *Party Memo* in your *Word Data* folder then click **Office Clipboard** on the Edit menu.

The Office Clipboard displays in the task pane.

2. Click the **Clear All button** [Clear All] to remove all items from the Clipboard, if necessary.

3. Find the words *Food and drinks* and close the Find and Replace dialog box, if necessary.

4. Select the sentence *Food and drinks will be provided, so come hungry.*

5. Click the **Cut button** ✂ on the Standard toolbar.

The selected sentence is removed from your document and appears on the Office Clipboard, as shown in Figure 1.7.

Word BASICS

Using the Office Clipboard
To copy and paste text:

1. Select the text to be copied.

2. Click the Copy button.

3. Click an insertion point in your document.

4. Click the Paste button.

To cut and paste text:

1. Select the text to be cut.

2. Click the Cut button.

3. Click an insertion point in your document.

4. Click the Paste button.

Figure 1.7
Clipboard with one cut item

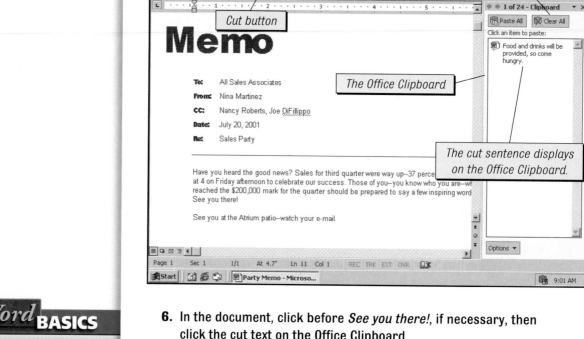

WORD 2002

Word BASICS

Using Drag-and-Drop

1. Select the text to be moved and point to the selected text.

2. Press and hold the left mouse button.

3. Drag the text to the new location.

4. Release the mouse button.

5. Adjust spacing between words, if necessary.

Another Way

To copy text using the drag-and-drop method, select the text, press and hold Ctrl, then drag-and-drop the selected text.

6. In the document, click before *See you there!*, if necessary, then click the cut text on the Office Clipboard.

The cut sentence is pasted back into the document. A Paste Options button appears in your document where you inserted the cut text. Clicking the Paste Options triangle button will reveal several formatting options.

7. Press Spacebar to insert a space after the pasted sentence. On the Clipboard, click the **Clear All button** 🔀 Clear All .

The cut text is removed from the Clipboard.

8. Select the name *Nina Martinez* after the *From:* heading and click the **Copy button** 🖹 on the Standard toolbar.

The selected text remains in place and is copied to the Clipboard.

9. Select the date and click the **Copy button** 🖹 on the Standard toolbar.

The date is copied to the top position on the Clipboard.

10. Click below the last line of the memo, press Enter↵ three times, and then click the **Paste All button** 🖹 Paste All on the Clipboard.

The name and the date are pasted side by side at the insertion point.

11. Insert a space between the name and the date.

12. Select the phrase—*you know who you are*—in the middle of the first paragraph.

13. Point to the selected text then press and hold the left mouse button.

A faint box appears below the pointer. The message *Move to where?* appears on the status bar.

NOTE *If you are not able to point to the selected text, the drag-and-drop option is turned off. To turn it on, click Options on the Tools menu. Click the Edit tab and then click* Drag-and-drop text editing.

14. Drag the selected text to position the insertion point between *quarter* and *should* which appear in the same sentence.

A faint dotted insertion point shows where the text will be dropped.

15. Release the mouse button.

The text appears in the new location, as shown in Figure 1.8.

16. Adjust space in the line before or after the text you just moved and between the words *you* and *who*, if necessary.

17. Save your document as *Revised Memo* in the *Tutorial* folder in your *Word Data* folder, then close the document.

18. Click **Close** ☒ to close the Clipboard.

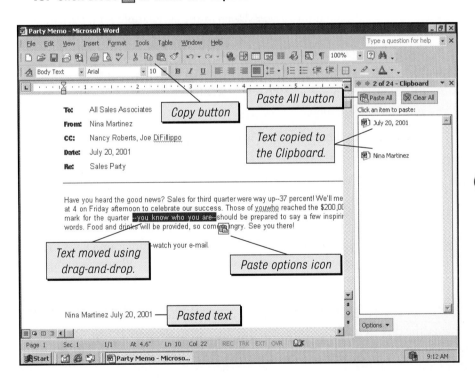

Figure 1.8
Text in new location

HANDS on

Using the Paste Special Command

In this activity, you will copy a memo header from a Word document then use the Paste Special command to paste it into another document that has been saved in a different file format. (You will learn more about file formats in the next activity.)

1. Open *Party Memo* in your *Word Data* folder.

2. Position your pointer in the selection bar at the upper-left corner of the document. When your pointer becomes an arrow, drag down in the selection bar to select all the material at the top of the document including the horizontal rule below *Re: Sales Party*.

The memo header material appears highlighted in the document.

3. Click the **Copy button** 📋, then click **Open** on the File menu and navigate to your *Word Data* folder, if necessary.

4. Click the **Files of type triangle button**, then click **Rich Text Format** to view only the files saved in that format.

5. Open the *Praise Memo* document.

The blinking insertion point appears next to the first character in the document.

6. Click **Paste Special** on the Edit menu.

7. Click the **Formatted Text (RTF) option** in the Paste Special list box and click **OK**.

The memo header is pasted into *Praise Memo* in the compatible RTF format.

8. Select *Sales Party* in the memo header and type Congratulations! to replace this text.

9. Save your document as *MKDesigns-RTF* in the *Tutorial* folder in your *Word Data* folder.

10. Close all open files; click **No** if prompted to save changes.

MANAGING FOLDERS AND CHANGING FILE TYPES

When you need to open a document, it is important to locate it quickly. One way to do that is to store related files together in a folder. Folders allow you to organize files by grouping related files together under a meaningful folder name. Creating a new folder can be accomplished in either the Save As or the Open dialog box—click the Create New Folder button 📁, enter a name for the new folder, and click OK. Change the drive letter or folder name that appears in the *Save in* text box (Save As dialog box) or the *Look in* text box (Open dialog box) to place your new folder in that location. Individual documents and folders with all their contents can also be deleted from the Save As or Open dialog box when they are no longer needed.

A **file type** or **file format** is a category or standard that is assigned to every file on a computer system. Common file types include *Word Document, Rich Text Format,* or *Text Only.* It is not unusual to save a Word file in a different file type so it can be accessed by another program. For example, if you want to share a document with a co-worker who has a different word processing program you may need to save your document in a format that is compatible with that program.

Since your Word files will usually be opened using the Word application software, in most cases you can simply accept the default file format *(Word Document)* in the

Save As dialog box. To save a document in a different file format, open the document and click Save As on the File menu to open the Save As dialog box. Then click the *Save as type* triangle button and choose a file format from the displayed list.

HANDS on

Changing File Types and Creating and Deleting Folders

In this activity, you will open a file in your *Word Data* folder then create a new folder in the *Tutorial* folder in which to save it. Before saving the file, you'll change the file format. Finally, you'll rename the folder then delete the new folder and its contents.

1. **Click Open on the File menu, navigate to your *Word Data* folder in the Open dialog box, then double-click *Australian Islands Article* to open it.**

2. **Click Save As on the File menu.**

The Save As dialog box appears containing the *Word Data* folders and files.

3. **Double-click the *Tutorial* folder.**

4. **Click the Create New Folder button 📁 on the dialog box toolbar.**

As shown in Figure 1.9, the New Folder dialog box appears requesting a name for the new folder. Note that the *Tutorial* folder is displayed in the *Save in* box of the Save As dialog box; this is where your new folder will be stored.

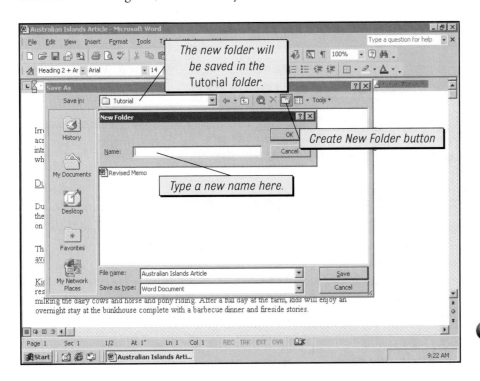

Word BASICS

Creating and Deleting Folders
Create a folder:

1. Click Open or Save As on the File menu and navigate to the location for your new folder.

2. Click the Create New Folder button, type the folder name, and press Enter⏎.

Delete a folder:

1. In the Open or Save As dialog box, click the folder you want to delete.

2. Click the Delete button.

Word BASICS

Changing a File Type

1. With the document open, click Save As on the File menu.

2. In the Save As dialog box, navigate to the location where you wish to save your file.

3. Click the *Save as type* triangle button, click a file type, and click Save.

Figure 1.9
Creating a new folder

5. Type *Australian Islands Files* in the *Name* text box and click **OK**.

The *Australian Islands Files* folder displays in the *Save in* box indicating this is where the open file will be stored.

6. In the *File name* text box, edit the existing file name to read *Australian Islands Article 1*.

7. Click the **Save as type triangle button**, click **Rich Text Format** on the drop-down list, then click **Save**.

The Save As dialog box closes and *Australian Islands Article 1* is saved in Rich Text Format within the new *Australian Islands Files* folder.

8. Close *Australian Islands Article 1*.

9. Click the **Open button** 📂.

The contents of the *Australian Islands Files* folder appear in the Open dialog box.

10. Click the **Up One Level button** 🖃.

The Open dialog box displays the contents of the *Tutorial* folder, including the *Australian Islands Files* folder.

11. Click the *Australian Islands Files* folder, then click the **Delete button** ✕ on the dialog box toolbar.

The Confirm Folder Delete dialog box asks if you want to remove the folder and its contents.

12. Click **Yes**.

The new folder and its contents are deleted.

13. Click **Cancel** to close the Open dialog box.

PREVIEWING AND PRINTING

Printing is a simple task in Word, whether you want to print a document, an envelope, or mailing labels. However, before you print any document, get into the habit of using the Print Preview button 🔍.

Previewing a Multi-Page Document

Print Preview lets you look at each page just as it will appear when printed. You can examine the format of up to six pages at once or one page at a time. In Print Preview, clicking a scroll arrow displays the next or previous page. You will notice that if you view the entire page at the default 40 percent size the text is too small to read; however, you can check that page breaks are satisfactory, margins are a consistent size, and headings are all the same style. You can see whether you need to make any adjustments prior to printing. If you wish to read the text at a certain place in the document, click that area to display the document at 100 percent; click the document again to return it to 40 percent.

Another Way

Build a folder structure of parent folders and subfolders within your Windows operating system. Using Windows Explorer, click the drive or folder where you want the new folders(s), point to New on the File menu, and click Folder.

Did you know?

You can print a document to a file so that you can later print the file on a different type of printer than the one used to create the document. For more information, enter the keywords *print to file* into the Ask a Question box.

Printing a Page and Printing Selected Pages

Clicking the Print button 🖨 on the Standard toolbar prints one copy (or **printout**) of all pages of your document. To print only certain pages, click Print on the File menu. Then, in the Print dialog box, specify whether you want to print just the current page (the page with the insertion point), only selected text (the *Selection* option), or several pages. Type page numbers with a hyphen or comma to tell Word which pages to print. To cancel a print job, double-click the printer icon (on the taskbar by the clock). In the printer window, select the job you want to cancel and click Cancel Printing on the Document menu.

Previewing and Printing a Multi-Page Document

In this activity, you will preview a multi-page document and then you will print selected pages from the document.

1. **Open *Atlas* in your *Word Data* folder.**

2. **Click the Print Preview button 🔍 on the Standard toolbar.**

The first page of *Atlas* appears at a reduced size in the Print Preview window.

3. **Click the Multiple Pages button ▦ in the Preview toolbar.**

A drop-down display of icons representing document pages appears.

4. **Point at the third icon in the first row (1 × 3 Pages) and click.**

The first three pages appear on the preview screen, as shown in Figure 1.10.

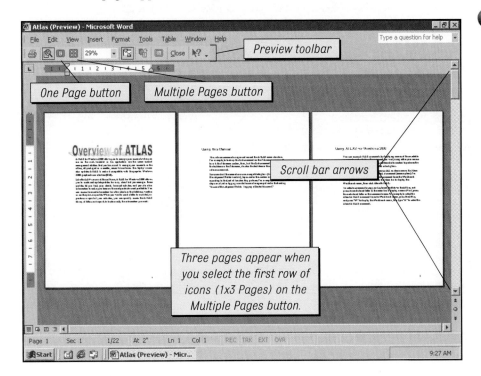

Figure 1.10
Print Preview window

5. Click the down scroll arrow.

The next three pages display.

6. Click the **One Page button** on the Preview toolbar to view one page on the preview screen.

7. On the vertical scroll bar, click once between the scroll box and the up arrow.

The previous page displays.

8. Click the document and watch it zoom to 100 percent size then click the document again to restore it to 40 percent size.

9. Click the **Normal View button** on the View toolbar.

The Print Preview window disappears and your document displays again in Normal View. Your preview of the document indicated that the layout is fine.

10. Click **Print** on the File menu to open the Print dialog box.

11. In the *Page range* section, select the **Pages option**.

12. Type 1,6,20 in the Pages text box.

Word will print these pages of *Atlas*.

13. Verify that *Number of copies* is set to 1, as shown in Figure 1.11. If not, click the triangle button until 1 appears in the list box. Then, click **OK**.

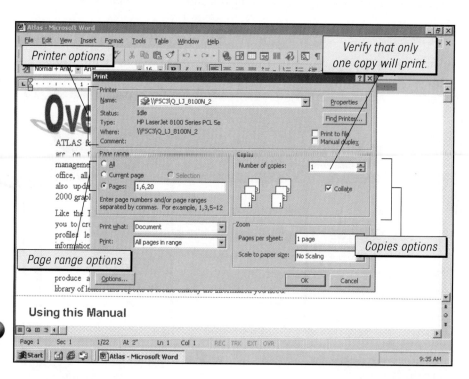

Figure 1.11
Print dialog box

Lesson 1

14. Navigate to page 3 of *Atlas* and click an insertion point on that page.

15. Click **Print** on the File menu.

16. In the *Page range* section of the Print dialog box, select **Current Page** and click **OK**.

Word prints the third page of *Atlas*.

17. Close the document.

Printing Labels and an Envelope

Through Word you can type addresses and print them on self-adhesive mailing labels or envelopes that can be fed manually through your printer. The self-adhesive mailing labels are commonly available at office supply stores.

In this activity, you will print a sheet of labels and attach an envelope to a letter, using Word's Envelopes and Labels tool. Check that the printer is switched on and secure permission to print the labels and an envelope before you start this activity.

> **NOTE** *If sheets of self-adhesive labels or envelopes are not available, this activity can be completed by printing on plain paper.*

1. Start Word, if necessary, then click the **New Blank Document button** .

2. Point to **Letters and Mailings** on the Tools menu, and click **Envelopes and Labels** on the submenu.

3. In the Envelopes and Labels dialog box, click the **Options button** on the Labels tab.

The Label Options dialog box appears.

4. Click the **Label products triangle button** and select a label product type to match your labels.

5. In the *Product number* section, select an Address label, such as *5260 - Address*, to match the number on your mailing labels then click **OK**.

> **NOTE** *Choose any label product type and address label if you intend to print on plain paper.*

6. Type a friend's name and address in the Address box then clear the *Use return address* check box, if necessary.

7. Click to select the *Full page of the same label* option, if necessary.

Printing a Label
To print a full page of the same label:

1. Point to Letters and Mailings on the Tools menu, then click Envelopes and Labels.

2. Click the Labels tab and the Options button.

3. Choose the label product and product number and click OK.

4. Type the address and select the *Full page of the same label* option.

5. Click the New Document button.

6. Click the Print button.

WORD 2002

NOTE *If you want to print just one label, click* Single label *and set the row and column list boxes to correspond to the desired label on the sheet of labels you will use.*

8. Click the **Options button** on the Labels tab of the Envelopes and Labels dialog box. Click the **Tray triangle button** and select **Manual Feed** (for commercial labels) or a plain paper tray if commercial labels are unavailable. Click **OK**.

At this point you could click the Print button in the Envelopes and Labels dialog box to print an entire sheet with the same address; however, proceed to the next step to see how different addresses can be printed on the same sheet.

9. Click the **New Document button**. Select the text in the first label, type a different address, then press Tab to move to the next label.

From this point you could continue to type various addresses to print on the same sheet.

10. Save the document as *Labels* in the *Tutorial* folder in your *Word Data* folder, then close the document.

11. Open *AHS Workshop* in your *Word Data* folder.

12. Point to **Letters and Mailings** on the Tools menu, then click **Envelopes and Labels** on the submenu.

13. Click the **Envelopes tab** in the Envelopes and Labels dialog box.

The address from *AHS Workshop* appears in the *Delivery address* section, as shown in Figure 1.12. Without the address from an open letter, you would simply type the address in this dialog box.

Printing a Label

To print a label file with different names and addresses:

1. Point to Letters and Mailings on the Tools menu, then click Envelopes and Labels.

2. Click the Labels tab and the Options button.

3. Choose the label product and product number and click OK.

4. Click the New Document button.

5. Type name and address in the first label; press Tab to move to the next label.

6. Print the label document.

Figure 1.12
Envelopes and Labels dialog box

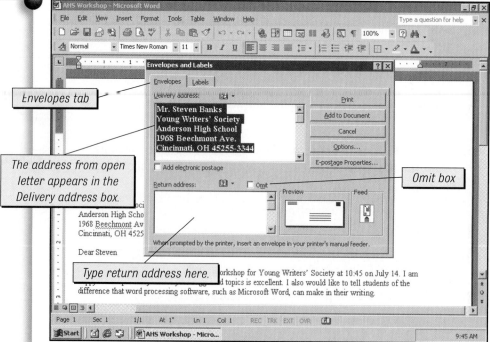

Envelopes tab

The address from open letter appears in the Delivery address box.

Omit box

Type return address here.

14. Clear the Omit box, if necessary. Type your name and address in the *Return address* box and click the **Add to Document button**.

15. Click **No** if a dialog box appears asking if you want to save the new return address as the default return address.

The envelope appears in the Word window with the delivery and return addresses.

16. Click **Print** on the File menu, select **Current page**, and click **OK** to print the envelope on plain paper.

17. Save the document as *Envelope* in the *Tutorial* folder in your *Word Data* folder then close the document.

NOTE *If you are printing on an envelope instead of plain paper, return to the Envelopes and Labels dialog box. Click Options on the Envelopes tab and choose the appropriate envelope size in the Envelope Options dialog box.*

CREATING A DOCUMENT FROM A TEMPLATE

You have learned that you can create documents by clicking the New Blank Document button 🗋. In many situations, though, you do not have to start new documents on a blank screen. Microsoft Word has preformatted **template** models that you can follow. A template includes necessary document parts, ordered and formatted. For example, the standard headings (*To:*, *From:*, and so on) and the current date are already displayed and properly arranged in the memo template. You replace the **variable information**—the text that is different in each memo you create. The template files are in the Templates box which you can access through the New Document task pane.

Each tab in the Templates dialog box represents a group of documents, such as *Letters & Faxes*, *Memos*, *Reports*, and *Web Pages*. To see the templates available in a group, click the tab. When you click the name of a specific template, a Preview box lets you see the template design. When you open the template you want to use, you are really working with a *copy* of it. That way, you can change the model document however you want and still have the original template unchanged.

Opening a Template and Replacing Variable Text

In this activity, you will open a memo template and use it to create a memo.

1. Start Word, if necessary, then click **New** on the File menu.

The New Document task pane displays.

2. Click **General Templates** in the New Document task pane.

3. In the Templates dialog box, click the **Memos tab**, if it is not on top.

Templates for creating memos appear.

Opening and Using a Template

1. Click New on the File menu.

2. Click General Templates in the New Document task pane.

3. Click the tab for the type of document in the Templates dialog box.

4. Click the template you want to use.

5. Verify that Document is selected in the Create New box.

6. Click OK.

7. Type to replace variable text, if necessary.

Additional templates are available at the Microsoft Office Template Gallery. Enter the keyword *templates* into the Ask a Question box and click the *About templates* Help topic to find the hyperlink to this page or search on the keywords *template gallery* at the *Microsoft.com* Web site.

4. Click the *Contemporary Memo* icon.

A preview of this template is displayed in the Preview window.

5. Click **Document** in the Create New box, if it is not selected, and click **OK**.

NOTE *If Template is selected when you click OK, you will open the actual template, not a copy of it. Then when you type, you would change the template.*

A copy of the *Contemporary Memo* template opens and the task pane closes. *Document* appears in the title bar followed by a number, like any other new document, because you opened a copy of the template. If you opened the actual template, the title bar would indicate *Template1*.

6. Click **Normal View** 📄 then scroll and read the document.

7. Click anywhere within the brackets after *To:*.

The text within the brackets is highlighted. You have selected variable text and now need to replace it with your information.

8. Type All Sales Associates to replace the variable text.

9. After *CC:* (meaning *copies to*), click the variable text and type Nancy Roberts, Joe DiFillippo.

10. Click the variable text after *From:*, and type your name.

Notice that on the next line Word has automatically inserted the current date.

11. After *Re:* (meaning *regarding*), click the variable text and type FOURTH QUARTER CONTEST.

12. Below the horizontal line, click before the first character and drag down to the end of the last paragraph to select the heading and all three paragraphs.

When you begin typing, you will replace the selected text.

13. Type the following message exactly as shown. Remember to use Backspace to erase errors as you type, and allow text to wrap at the end of each line. When finished, your memo should look like Figure 1.13.

Have you heard the good news? The Fourth Quarter Sales Contest has begun. We're tracking your sales and preparing for the best quarter ever.

The top five sales performers will receive an added bonus. Check your e-mail for more details on this exciting contest, and keep selling!

14. Save your document as *Template Memo* in the *Tutorial* folder in your *Word Data* folder, then close the document.

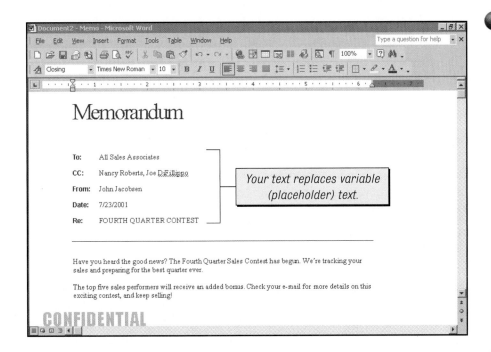

Figure 1.13
Memo created from a template

USING LANGUAGE AND GRAMMAR TOOLS

Even a good writer may make occasional errors in spelling, punctuation, subject-verb agreement, word choice, typing, verb tense, and so on. Good writers proofread their documents and correct their mistakes and declare a document final only when it is free of errors. Editing and proofreading are important for two reasons: communication and image. Errors in documents may cause readers to misunderstand your message, wasting your time and theirs. Besides, the documents you prepare—whether for yourself or an employer—represent you. Their quality and appearance convey a message about your attitude and competence.

No software can edit and proofread for you. Word provides tools to help you check spelling, grammar, and usage. The Spelling and Grammar tools flag potential errors and allow you to decide if a correction is needed in each instance. When Word detects a potential spelling or grammar error, the Spelling and Grammar Status icon on the status bar displays a red **X**. Word's AutoCorrect feature helps prevent some spelling, capitalization, and grammar errors by automatically correcting such errors as you type them. (To confirm the AutoCorrect settings on the computer you are using, click AutoCorrect Options on the Tools menu and click the AutoCorrect tab. Then select the options you want Word to automatically correct and click OK.) The Thesaurus tool (point to Language on the Tools menu) can find substitutes for words that are overused or used incorrectly in your documents. With the Replace feature you learned about earlier in this lesson, you can change occurrences of words used too often and correct repeated errors.

Checking Spelling and Grammar in a Document

The wavy, red lines in your documents mark words not in the Spelling dictionary. When you right-click one of these words, a **shortcut menu** appears. If the menu lists the correct spelling, click the correct word to replace the misspelled word. If the correct spelling is not on the shortcut menu, you may correct the spelling manually or click Ignore All. Clicking Ignore All tells Word to disregard all instances

NORTON
ONLINE

Visit **www.glencoe.com/norton/online/** for more information on Microsoft Word 2002.

of the underlined word in the current document. (Clicking Add to Dictionary puts the underlined word into the Spelling dictionary. You must not choose the Add option unless the computer belongs to you.) The wavy, red line disappears when you click one of these options. Another option on the shortcut menu is the Spelling command. Clicking it opens the Spelling dialog box, which is useful for checking spelling in long documents.

Wavy, green lines mark grammatical forms not found in the grammar rules for U.S. English usage. When you right-click this text, a shortcut menu displays. If the menu suggests an improvement to your text, you can click the suggested change if it truly improves your text. If the text is correct as is, you may click Ignore Once to remove the green underline.

When you click the Spelling and Grammar button , you can check spelling and grammar simultaneously throughout an entire document. The Spelling and Grammar tool goes automatically to the first potential spelling or grammar error and shows the sentence, with the problem highlighted. Spelling suggestions display in the Suggestions box. For grammar errors, suggestions display in the suggestions box, but a tip also displays, providing the related grammar rule and one or more examples. As soon as you choose to change or ignore the highlighted text, Word will move to the next possible error.

HANDS on

Checking Spelling and Grammar

In this activity, you will check the spelling and grammar of words and sentences identified by the Word spelling and grammar checker.

NOTE *Before beginning this activity, check that the Spelling and Grammar features are active. If necessary, click the New Blank Document button*  *to activate the menu bar, then click Options on the Tools menu. On the Spelling & Grammar tab, click to select these check boxes:* Check spelling as you type, Always suggest corrections, Check grammar as you type, *and* Check grammar with spelling. *Clear the other check boxes. Click the Custom Dictionaries button and verify that* CUSTOM.DIC *shows in the Custom Dictionaries dialog box. Check that* Grammar Only *appears in the* Writing style *list box. After you adjust these settings, close the Options dialog box and the blank document window.*

1. **Open** *Memo Draft* **in your** *Word Data* **folder then save the document as** *Memo Draft Revised* **in the** *Tutorial* **folder in your** *Word Data* **folder.**

2. **Point to the underlined name** *Riberts* **and right-click anywhere in the name.**

A shortcut menu opens showing the suggested word *Roberts* as a possible correction. You decide that the name is misspelled and should be *Roberts*.

3. **Click** *Roberts* **on the shortcut menu.**

The correct name replaces the misspelled name in your memo and the red, wavy underline disappears.

Word BASICS

Checking Spelling and Grammar

1. Right-click a word underlined in red (to correct spelling) or green (to correct grammar).

2. Click an option on the shortcut menu or type the correction in the document.

Or:

1. Click the Spelling and Grammar button on the Standard toolbar.

2. Click an option in the dialog box.

4. Click the **Spelling and Grammar button** 🔲 on the Standard toolbar.

The Spelling and Grammar dialog box appears displaying the first sentence, as shown in Figure 1.14. You may click Ignore Rule to ignore the highlighted error and similar errors (Ignore Rule can be useful in editing a long document). Click Change to implement the suggested correction. In this instance, you want more information about the possible error.

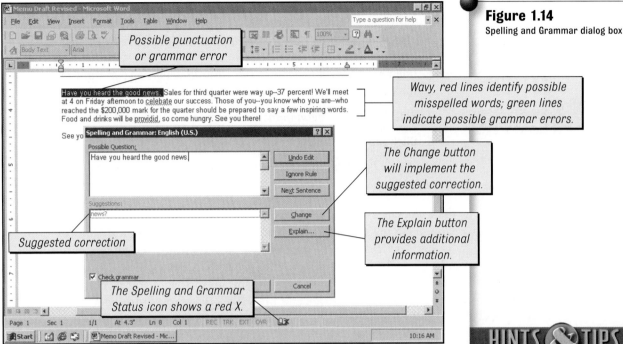

Figure 1.14
Spelling and Grammar dialog box

5. Click **Explain**.

The Office Assistant appears with additional information and examples.

WARNING *Not all suggested grammar changes are improvements. Read the information very carefully before deciding to change your text. Also, Word may not detect some errors.*

6. Read the information, then click **Change**.

The sentence is corrected—a question mark replaces the period and the green line disappears. The Spelling and Grammar dialog box moves on to a misspelled word and provides suggested changes.

7. Make appropriate changes in the Spelling and Grammar dialog box to correct the next two misspelled words.

WARNING *Never add words to a dictionary (Add to Dictionary button) unless you have permission to do so or you own the computer. In any case, always check a word carefully before adding it to the Word dictionary.*

The Office Assistant states that the spelling and grammar check is complete.

8. Right-click the **Office Assistant** then click **Hide** on the shortcut menu.

9. Save and close the document.

HINTS & TIPS

You can do a readability check through the Spelling & Grammar tab of the Options dialog box (Tools menu). Select *Check grammar with spelling* and *Show readability statistics.* Click the Spelling and Grammar button. When Word is finished with the Spelling and Grammar check, the Readability Statistics dialog box will appear with data about the document.

HINTS & TIPS

You can restore the spelling and grammar marks in a document that you (or another user) previously chose to ignore. Click Options on the Tools menu and click Recheck Document on the Spelling & Grammar tab.

Using the Thesaurus

The **Thesaurus** tool is a source of synonyms and antonyms that can help you find alternative words as you edit your document. If you tend to use the same words or phrases repeatedly, the Thesaurus tool can help you vary your vocabulary. In this activity, you will use the Thesaurus tool to find replacements for several words in the *Memo Draft Revised document.*

1. Open *Memo Draft Revised* in the *Tutorial* folder in your *Word Data* folder.

2. Select the word *good* in the first sentence of the document.

3. Click the **Tools menu**, point to **Language**, and click **Thesaurus**.

   WARNING *If the Thesaurus command does not appear on the Language submenu, see your instructor. You may need to install the Thesaurus.*

Using the Thesaurus

1. Select the word in question.

2. Click the Tools menu, point to Language, and click Thesaurus.

3. Click a synonym or type a word in the *Replace with Synonym* box.

4. Click Replace.

The Thesaurus dialog box appears, as shown in Figure 1.15. The word *good* appears in the *Looked Up* box and its meaning is defined in the *Meanings* box below. The *Replace with Synonym* box provides words and phrases with similar meanings that could substitute for *good*. Click any word in the *Meanings* box to view a list of corresponding synonyms for that word. Type a new word in the *Replace with Synonym* box and press Enter◄┘ to move it to the *Looked Up* box and view a new list of meanings and synonyms for that word.

Figure 1.15

Thesaurus dialog box

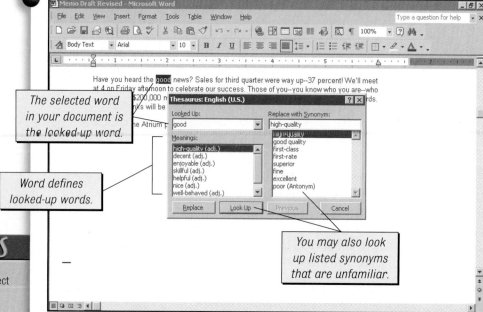

The selected word in your document is the looked-up word.

Word defines looked-up words.

You may also look up listed synonyms that are unfamiliar.

HINTS & TIPS

To find a synonym quickly, select the word you would like to replace and right-click. On the shortcut menu, point to Synonyms and then, if synonyms are suggested, click the option that fits the context of your sentence.

4. In the *Replace with Synonym* box, click *excellent* then click the **Look Up button**.

The word *excellent* now appears in the *Looked Up* box. As shown in the *Meanings* box, the word means outstanding—an appropriate replacement for *good*.

5. Click the **Replace button**.

The word *outstanding* replaces *good* in your document.

6. Save your changes as *Final Memo* in the *Tutorial* folder in your *Word Data* folder, then close the document.

Using AutoText, AutoComplete, and AutoCorrect

Many of your documents have repetitive elements that Word enables you to insert automatically so you can avoid typing them. AutoText is one such method of saving text or graphics for use elsewhere. When the AutoComplete feature is turned on, Word will display a ScreenTip when you type the first few characters of an AutoText entry. Pressing [Enter←] will place the AutoText suggestion in the document. In the same way, the current date and time can be easily inserted into a document using AutoComplete. Or you can use the Insert menu to choose from a large selection of various date/time formats. AutoCorrect automatically replaces typed characters with symbols or replaces incorrectly typed words with correctly spelled words as you type them.

Inserting Text Using AutoText, AutoComplete, and the Insert Menu

In this activity, you will add AutoText to the end of a document and you will use AutoComplete to insert the current date. You will then insert a new date format using the Insert menu and modify it to create a custom date/time format.

1. Open *Home Page Support* in your *Word Data* folder.

2. Press [Ctrl] + [End] to move the insertion point to the end of the document, then press [Enter←] two times.

3. Click the **View menu**, point to **Toolbars**, and click **AutoText**.

The AutoText toolbar appears below the Formatting toolbar.

4. Click the **All Entries button** [All Entries ▾] on the AutoText toolbar and point to Header/Footer.

The All Entries menu and the Header/Footer submenu display. (You'll learn more about creating and modifying actual headers and footers in Lesson 2.) Pointing to any of the items on the All Entries menu will display AutoText that can be inserted into your document.

5. On the Header/Footer submenu, click the **Filename option**.

The name of your file *(Home Page Support)* is inserted in the document. Whenever you change the name of this file, Word will automatically change this text in your document.

6. Click the **AutoText button** ▦, then click the AutoText tab of the AutoCorrect dialog box, if necessary.

WORD 2002

Word **BASICS**

Inserting AutoText

1. Point to Toolbars (View menu) and click AutoText to display the AutoText toolbar.

2. Click an insertion point for the AutoText.

3. Click the All Entries button, point to a category, and click the AutoText.

Inserting AutoText Using AutoComplete

1. Click the AutoText button and select the *Show AutoComplete suggestions* check box, if necessary.

2. As you type, watch for the AutoComplete ScreenTip to appear containing the text to be inserted.

3. Press Enter↵ if the AutoComplete text is appropriate; continue to type if it is not appropriate.

The AutoText tab displays a list of AutoText entries; clicking an item in the list displays the item in the Preview window as it would appear in a document.

7. Click to select the *Show AutoComplete suggestions* check box, then click **OK**.

8. Press Spacebar after the file name, type the current month, and press Spacebar again.

An AutoComplete ScreenTip appears prompting you to press Enter↵ to insert the date.

9. Press Enter↵ to automatically insert today's date, a comma, and the year.

10. Drag to select the date, then click **Date and Time** on the Insert menu.

11. In the Date and Time dialog box, click to select the **Update automatically check box**, if necessary.

Update automatically will cause the date in the file to be updated to the current date each time the file is printed. Notice the variety of date and time formats.

12. Click a different selection (a format like *Wednesday, March 20, 2001*) that does *not* display the time, then click **OK** to close the dialog box.

The date is inserted in the new format. By modifying the **field codes,** the hidden codes that automatically update the date and/or time, you can create a custom format not available as a selection in the Date/Time dialog box.

13. Right-click the date format in the document then click **Toggle Field Codes** on the shortcut menu.

The underlying field code is revealed representing the day, current month, date, and year in a format like *{DATE \@ "dddd, MMMM dd, yyyy"}*. (The exact code will vary depending upon the format you selected.)

 **BASICS**

Inserting a Date/Time Format

1. Click an insertion point in your document.

2. Click Date and Time on the Insert menu, and click the desired format.

3. Click to select the Update Automatically check box, then click OK.

14. Right-click the date format code and click **Edit Field** on the shortcut menu.

The Field dialog box appears with the current date format (such as *Wednesday, March 21, 2001*) highlighted in the *Field properties* list. The corresponding code for the current date format appears in the *Date formats* box.

15. Click after the last character of the code, press Spacebar, then type h:mm am/pm and click **OK**.

The Field dialog box closes. The time has been added to the date format in your document.

> **NOTE** *Learn more about editing field codes in date/time formats by entering keywords* field formats *in the* Ask a Question *box. Click the* Date-Time Picture (\@) field switch *link.*

16. Save the file as *Home Page Support Revised* in the *Tutorial* folder in your *Word Data* folder and close the document.

17. Click **View**, point to **Toolbars**, and click **AutoText** to close the AutoText toolbar.

HANDS on

Using AutoCorrect While Typing

In this activity, you will add a sentence to a letter while using the AutoCorrect tool to insert a symbol and correct your misspelled words.

1. Open the *AHS Workshop* document in your *Word Data* folder.

2. Click **AutoCorrect Options** on the Tools menu to open the AutoCorrect dialog box, then click the **AutoCorrect tab**.

3. Click to select any check boxes that do not have a check mark.

The *Replace text as you type* list box contains common typographical errors or typed symbols (left column) and corresponding corrections (right column), as shown in Figure 1.16. The copyright symbol appears at the top of the list.

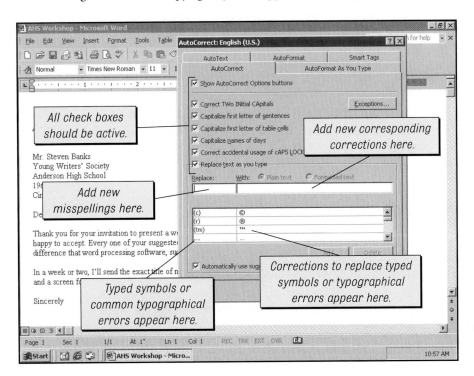

Figure 1.16
AutoCorrect dialog box

NORTON
ONLINE

Visit **www.glencoe.com/norton/online/** for more information on Microsoft Word 2002.

4. Scroll down in the *Replace text as you type* list box until you see the word *about* in the right column; make note of the corresponding typographical error in the left column.

5. Click **Cancel** to close the dialog box.

6. Click an insertion point at the end of the second paragraph in the *AHS Workshop* letter, then press [Enter⏎] twice.

AutoCorrect will replace a typed symbol or misspelled word as you type. To see the automatic correction, watch the Word window as you type the misspelled word *abbout* and the symbol *(c)* in the following step.

7. **Type these exact words (including misspellings):** I will let you know **abbout the copyright (c) 2004 issue pertanning to your documents.**

The misspelled word *abbout* changes to *about* as you type; the characters *(c)* are automatically replaced with the copyright symbol; however, the misspelled word *pertanning* is not corrected—it appears with a wavy, red underline. You could right-click this misspelled word and correct it on the shortcut menu; however, since you habitually type this word incorrectly it makes sense to add it to the AutoCorrect list.

8. **Right-click *pertanning*, point to AutoCorrect on the shortcut menu, then click AutoCorrect Options.**

9. **Type pertanning in the *Replace* box, press** `Tab`**, then type pertaining in the *With* box.**

10. **Click Add, then click OK to close the dialog box.**

11. **Select the sentence you just typed and press** `Delete`**, then retype it (including the errors) while watching for the replacement text to be inserted as you type:** I will let you know abbout the copyright (c) 2004 issue pertanning to your documents.

All the misspellings are automatically corrected and the copyright symbol is inserted.

12. **Point to the middle of the word *pertaining* and when a blue horizontal bar appears under the first two characters, point to the bar.**

The AutoCorrect Options button ⬛▾ appears.

13. **Click the AutoCorrect Options button ⬛▾.**

This button provides the options to restore the previous spelling or stop AutoCorrecting the word. Clicking Control AutoCorrect Options would take you back to the AutoCorrect Options dialog box.

14. **Click the option to stop automatically correcting the word *pertanning*.**

The incorrect spelling is restored; the red, wavy underline again appears under the word.

15. **Save your document as *Autocorrect Edits* in the *Tutorial* folder in your *Word Data* folder and close the document.**

Add a frequently used word or phrase to the AutoText tab of the AutoCorrect dialog box. Type the entry in the *Enter AutoText entries here* list and click OK. To delete an entry, click the entry and press the Delete button.

Using Help

Searching for a File

In this activity, you will explore Help to learn about using the Search feature to find a file on your computer.

1. In the Ask a Question box, type find a file and press Enter.

2. Click the <u>Find a file</u> link, click <u>Show All</u>, and read the information.

3. Close the Help window, then click the **Search button** on the Standard toolbar.

The Basic Search task pane displays.

4. Type Atlas in the *Search text* box, and click **Search**.

5. In a few moments, all documents containing *Atlas* will display in the Search Results task pane.

6. Click one of the files to open it, and then close the file and close the task pane.

Self Check

Test your knowledge by answering the following questions. See Appendix B to check your answers.

1. To count the number of lines in your document, click the _____ button.

2. Double-click the _____ button on the status bar to switch between Insert and Overtype modes.

3. The _____ can help you find alternative words as you edit a document.

4. The _____ is a temporary holding area for text that has been cut or copied.

5. To open a template, first click _____ on the File menu to activate the New Document task pane.

INSERTING HYPERLINKS

A hyperlink is a shortcut or jump that, when clicked, links you to another page, document, or Web site. Hyperlinks are usually easy to recognize within a document. For example, hyperlinks are often in a distinctive color and are often underlined. Typically, after you click a hyperlink, the link changes color to remind you that you already followed that link. In this activity, you will insert a hyperlink into a Web site within a document.

NOTE *Before starting this activity, connect to the Internet through your Internet Service Provider (ISP). If necessary, type your user name and password. If you are not sure how to connect to the Internet, ask your instructor for assistance.*

1. **Open** *Star Gazette Article* **in your** *Word Data* **folder then point to Toolbars on the View menu and click Web.**

The Web toolbar displays at the top of the document window. The Address box in the Web toolbar contains the path and file name of your open document. Table 1.4 provides a brief description of each button on the Web toolbar.

Table 1.4	The Word Web Toolbar	
Button	**Name**	**Description**
⇦	Back	Displays the previous Web site that you visited.
⇨	Forward	Displays the next Web site that you visited.
⊗	Stop	Stops the Internet connection in progress.
🗘	Refresh	Reloads the current site.
🏠	Start Page	Loads the Web site that you have specified as your starting point on the Web.
🔍	Search the Web	Loads the Web site that you have specified for launching Web searches.
Favorites ▾	Favorites	Provides access to your list of favorite Web sites.
Go ▾	Go	Allows you to access a Web site or document; also allows you to specify your Start and Search pages.
⬆	Show Only Web Toolbar	Hides or displays all visible toolbars except the Web toolbar.
http://www.microsoft.com	Address	Allows you to enter the location of a Web site you wish to open.
▾	Toolbar Options	Allows you to customize the toolbar by adding or removing buttons or reset the toolbar to display the default buttons.

2. Click the text within the Address box to select it then type the following address: http://www.eps.mcgill.ca/~bud/craters/FaceOfVenus.html. Verify that every character is accurate and no spaces appear between the characters, then press Enter⏎.

Word opens your browser at the *Face of Venus* Web site.

3. Close your browser window then scroll to the end of the open document and set the insertion point two lines below the last line.

4. Type Click here for Venus on the Web. Then select this sentence.

5. Click the **Insert Hyperlink button** 🔗 on the Standard toolbar.

The Insert Hyperlink dialog box appears as shown in Figure 1.17. The text you have selected as your hyperlink appears in the *Text to display* box.

6. Click **Existing File or Web Page** in the *Link to* bar, then click the **Address box triangle button** to display a list of recently visited Web sites.

7. Click the *Face of Venus* Web address which should be the first site in the list, then click **OK**.

8. Point to the hyperlink in the document, read the ScreenTip which includes the Web address, then press Ctrl and click the hyperlink.

Again, Word opens your browser at the *Face of Venus* site.

9. Close your browser to return to the Word window, then save the document as *Venus Link* in the *Tutorial* folder in your *Word Data* folder.

10. Close the Web toolbar, then close all open files and exit Word.

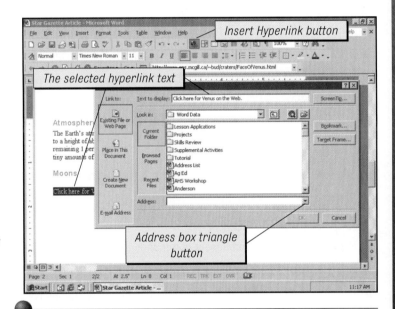

Figure 1.17
Insert Hyperlink dialog box

WARNING *You may proceed directly to the exercises in this lesson. If, however, you are finished with your computer session, follow the "shut down" procedures for your lab or school environment.*

SUMMARY AND EXERCISES

SUMMARY

More people use computers for word processing than any other task. Word is a powerful word processing application. Lesson 1 introduced basic word processing terms; explained how to start Word; and explored menus, toolbars, and other objects in the Word window. You learned to open, view, navigate, type, edit, preview, and print documents. You learned that Word offers a variety of templates that you can adapt to your needs. You used the Word language tools and the Copy, Cut, and Paste features to help edit documents. You inserted text into your document using the Insert menu, AutoText, AutoComplete, and AutoCorrect. You learned how to manage files and folders and how to change file types. Finally, you were introduced to the features of the Web toolbar and learned how to add a hyperlink to a document.

Now that you have completed this lesson, you should be able to do the following:

- Explain word processing. (page 39)
- Start Microsoft Word and name objects in the document window. (page 40)
- Provide a brief description of each menu on the Word menu bar. (page 41)
- Provide a brief description of each button on the Standard toolbar. (page 42)
- Look at documents in four different views. (page 44)
- Select single words or lines, whole paragraphs, or an entire document. (page 46)
- Find specific pages and text using the Find and Replace dialog box. (page 47)
- Edit text using the Insert and Overtype modes. (page 50)
- Rename and save a file. (page 51)
- Replace and delete text. (page 52)
- Use the Undo, Redo, and Repeat commands to edit text. (page 54)
- Use the Office Clipboard to cut, copy, and paste text. (page 56)
- Use the drag-and-drop method to move and copy text. (page 57)
- Create and delete folders and change file types. (page 60)
- Preview a document. (page 62)
- Print one page or selected pages of a multi-page document. (page 63)
- Print labels and an envelope. (page 65)
- Create a new document from a template. (page 67)
- Use the Spelling and Grammar tools to help edit documents as you type. (page 69)
- Use the Thesaurus tool to find alternate words. (page 72)
- Insert text using AutoText and AutoComplete. (page 73)
- Modify a date/time format using the Insert menu. (page 73)
- Use AutoCorrect to correct text while typing. (page 75)
- Search for a file on your hard drive. (page 77)
- Describe the Word Web toolbar features and insert a hyperlink into a document. (page 78)

CONCEPTS REVIEW

1 TRUE/FALSE

Circle T if the statement is true or F if the statement is false.

T   F   **1.** To select a sentence, press ⌈Ctrl⌉ and click anywhere in the sentence.

T   F   **2.** To select a paragraph, double-click anywhere within the paragraph.

T   F   **3.** The Normal View is the ideal choice for typing and editing text.

T   F   **4.** In Overtype mode, the text you type pushes existing text to the right.

T   F   **5.** The Find and Replace dialog box allows you to go to a specific page in a document.

T   F   **6.** To print all pages of a document, click the Print button on the Standard toolbar.

T   F   **7.** When you type to the end of a line, *word wrap* automatically moves the insertion point to the next line.

T   F   **8.** You can right-click a word underlined in red to correct its spelling.

T   F   **9.** When you *cut* text you do not remove it from its original location.

T   F   **10.** AutoCorrect and the Spelling and Grammar tools have eliminated the need for you to edit and proofread your documents.

2 MATCHING

Match each of the terms on the left with the definitions on the right.

TERMS	DEFINITIONS
1. selection bar	**a.** Allows you to quickly count characters, words, or lines of text in your document
2. Edit menu	
3. Word Count toolbar	**b.** Application that allows creation of text-based documents
4. AutoComplete	**c.** Includes the Find command
5. paste	**d.** A method of moving text without the Office Clipboard
6. status bar	
7. drag-and-drop	**e.** To insert text stored on the Office Clipboard
8. Print preview	**f.** Preformatted model documents
9. word processor	**g.** Invisible column between the left edge of the document window and the left margin of the page
10. templates	
	h. Displays your location within a document and the typing mode
	i. Automatically tries to finish what you are typing
	j. Allows you to see just how your document will look when printed

SUMMARY AND EXERCISES

3 COMPLETION

Fill in the missing word or phrase for each of the following statements.

1. Use the _____ key to erase errors to the left of the insertion point.

2. The Print Preview button is on the _____ toolbar.

3. To select a word, _____ it.

4. The blinking vertical bar where text is inserted when you type is called the _____ .

5. Word temporarily stores information that you have cut or copied from your document on the _____ .

6. To prepare a document by following a preset format, open a _____ .

7. The _____ appears at the right side of the application window when you first open Word.

8. The _____ button on the Standard toolbar removes text from your document and places the text on the Clipboard.

9. The quickest way to locate a particular word or phrase in a long document is to use the _____ command.

10. When you use _____ , the text you type is inserted into existing text, pushing the characters after it to the right.

4 SHORT ANSWER

Write a brief answer to each of the following questions.

1. Describe how to activate and deactivate Overtype mode using the mouse.

2. Name the four document views and describe each view briefly.

3. Describe how to start Microsoft Word.

4. Explain the advantages of using a template.

5. Describe three features of the Word Web toolbar.

6. Describe two ways to navigate a document without using the scroll bars.

7. Explain why you might need to save a document as a different file type (file format).

8. Describe how to save an existing document under a new name.

9. Explain how to create a new folder and how to delete a folder.

10. Explain the advantages and limitations of using AutoCorrect and the Word Spelling and Grammar tools to edit and proofread documents.

5 IDENTIFICATION

Label each of the elements of the Word window in Figure 1.18.

Figure 1.18

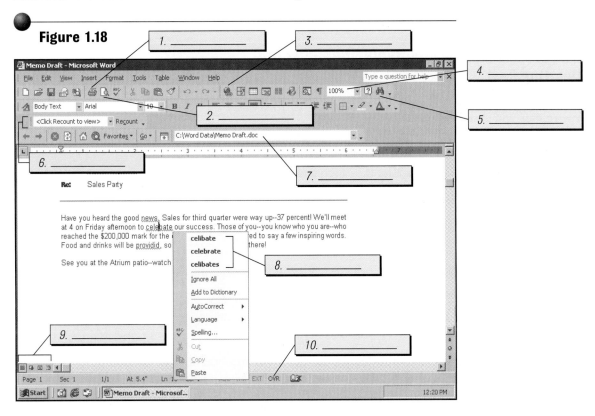

SKILLS REVIEW

Complete all of the Skills Review problems in sequential order to review your skills to start Word; identify objects in the document window; view documents; navigate a document and replace, select, and delete text; insert a paragraph; use Undo, Redo, and Repeat; move, copy, cut, and paste text; use the Paste Special command; create and delete folders and rename and save files in a new format; preview and print; create a document from a template; check spelling and grammar; use the Thesaurus; and insert text using AutoText, AutoCorrect, AutoComplete, and the Insert menu.

1 Starting Word and Viewing a File

1. Click the **Start button** ![Start], point to **Programs**, and click **Microsoft Word**.

2. Click the **Open button** on the Standard toolbar.

3. Click the **Look in triangle button**; then click the drive (and open the folder, if necessary) that contains your *Word Data* folder.

4. Double-click *Star Gazette Article*.

5. Click the **Print Layout View button** .

6. Scroll to the left and right and examine the width of the side margins.

7. Click the **Web Layout View button** .

8. Scroll rapidly to the end of the document; click an insertion point; then press `Ctrl` + `Home` to go to the beginning of the document.

9. Click the **Normal View button** `≣`.

2 Navigating a Document and Replacing, Selecting, and Deleting Text

1. With *Star Gazette Article* open in your document window, click the **Find button** `🔍`, type **roman**, and click **Find Next**.

2. Activate Overtype mode in the status bar, and change *r* to *R*.

3. Find *nitrogen* and change the comma after it to a semicolon.

4. In the same sentence, change the comma after *oxygen* to a semicolon.

5. Search for *it's* and delete the apostrophe; click **Find Next** again and delete the apostrophe in the second occurrence.

6. Click **Find Next**. A dialog box indicates that the search is complete; click **OK**.

7. Click the **Replace tab**. In the *Find what* box, type **Venus's**; in the *Replace with* box, type **Venus'**. Click **Find Next** then click **Replace**. Continue searching to correct all occurrences.

8. Click the **Find tab**, scroll to the top of the document, click an insertion point, then find the second occurrence of *drift*. Select the sentence in which it occurs and delete it.

9. Click the **Go To tab**. In the *Go to what* list box, click **Page** and type 2 in the *Enter page number box*. Then click the **Go To button**.

10. In the *Enter page number* box, type −1 and click the **Go To button**.

11. Close the Find and Replace dialog box, save your document as *Star Gazette Edited* in the *Skills Review* folder in your *Word Data* folder, then close the document.

3 Inserting a Paragraph and Using the Word Count Toolbar

1. Open *Star Gazette Article* in your *Word Data* folder, and press `Ctrl` + `End` to go to the end of the document.

2. Point to **Toolbars** on the View menu, and open the Word Count toolbar.

3. Click the **Word Count Statistics triangle button** `520 Lines ▾` and click **Words** to count the number of words in the file.

4. Press `Enter↵`, and type the following paragraph using Insert mode. Correct your errors using `Backspace` and `Delete`.

The Earth's single moon is large in comparison with the natural satellites of all the other planets except for Pluto. Astronomers actually consider the Earth-Moon system to be a double planet. Its size gives the moon a significant gravitational influence on the Earth, causing our oceans to have tides.

5. Click the **Recount button** Recount to count the number of words in the file.

6. Save your document as *Star Gazette Addition* in the *Skills Review* folder in your *Word Data* folder and close the document. Close the Word Count toolbar.

4 Undoing, Redoing, and Repeating Actions

1. Open *Star Gazette Article* in your *Word Data* folder.

2. Click the **Find button** and find the word *percent* using the Find and Replace dialog box. Select the word, then type the percent sign (*%*).

3. Find the next two occurrences of the word *percent* and in each instance click **Repeat Typing** on the Edit menu to replace it with the percent sign (*%*).

4. Close the Find and Replace dialog box.

5. Click the **Undo button** until each occurrence of the word *percent* is restored.

6. Click the **Redo button** to restore the percent sign (*%*) in all instances; then click Undo again to reverse those actions and restore all the occurrences of *percent*.

7. Close the document; click **No** if prompted to save changes.

5 Moving and Copying Text

1. Open *Write this Way* in your *Word Data* folder.

2. Click **Office Clipboard** on the Edit menu to display the Clipboard task pane, then click **Clear All** Clear All.

3. Triple-click to select the next-to-last paragraph in the document, then click **Cut**.

4. Paste the cut text from the Clipboard into a new line at the end of the document.

5. Type **Which of these titles do you like best?** and press Enter.

6. Scroll to the top of the document and copy the document title and subtitle to the Clipboard as separate items. Scroll to the end of the document and click below the last line.

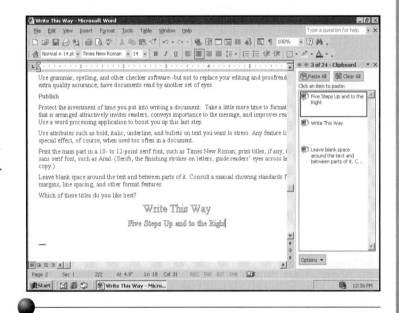

Figure 1.19

7. Click **Write This Way** on the Clipboard, then click *Five Steps Up and to the Right* on the Clipboard. (Your document should look like Figure 1.19.)

8. Next, find and select the question *Is the tone positive?*

9. Drag the sentence to the right to drop it at the end of the next sentence.

10. Save the document as *Write Revised* in the *Skills Review* folder in your *Word Data* folder then close the document and close the Clipboard.

SUMMARY AND EXERCISES

6 Using the Paste Special Command

1. Open *Australia Tour Pricing* in your *Word Data* folder.

2. Select the *Glen Travel Agency* header down to and including the date, and click **Copy** 🖹.

3. Click **Open** 📂, then click the **Files of type triangle button** and click **Rich Text Format**.

4. Open *Glen Travel Prices* in your *Word Data* folder, click **Paste Special** on the Edit menu, then click **Formatted Text (RTF)** in the Paste Special dialog box and click **OK**.

5. Save the document as *Glen Travel Prices RTF* in the *Skills Review* folder in your *Word Data* folder, then close all documents.

6. Click **Open** 📂, click the **Files of type triangle button**, click **All Files**, then click **Cancel**.

7 Creating and Deleting Folders

1. Click **Open** 📂 and navigate to the *Skills Review* folder in your *Word Data* folder.

2. With the *Skills Review* folder in the *Look in* box, click **Create New Folder** 📁.

3. Type **Star Gazette Docs** as the new folder name and click **OK**.

4. Click **Create New Folder** 📁, type **Correspondence**, and click **OK**.

5. Click the **Up One Level button** 🔼 twice, click the *Star Gazette Docs* folder, then click **Delete** ✖. Click **Yes** to confirm the deletion.

8 Renaming and Saving Files in a New Format

1. Navigate to the *Skills Review* folder in your *Word Data* folder and click *Glen Travel Prices RTF*.

2. Click **Tools** Tools ▾, click **Rename**, then type **Glen Travel Agency Prices RTF** as the new file name and press Enter↵.

3. Open *Glen Travel Agency Prices RTF* and click **Save As** on the File menu.

4. Type **Glen Travel Rates** in the *File name* box, click **Word Document** on the *Save as type* drop-down list, click **Save**, and close the document.

9 Previewing and Printing a Document

1. Open *Atlas* in your *Word Data* folder, and click the **Print Preview button** 🔍.

2. Click the **Multiple Pages button** 🔲, and select **2 × 3 pages** to view pages 1–6.

3. Click the **down scroll arrow** to preview pages 7–12.

4. Click twice anywhere on page 12 (bottom right) to enlarge the page to 100 percent.

5. Click the page again to return to the 2 × 3 layout, then continue scrolling to the end of the document.

WORD 2002

6. Click the **Print Layout View button** .

7. Scroll to page 14 and click anywhere on the page.

8. Click **Print** on the File menu.

9. In the *Print range* section, click the **Current page option**.

10. Verify that the Number of copies is set to 1, and click **OK**.

11. Close the document.

10 Printing Labels and Envelopes

1. Click the **New Blank Document button** , point to **Letters and Mailings** on the Tools menu, and click **Envelopes and Labels**.

2. Click the **Options button** on the Labels tab and select the appropriate label product and product number, if you are printing on commercial labels.

3. Click the **Tray triangle button**, click the appropriate paper tray, and click **OK**.

4. Type a relative's name and address in the Address box, select the **Full page** of the same label option, then click **Print**.

5. Point to **Letters and Mailings** on the Tools menu and click **Envelopes and Labels**.

6. Type a delivery address and return address on the Envelopes tab, and click **Add to Document**; click **No** if prompted to save the return address.

7. Click **Print** on the File menu, click the **Current Page option**, and click **OK** to print on plain paper.

8. If you are printing on an envelope, reopen the Envelopes and Labels dialog box; click **Options** on the Envelopes tab; and choose the appropriate envelope size in the Envelope Options dialog box. Print the envelope.

9. Close the document. Click **No** if asked to save changes.

11 Creating a Document From a Template

1. Click **New** on the File menu. In the New Document task pane, click **General Templates**.

2. In the Templates dialog box, click the Letters & Faxes tab, then click the **Professional Fax template** (see Figure 1.20).

3. Verify that the Document option is selected in the *Create New* box, and click **OK**. Save the document as *Template Fax* in the *Skills Review* folder in your *Word Data* folder.

Figure 1.20

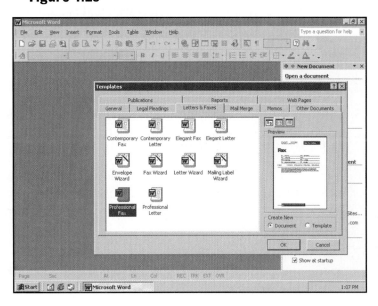

4. Select the *Company Name Here* header and type your name. Click the return address notation (upper left) and type your address.

5. Compose a fax message to your instructor. Click each area containing variable text (except for the current date) and type a fictional fax and phone number, if necessary. Indicate with an **X** that the material is for review. In the *Comments* section, describe the three most useful things you learned in this lesson.

6. Save and close the file.

12 Checking Spelling and Grammar

1. Open *Step Write Article* in your *Word Data* folder and save it as *Step Write Edited* in your *Skills Review* folder.

2. In the first paragraph, right-click each word underlined with a wavy, red line and make the necessary corrections.

3. Right-click the first word in the first paragraph (*paid*) and click **Grammar** on the shortcut menu. Click **Explain** to read the grammar rule. Click **Change** and change it to *Paid*, as suggested.

4. Press Ctrl + Home to move to the top of the document and click the **Spelling and Grammar button** .

5. Read the suggestion in the Spelling and Grammar dialog box and make the appropriate change.

6. Proceed through the document and study each spelling and grammar question before choosing an option. Do not add words to the spelling dictionary. Click **Ignore** if you are unsure of the correction.

7. Save and close the document.

13 Using the Thesaurus

1. Open *Ag Ed* in your *Word Data* folder then find and select the word *cogent*.

2. Click the **Tools menu**, point to **Language**, and click **Thesaurus**.

3. In the *Replace with Synonym* box, click *sound*; then click **Replace**.

4. Find and select *empirical* and replace it with a synonym.

5. Find and select *expenditure* then click **Thesaurus** on the Tools menu. Click *disbursement* in the synonym list and click **Look up**. Replace the original word with a synonym of *disbursement*.

6. Navigate to the top of page 1 using the Find and Replace dialog box. On the Replace tab, type **expenditure** in the *Find what* box, if necessary, and type **payout** in the *Replace with* box. Click **Find Next**. Follow Table 1.5 to determine in which instances to replace *expenditure*.

7. Navigate again to the top of page 1 and type **regarding** in the *Find what* box; type **about** in the *Replace with* box, and click **Replace All**. Click **OK** to acknowledge the global replacement.

8. Close the Find and Replace dialog box and save the document as *Ag Ed Revised* in the *Skills Review* folder in your *Word Data* folder. Close the file.

14 Inserting a Date/Time Format Using the AutoText Toolbar and Insert Menu

1. Open *Star Gazette Article* in your *Word Data* folder, then press [Ctrl] + [End] and press [Enter←] two times.

2. Click the **View menu**, point to **Toolbars**, and click **AutoText**.

3. On the AutoText toolbar, click the **All Entries button** [All Entries ▾], point to **Header/Footer**, and click **Filename**.

4. Press [Enter←] then click **Date and Time** on the Insert menu.

5. Click a month/year format *without* today's date (like *July 01*), and click **OK**.

6. Right-click the month/year format and click **Toggle Field Codes** on the shortcut menu. Right-click the code, then click **Edit Field**.

7. In the *Date formats* box, click before the first *y*, type **dd**, and press [Spacebar]. (The Field dialog box should look like Figure 1.21.) Click **OK**.

8. Close the AutoText toolbar. Save your document as *Star Gazette AutoText* in the *Skills Review* folder in your *Word Data* folder, then close the document.

15 Inserting Text Using AutoCorrect and AutoComplete

1. Open *AHS Workshop* in your *Word Data* folder.

2. Click after the last word in the second paragraph and press [Enter←] twice.

3. Type the following sentence, including the typographical errors in the words *copy, article,* and *global.* When you press [Spacebar] after typing these words, watch the Word window to see if AutoCorrect corrects the misspellings.

   As you requested, I'll send a cpoy of my recent articel on the gloabl economy.

4. Select the word *Sincerely* then slowly type **Best regards** watching for the AutoComplete ScreenTip. Press [Enter←] when prompted to insert the text.

5. Save the document as *AHS Workshop Corrected* in the *Skills Review* folder in your *Word Data* folder, then close the document.

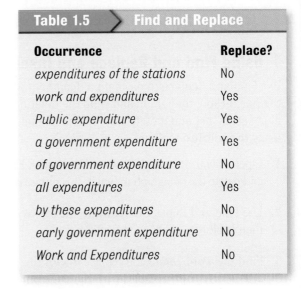

Table 1.5	Find and Replace
Occurrence	**Replace?**
expenditures of the stations	No
work and expenditures	Yes
Public expenditure	Yes
a government expenditure	Yes
of government expenditure	No
all expenditures	Yes
by these expenditures	No
early government expenditure	No
Work and Expenditures	No

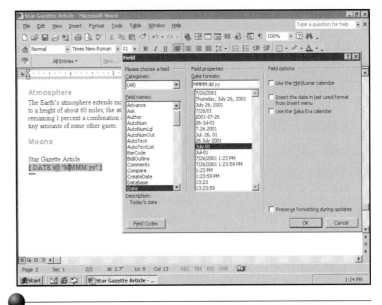

Figure 1.21

SUMMARY AND EXERCISES

LESSON APPLICATIONS

1 Using Find and Replace and Inserting a Date/Time Format

Use Find and Replace to navigate a document and find a paragraph. Select and delete the paragraph, then undo and redo the deletion. Find and replace specific words and phrases. Insert and modify a date/time format using the Insert menu. Insert AutoText using the AutoText toolbar.

1. Open *Nonprinting* in your *Word Data* folder. Find the phrase *A good approach*. Select and delete the paragraph in which this phrase occurs, then undo and redo the deletion.

2. Use Find and Replace to return to the top of the document. Go to the top of page 3, then back to page 1.

3. Find the word *entails* and replace it with the word *means*. Find the phrase *questions-and-answers* and replace it with the same phrase but without the hyphens between the words.

4. Navigate to the last page of the document and press [Enter←] twice at the end of the last paragraph.

5. Type **This file was last updated on** then use the Insert menu to insert a date format to be updated automatically. View the field codes in the document, then edit the codes to create a new custom date/time format. Adjust spacing as necessary.

6. Activate the AutoText toolbar. On a new line, insert Header/Footer AutoText showing the file name. Close the AutoText toolbar.

7. Save your document as *Nonprinting Updated* in the *Lesson Applications* folder in your *Word Data* folder. Close the document.

2 Copying, Cutting, Pasting, and Editing Text

Copy and cut text and paste it into a new location using the Clipboard. Move text using drag-and-drop. Type and edit a new paragraph using Insert and Overtype modes.

1. Activate the Clipboard task pane and clear the Clipboard. Open *Nonprinting* in your *Word Data* folder. Find the phrase *Marginal Notes* and copy the paragraph in which it occurs to the Clipboard.

2. Find the phrase *Update the substance* and cut the paragraph in which it occurs.

3. Find the phrase *Ask a cadre*. Paste the *Marginal notes* paragraph on a new line following the *Ask a cadre* paragraph. Paste the *Update the substance* paragraph on a new line following the *Marginal notes* paragraph. Adjust vertical spacing as necessary between paragraphs (see Figure 1.22).

4. Find the two occurrences of the phrase *Copyedit the text*. In these sentences, drag-and-drop the word *wordiness* to place it before the phrase *misspelled words*. Correct punctuation and adjust spacing between words, if necessary.

5. Enter the following new paragraph on a new line at the end of the section entitled *What WPS Can Do:* **WPS maintains close relationships with a number of superb outside suppliers who share our concern for quality.** Select the word *close*, and type **excellent** using Insert mode. Activate Overtype mode and overtype the phrase *concern for quality* with the words **determination to provide outstanding service.**

6. Save the document as *Nonprinting Revised* in the *Lesson Applications* folder in your *Word Data* folder. Clear and close the Clipboard, then close the document.

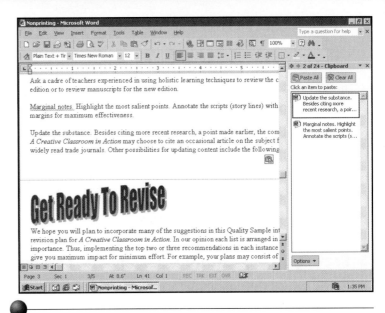

Figure 1.22

3 Copying a Header With the Paste Special Command

Copy a memo header, use Paste Special to change its file type, then paste it into another document.

1. Open *Nonprinting* in your *Word Data* folder. If necessary, open and clear the Office Clipboard.

2. Click in the selection bar to select the *A Creative Classroom in Action* header (at the top of the document), then copy the header to the Clipboard (see Figure 1.23).

3. Open the *Word Data* folder. View only those files in Rich Text Format. Open *Memo Format*. Reopen the Clipboard task pane, if necessary.

4. Use the Paste Special command to paste the header from the Clipboard into the top of the *Memo Format* document in the compatible RTF format.

5. Save *Memo Format* as *Memo Format RTF* in the *Lesson Applications* folder in your *Word Data* folder. Close all documents and clear and close the Clipboard.

4 Managing Folders and Files

Create a new folder. Change a document file type and save the file with a new name. Rename a document.

1. Open *Report Memo* in your *Word Data* folder.

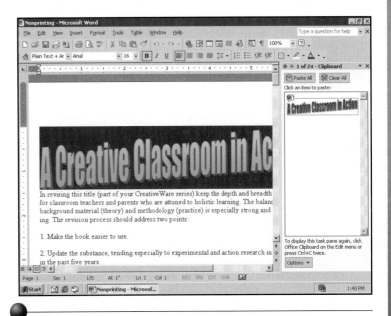

Figure 1.23

2. Change the file type to *Rich Text Format* in the Save As dialog box.

3. Save the document as *Report Memo RTF* in the *Lesson Applications* folder in your *Word Data* folder, and close the file.

4. In the Open dialog box, navigate to the *Lesson Applications* folder in your *Word Data* folder and view All Files.

5. Create a new folder within your *Lesson Applications* folder named *Sales Memos*.

6. Open *Report Memo RTF* in your *Lesson Applications* folder then save it as *Sales* in the new *Sales Memos* folder. Close the document.

7. Open the *Sales Memos* folder in the Open dialog box. Rename the *Sales* document as *Jan Sales Results*, then close the dialog box.

5 Previewing and Printing Documents, Envelopes, and Labels

Preview a document using Print Preview, then print specific pages. Print envelopes and labels.

1. Open *Ag Ed* in your *Word Data* folder and activate Print Preview. Preview pages 1–4 of the document.

2. Switch to Normal View. Click Print on the File menu and print pages 1, 3, and 4. Close the document.

3. Open a new, blank document. In the Envelopes and Labels dialog box, enter the delivery address of a friend and your return address on the Envelopes tab. Check that the Envelope size is correct. Print the envelope.

4. On the Labels tab of the Envelopes & Labels dialog box, enter the delivery address you typed for the envelope if necessary. Select the appropriate label product, product number, and paper tray. Print a single label.

6 Checking Spelling and Grammar and Using the Thesaurus

Check spelling and grammar in a document. Use the Thesaurus tool to find synonyms. Use Find and Replace to replace words throughout a document. Use AutoCorrect to correct typographical errors as you type.

1. Open the *Woodsy View News* document in your *Word Data* folder and save it as *Woodsy News Edited* in the *Lesson Applications* folder in your *Word Data* folder.

2. Check and correct spelling and grammar for the entire document. Assume that all names are spelled correctly as you respond to the spelling and grammar problems. Read the grammar rules, if necessary.

3. Navigate to the beginning of the document.

4. Find the word *capacity* and use the Thesaurus to replace it with a synonym. Find the word *trash* and replace each occurrence with a synonym.

5. Use Replace All to change *Kay Gradison* to *Kathryn Gradison* throughout the document.

6. Open the AutoCorrect tab of the AutoCorrect dialog box. Scroll through the *Replace text as you type* list. Make note of these misspelled words in the *Replace*

column and the corresponding corrections in the *With* column: *instaleld (installed)*; *int he (in the)*.

7. On a new line at the end of the *Work, Work, Work* section of the open document, type this sentence with errors to correct misspellings automatically: **Last month the Gas Co. instaleld new meters int he rear of five houses on Charles St.**

8. Save your changes and close the document.

7 Creating a Memo From a Template

Create a memo from a Word template and save it as a document.

1. Click New on the File menu and click General Templates.

2. Click the Memos tab and open *Contemporary Memo* as a new document. Save the document as *Contemporary Memo* in the *Lesson Applications* folder in your *Word Data* folder.

3. Write a short memo directed to a classmate describing two academic or career objectives you'd like to accomplish within the next five years. Save your changes, and close the document.

PROJECTS

1 Write This Way

An article you wrote needs more work before you can fax it to the publisher. Open *Step Write Article* in your *Word Data* folder. Save the document as *Step Write Released* in the *Projects* folder in your *Word Data* folder. Search for the sentence containing the word *wake*. Insert the following two paragraphs on a new line below that sentence (see Figure 1.24):

Common faults include excess words, which waste time for both writer and readers; impressive-sounding words and jargon, which often block communication; indefinite words, which are colorless and boring; long words and sentences, which raise reading difficulty; and passive voice, which hides meaning by omitting action words.

Use grammar, spelling, and other checker software—but not to replace your editing and proofreading. For extra quality assurance, have documents read by another set of eyes.

Proofread and edit the entire document using Word's spelling and grammar tools as an aid. Watch for misspelled words, incorrect words, and punctuation errors. On a new line at the end of the document, insert your name in parentheses. Insert AutoText at the end of the document in a format indicating the file name

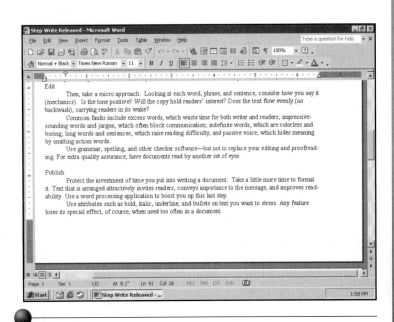

Figure 1.24

and the date the file was created and last printed. Preview the document and print it. Save and close the file.

2 Just the Fax

You need to create a cover page to fax to *The Small Business Journal* along with the article you wrote in Project 1. Open the *Elegant Fax Word* template (or another template of your choice) to create a fax cover page. In the fax template, replace the FROM information with your name; replace the Company name with *The Small Business Journal*; and replace the RE information with an appropriate subject line. Type the number of pages to be faxed. Create a name and phone numbers for the TO, PHONE, and FAX information. Create a company name and address for yourself. Delete any sample text in the header that you do not need to use. Compose a brief note as the text of the fax mentioning that you are faxing the document for publication. At the bottom of your document, insert the date (with Update Automatically activated in the Date and Time dialog box). Save the cover sheet as *Fax Article* in the *Projects* folder in your *Word Data* folder and close the document.

3 Organizing Files

You just learned that you will be writing more articles for publication in *The Small Business Journal*, so you decide to organize your files to make them easier to retrieve. Also, your editor has asked that you send your articles to the *Journal* electronically in RTF format. Open *Fax Article* (saved in Project 2) in the *Projects* folder in your *Word Data* folder (see Figure 1.25). (If you did not complete Project 2, open *Fax Info* from your *Word Data* folder.) Create a new folder named *My Faxes* in the *Projects* folder. Save *Fax Article* (or *Fax Info*) in the new folder as *Fax Article RTF* in Rich Text Format (*RTF*) so it is ready to copy to a disk to be sent to the *Journal*. Close the document.

4 My Bio From a Template

Since you often give presentations to people in your field, you need to write your biography (a brief account of your life). Then you can give a copy to program planners who may print the information in their program and/or prepare to introduce you to meeting participants. A sample bio appears in your *Word Data* folder: *Tony Denier's Bio*. Choose a Word Report template to create your own bio. (*Note:* The Word Report templates may need to be installed from your Office XP CD-ROM.) You may copy part or all of *Tony Denier's Bio* and then delete and replace text to create your own document. (*Hint:* Navigate between the two open files using taskbar buttons or use Arrange All on the Window menu.)

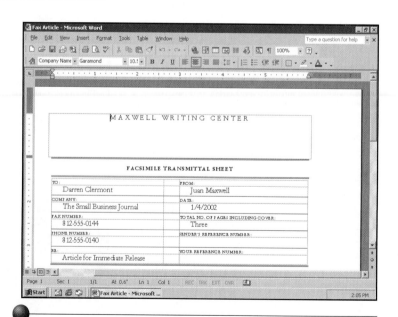

Figure 1.25

Your bio should have at least two short paragraphs and should mention your education, career achievements and/or goals, hobbies, and special interests. Edit your document carefully, checking spelling and grammar. Save the document as *My Bio* in the *Projects* folder in your *Word Data* folder. Close the file.

5 What's a Wizard?

Open a new, blank document and save it as *Wizard* in the *Projects* folder in your *Word Data* folder. Explore Help to learn more about wizards by entering *wizard* in the *Ask a Question* box, then clicking the <u>About installing wizards</u> link. Click <u>Show All</u> in the Help window to read the definition of the word *wizard*. Read the Help page and explore the links, then close the Help window. Now you will determine the types and number of wizards available on each tab of the Templates dialog box. Create a table to summarize the information you gather. (Type the entry in the first column, then press Tab to type the second column.) Your text should contain two columns, similar to Table 1.6. (Table 1.6 is a list of all the tabs in the Templates dialog box.)

In the Templates dialog box, count the files on each tab that contain the name *Wizard* and complete the second column of information, omitting any category (tab) that contains no wizard. Above your table, type a heading and a statement to introduce the data. Save and close the file.

Table 1.6	
Category (Tab)	**Number of Wizards**
General	
Legal Pleadings	
Letters & Faxes	
Mail Merge	
Memos	
Other Documents	
Publications	
Reports	
Web Pages	

6 AutoCorrect It

Word's AutoCorrect feature is designed to automatically correct the most common errors made while typing. However, each user makes unique errors that may not be in the AutoCorrect list. Identify common errors that you make by quickly typing a few paragraphs. (Find the text within a textbook, newspaper, or periodical.) Check to see if your errors are in Word's AutoCorrect list. Add two words to the list and type a few sentences containing the intentional misspellings to observe the AutoCorrect feature in action. For help, enter the keyword *AutoCorrect* into the *Ask a Question* box, and click the *Create or change AutoCorrect entries* Help topic (see Figure 1.26).

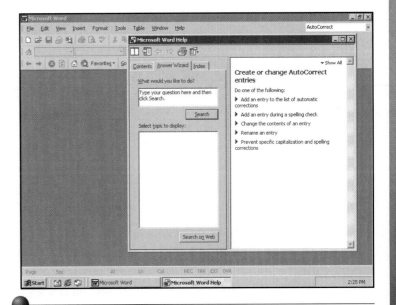

Figure 1.26

SUMMARY AND EXERCISES

 **7 Write This Way on the World Wide Web**

Open a new, blank document and save it as *Web Link* in the *Projects* folder in your *Word Data* folder. Write a paragraph explaining why it is important to proofread a document. At the end of the document, insert hyperlinks to the following Web sites. Change the descriptive text as desired for each hyperlink.

Proofreading & Editing Tips	http://www.lrcom.com/tips/proofreading_editing.htm
Ten Proofreading Tips	http://www.ascs.org/10tips.html
Successful Proofreading Strategies	http://www.temple.edu/writingctr/cw06005.htm

Follow the links to all three sites. Of the three sites, choose two that are the most helpful to you. Delete the link to the third site. Arrange the links in the desired order in your document. Save and close the document.

If you have difficulty following one or more of the hyperlinks, it is possible the Web address may have changed. If this occurs, click Search the Web on the Word Web toolbar. Then perform a search in your browser on the keyword *proofreading*. Explore the search results to find a substitute site.

 ## Project in Progress

8 Now You're in Business

Savvy Solutions, your new company, will provide a variety of writing, editing, and training services for small and medium-sized organizations. Today you received a letter from a local high school student asking if you would present at their annual Writer's Workshop. The letter asked you to propose a topic or to select one of these topics: Writing School Papers, Writing in Business, Writing for Newspapers and Magazines, or Writing for the Web. Use a letter template of your choice to create a new document with the following information:

Letter address:

Mr. Steven Banks
Young Writers' Society
Anderson High School
1968 Beechmont Ave.

[Your City, ST 00000]

Body:

Thank you for your invitation to present a workshop for Young Writers' Society at 10:45 on [insert a date]. I am very happy to accept.

Every one of your suggested topics is excellent, and I would love to discuss Writing in Business with the students. I will stress the importance word processing software, such as Microsoft Word, can have to their documents.

I'll send the exact title of my presentation and my bio in a week or two. Please arrange an LCD computer and a screen for my PowerPoint slides for the day of the workshop.

Insert today's date and a salutation. At the end of the letter, include a complimentary close with your name as the sender, and a title such as Writing Consultant. Add, delete, or change any information to suit your preferences. Edit and proofread with the help of the Word Thesaurus, Spelling, and Grammar tools.

Save your document as *Writing Workshop* in the *Projects* folder in your *Word Data* folder. Create a new folder in your *Projects* folder and name it *Writing Projects*. Save *Writing Workshop* in Rich Text Format (RTF) as *Writing Workshop RTF* within your *Writing Projects* folder. Save, preview, and print *Writing Workshop*. Create and print a mailing label and an envelope for your letter. Close the document and exit Word.

LESSON 2

Formatting Documents

CONTENTS

- Reformatting Text
- Maintaining Consistency in a Document
- Enhancing the Appearance of a Document
- Inserting and Formatting Graphics
- Sorting Words or Numbers
- Adding Reference Features
- On the Web: Naming Favorites

OBJECTIVES

After you complete this lesson, you will be able to do the following:

► Insert and modify page and section breaks.

► Change margins and vertical alignment.

► Modify horizontal alignment and indentation style.

► Set character, line, and paragraph spacing and tab stops.

► Apply and modify newsletter-style formats.

► Use Reveal Formatting to check paragraph alignment and check for consistency of spacing in headings, between paragraphs, and in tabs.

► Enhance the appearance of text by applying bold, italic, and underline as well as superscripts and subscripts.

► Apply text animation, a border, shading, and highlighting.

► Use Format Painter to change text formats.

► Use the Style command to reformat documents.

► Search the Clip Organizer for an image, insert the image into a document, and edit the image.

► Sort a list alphabetically.

► Add and edit bullets, numbers, and outline numbers in a list.

► Add and modify page numbers in a document; insert and edit headers and footers.

► Insert a footnote and table of contents.

► E-mail a Word document.

► Add favorites in Word and Internet Explorer.

MOUS Objectives
In this lesson:
W2002-1-2
W2002-1-4
W2002-1-6
W2002-2-1
W2002-2-2
W2002-2-3
W2002-2-4
W2002-3-1
W2002-3-2
W2002-3-3
W2002-5-1
See Appendix D.

REFORMATTING TEXT

After you have entered and edited all text in a document, you will want to make sure the formatting of your document appears professional. The format of a document is the **layout**—the arrangement and spacing of various parts of the document in relation to the edges of the page. Much reformatting may be done with the buttons on the Formatting toolbar. The File menu, Insert menu, Format menu, and horizontal ruler are also involved in reformatting a document.

NOTE *Formatting is described in relation to a printed document. The term* **page** *usually refers to the standard paper size (8.5 by 11 inches) on which most documents are printed.*

Inserting Page Breaks and Changing Margins

In Normal View, faint, dotted horizontal lines indicate automatic **page breaks.** Page breaks are more clearly defined in Print Layout View. The blank areas forming the border from the text to the edge of the paper are called **margins.** So far, you have used the default (preset) margins for your documents. In Word, each margin (top, left, right, and bottom) is a conventional width: 1 inch. You can change these margin widths. Narrow margins let you type more text on a page, but wide margins make a page look easier to read.

Page breaks divide text into separate pages. By default, the print area is 9 inches top to bottom; and Word will fill that area unless you tell it not to. Wherever you want to start a new page you can insert a **manual page break** to override Word's **automatic page breaks.** For example, you might insert page breaks between chapters or main topics of a report. The manual page breaks you insert are labeled *Page Break* so that you can tell them from Word's automatic page breaks.

You can also control where automatic page breaks occur. By default, Word will prevent widows and orphans from occurring within a document. A **widow** is the last line of a paragraph printed by itself at the top of a page. An **orphan** is the first line of a paragraph printed by itself at the bottom of a page. If you want to prevent an automatic page break from occurring within certain text (such as a heading and the following paragraph or several paragraphs), select the text that you want to remain together and right-click. Click Paragraph on the shortcut menu and click the Line and Page Breaks tab in the Paragraph dialog box. To avoid an automatic page break within a paragraph, select the *Keep lines together* option in the Paragraph dialog box and click OK; to avoid an automatic page break between two paragraphs, select the *Keep with next* option and click OK.

Margin settings and vertical and horizontal alignment define page setup. In Word, margins may be as narrow as one-quarter inch or as wide as possible for the paper size. Margins of one inch to two inches are typical.

Setting Up Pages

The **vertical alignment**—or relationship of text to the top and bottom edges of a page—is also part of setting up (reformatting) text. Text is **top aligned** by default which means the first line of text always appears at the top margin. You can change this vertical alignment so that the last line of text prints at the bottom margin **(bottom alignment),** regardless of where the top and bottom margins are set. Another alternative is to place text an equal distance between the top and bottom margin **(centered alignment).**

The **justified** setting distributes *paragraphs* between the top and bottom margins. Justified alignment looks the same as top alignment, if the page contains only one paragraph. However, with two paragraphs on a page, one will be top aligned; the other will be bottom aligned. With three paragraphs on a page, one will be aligned at the top, one at the center, and one at the bottom.

Inserting Section Breaks

Varying the margin settings or vertical alignment within a document calls for **section breaks.** A section break shows up in Normal View as a dotted double line

NORTON
ONLINE

Visit **www.glencoe.com/norton/online/** for more information on page layout.

labeled *Section Break* and either *(Next Page)*, *(Continuous)*, *(Odd Page)*, or *(Even Page)*. Table 2.1 explains the different types of section breaks. Section breaks do not show in Print Layout View or on a printed page.

Table 2.1	Types of Section Breaks
Section Break	**Description**
Next Page	The following section starts at the top of the next page.
Continuous	The following section starts on the same page.
Even page or Odd page	The following section starts on the next even- or odd-numbered page.

HANDS on

Breaking Pages

In this activity, you will insert page breaks into a document.

1. Open *Astronomy 110* in your *Word Data* folder and save it as *Reformatted* in the *Tutorial* folder.

With the file saved in a different folder with a new name, you can easily save changes as you work. First, you will add pages by inserting page breaks. Then you will type a few words on each new page.

2. Click **Print Layout View** 🔲 to view the document; then click **Normal View** 🔳 to reformat it.

3. Click before the first character in the first paragraph, then click **Break** on the Insert menu.

The Break dialog box appears, as shown in Figure 2.1.

4. Click **Page break**, if necessary, and click **OK**.

You have added a page at the beginning of the document. The *Venus* heading is on page 1 and the text is now on page 2, as shown on the status bar.

5. Click the Page Break line and type the following text: Venus: Roman goddess of gardens and fields, of love and beauty

WARNING *Do not select the Page Break line. If you do, you will replace the line with the text you type. If this happens, click the Undo button*  *and repeat step 5.*

Now you will add a new page in the middle of your document and another page at the end.

6. Scroll down to locate the heading *Earth*, then click an insertion point before the first character in the heading.

WORD 2002

Figure 2.1
Break dialog box

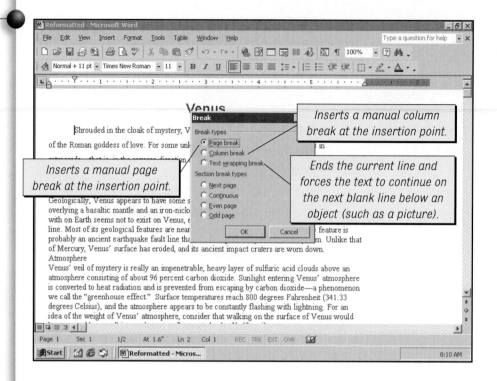

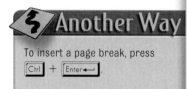

7. Click **Break** on the Insert menu, click **Page break**, then click **OK**.

8. Click **Repeat Insertion** on the Edit menu to insert another page break.

Your document looks like Figure 2.2. The insertion point is now at the top of page 4. Page 3 is represented by the narrow space between the two Page Break lines.

To insert a page break, press Ctrl + Enter↵.

Figure 2.2
Manual page breaks

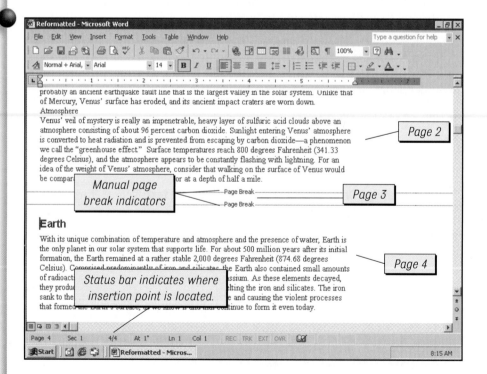

9. Click the Page Break line directly above *Earth* and press Enter⏎.

10. Click in the middle of page 3 and type the following text, with one space before the dash: Our roots are in the dark; the earth is our country. —U. LeGuin

11. Scroll to the end of the document, insert a page break below the last line, and type Bibliography on the new page 5.

12. Click **Save** on the File menu and close the document.

Changing Margins, Breaking Sections, and Aligning Vertically

In this activity, you will change margins, insert section breaks, and change the vertical alignment.

1. Open *Reformatted* in the *Tutorial* folder in your *Word Data* folder, and save it as *Reformatted Margins* in the *Tutorial* folder.

2. Click **Page Setup** on the File menu, and click the **Margins tab**, if necessary.

The Page Setup dialog box appears, as shown in Figure 2.3.

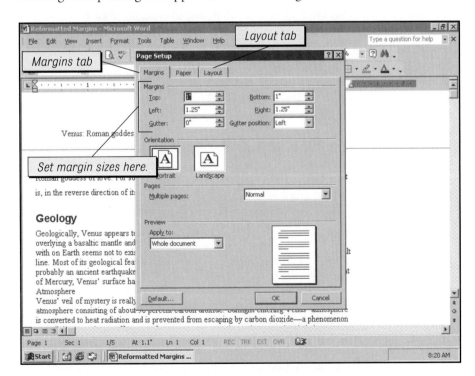

Figure 2.3
Page Setup dialog box

3. In the *Margins* section, change the top and left margins to 1.5″; change the right margin to 1″.

Reformatting Pages

To change margins:

1. Click an insertion point where a margin change is desired.

2. Click Page Setup on the File menu.

3. Click the Margins tab in the Page Setup dialog box.

4. Adjust the margin settings.

5. If necessary, choose an option in the *Apply to* box.

To change vertical alignment:

1. Click Page Setup on the File menu.

2. Click the Layout tab in the Page Setup dialog box.

3. Select a vertical alignment option.

4. If necessary, choose an option in the *Apply to* box.

To insert section breaks:

1. Click Break on the Insert menu.

2. Click one of the four section break types in the Break dialog box.

---

4. Click the **Layout tab** and verify that *Top* appears in the *Vertical alignment* box, then click **OK**.

5. Click **Print Layout View** 🗎 then scroll to view your new margin settings.

The margins are fine, but perhaps the single line of text on page 1 would look better if it were halfway down the page.

6. Click **Normal View** 🗎 and click at the end of the single line of text on page 1.

7. Click **Break** on the Insert menu. Under *Section break types*, click **Next page** and then click **OK**.

A Next Page section break appears in your document. Page 1 is now a separate section from the rest of the document. That means you can change the alignment on it without affecting other pages. You no longer need the manual page break.

8. Click the Page Break line under the Section Break, if necessary, then press ⌷Delete⌷.

9. Click the *Venus* heading on page 1, click **Page Setup** on the File menu, then click the **Layout tab**. In the *Vertical alignment* box, select **Center**. Verify that *This section* shows in the *Apply to* box, then click **OK**.

10. Click **Print Layout View** 🗎 and scroll to see the text on page 1 which is now centered vertically on the page between the top and bottom margins. Scroll to page 2 and note that text on this page is still top aligned (it begins at the top margin).

Page 3 also consists of a single line of text. To center it vertically, you will need a section break before and after the text to separate it from the preceding and following pages.

11. Click **Normal View** 🗎 , then go to the top of page 3.

12. Click before the first character in the text on page 3, click **Break** on the Insert menu, then click **Next Page** under *Section break types* and click **OK**.

13. Click at the end of the text on page 3 then click **Repeat Insertion** on the Edit menu.

14. Click each Page Break line (before and after the section breaks) then press ⌷Delete⌷. Your document should now resemble Figure 2.4.

15. Click before the first character on page 3, click **Page Setup** on the File menu, then click the **Layout tab**. Click **Center** on the *Vertical alignment* box, verify *This section* appears in the *Apply to* box, and click **OK**.

The text alignment is not apparent in Normal View.

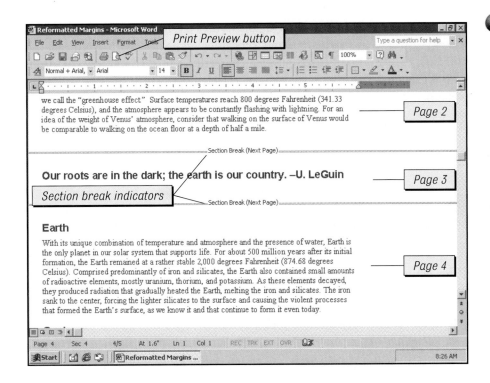

Figure 2.4
Next Page section break

Print Preview button

Page 2

Section break indicators

Page 3

Page 4

WORD 2002

Another Way

- To change margins, switch to Print Layout View. Point to a margin boundary on the horizontal ruler (left and right margins) or vertical ruler (top and bottom margins) and drag the boundary. Press Alt as you drag to display the width of the print area.

- To open the Page Setup dialog box, double-click the shaded part of the ruler that extends over the right margin.

16. Click **Print Preview** 🔍, click the **Multiple Pages button** ▦, then click the **2 x 3 Pages icon.**

Though the text is not readable, you can see that the line on page 3 is centered vertically and you can see the alignment on the other pages in the document.

17. Click **Normal View** ▤, click **Save** 🖫, and close the document.

Formatting Paragraphs

The way that text lines up in relation to the left and right margins is called **horizontal alignment.** In the Word window, text is automatically **left aligned.** Every line begins flush with the left margin, making the left margin perfectly even. You can change this alignment. Text may be **right aligned;** that is, all lines are flush with the right margin. Text may be **justified** or aligned so that it is flush with both margins. Text may be **center aligned,** or centered. With this alignment, short lines of text are placed an equal distance from the left and right margins and neither margin appears perfectly even. The Formatting toolbar provides all four options.

The term **indentation** refers to variations in the left and right side margins of lines in a paragraph and paragraphs on a page. A **first-line indentation** of one-half inch is conventional. **Hanging indentation**—the second and subsequent lines of a paragraph indented under the first line—is also common. In Word, a first-line or hanging indentation may be any width; and whole paragraphs may be indented on the left and/or right any amount of space the user desires.

The amount of white space between text lines is called **line spacing.** Most business documents use single spacing (the default line spacing). Double spacing (a blank line between each line of text) and 1.5 spacing (one-half blank line between each line of text) are also common. You may insert additional space above and below

Did you know?

You can *hyphenate* your text automatically as you type. Word breaks long words at the ends of lines and inserts hyphens at the proper place. To turn on the Hyphenation feature, click the Tools menu, point to Language, and click Hyphenation. Select the desired options.

paragraphs. Adding **paragraph spacing** opens up a page and makes paragraph side headings easy to see. Paragraph spacing is measured in **points.** With Word, you can also adjust the amount of space between characters, called **character spacing.** If you want to affect the spacing between all selected characters, you can expand or condense the space. If you want to affect the spacing of particular letters, choose the kerning option.

HANDS on

Changing Horizontal Alignment and Indentation Style

In this activity, you will reformat a document by changing the horizontal alignment and indentation options.

Word BASICS

Changing Horizontal Alignment

1. Select the text to be aligned.

2. Click the Align Left, Center, Align Right, or Justify button on the Formatting toolbar.

1. Open *Venus Information* in your *Word Data* folder and save it as *Venus Aligned* in your *Tutorial* folder.

2. Click **Normal View** ▤, if necessary. Click the line of text on page 1 and click the **Center button** ▤ on the Formatting toolbar.

3. Click the *Venus* heading at the top of page 2, and click **Repeat Paragraph Alignment** on the Edit menu.

The text appears centered on page 1 and the *Venus* heading appears centered at the top of page 2.

4. Click anywhere in the first paragraph of text on page 2, then click the **Justify button** ▤.

Both the left and right paragraph margins appear even, as shown in Figure 2.5.

Figure 2.5
Centered and justified text

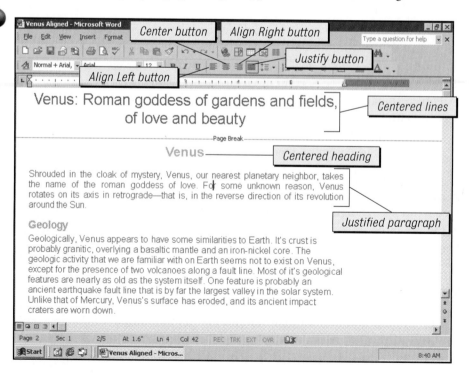

HINTS & TIPS

You can use the Reveal Formatting feature to change formatting in a paragraph. Click Reveal Formatting on the Format menu. In the Reveal Formatting task pane, click the blue underlined text and then make the changes in the dialog box that opens.

5. Navigate to the end of page 4 and click after the last character of the last paragraph. Press [Enter←] two times, then type the following text, replacing *Your name* and *Current date.*

Your name
Submitted to Professor Dowdell
AST 110, Section F3
Current date

6. Select the four lines of text you just typed, and click the **Align Right** button ▤.

The text aligns on the right margin. Now you will begin changing the indentation style of some paragraphs.

7. On page 5, click after the word *Bibliography*, press [Enter←] twice, and type the following reference at the left margin: Author, F. M. Venus Overview. [Online] Available: http://www.eps.mcgill.ca/~bud/craters/FaceOfVenus.html [February, 2001].

NOTE *The Web address you typed may be automatically formatted as a hyperlink (underlined and in color). If so, right-click the hyperlink and click Remove Hyperlink on the shortcut menu.*

8. Click anywhere in the text you just typed, then click **Paragraph** on the Format menu.

The Paragraph dialog box appears.

9. Click the **Indents and Spacing tab.** Click the **Special box triangle button** and click **Hanging.** Select the numbers in the *By* box and type *.75.* See the Preview box (Figure 2.6).

Word BASICS

Changing Indentations
Entire paragraph:

1. Click the paragraph to be changed.

2. Click the Increase Indent or Decrease Indent button on the Formatting toolbar.

Or:

1. Click the text and click Paragraph on the Format menu.

2. On the Indents and Spacing tab, set the desired Indentation options for the left and right margins in the Paragraph dialog box.

First line indentation:

1. Click the text and click Paragraph on the Format menu.

2. On the Indents and Spacing tab, select either First line or Hanging in the *Special* list box.

3. Select or type the indentation value in the *By* box.

HINTS & TIPS

To indent the first line of a paragraph one-half inch, use Word's default tab stops: Click before the first character and press [Tab].

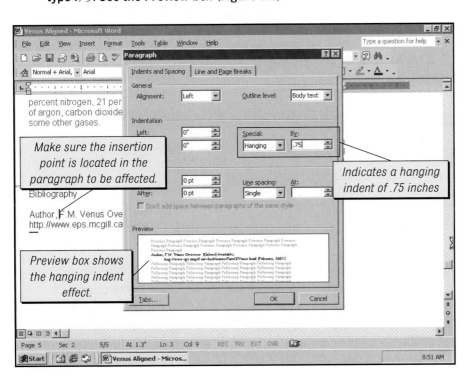

Make sure the insertion point is located in the paragraph to be affected.

Indicates a hanging indent of .75 inches

Preview box shows the hanging indent effect.

Figure 2.6
Paragraph dialog box

The second and third lines are indented three-quarters of an inch under the first line in hanging-indent style.

10. Click within the paragraph under the heading *Atmosphere* on page 4, then click **Paragraph** on the Format menu. Click **First line** in the *Special* box and type *.75* in the *By* box. Check the Preview window and click **OK** to close the dialog box.

The first line of the paragraph is indented three-quarters of an inch from the left margin.

11. Save your changes and close the document.

HANDS on

Setting Spacing Options

In this activity, you will change character, line, and paragraph spacing in a document.

1. Open *Venus Aligned* in the *Tutorial* folder in your *Word Data* folder and save it as *Venus Spacing* in the *Tutorial* folder.

2. Select the *Venus* heading on page 2.

3. Click **Font** on the Format menu, and click the **Character Spacing** tab. In the *Spacing* box, click the **Expanded option**. Verify that the number in the *By* box is 1 pt, and click **OK**.

The spacing between the letters in the heading expands slightly.

4. Select the first paragraph on page 4 (under the *Earth* heading). Click the **Increase Indent button** on the Formatting toolbar.

The paragraph is indented one-half inch from the left margin.

5. With the paragraph still selected, click the **Line Spacing triangle button** on the Formatting toolbar and click **1.5**. Click to deselect the paragraph.

The line spacing has increased to 1.5, as shown in Figure 2.7. Now you will change line spacing and paragraph spacing.

6. Select the second paragraph on page 4 (under the *Geology* heading) then click **Paragraph** on the Format menu.

The Paragraph dialog box appears.

7. Click the **Indents and Spacing tab**, if necessary. In the *Spacing* section, change the *Before* spacing to **6 pt** and the *After* spacing to **12 pt**. Set the *Line spacing* to **Double**. In the Indentation section, set the Indentation for the right margin at **.5″**. Look at the Preview box and click **OK**.

Word BASICS

Setting Spacing Options
To change character spacing:

1. Select the characters to be changed.

2. Click Font on the Format menu.

3. On the Character Spacing tab in the Font dialog box, select the desired options.

To change line spacing:

1. Click the paragraph or select consecutive paragraphs to be changed.

2. Click the Line Spacing triangle button on the Formatting toolbar, and click the desired spacing.

To change paragraph spacing:

1. Select the paragraph or paragraphs to be changed.

2. Click Paragraph on the Format menu and click the Indents and Spacing tab.

3. In the Spacing section, increase or decrease the space above or below the paragraph.

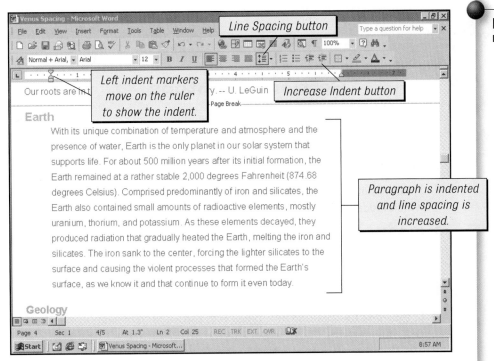

Figure 2.7
Indentation and line spacing changes

The line spacing and indentation appear changed in the selected paragraph.

8. Again select the first paragraph on page 4 under the *Earth* heading, then click **Paragraph** on the Format menu. Change the paragraph spacing to **6 pt** in the *Before* box and **12 pt** in the *After* box and click **OK**.

9. Click the document to deselect the text. Click **Print Layout View**  and scroll to view the two reformatted paragraphs.

10. Click **Normal View** then again select the first paragraph on page 4. Click the **Decrease Indent button** on the Formatting toolbar. Click the document to deselect the text.

The indentation is adjusted in the selected paragraph.

11. Click **Save** and close the document.

Did you know?

The abbreviation *pt* stands for *point* which is a unit of measure ($1/72$ of an inch) relating to the height of a printed character.

Tabulating Text

Instead of paragraphs, a columns-and-rows arrangement (a tabular format) makes some text easier to read. This format involves **tab stops** that specify where listed items begin in relation to the left margin as well as the distance between columns of listed items. The default tab stops in Word are *left tabs* at half-inch intervals; they align columns on the left. When you set custom tabs, it is best to clear the default tabs. You may prefer centered tabs for some columns, and columns containing numbers are often best aligned at the right or at decimal points. In addition, the *bar* option will insert a vertical line in the column. All these options are available in the Tabs dialog box (Format menu).

HANDS on

Setting Tab Stops

In this activity, you will set tab stops and type tabulated text on a separate page of the original *Venus Information* document.

1. Open *Venus Information* in your *Word Data* folder.

2. Find the phrase *worn down*, click at the end of the sentence in which it occurs, and press [Enter←] twice.

3. Click **Tabs** on the Format menu.

The Tabs dialog box appears.

4. Click the **Clear All button** to delete the current tabs.

5. In the *Tab stop position* box, type .5; in the *Alignment* section, click **Left**, if necessary. Click the **Set button**.

The Tab setting appears in the *Tab stop position* box as shown in Figure 2.8.

Word BASICS

Setting Tab Stops

1. Click Tabs on the Format menu.

2. Click the Clear All button in the Tabs dialog box to delete existing tabs.

3. Type the Tab stop position and click the desired alignment button.

4. Click the Set button for each tab entry.

5. When all tabs are set, click OK.

Did you know?

You can set tab stops with *leader* characters (the little dots or other graphics that lead a reader's eye from left to right). In the Leader section of the Tabs dialog box, select one of three leader options when you set the tab stop position and alignment.

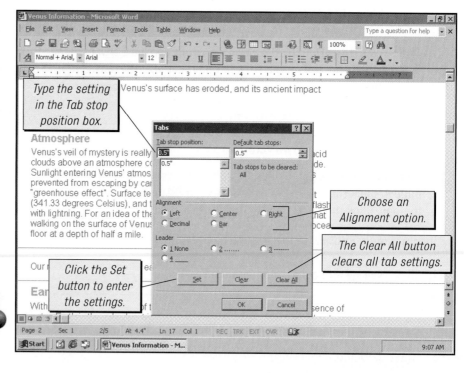

Figure 2.8
Tabs dialog box

6. Type 2 in the *Tab stop position* box, click the **Center option**, and click **Set**. Repeat this procedure to set a left tab at 3″ and a right tab at 5.75″.

All four tab stops appear in the *Tab Stop position* list.

7. Click **OK** to close the dialog box and return to the document.

The tab stops show on the ruler. Distinctive symbols represent the left tab, the center tab, and the right tab.

8. Press `Tab` and type the first word in the table below, watching the screen to see how the text aligns to the left tab. Press `Tab` to move to the next stop (a center tab) and type the column entry. Continue to press `Tab` and type the remaining entries in the first line. At the end of the first line, press `Enter←` to move to the second line.

Mission	Launch Date	Key Event	Key Event Date
Mariner 2	8/27/62	Passed near Venus	12/14/62
Mariner 5			

Your tabulated text should resemble Figure 2.9.

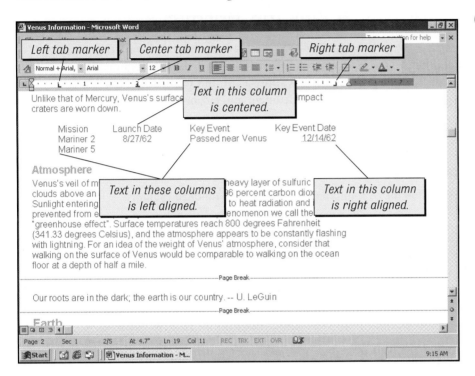

Figure 2.9
Left, centered, and right tab stops

9. Save your changes as *Venus Tabs* in the *Tutorial* folder in your *Word Data* folder, and close the document.

Formatting Newsletter Columns

A multiple-column format is typical in newsletters, newspapers, magazines, brochures, catalogs, directories, flyers, and Web pages. Often certain sections of other documents, including reports, legal documents, and resumes may use a column format. Generally, more text fits attractively on a column-formatted page; and columns are often easier to read than long lines of text.

The Columns button  on the Standard toolbar formats text in one to four columns. The column width is equal and the space between columns is a standard 0.5". Although two- and three-column formats are most common, you can set the number of columns from 1 to 12. You can vary the column widths on a page and specify the amount of space between columns. Preset options include wide columns (6") and narrow columns (under 2"). You can also select an option to draw a vertical line between columns.

Another Way

Click the Tab button at the left end of the ruler repeatedly to find the tab alignment you want, then click the ruler at the desired tab stop position to set the tab. The symbol that appears at the left end of the ruler will correspond to the symbol in the Tab button (Left, Center, Right, Decimal, or Bar tab).

WORD 2002

Did you know?

If you double-click the shaded area of the ruler, the Page Setup dialog box will appear.

HINTS & TIPS

In Normal View, multiple-column formats appear as one long column. Switch to Print Layout View to manipulate column formats.

After you insert columns, inspect your document for balance. The basic format is **newsletter columns;** that is, side-by-side columns. Word fills the first column on a page. When that column is full, the text snakes to the next column which may end short of the bottom margin. According to your preference, you can change the vertical balance of columns by inserting a continuous section break into the document.

HANDS on

Creating and Modifying a Column Format

In this activity, you will apply newsletter-style column formatting to a document then you will insert a column break, change the text alignment, and apply a new column format. You will apply a column format to a new blank document then paste text into the document and balance the columns.

1. Open *Woodsy View News* in your *Word Data* folder and save it as *Columns* in the *Tutorial* folder.

2. Click **Select All** on the Edit menu to select the entire document.

3. Click the **Columns button** on the Standard toolbar.

A drop-down panel appears containing four column icons, as shown in Figure 2.10.

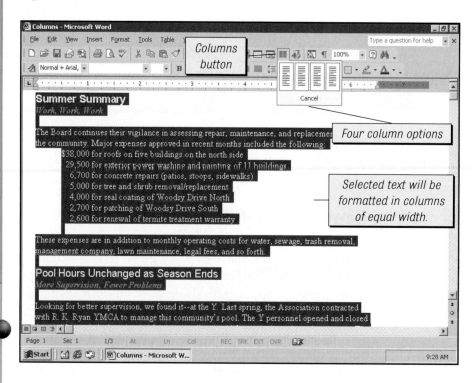

Figure 2.10
Columns menu

4. Point to the **2 Columns icon** then click.

The document is now arranged in two columns. Also, Word switched to Print Layout View so you could see the results of your action.

5. Click the document to deselect the text, then scroll through the document to observe the two-column format.

6. Click **Select All** on the Edit menu, then click **Columns** on the Format menu.

The Columns dialog box appears, as shown in Figure 2.11, showing five presets and list boxes for specifying the number of columns, width, and spacing.

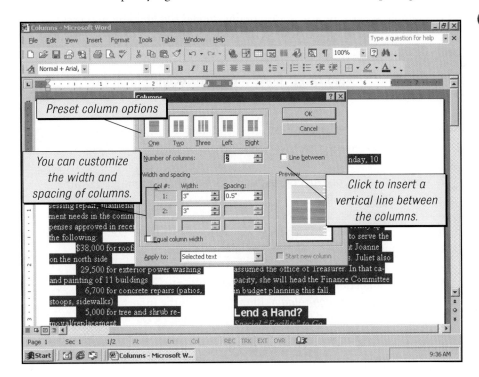

Figure 2.11
Columns dialog box

7. Click the **Three column icon** in the *Presets* section to revise the column layout from two to three columns. Click the **Line between option** to insert a vertical line between columns, then click **OK**.

Your document now appears in a three-column format, and a vertical line extends from the top margin to the bottom margin between the columns.

8. Click the document to deselect the text, then scroll to the bottom of page 1 and click an insertion point before the first character in the heading at the bottom of the first column.

9. Click Break on the Insert menu, select the **Column break option** in the Break dialog box, and click **OK**.

The heading moves to a better location at the top of the next column.

10. Click **Select All** on the Edit menu then click Justify ▤ on the Formatting toolbar. Deselect the text then scroll through the document to observe the modified alignment.

11. Save and close the document.

12. Click the **New Blank Document button** 🗋 and click **Print Layout View** ▣, if necessary.

NORTON
ONLINE

Visit **www.glencoe.com/norton/online/** for more information on creating a column format.

13. Click **Columns** on the Format menu. In the *Presets* section of the Columns dialog box, click the **Three column icon** and click **OK**.

The default column settings appear on the horizontal ruler.

14. Save the new document as *New Columns* in the *Tutorial* folder in your *Word Data* folder.

15. Open *Ag Ed* in your *Word Data* folder. Select the heading and text from the top of the document through . . . *diffusion of agricultural technology* at the end of the third paragraph.

16. Click the **Copy button** 📋. Close the *Ag Ed* document. Click **Paste** 📋.

The copied text is pasted into the *New Columns* document in the three-column format. A few lines run over to a second page.

17. Click **Select All** on the Edit menu. Click the **Line Spacing triangle button** ≡▾ and click **1.5**.

The line spacing is adjusted so the text fits on page 1, but the columns are not in vertical balance (the third column runs short).

18. Click an insertion point after the last line in the document (next to the period after *technology*). Click **Break** on the Insert menu, click **Continuous** under *Section break types*, and click **OK**.

19. Click **Print Preview** 🔍 to view the document.

The columns appear balanced vertically.

20. Close the Print Preview window, then save and close the document.

MAINTAINING CONSISTENCY IN A DOCUMENT

Word provides tools to help check for consistency in alignment and formatting of a document. The Show/Hide button ¶ (Standard toolbar) reveals a **paragraph mark** wherever you pressed ⏎ Enter , a dot wherever you pressed ␣ Spacebar , and an arrow wherever you pressed ⭾ Tab . These symbols help you detect inconsistencies in vertical and horizontal spacing and indenting. With the Show/Hide feature you can visually inspect the document to eliminate extra or missing blank lines between paragraphs, spaces between words, or indentations.

The Reveal Formatting task pane shows the current font, paragraph, spacing, image, and table properties for any point in your document and allows you to change any of these properties.

The Find and Go To features, which you learned about in Lesson 1, can also help you check alignment in a document.

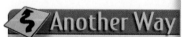

HINTS & TIPS

Use the Find and Replace dialog box to find text of similar formatting.

Another Way

To show all formatting marks in a document, click *Show all formatting marks* in the Reveal Formatting task pane.

HANDS on

Checking Consistency in Spacing and Alignment

In this activity, you will check the spacing in headings and between paragraphs; then you will check the tabs (indentations). Finally, you will use Reveal Formatting to change paragraph alignment.

1. Open *Creative Classroom* in your *Word Data* folder and save it as *Quality Assurance* in the *Tutorial* folder.

2. Click the **Show/Hide button** ¶ on the Standard toolbar.

The paragraph and spacing marks are revealed in the document. Notice that two dots appear after the word *Classroom* in the main heading at the top of page 1.

3. Click to the left of one of the dots between *Classroom* and *in* and press Delete.

4. Click the Find button 🔍 then click the **Go To tab**.

5. Click **Heading** in the *Go to what* box, as shown in Figure 2.12.

WORD 2002

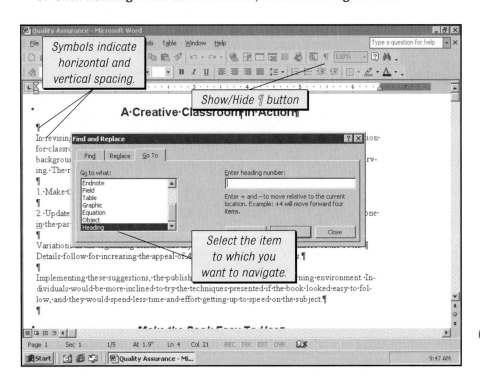

Symbols indicate horizontal and vertical spacing.

Show/Hide ¶ button

A·Creative·Classroom¶in·Action¶

Select the item to which you want to navigate.

6. Click **Next** to advance to the next centered heading.

7. Check the spacing indicated by dots in the heading and edit appropriately. Check all the remaining headings in the document.

8. Click **Page** in the *Go to what* box, and type 1 in the *Enter page number* box. Click the **Go To button**.

Word **BASICS**

Checking Spacing and Alignment
To check a heading:

1. Click the Show/Hide button (¶) on the Standard toolbar to reveal spacing characters.

2. On the Go To tab in the Find and Replace dialog box, click Heading in the *Go to what* list box.

3. Click Find Next.

To check paragraph marks and tabs:

1. Click the Show/Hide button (¶) on the Standard toolbar to reveal spacing characters.

2. On the Find tab in the Find and Replace dialog box, click More, and then click Special.

3. Click Paragraph Mark or Tab Character.

4. Click Find Next.

Figure 2.12
Go To tab

Now you will check paragraph marks throughout the document, using the Find feature.

9. On the Find tab, click the **More button** to expand the dialog box. Click the **Special button**.

The Special menu displays, as shown in Figure 2.13.

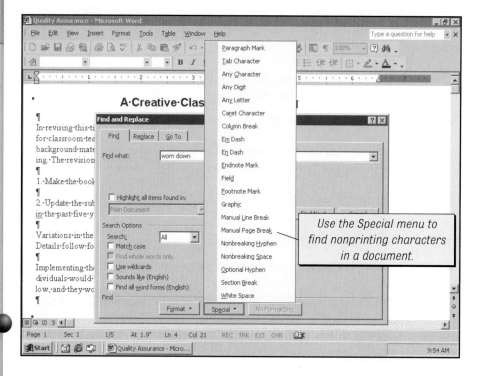

Use the Special menu to find nonprinting characters in a document.

Figure 2.13
Special menu

10. Click **Paragraph Mark** then click the **Less button** to collapse the dialog box.

11. Click the **Find Next button**.

Word jumps to the first paragraph mark at the beginning of the document.

12. Click **Find Next** three times.

The paragraph mark to the right of the main heading is selected.

13. Click **Find Next** again.

Word jumps to the paragraph mark on the next line. This pattern of paragraph marks should appear consistent throughout the document. One paragraph mark should appear at the end of each partial line and one paragraph mark should appear on the next line.

14. Continue checking for extra or missing paragraph marks by clicking **Find Next**. To insert a missing paragraph mark, click the document and press [Enter ↵]; to remove an extra paragraph mark, click the document and press [Delete]. (Do not add extra paragraph marks in the bulleted list in the document.) Stop when Word returns to the top of the document.

Now you will check the consistency of tabs in the document. The document format involves no paragraph indentations; therefore, no tab characters (or arrow symbols) should appear.

15. On the Find tab, click the **More button** and click the **Special button**. In the Special menu, click the **Tab Character option**. Click the **Less button** and then search the document.

No tabs are found; a message appears indicating that the search is complete.

16. Click **OK** in the message box. Close the Find and Replace dialog box and click the **Show/Hide button** ¶.

17. Select the last two paragraphs in the document (under the *Project Management* heading) and click **Reveal Formatting** on the Format menu.

The paragraph alignment is shown as *Left* in the Reveal Formatting task pane (see Figure 2.14).

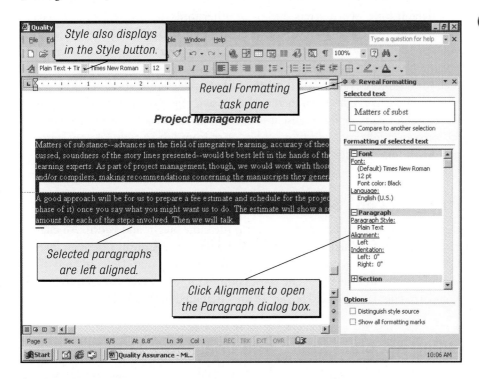

Figure 2.14
Reveal Formatting task pane

18. Click **Alignment** in the Paragraph section of the task pane.

19. The Paragraph dialog box appears.

20. Click the **Indents and Spacing tab** in the Paragraph dialog box. In the General section, click the **Alignment box triangle button**, click **Centered**, and click **OK**.

Both of the selected paragraphs become centered.

21. Close the Reveal Formatting task pane, click **Save** 🖫, and close the document.

ENHANCING THE APPEARANCE OF A DOCUMENT

An effective way to enhance the appearance of a document is to modify some attributes of the characters. For example, you can select a new font or change the font size; add bold, italic, and underline; add color; or even add borders, shading, and highlighting.

These style choices can be attractive additions to edited, reformatted documents. Certain font characteristics can help to set off special copy, such as headings. For example, the characters in a heading may contrast in design, size, darkness, and color. Such contrast makes documents inviting to readers. Setting off text in this way may also provide clues to how document content is organized.

Changing Font Design

A **font** is a set of characters of one design. In Word, a font named **Times New Roman** is the default font. Word offers dozens of other fonts, as you will soon discover. However, the fonts available to you depend upon the printer you are using. A certain printer may convert a fancy Word font to less desirable characters or may not print the font at all. Some fonts are ideal for ordinary copy, while others are best suited for headings. A few special-purpose fonts are designed more for Web pages, posters, and the like rather than memos, letters, and reports. The Times New Roman font is ideal for paragraphs because it is a **serif** font. That is, the characters have *feet* that form a straight line, guiding readers' eyes from left to right. A font without feet—**Arial,** for example—is best for headings. These fonts are called **sans serif.**

Changing Font Size

When you start a new document, all text is the same height and width. All characters are the same **font size** (sometimes called point size). A **point** ($\frac{1}{72}$ of an inch) is a unit of measure applied to fonts. The default size is 12 point. (Files in your *Word Data* folder vary in font size.) The most common font sizes for paragraphs are 10, 11, and 12. Font sizes of 14, 16, and 18 are often used for headings.

Adding Special Effects and Character Effects

Another way to enhance text is to add one or more special effects. You can use the **bold** style attribute to make words stand out from the surrounding copy. Bold is a heavier type style that helps readers see important points or technical terms at a glance. **Italic** is another common style attribute. Italic text has thin, delicate characters that slant to the right. A large block of italic text is hard to read, but italic is an attention-getter when used sparingly. Another way to call attention to certain words is to underline them. Besides the standard solid line, Word offers more than a dozen **underline** styles—solid, dotted, dashed, and wavy. In addition, you can apply **character effects,** such as subscript, superscript, or small caps. There are also a variety of **animations** available that you can apply to text including selections that make text shimmer or sparkle in the document window. The key to using various text effects and style attributes effectively is to avoid using them too much.

WORD 2002

Changing Font Color

The default font color is black on a white background. As a Word user, though, you are certainly not limited to black-and-white documents. More than forty basic font colors are provided, along with the tools to create many, many more. (Background colors are equally numerous. Changing the background color, however, switches the document automatically to Web Layout View—not the best view for editing and formatting tasks.)

If your document happens to be a Web page, the use of various colors is critical to attracting and holding the attention of site visitors. Nowadays, too, many offices are equipped with an **intranet**—a Web-like network for communicating within an organization. As a result, many documents never make it to paper; they are published on the intranet instead, and read by company employees from their computer screens. In some schools today, students create documents on the computer and submit them via e-mail or save them to a network drive. These documents, too, never get on paper. Instructors and other students read the documents on their computers. Also, color printers are rapidly becoming standard office equipment. On some black-and-white printers, different font colors appear as various shades of gray.

Adding Borders, Shading, and Highlights

You can make a paragraph or page stand out by adding a border on any or all sides of it or by adding **shading,** a color that will fill the space inside a border. Add a **highlight** if you want a color background to appear over selected text much like a highlighter.

HANDS on

Enhancing Text

In this activity, you will change the font design, size, and color of selected text in a document. You will apply bold, italic, and underline; apply superscript and subscript character effects; add a text animation; and add a border, shading, and highlighting.

1. Open *Venus Information* in your *Word Data* folder, and save the file as *Venus Enhanced* in the *Tutorial* folder in your *Word Data* folder.

2. Select the line of text on page 1 and click the **Font triangle button** [Arial ▾] on the Formatting toolbar.

The Font list box displays. The font names are listed in alphabetic order. Recently used fonts form a short list at the top of the Font list box.

3. Scroll down, if necessary, in the Font list box and click **Times New Roman**.

The font style changes.

Enhancing Text

To change font design or size:

1. Select the text to be changed.

2. Click the Font triangle button (to change design) or the Font Size triangle button (to change size).

3. Click the desired font name or size.

To change the font style attributes:

1. Select the text to be changed.

2. Click the toolbar button(s) for the desired attribute (bold, italic, or underline).

To add character effects:

1. Select the text to be changed.

2. Click Font on the Format menu.

3. On the Font tab, select the desired character effect and click OK.

Figure 2.15
Enhanced text

Enhancing Text

To change the font color:

1. Select the text to be changed.

2. Click the Font Color triangle button on the Formatting toolbar.

3. Click the desired color sample.

To add borders:

1. Select the text to be defined by a border.

2. Click Borders and Shading on the Format menu.

3. On the Borders tab, click the desired options and click OK.

4. Click the **Bold button** ▣. Click anywhere on the screen to deselect the text.

5. Click **Find** 🔍, find the word *roots*, then close the Find and Replace dialog box. Select the entire line of text in which the word *roots* occurs. Click the **Font Size triangle button** 12 ▾, click **14**, and then click the **Italic button** *I*.

Since the italic effect should be applied to the quotation only and not the writer's name, you need to reformat part of the line.

6. Select the name and the dash in front of it, and click the **Italic button** *I* to *remove* the effect. Click the document to deselect the text.

7. After the last character in the author's name, type 1 then select it.

8. Click **Font** on the Format menu. On the Font tab, click to activate **Subscript** in the *Effects* section, then click **OK**.

The number 1 appears in the subscript position, slightly below the line of text.

9. With the number still highlighted, click **Font** on the Format menu, select **Superscript**, and click **OK**.

10. Click anywhere in the document to deselect the text.

Your screen should appear similar to Figure 2.15.

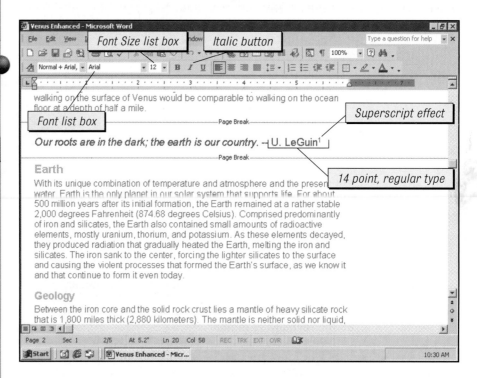

11. Navigate to page 2, select the *Venus* heading at the top of page, and click the **Font Color triangle button** ▲▾.

The Font Color palette appears. When you point to a color square on the palette, a ScreenTip appears with the color name.

12. Point to the **Sky Blue sample** and click, as shown in Figure 2.16. Click the document to deselect the text.

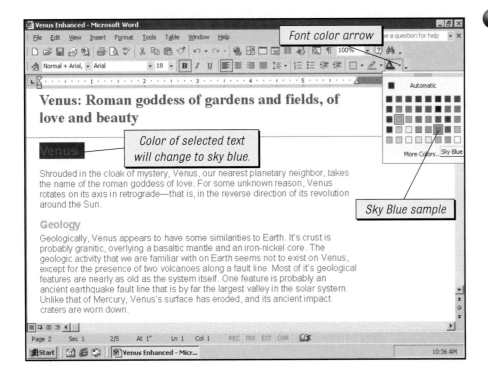

Figure 2.16
Font Color palette

Word BASICS

To add shading:
1. Select the text to be shaded.
2. Click Borders and Shading on the Format menu.
3. On the Shading tab, click the shading options and click OK.

To highlight text:
1. Select the text to be highlighted.
2. Click the Highlight triangle button on the Formatting toolbar.
3. Click the desired color sample.

To apply animation:
1. Select the text to be animated.
2. Click Font on the Format menu.
3. On the Text Effects tab, click the desired animation effect and click OK.

13. Scroll through the document, select each additional heading, and click **Repeat Font Color** on the Edit menu to change all heads to sky blue.

14. Select the *Earth* heading on page 4, and click the **Underline button** 🔲.

A solid, single line appears under the selected word.

15. Click Font [Arial ▼] and click **Times New Roman**. Select the number in the Font Size box [16 ▼], type 17 and press [Enter↵].

NOTE *Because 17 point is not listed in the Font Size list, you must type it in the Font Size box.*

16. Click to deselect the heading, then click **Find** 🔍 and find the word *subduction*. Close the Find and Replace dialog box, then right-click on the word *subduction*, and click **Font**.

17. On the Font tab, click the **Underline style triangle button** and click the single wavy line near the bottom of the list box. Click the **Underline color triangle button** and click a **Gray color sample**. Look at the Preview window and then click **OK**.

18. Select the word *Bibliography* on page 5 and click the **Highlight triangle button** 🖊▼. Select the **Yellow color sample** in the palette.

The word *Bibliography* is highlighted. Now you will add a border and shading to selected text.

19. Select the entire line on page 3, and click **Borders and Shading** on the Format menu.

20. On the Borders tab, click the **Box option**. On the Shading tab, click the **Light Yellow color** in the Fill palette, and click **OK**.

21. Click the document to deselect the text and view the border and shading.

22. Click the selection bar to again select the line on page 3.

23. Click **Font** on the Format menu. On the Text Effects tab, click **Marching Red Ants** in the Animations list box and click **OK**.

24. Deselect the text to view the moving red border.

25. Click **Save** 🖫 and close the document.

HANDS on

Using Format Painter

The Format Painter 🖌 allows you to quickly copy text formats from one part of a document to another. Select the text format you wish to copy, click 🖌, then simply *brush* over the text you want to change with the paintbrush pointer. The new text will assume the same font style, line spacing, indentations, and so on, as the text you copied from.

In this activity, you will use Format Painter to change the plain text in your document to match the text that has already been formatted and enhanced.

1. Open *Astronomy 110* in your *Word Data* folder.

2. Click **Find** 🔍 and find the italicized word *subduction*. Close the Find and Replace dialog box and click the **Format Painter button** 🖌 on the Standard toolbar.

A paintbrush appears beside the I-beam pointer.

3. In the same sentence, select the words *sea-floor spreading*.

As you release the mouse button, the selected text becomes italic.

4. Click the bold, red *Geology* heading at the top of page 1; then click the **Format Painter button** 🖌.

5. Click the *Atmosphere* heading that appears in plain text in the next paragraph on the same page.

The 14-point Arial font, bold effect, and red color are copied to this heading. Your screen should now resemble Figure 2.17.

6. Triple-click the paragraph under the *Venus* heading on page 1 to select the paragraph.

7. Click the **Format Painter button** 🖌. Then click anywhere in the paragraph below the *Geology* heading in the next paragraph on page 1.

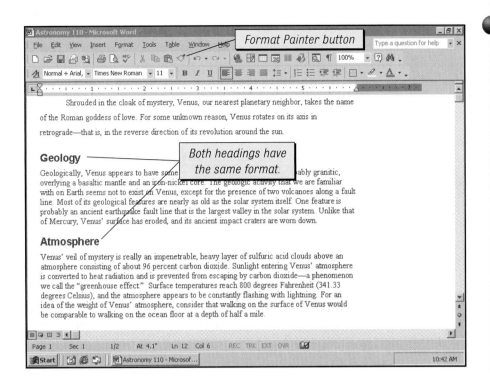

Figure 2.17
Copied text format

WORD 2002

8. Select the *Geology* paragraph you just formatted on page 1, and double-click the **Format Painter button** .

9. Scroll down to the next single-spaced paragraph (under *Atmosphere*) and click anywhere in it to change the spacing. Scroll down and click each of the remaining single-spaced paragraphs in the document.

10. Click the **Format Painter button** to deactivate it or press Esc.

11. Select the *Venus* heading at the top of page 1, and use Format Painter to copy the attributes of the *Venus* heading to the *Earth* heading on page 1.

12. Save the document as *Astronomy Enhanced* in the *Tutorial* folder in your *Word Data* folder, and close the document.

Using the Style Command

Using the Style feature is a quick way to format and enhance documents at the same time. A **style** combines format properties (alignment, indentations, and line spacing) and appearance properties (font and font size and bold, italic, or underline). Thus, when you choose a style, one click takes care of all these factors at once. In a new blank document, the text you type uses the **Normal style**—the base style for the Normal template in Word.

You can apply four different types of styles in a Word document. **Paragraph style** controls all aspects of a paragraph's appearance, such as text alignment, tab stops, line spacing, and so on. **Character style** affects selected text within a paragraph, such as the font and size of text and bold and italic formats. **Table style** provides a consistent look to borders, shading, alignment, and fonts in tables. **List style** applies similar alignment, numbering, or bullet characters and fonts to lists of text. You can also create your own styles.

Did you know?

You can create your own styles or modify existing styles and give them descriptive names. You should neither create nor modify styles on a computer that you do not own, however, unless you have approval to do so. By using the Styles and Formatting task pane, you can also reuse formatting within a document without creating a new style.

Word provides more than one style list. One list is *All styles*; another is *Available styles*. A third option, *Custom*, would contain only those styles that a Word user created. Therefore, the Custom list would vary greatly from one computer to another. The *All styles* list is used in the following activity.

HANDS on

Applying and Creating Styles

In this activity, you will apply paragraph styles and character styles to reformat and enhance a document. You will then create a character style.

1. Open *Astronomy Unformatted* in your *Word Data* folder and save it as *Styles* in the *Tutorial* folder.

2. Select the *Venus* heading at the top of the document, and click the **Styles and Formatting button** 🖼.

The Styles and Formatting task pane appears.

3. Click the **Show box triangle button** at the bottom of the task pane and click **All styles**.

In the Styles and Formatting task pane, the name of each style indicates its intended use. For example, *header* indicates a paragraph heading; and *body text* indicates a paragraph itself. Each style also shows how your text will look (font, font color, and alignment or indentation). The symbols in the right column of the list indicate whether a style involves paragraph style (¶), character style (a), list style (▤), or table style (⊞). The list also shows the font size and, for paragraph styles, the horizontal alignment. Pointing to a style will display a ScreenTip box containing style and formatting information.

4. Scroll through the *Pick formatting to apply* box and click **Heading 1**.

The style is applied to the *Venus* heading.

5. Select the heading *Geology* that appears a few lines below the *Venus* heading and click **Heading 2**.

6. Select the first paragraph of text (under *Venus*). Scroll through the Style list and click **Body Text Indent 2**, a 12-point body text style.

The style—which includes font size, indentation, line spacing, and paragraph spacing—is applied to the paragraph.

7. Find and select the heading *Earth*. Point to the **Heading 1 style** in the *Pick formatting to apply* box as shown in Figure 2.18.

The ScreenTip box displays the style properties.

8. Click **Heading 1**.

The heading *Earth* is changed to the Heading 1 style.

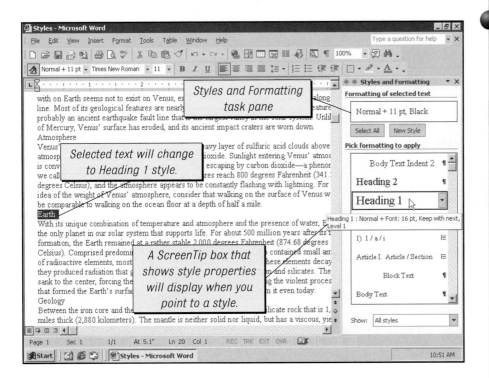

Figure 2.18
Styles and Formatting task pane

9. Read the ScreenTip description of the Heading 2 style and change the style of the next heading, *Geology*, to **Heading 2**.

NOTE *You can make additional changes to text after a style is applied—for example, you may add underline or other attributes.*

10. Change the style of the *Geology* paragraph to **Body Text Indent 2**.

11. Find and select the word *subduction* and scroll in the *Pick formatting to apply* box to find and apply the character style **Emphasis**.

Now you will create a new character style.

12. Find and select the words *continental drift*, and click the **New Style button** in the Styles and Formatting task pane.

The New Style dialog box appears.

13. Type Terms in the *Name* box, click the **Style type triangle button** and select **Character**.

14. In the *Formatting* section, click the **triangle buttons** to select **Arial** as the font and **10** as the font size; click the **Bold** button (see Figure 2.19); and then click **OK**.

The *Terms* style appears in the *Pick formatting to apply* box.

15. With *continental drift* still selected, click **Terms** to change the selected text to the new style.

16. Close the Styles and Formatting task pane.

17. Save your changes and close the document.

Figure 2.19
New Style dialog box

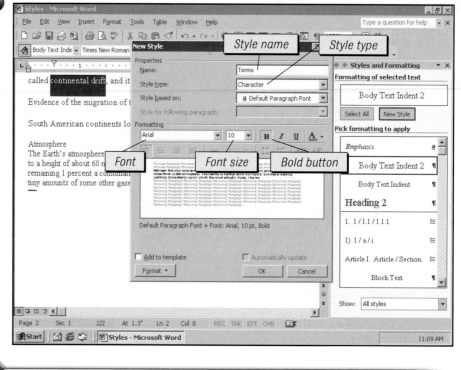

INSERTING AND FORMATTING GRAPHICS

Sometimes it is difficult to get a point across with text alone. In such cases, you can add a **graphic** (also called an **object** or **image**) to a document. A graphic is any element in a document that is not text. Examples include a drawing object made with lines, curves, or decorative text (called **WordArt**) or pictures (clip art or a photograph). Word has an entire folder called the **Clip Organizer** which includes professionally designed objects (pictures, photographs, sound, and video clips) from which you can choose to complement many different subjects in your documents. The graphics in the Clip Organizer are called **clip art,** or clips. The Drawing toolbar has tools that help you draw geometric shapes and other objects, insert WordArt, and access the Clip Organizer.

Browsing the Clip Organizer

The Insert Clip Art button 📷 on the Drawing toolbar opens the Insert Clip Art task pane. Clips are organized by pictures, sounds, and motion clips and in subject categories identified by keywords such as Animals, Buildings, Character Collections, Food, Healthcare, People, and Travel. You can open the Clip Organizer and browse the categories that fit your subject, or you can search for related clips with keywords. Before you insert a clip into your document, you can preview it.

If the graphic you want to insert into your document is in another location, such as in a program, on the Web, or on a disk, Word will allow you to **import** (or insert) many popular types of graphic files directly into your document. Click the Insert menu, point to Picture, and then click From File or simply click the Insert Picture button 🖼. When you locate the file you want to insert, just double-click it. If you want to import a free image from a Web site, you often must copy and save the image to a local drive.

WARNING *You can use any Clip Organizer image in the documents you create—as long as you are not selling the documents with the image. Before you add any graphic to a document, be sure to verify the legal restrictions for using it. Always secure permission from your instructor before you add a graphic to the Clip Organizer.*

Working With an Image

An inserted clip may be the wrong size and in the wrong place. Therefore, you must be able to resize, move, and align the image on the page. You can perform these tasks with resize handles. To move or resize an image, you must first select the image by clicking it. The **resize handles** surrounding the image allow you to **resize** it. Point to a handle until a two-way arrow appears. To change only the height of an image, drag a vertical two-way arrow until you see the desired image size. To change only the width of an image, drag a horizontal two-way arrow. To maintain the image proportions while you resize it, drag a corner or diagonal resizing handle. To move an image, click the selected object and drag it to the new location.

Tools on the Picture toolbar allow you to handle images more precisely, however, than using sizing handles. When you select a picture, the Picture toolbar appears with editing tools. You can, for example, change the contrast between light and dark colors, **crop** (cut off) unnecessary parts of the picture, and change the size and **layout** (how text aligns and wraps in relation to the picture).

Before you change the height and/or width of an image (in the Format Picture dialog box), you need to guard against distortion. If you make a clip wider, for example, without changing the height an equal amount, you change its height-width relationship, or **aspect ratio.** Before you change either the height or the width, you need to lock the aspect ratio. Thus, when you change either dimension, Word changes the other dimension proportionately. (If you forget to lock the aspect ratio, or otherwise make a mistake in resizing, you can click the Reset Picture button 📷 to restore the image to original size.)

Graphics almost always share a page with paragraph copy. The **wrapping style,** or text wrapping, refers to the visual relationship of the text and the image. You cannot use the buttons for aligning text (on the Formatting toolbar) to align pictures. Instead, you align objects horizontally by clicking the Format Picture button 📷 on the Picture toolbar. In a finished document, text and graphics should complement each other. If they compete for readers' attention, you should change the text appearance or the size, wrapping style, and/or alignment of the graphic.

Inserting, Editing, and Formatting an Image

In this activity, you will search for an image, insert the image into a document, and then edit and format the image.

1. Open *Sandy Reef Island Tour* in your *Word Data* folder and save the file as *Clip Art* in the *Tutorial* folder. Read the document, which describes Sandy Reef Island.

Another Way 💲

To open the Insert Clip Art task pane, click the Insert menu, point to Picture, and click Clip Art.

WORD 2002

Inserting an Image

1. Click an insertion point where you want the image.

2. Click the Insert Clip Art button on the Drawing toolbar.

3. Type keywords in the Insert Clip Art task pane and click the Search button.

4. Click an image to insert it into the document.

2. Point to **Toolbars** on the View menu and click **Drawing**.

The Drawing toolbar appears beneath the document window above the status bar.

3. Position an insertion point two lines below the last line of text in the document, then click the **Insert Clip Art button** 🖼 on the Drawing toolbar.

The Insert Clip Art task pane displays.

4. In the Search text box, type travel and click the **Search button**.

Travel-related images display in the task pane, as shown in Figure 2.20.

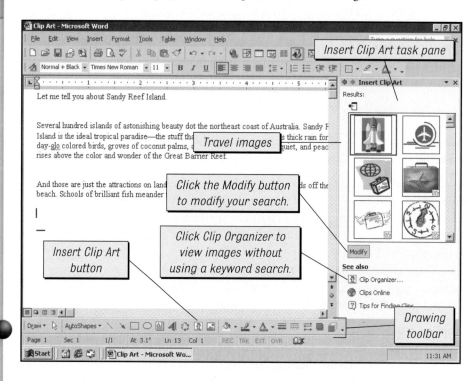

Figure 2.20
Insert Clip Art task pane

NOTE *If you want to view additional images, click Clip Organizer in the See also section of the Insert Clip Art task pane. Select a folder in the Collection List box. Available images will display in the right side of the Microsoft Clip Organizer box. The Office clip art images are arranged by category in the Office Collections subfolders.*

5. Click one of the travel images to insert it into your document.

The clip art is inserted at the end of the document.

WARNING *The Clip Organizer graphics must be installed on your computer to view clips from the Clip Organizer. If no pictures, sound files, or motion clips exist in the Clip Organizer, see your instructor. If you have access to the Microsoft Office CD and receive a message that additional clips are on the Microsoft Office CD-ROM, click OK to continue. If you receive a message that Word is indexing clips from previous editions, click Postpone.*

6. Close the Insert Clip Art task pane.

Now you will edit and format the image you just inserted.

NORTON ONLINE

Visit www.glencoe.com/norton/online/ for more information on importing graphics.

7. Click anywhere in the clip to select it.

The Picture toolbar floats in the document window. A small box called a *handle* appears at each corner and at the middle of each side of the image. Drag any of the corner handles to resize the image while maintaining its height-to-width proportions (aspect ratio). Resize an image using a center handle to distort the image vertically or horizontally.

8. Click the **Format Picture button** 🖼 on the Picture toolbar, and click the **Size tab** in the Format Picture dialog box. Your document window should look similar to Figure 2.21.

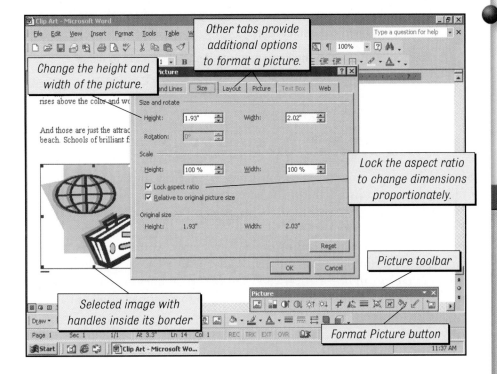

Figure 2.21
Size tab in the Format Picture dialog box

9. Under Scale, select the **Lock aspect ratio check box**, if necessary.

10. In the *Size and rotate* section, increase the number in the **Height box** to approximately 2″.

The number in the Width text box changes automatically because you selected *Lock aspect ratio*.

11. On the Layout tab, click the **Square icon** under *Wrapping style*. Under *Horizontal alignment*, click **Right**; then click **OK**.

The dialog box closes and the image moves to the right below the text. The clip is still selected except now the border is gone and white resize handles surround the image.

12. Point to the center of the clip art image, press and hold the left mouse button, and drag this image to the top of the right side of the document.

Another Way

To format a picture, click anywhere in the clip to select it, then right-click and click Format Picture. Make the necessary changes in the Format Picture dialog box.

A dotted line indicates where the clip will be located.

13. Release the mouse button to place the image on the right side of the text.

14. Click the document to deselect the image and close the Picture toolbar, then scroll to view the document.

NOTE *If you want to select another wrapping style to improve the overall appearance of your document, select the clip and click the Text Wrapping button* ▦ *on the Picture toolbar. Then click an option.*

15. Move or resize the picture, if desired.

16. Change the text appearance as desired for the text and the picture to complement each other.

17. Point to **Toolbars** on the View menu and click **Drawing** to close the toolbar. Save and close the document.

SORTING WORDS OR NUMBERS

Many documents contain lists—sometimes arranged in alphabetic or numeric order. You can **sort** lists manually by cutting and pasting or dragging and dropping. However, a faster, more accurate way to sort a list is to use the Sort feature on the Table menu. With the Sort feature, you can specify whether you want items sorted in **ascending** or **descending** order. You can sort words, numbers, or dates that appear as text or in tables; the items must be listed vertically, though. Any column in tables can be sorted. If you want to sort all lines in a document, just issue the Sort command. If, however, you want to sort particular lines in a document, select the lines and then sort.

HANDS on

Sorting a List

In this activity, you will sort a list alphabetically in ascending order.

1. Open *Bookmark* in your *Word Data* folder, and save the file as *Sort* in the *Tutorial* folder.

You want to sort a list of software features near the end of this document, so you must select the items to be sorted.

2. Navigate to the top of page 13. Select all the text under the *Word Processing* heading from the words *Block Delete* through *Special characters* (on page 14).

3. Click **Sort** on the Table menu.

The Sort Text dialog box appears. The default options are set to sort text by paragraph in ascending order.

Word BASICS

Sorting a List

1. Select the text to be sorted.

2. Click Sort on the Table menu.

3. Click a *Sort by* option in the Sort Text dialog box.

4. Click a Type option.

5. Click Ascending or Descending.

6. Click Header row, if necessary, and click OK.

4. Click **OK** to accept the default settings.

Word rearranges the selected items in alphabetic order.

5. Find the phrase *Formula bar* and select the text from *Formula bar* through the last line of text in the document.

6. Click **Sort** on the Table menu. Confirm the options are set to sort the paragraphs of text in ascending order and click **OK**.

7. Save and close the document.

ADDING REFERENCE FEATURES

You can add reference features to long documents to help readers find information and to provide supporting facts or sources. Such reference features include bullets or numbers to highlight listed items, page numbers, headers and footers, footnotes, and a table of contents.

Using Bullets and Numbers

A **bullet** is a character, typographical symbol, or graphic used as a special effect to highlight an item. Word provides bullet characters, including dots, squares, arrows, and check marks; the Clip Organizer also includes images that you can use as a bullet. You can use bullets to distinguish main items from secondary items when the order of items is not critical. You may add bullets to an existing list or add them as you type.

If priority is important in a list of items, use numbers to indicate the order of importance in the list. Also, use numbers when you want the reader to know that the items or steps must be completed in sequence. As with bullets, you may add numbers to an existing list or add them as you type. You may also create an outline numbered list.

HANDS on

Adding Bullets, Numbers, and Outline Numbers to Lists

In this activity, you will add bullets and numbers to a list of items; change existing bullets; create a list while adding bullets as you type; and create a list while adding outline numbers.

1. In your *Word Data* folder, open *Series* and save the document as *Bullets & Numbers* in the *Tutorial* folder.

2. Find *Table of Contents*. Click in the selection bar and drag down to select the text from *Table of Contents* through the end of the paragraph with the *Feedback form* heading (in the middle of the following page).

3. Click the **Bullets button** ☰ on the Formatting toolbar and then deselect the text and scroll up to view the formatting.

A bullet appears to the left of each selected item, similar to Figure 2.22. The bullet character in your document may differ, depending upon which bullet character is selected in the Bullets and Numbering dialog box.

Figure 2.22
Bulleted list

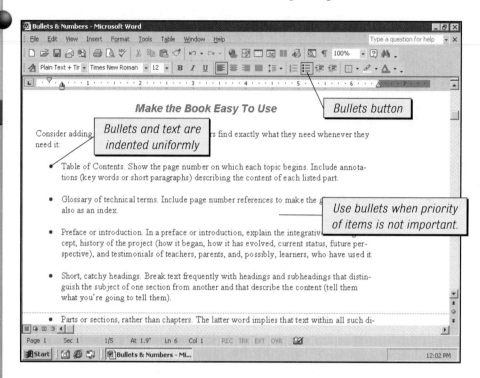

Inserting Bullets and Numbers

To insert bullets:

1. Select the items to be bulleted.

2. Click the Bullets button on the Formatting toolbar.

To insert numbers:

1. Select the items to be numbered.

2. Click the Numbering button on the Formatting toolbar.

To insert outline numbers:

1. Select the items to be numbered.

2. Click Bullets and Numbering on the Format menu.

3. Click the Outline Numbered tab in the Bullets and Numbering dialog box.

4. Click the style you want and click OK.

4. Select the bulleted items again and click **Bullets and Numbering** on the Format menu. Click the **Bulleted tab**.

The Bulleted tab displays seven bullet options.

5. Click a bullet option that differs from your document and click **OK**.

Word changes the bullet in your document to the bullet character you chose.

6. Find *What WPS Can Do*. Select the bulleted list in this section of the document, and click the **Bullets button**.

The bullets disappear and the selected text moves to the left margin.

7. Click the **Bullets button** again.

Word inserts the bullet design you selected in step 5. The bullets and text are uniformly indented from the left margin, 0.25" and 0.5", respectively.

NOTE *Before proceeding to the next step, click the Tools menu and click AutoCorrect Options. On the AutoFormat As You Type tab, select the* Automatic bulleted lists *check box and click OK.*

8. Click the **New Blank Document button**. In the new document, type an asterisk (*) and press Spacebar. Then type Bookmark and press Enter.

Your text is automatically changed to a bulleted list.

9. Type the following items. Press  after each item:
Bullets, Find, Go To, Replace, Sort.

10. After the last item, press <kbd>Enter↵</kbd> twice to turn off the automatic bullets.

11. Click **Bullets and Numbering** on the Format menu and click the **Outline Numbered tab**.

12. Click the option that uses Arabic numbers for first-level items and indents the next level with Arabic numbers, as shown in Figure 2.23. If this option is not available, click any option that does not have the word *Heading* on the sample. Click **OK**.

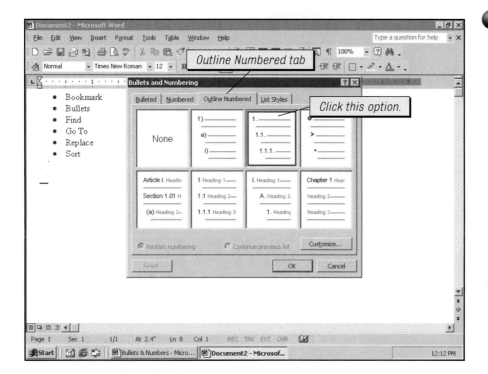

Figure 2.23
Outline Numbered tab

13. Type the following partial outline. Press <kbd>Enter↵</kbd> after each item except the last item. Do not press <kbd>Tab</kbd>. All items will be numbered automatically as first-level items as you type.

Planning Phase
Identifying Potential Employers
Where to Look
Checking and Choosing
Analyzing Jobs and Qualifications
Writing Phase

14. Select the second and third items on the list.

15. Click the **Increase Indent button**  on the Formatting toolbar.

The indent increases and the selected items become numbered as subordinate (lower-level) items.

16. Select the last two items in the outline; click the **Increase Indent button** .

Again, the demoted items indent and are renumbered appropriately.

Another Way

To insert numbering automatically as you type, select the *Automatic numbered lists* option on the AutoFormat As You Type tab of the AutoCorrect dialog box (Tools menu).

17. Save the document as *Outline List* in the *Tutorial* folder, and close the document.

18. Go to the top of the *Bullets & Numbers* document. Find the word *Incorporate*. Select this line and the balance of text above the *What WPS Can Do* heading.

19. Click the **Numbering button** 📄 on the Formatting toolbar.

Each selected item is indented and numbered with an Arabic number. The numbering style in your document depends upon which numbering style is selected in the Bullets and Numbering dialog box.

20. Save and close the document.

Numbering Pages

Word adds page numbers to documents automatically. If you should add or delete a page, Word renumbers the pages automatically, too. Page numbers are printed in the margin area at the top or bottom of pages and aligned at the left, center, or right, as you choose. Different types of page numbering are available, including lowercase and uppercase letters and Roman numerals or Arabic numbers. By dividing documents into sections, you can use different numbering in each section.

HANDS on

Adding Page Numbers

In this activity, you will number pages in a document and then modify the original page numbering.

1. Open *Ag Ed* in your *Word Data* folder and save it as *Reference Features* in the *Tutorial* folder.

2. Click **Page Numbers** on the Insert menu.

The Page Numbers dialog box displays, as shown in Figure 2.24.

3. Click the **Position triangle button** then click **Bottom of page (Footer)**. Click the **Alignment triangle button** and click **Center**. Preview the document and then click **OK**.

Word switches to Print Layout View.

4. Scroll down and view the page number at the bottom center of the first page. Navigate to the end of the document and view the page number on the last page.

The page numbers appear dim—they are inactive. The number can only be edited by clicking Header and Footer on the View menu or by double-clicking the number. (You will work with headers and footers in the next activity.) You will now divide the document into three sections and use different numbering for each section.

Word BASICS

Inserting Page Numbers

1. Click Page Numbers on the Insert menu.

2. In the Page Numbers dialog box, click a position and alignment option. If the position is Bottom of page (footer), click *Show number on first page*.

3. Click Format and set the desired options.

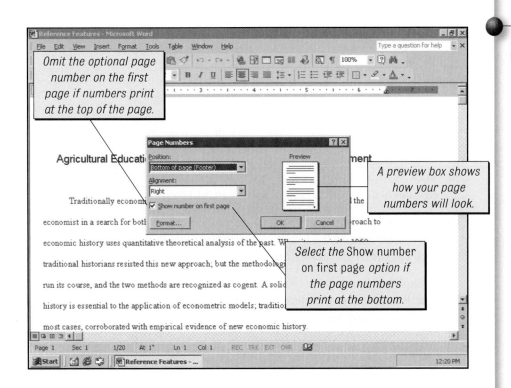

Omit the optional page number on the first page if numbers print at the top of the page.

A preview box shows how your page numbers will look.

Select the Show number on first page *option if the page numbers print at the bottom.*

Figure 2.24
Page Numbers dialog box

5. Navigate to the top of the document. Click before the main heading then click **Break** on the Insert menu. Click **Next Page** under Section break types and click **OK**.

6. Click **Normal View** 📄. Scroll up if necessary.

The section break appears at the end of page 1 above the main heading.

7. Click **Print Layout View** 📄 so you can see the page numbers as you work.

8. Click page 1. Click **Page Numbers** on the Insert menu. Click the **Alignment triangle button** and click **Right**. Then click the **Format button**.

The Page Number Format dialog box appears.

9. Click the **Number format triangle button** and click the **i, ii, iii, ... option**. Click **OK**, preview the page in the Page Numbers dialog box, and click **OK**.

The number *i* appears in the bottom-right corner of the first page. Notice the same style page number on the status bar also. Now you will number pages in the main part of the document with Arabic numbers, starting with 1.

10. Click to the left of the heading at the top of page 2, then click **Page Numbers** on the Insert Menu. Click the **Format button** in the Page Numbers dialog box.

Under Number format, the Arabic numbers format (1, 2, 3 . . .) is already selected; you want to start this numbering at page 1.

You can use the Inside and Outside alignment options to insert page numbers for bound documents. The Inside option aligns the number on the right of even-numbered pages and on the left of odd-numbered pages. The Outside option does just the opposite.

11. In the *Page numbering* section, type 1 in the *Start at* box, and then click **OK**. Click **OK** again to close the Page Numbers dialog box.

The page number in the status bar changes to *Page 1*. Scroll down to verify the number at the bottom of page 1.

12. Go to the *Bibliography* heading. Click at the bottom of the page and insert a *Next page* section break.

13. Click **Normal View** ▤, click the manual Page Break (after the Section break) and press ⌷Delete⌷. Click **Print Layout View** ▣.

14. Go to the *Appendix A* heading, click before the heading, and click **Page Numbers** on the Insert Menu. In the Page Numbers dialog box, click the **Format button**.

15. Click the **A, B, C, ... option** number format. Type A in the *Start at* box, if necessary; and click **OK**. Click **OK** again to close the Page Numbers dialog box.

The status bar now displays *Page A   Sec 3*.

16. Click the **Print Preview button** 🔍 then the **Multiple Pages button** ▦ (2 x 2 Pages). Click the page number on the last page twice.

The page enlarges so that you can see the page number *B* clearly.

17. Click the page number again to reduce the page size. Click the top-left page, then click the page number—the Arabic number *18*. Click again to reduce the page size.

18. Scroll to the top of the document in the Preview window. Click the page number on the top-left page—the Roman numeral *i*. Click again to reduce the page. Then, click the **Print Layout View button** ▣ to close Print Preview.

As you observed, you used a different page numbering style in each of the three sections of your document.

19. Save your changes and close the document.

Creating and Modifying Headers and Footers

In long documents, other pieces of information besides the page number are often printed in the top and/or bottom margin to guide readers who may be looking for a specific topic. For example, on time-sensitive documents, the date and time may appear at the top or bottom of every page. That way readers know they are reading current information. Information repeated in the top margin is called a **header;** information in the bottom margin is called a **footer.** To specify the information, you will work in the Header and Footer view, where you can insert information by using the Click and Type feature, by selecting AutoText items, or by clicking buttons on the Header and Footer toolbar. (In Print Layout View, the **Click and Type** feature automatically applies paragraph formatting when you double-click certain sections of a document. You can then insert text or an image where the insertion point is located. The pointer shape is a clue to the formatting that Click and Type will apply in any one area of a document.)

Adding Headers and Footers

In this activity, you will insert a header to all pages of a document. The header will contain the file name of the document and the date. Then you will insert a page number in a document footer.

1. Open *Reference Features* in the *Tutorial* folder in your *Word Data* folder and save it as *Header and Footer* in the *Tutorial* folder.

2. Click **Normal View** ▤, if necessary, to view the section breaks. Click anywhere within page 1 of section 2.

3. Click **Header and Footer** on the View menu.

The Header and Footer toolbar appears, as shown in Figure 2.25. Text in the main view of the document is inactive (it appears dim). You must insert header information (text or graphics) in the dotted Header box.

WORD 2002

Word BASICS

Creating a Header or Footer

1. Click Header and Footer on the View menu.

2. Type or insert the desired information (such as the date, time, page number, or other text).

3. Click the Close button.

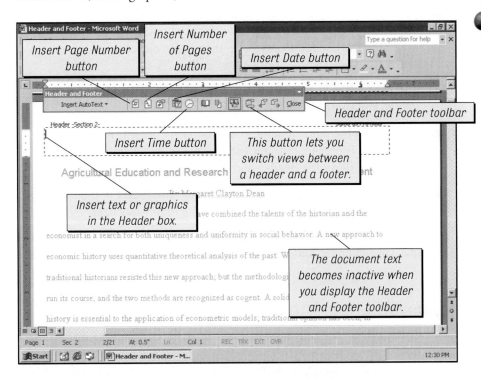

Figure 2.25
Header and Footer toolbar

4. With the insertion point at the left margin in the Header box, click the **Insert AutoText button** [Insert AutoText ▾] on the Header and Footer toolbar. Click **Filename** to automatically insert the document name.

5. Double-click at the right end of the Header box. Click the **Insert Date button** 🗓 on the Header and Footer toolbar.

HINTS & TIPS

If your document contains section breaks, you can insert a different header or footer for each section. Click a section where you want the different header or footer, then click the Same as Previous button. Type the new header or footer.

The date is inserted into the header.

6. Close the Header and Footer toolbar. Click **Print Layout View** 🗏 and scroll through the document.

The header has been inserted into all pages of the document. The header appears inactive while the main text appears normal.

7. Navigate to the top of page i and double-click the header.

The Header and Footer toolbar displays. The header is now active.

8. Double-click the center of the dotted Header box to place an insertion point at the center of the header. Click the **Insert Page Number button** ⊞ on the Header and Footer toolbar, press [Spacebar], type of, press [Spacebar], then click the **Insert Number of Pages button** ⊡.

The page number *(i of 21)* appears in the header.

9. Click the **Switch Between Header and Footer button** 🗐.

Word displays the Footer box on the same page with the insertion point at the left margin.

10. Type Author: Margaret C. Dean. Click the **Switch Between Header and Footer button** 🗐 and select the page number (i of 21) in the header. Press [Delete], then again click the **Switch Between Header and Footer button** 🗐.

11. Select the letter C. in the footer and type Clayton, then close the Header and Footer toolbar.

12. Double-click the page number in the footer on page 1. When the Header and Footer toolbar appears, select the page number and press [Delete]. Close the Header and Footer toolbar.

13. Scroll the document to examine the header and footer in the three sections. Note that the page number in the footer has been deleted throughout the entire document.

14. Save your changes and close the document.

Using Footnotes

Footnotes may occur at the bottom (or foot) of a page to explain or expand upon key points or provide source information. Footnotes invariably refer to a specific word, sentence, or paragraph. Labeling the footnote and the text it refers to with the same label—a superscripted number or symbol—shows this relationship. A documentation footnote typically has four divisions: author name(s), title, publication date, and page reference. The arrangement and punctuation may vary, depending upon the type of publication noted and the style manual followed.

When you type text that requires a footnote, you must use the Footnote command to insert a footnote. You will then verify that you want the footnotes numbered sequentially with Arabic numbers and type the footnote text in Footnote view. Word will automatically number and place the footnotes below a short horizontal line at the left margin between your main text and the footer.

The footnote text style is based on the Normal style. When you point to a note reference number, the note text displays above the reference number as a ScreenTip. Later, if you want to delete a footnote, you have only to delete the reference number in the main text. If you want to move a footnote to another location, select the reference number and use the Cut and Paste method. Word will renumber automatically and move the footnote to the new location. If you need to edit footnote text, double-click the reference number or click Footnotes on the View menu. (Some writers use **endnotes** instead of footnotes. Endnotes serve the same purpose as footnotes, but they appear together on a separate page at the end of a document. The same Word feature that inserts footnotes also inserts endnotes.)

Inserting Footnotes

In this activity, you will insert footnotes in a multiple-section document.

1. Open *Header and Footer* in the *Tutorial* folder in your *Word Data* folder, and save it as *Footnote* in the *Tutorial* folder. Click **Print Layout View** 🔲, if necessary.

2. Find the second occurrence of the words *economic history*. Click an insertion point after the period that ends the sentence.

3. Point to **Reference** and click **Footnote** on the Insert menu.

The Footnote and Endnote dialog box displays, as shown in Figure 2.26.

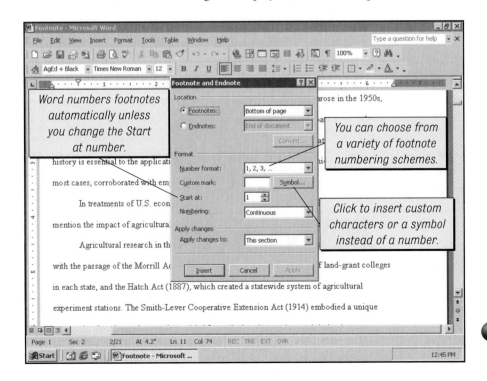

WORD 2002

Word BASICS

Inserting Footnotes

1. Click an insertion point in the document for the footnote number.

2. Point to Reference on the Insert menu, and click Footnote.

3. In the Footnote and Endnote dialog box, click Insert to insert continuously numbered (Arabic) footnotes at the bottom of pages.

4. Type the footnote text.

Figure 2.26
Footnote and Endnote dialog box

WORD 2002

4. Click **Insert**.

Word places the superscript number 1 at the bottom of the page.

5. **Scroll up three paragraphs to view the corresponding superscript number inserted after** *economic history*.

6. **Scroll back to the bottom of page 1 and type the following footnote text next to the superscript number:** Neimi, A. W., U.S. Economic History (1975), pp. 2–3.

NOTE *Do not press* Enter⏎ *after you type the footnote. Word will automatically adjust the spacing if another footnote appears on the same page.*

7. **Click the paragraph above the footnote.**

8. **Find the words** *major force* **and click an insertion point after the period at the end of this sentence. Click the Insert menu, point to Reference, and click Footnote.**

9. **Click Insert to accept the footnote settings.**

Word inserts the footnote number (2) at the bottom of the page and also at the insertion point (after *major force*) in the document.

10. **Type the following footnote text:** Ibid., p. 230.

Ibid. is an abbreviation of the Latin word *ibidem*, which means *in the same place*. In other words, footnote 2 refers to the same publication as footnote 1.

11. **Save your changes and close the document.**

Creating a Table of Contents

A **table of contents** (or **TOC**) is a list of the headings and subheadings and the page numbers on which they are found in the document. A table of contents typically appears at the beginning of a document.

Word will create a table of contents on the basis of the heading styles used in your document. Several different arrangements are available. Word automatically inserts a hyperlink for each heading that appears in a table of contents. Thus, you can click headings in the TOC to jump to the corresponding page in your document. If you add text or headings to your document, you can automatically update the table of contents by selecting it and pressing F9.

HANDS on

Inserting a Table of Contents

In this activity, you will create and modify a table of contents for a document.

1. **Open** *Footnote* **in the** *Tutorial* **folder in your** *Word Data* **folder and save it as** *Contents* **in the** *Tutorial* **folder.**

2. Click the heading on page 1 of Section 2; then click the **Styles and Formatting button** to open the Styles and Formatting task pane. Click **All styles** in the *Show* box, if necessary.

Heading 2 displays in the *Formatting of selected text* box at the top of the task pane.

3. Close the Styles and Formatting task pane. Go to the next heading in the document using the Go To tab of the Find and Replace dialog box. Click the *Land-Grant Colleges* heading and verify that Heading 4 appears in the Style button on the Formatting toolbar.

4. Verify the heading styles throughout the document by advancing to each using Go To. Click each head and examine the Style button on the Formatting toolbar.

5. Navigate to the top of the document and click an insertion point on page i.

6. Click the **Insert menu**, point to **Reference**, and click **Index and Tables**. Then click the **Table of Contents tab**.

The Index and Tables dialog box displays with the Table of Contents tab on top, as shown in Figure 2.27.

WORD 2002

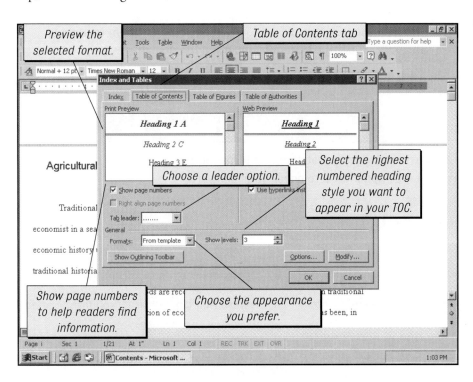

Figure 2.27
Table of Contents tab

7. Click the **Show page numbers option**, if it is not selected. Change the Tab leader to the **solid line option**, if necessary.

8. Click the **Formats triangle button**, and click **Distinctive**.

The tab leader and format display in the Print Preview window. You want to show Heading levels 1–4 in your TOC.

NORTON ONLINE

Visit **www.glencoe.com/norton/online/** for more information on creating a table of contents.

9. Click the **Show levels up triangle button** and change the setting to **4**.

The Heading 4 level appears in the Print Preview window.

10. Click **OK** to create the table of contents.

Word inserts the table of contents at the insertion point.

11. Click an insertion point above the first line of the table of contents and type Table of Contents. Select *Table of Contents*, click the **Style button** [Normal ▾], and click **Heading 2**.

Now you will update the TOC to include the *Table of Contents* heading you just typed above it.

12. Select the *Table of Contents* heading and the entire TOC. Then press [F9].

The Update Table of Contents dialog box appears.

13. Click the **Update entire table option** and click **OK**.

Word adds the *Table of Contents* heading and page number to the TOC.

14. Deselect the text, then press [Ctrl] and click *Bibliography* to jump to the page where the heading appears in the document.

15. Save and close the document.

Test your knowledge by matching the terms on the left with the definitions on the right. See Appendix B to check your answers.

TERMS	DEFINITIONS
_____ **1.** bullet	**a.** Distance of text from the left or right page margins
_____ **2.** subscript	**b.** A set of characters of one design
_____ **3.** Format Painter	**c.** Feature that copies paragraph format and character appearance
_____ **4.** indentation	**d.** May be a dot, arrow, square, or check mark
_____ **5.** font	**e.** Character or symbol that is positioned slightly lower than other text.

E-Mail a Word Document

In this activity, you will explore Help to learn about the features of your e-mail program and how to use Word to send an **e-mail** (electronic mail) message with a document attachment. Before you begin this activity, secure permission from your instructor.

1. Type e-mail messages in the *Ask a question box* and press ⌷Enter⌷. Click the **Create a new e-mail message link**. Click **Show All** in the Help window, and read the information. Close the Help window.

2. Open the *Woodsy View News* document in your *Word Data* folder, then click the **E-mail button** 🖻 on the Standard toolbar.

Word displays an e-mail header. By default, the file name of the open document appears in the *Subject* box of the e-mail header, as shown in Figure 2.28.

3. In the *To* box, type an e-mail address of a friend, a student, or your instructor. (Your instructor may provide the address.) Press ⌷Tab⌷ twice to move to the *Subject* box. (Word will include your e-mail address automatically in a *From* box that doesn't display in the e-mail header.)

4. Select the text in the *Subject* box and type Newsletter and press ⌷Tab⌷. In the *Introduction* box, type the name of the person to whom you are writing, followed by a comma, then type the Woodsy View Association newsletter is attached.

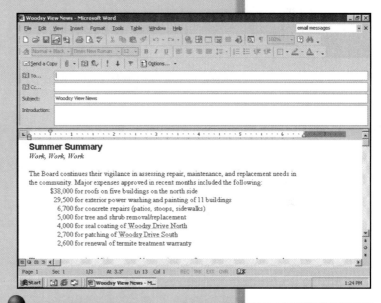

Figure 2.28
E-mail header in the Word window

5. To send the e-mail message and the attachment, click the **Send a Copy button** 🖃 Send a Copy. If you are connected to the Internet, Word will send your message to the address in the *To* box and close the e-mail header. If you are not connected, you will receive a message asking you to connect to the Internet.

6. Close your document.

NAMING FAVORITES

As you probably know, hundreds of thousands of Web sites are available at the click of your mouse. With so many sites available, you may have difficulty keeping track of those that you would like to revisit. Word and Internet Explorer provide an easy way to do just that. You can keep a list of **favorites** or **bookmarks** to which you can return quickly. In this activity, you act as a personal travel consultant for GlenTravel Agency. You will designate a Web page and a document as favorite places.

> **NOTE** *Steps for this activity assume your default Web browser is Internet Explorer. If you are using a different Web browser, the steps may be slightly different. If you are unsure of how to add a favorite (or bookmark) to your particular browser, search your Help menu for information.*

1. Connect to the Internet. Open *Australia Tour Pricing* in your *Word Data* folder. Point to **Toolbars** on the View menu and click **Web**.

2. Click the text in the Address bar of the Web toolbar, type www.travel.com, and press `Enter←`.

Your Web browser launches, and the *Travel.com* home page appears.

> **NOTE** *If you have trouble connecting to the* Travel.com *home page, locate an alternative site by clicking Search* `🔍Search` *on the Internet Explorer toolbar and search for Web sites containing the keyword* Travel.

3. Explore the links at this site to find information about Australia that you and other travel agents could use to promote tours of Australia.

4. Return to the *Travel.com* home page by clicking the **Back button** `⇐ Back ▾` or by typing the *Travel.com* address in the Address bar.

5. Click Favorites `Favorites ▾` on the Explorer toolbar to open the Favorites pane. Click Add `📑 Add...` and click **OK** in the Add Favorite dialog box to add this site to your list of favorite places.

Travel.com has been added to the list of sites in the Favorites pane. (It has also been added to your Favorites list in Word.) Now at any time you can click the Favorites button `⭐Favorites` in your browser (or Word) to access this link.

6. Click the **Australia Tour Pricing taskbar button** to return to the Word document.

In addition to Web sites, Word also allows you to add documents to your Favorites list. You can use this feature to quickly open documents that you often use.

7. Click the **Favorites button** `Favorites ▾` on the Web toolbar and click **Add to Favorites**.

8. In the Add To Favorites dialog box, type Australia Tour Pricing in the File name box, as shown in Figure 2.29.

9. Click the **Add button**.

Figure 2.29
Add To Favorites dialog box

10. Close the *Australia Tour Pricing* document.

Now you can return easily to the Web site and document designated as favorites.

11. Click the **Favorites button** `Favorites ▾` on the Word Web toolbar, and click the **Open Favorites folder**. Click *Australia Tour Pricing* and click **Open**.

Word remembers where the document is stored and automatically opens the file.

12. Close the document. Click **Favorites** `Favorites ▾` again on the Web toolbar and click the *Travel.com* link.

Your browser launches and loads the *Travel.com* Web site. The Favorites pane appears to the left of the browser window.

13. Right-click the *Travel.com* link in the Favorites pane, click **Delete** on the shortcut menu, then click **Yes** to send the link to the Recycle Bin. Close the browser.

14. Click **Favorites** `Favorites ▾` on the Word Web toolbar and click **Open Favorites**. Right-click *Australia Tour Pricing*, click **Delete** on the shortcut menu, then click **Yes** to delete the link to this file (this will just delete the link; it will not delete the file).

15. Close the Favorites dialog box and the Web toolbar. Close Word. Close your browser and disconnect from the Internet.

> **WARNING** *You may proceed directly to the exercises in this lesson. If, however, you are finished with your computer session, follow the "shut down" procedures for your lab or school environment.*

SUMMARY AND EXERCISES

SUMMARY

WORD 2002

Word provides many features for formatting text. Options such as bold, underline, and italic are available for enhancing the appearance of a document. Word enables you to easily format text in newsletter columns. The Format Painter and Style features are handy tools for quickly changing format and appearance. Images add interest to documents; Word equips users with tools to find, insert, and edit images. Word makes short work of page numbering and quickly adds headers and footers, footnotes, or a table of contents. You can send an e-mail right from a Word window and attach a Word document to an e-mail. In addition, Word provides a feature for you to add favorites in both Word and your Web browser so you can quickly return to a document or a Web site.

Now that you have completed this lesson, you should be able to do the following:

- Insert and modify page and section breaks. (page 101)
- Distinguish between a manual and automatic page break. (page 101)
- Define a *widow* and an *orphan.* (page 100)
- Change margins and vertical alignment. (page 103)
- Describe the types of text alignment and indentations involved in page setup. (page 105)
- Modify horizontal alignment and indentation style. (page 106)
- Set character, line, and paragraph spacing and tab stops. (page 108)
- Describe the types of tab stop options and how they align text. (page 109)
- Explain the advantages to formatting text in a newsletter style. (page 111)
- Apply and modify newsletter-style column formats. (page 112)
- Use Reveal Formatting to check paragraph alignment and check for consistency of spacing in headings, between paragraphs, and in tabs. (page 115)
- Explain the purpose of using attributes such as bold or italic or contrasting fonts. (page 118)
- Define *serif* and *sans serif.* (page 118)
- Enhance the appearance of text by applying bold, italic, and underline as well as super-scripts and subscripts. (page 119)
- Apply text animation, a border, shading, and highlighting. (page 119)
- Use Format Painter to change text formats. (page 122)
- Define the word *style* and describe the four style types: Paragraph, Character, Table, and List. (page 123)
- Use the Style command to reformat documents. (page 124)
- Search the Clip Organizer for an image, insert the image into a document, and edit the image. (page 127)
- Sort a list alphabetically. (page 130)
- Add and edit bullets, numbers, and outline numbers in a list. (page 131)
- Add and modify page numbers in a document. (page 134)
- Insert and edit headers and footers. (page 136)
- Insert and edit a footnote. (page 138)
- E-mail a Word document as an attachment. (page 143)
- Add favorites in Word and Internet Explorer to a Web site and to a document. (page 144)

CONCEPTS REVIEW

1 TRUE/FALSE

Circle T if the statement is true or F if the statement is false.

T   F   **1.** A footer is the same as a footnote.

T   F   **2.** The font Times New Roman is often used for paragraph text.

T   F   **3.** Character style controls all aspects of a paragraph's appearance.

T   F   **4.** For the body text of letters and memos, a font size of 6 to 8 is recommended.

T   F   **5.** You can use the Reveal Formatting task pane to change formatting in a paragraph.

T   F   **6.** The Align Right button makes text even on both side margins.

T   F   **7.** You can add a Web site to Favorites the first time you visit it.

T   F   **8.** Page numbers may be placed at the top or bottom of pages.

T   F   **9.** Open the Paragraph dialog box to choose hanging indentation style.

T   F   **10.** You can use photographs as clip art.

2 MATCHING

Match each of the terms on the left with the definitions on the right.

TERMS	DEFINITIONS
1. serif	**a.** Most common type of font used for paragraph text
2. bold	**b.** Group of characters that share a common design
3. columns	**c.** Vertical measure between lines of text within paragraphs
4. superscript	**d.** Text that looks thick and dark
5. font	**e.** Often used within footnotes
6. clip	**f.** A ready-made image
7. line spacing	**g.** May be a dot, square, arrow, or even a picture
8. widow	**h.** Used to format a newsletter or newspaper
9. styles	**i.** Sets of text characteristics with names like Body or Title
10. bullet	**j.** The last line of a paragraph printed by itself at the top of a page

SUMMARY AND EXERCISES

3 COMPLETION

Fill in the missing word or phrase for each of the following statements.

1. To find the headings in a document, use the _____ tab of the Find and Replace dialog box.

2. Information that repeats at the top or bottom of each page of your document is called a _____ or _____ .

3. To change margins or vertical alignment, select _____ on the File menu.

4. Small boxes called _____ surround a selected clip or drawing.

5. To align all lines of a paragraph so they are flush at both the right and left margins, use the _____ button.

6. If priority is important in a list, use numbers; however, use _____ when all items have the same priority.

7. Drag a corner handle to resize an image and maintain its height-width proportions, also called _____ .

8. The _____ dialog box has Set, Clear, and Clear All buttons.

9. The _____ command on the Insert menu lets you insert page breaks and section breaks.

10. In a new blank document, the text you type uses the _____ style—the base style for the Normal template in Word.

4 SHORT ANSWER

Write a brief answer to each of the following questions.

1. Briefly describe how to copy double spacing and italic from one paragraph to another.

2. Explain how to create an outline numbered list.

3. Define paragraph spacing and explain how it differs from line spacing.

4. Describe the four main horizontal alignment options you can apply from the Formatting toolbar.

5. Describe the Insert Clip Art task pane and how it can be used to locate images and insert them into a document.

6. Describe the use and purpose of the Style button on the Formatting toolbar.

7. Explain how to find all formatting marks in a document.

8. Describe the purpose of favorite places.

9. Explain the purpose of section breaks and name two kinds.

10. Besides font and indents, what factors should you consider in creating a paragraph style?

5 IDENTIFICATION

Label each of the elements in Figure 2.30.

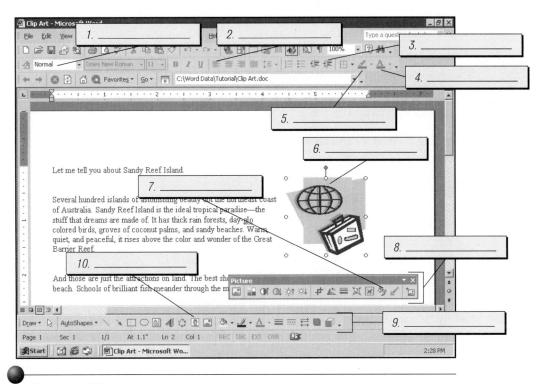

Figure 2.30

SKILLS REVIEW

Complete all of the Skills Review problems in sequential order to review your skills toreformat pages and paragraphs; maintain consistency in a document; enhance the appearance of documents; add tabs and special effects; insert, edit, and format an image; apply styles; work with columns; add a header and footer; sort a list; and add reference features.

1 Reformat Pages and Paragraphs

1. Open *Write this Way* in your *Word Data* folder and save it as *Reformat* in the *Skills Review* folder.

2. Find the word *stopping* and click after the end of this sentence. Click **Break** on the Insert menu, click **Page break**, then click **OK**.

3. Click **Page Setup** on the File menu. Change the margins as follows: Top: 2"; Bottom: 1.25"; Left: 1.25"; Right: 1.25". Click **OK**.

4. Click at the end of the last line on page 1 and press `Enter`. Click **Break** on the Insert menu, click **Next page** under Section break types, and click **OK**.

5. Click **Normal View** if necessary, click the manual Page Break and press `Delete`.

6. Click **Show/Hide** ¶ and delete any paragraph marks at the top of page 2. Click page 2 then click **Page Setup** on the File menu and change the top margin to 1.25"; in the Preview section, click **This section** in the *Apply to* box, if necessary, and click **OK**. Click **Show/Hide** ¶, click **Print Layout View** ▣, and scroll to view the document.

7. Click page 1, click **Page Setup** on the File menu, and change the top margin to 1.25". Under *Apply to*, click **This section**. On the Layout tab, change the vertical alignment to **Center**, and click **OK**.

8. Select the main title and subtitle and click the **Align Right button** ▤.

9. Select *Plan* (the paragraph heading on page 1) and click **Align Right** ▤. Select the *Draft* heading on page 1 and click **Align Right** ▤.

10. Select the first paragraph on page 1 below *Five Steps Up and to the Right*, and click **Increase Indent** ▤. Then click the **Line Spacing button** ▤ and click **1.5**.

11. Select the first paragraph under the *Plan* heading, right-click, then click **Paragraph**. On the Indents and Spacing tab, click **Justified** in the alignment box. Type 0.5" as the left and right indentation and click **(none)** in the Special list box, if necessary. In the Spacing section, click **12 pt** in the Before and After box and click **OK**.

12. Select the other three paragraphs under *Plan*, right-click, click **Paragraph**, then click the **Indents and Spacing tab**. In the Special section, click **First line by 0.5"**; under Spacing, click **Double** in the Line-spacing box; click **6 pt** before and after. Click **OK**.

13. Save your changes and close the document.

2 Check Spacing and Indentations

1. Open *Creative Classroom* in your *Word Data* folder and save it as *Consistency* in the *Skills Review* folder.

2. Click the **Show/Hide button** ¶ to display the nonprinting characters. Navigate to the end of the document and click an insertion point at the end of the last line.

3. Click the Find button ▥. Click the **More button**. Click the **Special button** then click **Paragraph Mark**. In the Search options list box, click **Up**. Click the **Less button**.

4. Click **Find Next** to advance through the document and verify that each partial line (the end of each paragraph) ends with a paragraph mark and that paragraphs are separated by one blank line (another paragraph mark). Delete extra paragraph marks and insert missing ones. Do not add extra paragraph marks in the bulleted list. Delete extra paragraph marks at the top of the document.

5. When you finish your check of the document, click **More** in the Find and Replace dialog box. Click **All** in the Search Options list then click **Less** to collapse the dialog box.

6. On the Go To tab, click **Heading** in the *Go to what* box (see Figure 2.31). Click **Next** to navigate to each heading and delete extra spaces between the words in the headings. Close the Find and Replace dialog box. Click **Show/Hide** ¶.

7. Save and close the document.

3 Set Tab Stops and Apply Special Effects

1. Click **New Blank Document** 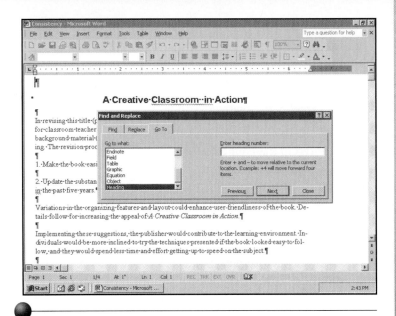 and save the new document as *Decimal Tabs* in the *Skills Review* folder in your *Word Data* folder.

2. Click **Tabs** on the Format menu and click **Clear All** to clear the default tabs. Click **Left** in the Alignment section then type 2 in the Tab stop position box and click **Set**. Continue to set left tabs at each of these positions: 3", 3.75", and 4.75". Click **OK** to close the Tabs dialog box.

3. Press [Tab] to advance to the first stop. Type the following as column headings pressing [Tab] after each word: **Actual, Budget, Variance, Total Budget**.

Figure 2.31

4. Press [Enter←], then click **Tabs** on the Format menu. Click **Clear All** and set these new tabs: Left: 1"; Decimal: 2.25"; Decimal: 3.25"; Decimal: 4"; Right: 5.5". Click **OK**.

5. Press [Tab] then type the entries below. Press [Tab] after each entry and press [Enter←] at the end of each line.

| Income | 9,438.00 | 10,000.00 | 562.00 | 120,388.00 |
| Expenses | 10,000.00 | 9,997.00 | 3.00 | 196,519.00 |

6. Select the column headings and click **Bold** [B]. Select each side heading and click **Bold** [B]. Select the *Total Budget* heading and click **Italic** [I]. Select the numbers in the *Expenses* row and click **Underline** [U].

7. Select *Total Budget*, click the **Highlight triangle button** [✎▾], and click **Turquoise**.

8. Select *Total Budget*, and click **Borders and Shading** on the Format menu. On the Borders tab, click the **Shadow option**, and click **OK**.

9. With *Total Budget* still selected, click **Font** on the Format menu. On the Text Effects tab, click **Sparkle Text** and click **OK**. Deselect the heading to view the effects.

10. Select the *Actual, Budget,* and *Variance* headings, and click **Borders and Shading** on the Format menu.

11. On the Shading tab, click the **Turquoise color** on the Fill palette. Click **Text** in the *Apply to* box, if necessary, and click **OK**.

12. Save your changes and close the file.

SUMMARY AND EXERCISES

4 Enhance Text and Use Format Painter

1. Open *Write this Way* in your *Word Data* folder and save it as *Write Enhanced* in the *Skills Review* folder.

2. Select the title and the subtitle. Click the **Font triangle button** [Times New Roman ▾] and click **Arial** or another sans serif font.

3. With the headings still selected, click **Font** on the Format menu. On the Font tab, click **Red** in the Font color box, click to deselect **Outline** in the Effects section, and click **OK**. Deselect the text.

4. Select *Write this Way*, right-click, and click **Font** on the shortcut menu. Click **20** in the Size list box and click **OK**.

5. Select *Five Steps Up and to the Right*, right-click, and change the font size to **16**.

6. Select the opening paragraph, click the **Font color triangle button** [A ▾], and click **Red**. Click **Font** on the Format menu, type **13** in the Size list box, and click **OK**.

7. Select the *Plan* heading, click the **Font triangle button**, and click the same sans serif font you used for the title. Change the font color to Red and change the Font size to 14.

8. Select the first two paragraphs beneath *Plan* and change the font size to 12.

9. Select the *Plan* heading, double-click the **Format Painter button** [⊿], and paint the *Draft* heading.

10. Scroll down and paint the *Revise* heading; then continue to scroll down to paint the *Edit* heading and the *Publish* heading.

11. Click the **Format Painter button** [⊿] to deactivate it.

12. Use Format Painter to copy the paragraph formatting of the first paragraph under *Plan* (on page 1) to the first paragraph under *Draft*. Then copy the paragraph formatting of the second paragraph under *Plan* to the second paragraph under *Draft*.

13. Preview the document, save your changes, and close the document.

5 Apply and Create Styles

1. Open *Application Followup* in your *Word Data* folder and save it as *Letter Styles* in your *Skills Review* folder.

2. Select the date. Click the **Styles and Formatting button** [⊿]. Click **All Styles** in the *Show* box in the Styles and Formatting task pane. (Each time you open this task pane, verify that you are selecting from the *All styles* list.)

3. Scroll in the *Pick formatting to apply* box and click the **Date style**. Close the Styles and Formatting task pane.

4. Select the name and address. Click the **Style triangle button** [Normal ▾], then scroll the Styles list and click the **Plain Text style**.

5. Select *Dear Mr. Olivo*, click the **Style triangle button** [Normal ▾], then scroll the style list and click **Salutation**.

6. Select *APPLICATION FOLLOWUP* and use the **Style button** [Normal ▾] to apply the **Strong character style**; select the body of the letter and apply the **Body Text style**; select *Sincerely* and apply the **Closing style**.

7. Click an insertion point after *Sincerely*, press [Enter ←], and type your name.

8. Click the body text of the letter. Click the **Styles and Formatting button** [A]. (Your document window should appear similar to Figure 2.32.)

9. Click **New Style** in the Styles and Formatting task pane and type **Position** in the *Name* box. Click **Arial, 11 pt**, and **Red** in the Formatting section and click **OK**.

10. Select the words *Legal Assistant* in the body of the letter and click the **Position style** in the *Pick formatting to apply* box.

11. Close the Styles and Formatting task pane. Save and close the document.

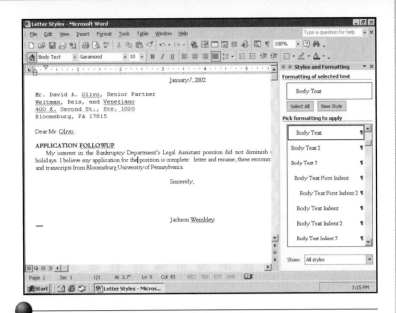

Figure 2.32

6 Insert, Edit, and Format an Image

1. Open *Write This Way* in your *Word Data* folder and save it as *Insert Clip* in the *Skills Review* folder. Click **Print Layout View** [▣], if necessary.

2. Click an insertion point after the end of the last line of the first paragraph, and press [Enter ←]. Point to **Toolbars** on the View menu and click **Drawing**. Click the **Insert Clip Art button** [▨].

3. Type the keyword **business** in the *Search text* box in the Insert Clip Art task pane, and click **Search**.

4. Click a clip in the Results box to insert it. Close the Insert Clip Art task pane.

5. Click the image to select it and point to the handle in the lower-right corner. Click when the pointer becomes a diagonal double-headed arrow and drag up and to the left to decrease the image size by about half. (If you make a mistake, click **Undo** [↶ ▾] and try again.)

6. Click the **Text Wrapping button** [▨] on the Picture toolbar and click **Square**.

7. Drag to place the image on the right margin to the right of the first two paragraphs at the beginning of the document.

8. Click the document to deselect and view the image. Close the Drawing toolbar, then save and close the document.

7 Sort a List and Add Bullets and Numbers

1. Open *Bookmark* in your *Word Data* folder and save it as *Bookmark Sorted* in the *Skills Review* folder.

2. Navigate to the *Master List of Suite Features* heading and scroll down to find the *Spreadsheet* list.

3. Type 5 and press ⌞Spacebar⌟ in front of the following items: AVERAGE function, COUNT function, IF function, MAX function, MIN function, NOW function, SUM function, TODAY function.

4. Select the list items from *Absolute and relative cell references* to *Paste command* at the end of the spreadsheet list.

5. Click **Sort** on the Table menu. Click **Field 1** in the *Sort by* box, click **Number** in the *Type* box, and click **Ascending**. Click **OK**. (The numbered items form a separate alphabetized list at the bottom of the selected text. The other listed items are not alphabetized since you are sorting only items with a number.)

6. Navigate up to the *Word Processing* list. Select all items that end with a 2 and click the **Bullets button** ▤. Click the **Decrease Indent button** ▤ to decrease the indentation.

7. Select all items that end with a 4, then click **Bullets and Numbering** on the Format menu. On the Bulleted tab, click a bullet icon that is different than the one you just inserted, and click **OK**.

8. Select all items in the Spreadsheet list excluding the items starting with 5.

9. Click the **Numbering button** ▤. Click **Sort** on the Table menu and accept the defaults by clicking **OK** to sort paragraphs of text in ascending order.

10. Select numbered items 20–29, right-click, and click **Restart Numbering** to number the selected items from 1–10. Right-click again and click **Bullets and Numbering**. On the Outline Numbered tab, click a numbering icon (*do not* click an icon that includes headings). Click **OK**.

11. Deselect the text, click the number *2* (in item 2), and press ⌞Tab⌟. (Item 2 becomes subordinate and the subsequent items are renumbered.)

12. Click the next item (the new item 2), and click **Increase Indent** ▤ twice to make it a subordinate item.

13. Save and close the document.

8 Insert Page Numbers and Add a Header and Footer

1. Open *Bookmark* in your *Word Data* folder and save it as *Bookmark Header* in the *Skills Review* folder.

2. Click **Page Numbers** on the Insert menu.

3. Click **Top of page (Header)** in the Position box. Click **Right** in the Alignment box. Clear the *Show number on first page* check box. Click **OK**.

4. Click **Print Layout View** 🔲, if necessary, and navigate to page 2 to verify the page number. Click at the top of page 2.

5. Click **Header and Footer** on the View menu. Click the **Switch Between Header and Footer button** 🔳.

6. Click **Insert AutoText** [Insert AutoText ▾] on the Header and Footer toolbar, and click **Filename** to insert the file name on the left side of the footer. Double-click the center of the footer area and click **Insert Date** 🔳 on the Header and Footer toolbar.

7. Double-click the right side of the footer area then click **Insert Page Number** 🔳. Click after the page number and type [Spacebar] of [Spacebar]. Click **Insert Number of Pages** 🔳 on the Header and Footer toolbar.

8. Close the Header and Footer toolbar. Scroll through the document to see the footer.

9. Save and close the document.

9 Insert Footnotes and a Table of Contents

1. Open *Book Revision* in your *Word Data* folder, and save it as *Book Revision TOC* in the *Skills Review* folder.

2. Click **Print Layout View** 🔲, if necessary. Click after the colon at the end of the last sentence in the first paragraph.

3. Point to **Reference** on the Insert menu and click **Footnote** to open the Footnote and Endnote dialog box. In the Format section, verify that *Continuous* is selected in the Numbering box and click **Insert**.

4. Type the following as the footnote text: King, E. E., *How to Design the Perfect Book* (2000), p. 101.

5. Click **Normal View** 🔳. Click at the top of the document and find *The following design factors* in the document. Click at the end of the sentence, point to Reference on the Insert menu, and click **Footnote**. Click **Insert**. Type this footnote text: Ibid., p. 103. (Your document should look like Figure 2.33.) Click **Close** on the Footnote pane.

6. Navigate to the top of the document and click before the main heading. Click **Break** on the Insert menu; click **Page break**, if necessary, and click **OK**.

7. Click **Find** 🔳 to open the Find and Replace dialog box. On the Go To tab, click **Heading** in the *Go to what* box.

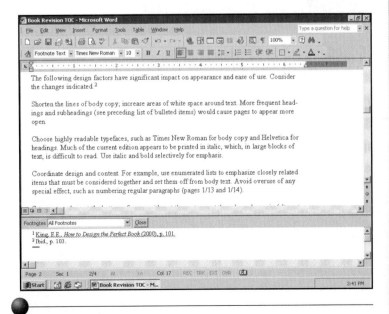

Figure 2.33

8. Click **Next** then click the heading to check the heading levels in the Style button [Normal ▾]. Repeat this process to confirm all the heading levels in the document.

9. Go to page 1. Click the **Insert menu**, point to **Reference**, and click **Index and Tables** to open the Index and Tables dialog box. Click the **Table of Contents tab**.

10. In the Formats box, click **Simple**. Select the **Show page numbers check box**, if necessary. Set the *Show levels* box to **2** and click **OK**.

11. Click **Print Preview** 🔍 and navigate to view your TOC. Close Print Preview, then save and close the document.

10 Apply and Modify a Column Format

1. Open *Book Revision* in your *Word Data* folder, and save it as *Book Column* in the *Skills Review* folder. Click **Print Layout View** 🔳, if necessary.

2. Click **Select All** on the Edit menu to select all text in the document.

3. Click **Columns** on the Format menu to open the Columns dialog box.

4. Click the **Two-column icon**, then click the **Line between check box** to insert a vertical line between the columns. Click **OK**.

5. With the columns still selected, click **Justify** 🔳. Deselect the text then scroll to view the document.

6. Click **Select All** on the Edit menu. Click **Columns** on the Format menu, click the **Three-column icon**, and click **OK**.

7. Deselect the text and view the document. Save and close the document.

LESSON APPLICATIONS

1 Reformat and Enhance a New Document

Create an announcement for a workshop scheduled in your area by typing columns in a tabular format. Change font size and attributes and apply font effects, borders, shading, highlighting, animation, and color.

1. Open a new, blank document and save it as *Workshop Announcement* in the *Lesson Applications* folder in your *Word Data* folder.

2. Change all the margins to 2"; change the vertical alignment to Center.

3. Set two tabs: Left tab at 1.5"; Center tab at 4".

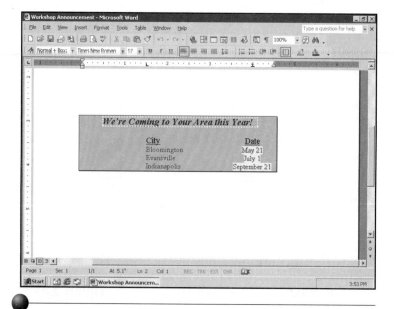

Figure 2.34

4. Type **City** and **Date** at the tabs; underline and change these headings to a larger font.

5. Beneath the headings, type three cities in your state and three dates (omit the year).

6. Above the headings, type: **We're Coming to Your Area this Year!**

7. Add enhancements of your choice, including bold or italic; font effects, such as Outline or Shadow; borders and shading; highlighting; animation; and font color. Your finished document might resemble Figure 2.34, but it will differ somewhat depending on the enhancements you choose.

8. Save and close the document.

2 Insert a Clip and Apply Column Formats

Insert a clip into a document in your *Word Data* folder; format the document in columns.

1. Open *Australian Islands Article* in your *Word Data* folder and save it as *Picture This* in the *Lesson Applications* folder.

2. Open the Insert Clip Art task pane and search for a clip art using the keyword *leisure*. If you don't find a suitable clip, browse the Clip Organizer or insert another clip of your choice.

3. Resize the clip to approximately half its initial size and place it at the very top of the document.

4. Select all the text in the document except the main heading; do not select the graphic.

5. Format the text in two-column format, deselect the text, and view the document. Reformat the columns with a different horizontal text alignment.

6. Select all the text again, excluding the graphic and main heading. Change to a 3-column format with a vertical line between the columns.

7. Save and close the document.

3 A Different Sort

Create and apply styles; apply bullets, numbering, and outline numbering; indent paragraphs; and sort paragraphs alphabetically.

1. Open *Woodsy View News* in your *Word Data* folder and save it as *Woodsy View News Sort* in the *Lesson Applications* folder.

2. Change all of the headings that appear in blue font color as Heading 1 style and change all of the headings that appear in pink font color as Heading 3 style.

3. Under *Memory Joggers*, type a heading, a period, and a space at the beginning of each paragraph as follows: **Water, Carports, Repairs, Gutters, Trash, Trash, Pets, Repairs.** Create a new character style for these headings named *Line Heading,* and apply the new style to each heading.

4. Sort the eight paragraphs in the *Memory Joggers* section alphabetically (in ascending order) then apply a bullet format. Sort the *Thank You* paragraphs (below *Memory Joggers*) in descending order; apply bullets.

5. Number the list under *Summer Summary* at the top of the document. Using the Numbered tab in the Bullets and Numbering dialog box, select the style with a parenthesis after the number. Reduce the list indent so the list begins at the left margin.

6. Insert a page break at the end of the document, and type the following list.

Be sure to attend next month's meeting to learn more about the following:
Swimming Pool
Hiring Lifeguard
Heating Pool
Adding Whirlpool
Winter Contingency Plans
Purchasing New Snow Plow
Salting Roads

7. Select the seven items in the list and apply an outline numbered list format.

8. Make items 2–4 and items 6 and 7 second-level (subordinate) items.

9. Save and close the document.

4 A Contents Set in Style

Number pages and insert a footer. Apply heading styles and insert page and section breaks. Insert a table of contents.

1. Open *Australian Islands Article* in your *Word Data* folder. Save it as *Australian Islands TOC* in the *Lesson Applications* folder.

2. Insert a footnote at the end of the first paragraph. Type **Wilhelm, Gunnar, Visiting Australia (2002), p. 47.** as the footnote text.

3. Apply Heading 1 style to the main heading and Heading 2 style to the other headings.

4. Insert page breaks to put each heading at the top of a new page.

5. Insert a Next page section break at the top of the document.

6. Number the pages at the top center. Change the line spacing in the document to Double.

7. Change the page numbering so Section 1 begins with *i* and Section 2 begins with *1*.

8. Insert a table of contents in Section 1 containing all headings in the document and the corresponding page numbers. Try to use a format and leader character that you have not previously used.

9. Create a footer on all pages of the document showing the file name, today's date, and Page *x* of *y* (where *x* is the page number and *y* is the number of pages).

10. Save and close the document.

PROJECTS

1 My Bio Enhanced

As a legal assistant for a prominent firm, you want your professional biography to be inviting in appearance and stand out from others. Therefore, it is important that you enhance it effectively. Open *My Bio* in your *Word Data* folder and save it in the *Projects* folder as *My Bio Enhanced*. Change the margins and line spacing in the document and indent the first line of each paragraph. Reformat and enhance your bio to project an image in keeping with your personality and apply various font effects and color, as appropriate. Use the Styles and Formatting task pane to create at least one new style and apply it to the document. Check consistency of alignment and formatting in the document, then send it to a classmate as an attachment to an e-mail message.

2 By Design

As a recent graduate seeking a position as a graphic designer, you decide to create your own personalized letterhead to display your abilities. Open a new, blank document and save it as *Personal* in the *Projects* folder in your *Word Data* folder. Design a letterhead for yourself, using fonts, font sizes, font colors, special effects, and character effects of your choice. (Explore Help to learn about other features, such as WordArt.) Remember to use Format Painter to help in copying formats. Before adopting a particular font, verify that the printer you use can print the font. In addition to your name and address, include a telephone number and an e-mail address. Include additional information, such as a favorite quotation, if you wish. (*Hint:* You will want to use a very narrow top margin so that

Figure 2.35

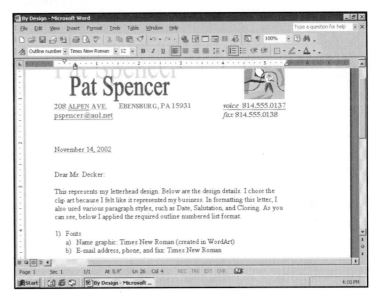

the design is as close to the top edge of the page as possible when the letterhead is printed.) Insert clip art of your choice; size it and position it attractively. Save the file. When finished, write a brief message to your instructor on the letterhead. In the message, name the fonts, font sizes, and effects used in the letterhead. Under each of these categories (fonts, font sizes, and effects) list the information then format this text as an outline numbered list. Describe why you chose the image you inserted. Save the message as *By Design* in the *Projects* folder in your *Word Data* folder. An example is shown in Figure 2.35.

3 Hot Button Sort

In a new, blank document, type a list of five Word toolbar buttons you use most often (type each button name on a separate line). Beneath it, list five additional buttons that you rarely or never use. Add an overall heading (example: *Word Toolbar Buttons*) to introduce your lists. Sort each list in alphabetic order. Increase the font size and add a border and a color fill (shading) to the heading. Apply highlighting and an animation effect to the list of five frequently used buttons and add a footnote explaining their significance. Add one or more font effects (such as Shadow or Outline) to the list of infrequently used buttons. Adjust font sizes as appropriate. Edit, format, and enhance the document according to your preferences. Save the document as *Buttons* in the *Projects* folder in your *Word Data* folder.

4 Tip of the Day

You already knew Microsoft Word features when you started your company Savvy Solutions. You have determined that some employees, though, are still not up to speed. You have decided to encourage employees to teach themselves before investing in formal Word training sessions. To start, you will circulate a how-to sheet to encourage the use of Help (an example appears in Figure 2.36). Soon you will e-mail the information sheet each morning, and eventually such information will be standard fare on Savvy Solutions' intranet (the company's internal network).

In a new document, compile several tips for the information sheet by copying Microsoft Word Help screens for copying, deleting, moving, and renaming files.

Figure 2.36

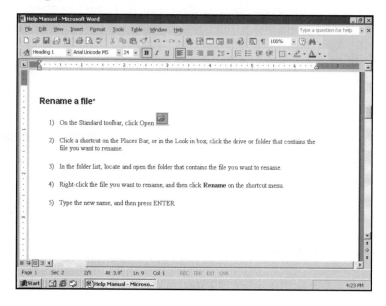

Change the numbered list format in the copied text. Create a table of contents in a separate section at the beginning of the document. Insert a footnote on each page to document the source of the information and encourage users to search Help for more information. Insert page numbers and the file name at the top of each page in the second section—begin the first page of the second section as page 1. Save the document as *Help Manual* in the *Projects* folder in your *Word Data* folder.

5 Travel Brochure

You are one of the three owners of a successful travel agency. The owners have decided it would be a good idea to create a one-page travel advertisement to mail to prospective customers. The owners have already written the text and have decided to meet for the third time to brainstorm about the design of the brochure (the previous two meetings have lacked focus and been unsuccessful). You have decided to create a mock-up of the document with sample illustrations since the other owners are having a hard time imagining the layout. Open *Travel Text* in your *Word Data* folder which contains the text for the advertisement. Save the document as *Travel Ad* in your *Projects* folder. Read the text to get a sense of the theme, then search the Clip Organizer for three representative images you could use in the brochure (search Clips Online, if necessary). Apply styles to the headings and text. Format the document in newsletter-style columns and experiment with different column formats and column text alignment. Place the last line of the document

(Call Kelly Travel right now . . .) in a prominent location in the brochure. Apply a character effect, color, and/or highlighting to this text to make it stand out.

6 My Favorite Cards

Several friends sent you animated greeting cards on your most recent birthday. You enjoyed receiving birthday greetings by e-mail—especially the ones that included a peppy tune—and you also want to be prepared to send e-cards on special occasions. Open your browser and visit each of the following Web sites that offer animated greeting cards: *www.americangreetings.com*, *www.bluemountain.com*, *www.hallmark.com*.

Rate the sites (based on your personal opinion) on the following factors, using a scale of 1 to 10 for each factor: appearance of the home page (color, arrangement, and so on); number of card categories; number and variety of cards in the Birthday category; and clarity of directions for ordering an electronic greeting. Calculate the total rating for each site and add the site(s) with the highest rating(s) to your list of favorites (bookmarks). Set tab stops in a new blank document to display the information in columns in a readable format. Use Styles to create a main heading *(My Favorite Cards)*, a secondary heading *(Online Greetings)*, and column headings *(Company, Ratings)*. Type company names *(American Greetings, Blue Mountain, Hallmark)* in the first column and your ratings in the second. Reformat and enhance the text to make it attractive and easy to read. Add a border, shading, and highlighting to the document. Save the file as *Greeting Cards* in the *Projects* folder in your *Word Data* folder.

Project in Progress

7 Following Through

As the founder-owner of Savvy Solutions, you recently accepted an invitation to present a workshop at Anderson High School. Now it's time to organize the handouts you will take to the workshop. In a new document, list five Word features you learned in Lesson 2 to emphasize at the workshop. For each feature, write a sentence describing what the feature does and give an example of when the students might use it. Include two or three keywords for finding information about the feature in Help. Set up the information in columns using tabs. Use styles attractively. Number the pages. Create a table of contents and add a footnote, giving copyright information for Microsoft Word. *(Hint:* For copyright details, see *About Microsoft Word* on the Help menu.) For the footnote, try inserting a symbol instead of a number. Each feature and the TOC should appear on a separate page. Create an attractive cover sheet for your handouts. Set up the cover sheet as a separate section at the beginning of the file. On the cover sheet, insert clip art that relates in some way to the topic of writing. Size and position the image as desired. Include the title of your presentation, your name, and the date of the presentation on the cover sheet. Reformat and enhance the cover as desired. Check the document for consistency in alignment and formatting, and make any necessary changes. Save the document as *Word Power* in the *Projects* folder of your *Word Data* folder and close the document.

LESSON 3

Advanced Document Creation

CONTENTS

OBJECTIVES

After you complete this lesson, you will be able to do the following:

- ► Insert a table into a document.
- ► Draw a table in a document.
- ► Change page orientation.
- ► Enter and modify table data.
- ► Insert and delete table rows and columns.
- ► Change table cell alignment and enhance text.
- ► Move and resize tables.
- ► Add borders and shading to table cells.
- ► Use Table AutoFormat.
- ► Insert a watermark into a document.
- ► Create and modify a chart.
- ► Insert a diagram from the Diagram Gallery.
- ► Use Mail Merge to create form letters and labels.
- ► Track changes made by multiple reviewers.
- ► Compare and merge edited documents.
- ► Insert handwriting using Word's Handwriting Recognition feature.
- ► Set up a voice recognition profile.
- ► Use speech recognition to insert text using Voice Command and Dictation modes.
- ► Perform an advanced Internet search using a search engine.

MOUS Objectives
In this lesson:
W2002-3-3
W2002-3-4
W2002-5-2
W2002-6-1
W2002-6-2
See Appendix D.

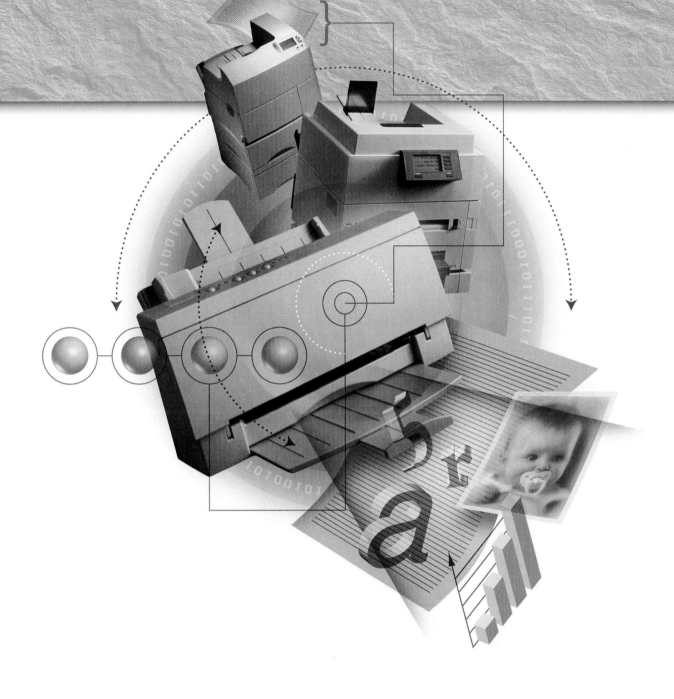

CREATING AND FORMATTING TABLES

Imagine that you are responsible for collecting a monthly fee from residents of a condominium community. At the end of each month, you summarize information for individuals whose payments are more than 15 days overdue. For each late payment your summary includes a unit number, an occupant number, the occupant's name, the beginning balance, charges added, payments made, the current balance, and the date of the last payment. If there were twenty homeowners, you would need eight columns and twenty or more rows to prepare your summary report.

Setting tabs, as you did in Lesson 2, can be tedious and time-consuming when you have more than three or four columns. However, with Word's Table feature you can easily create a grid containing the required number of columns and rows. The Tables and Borders toolbar provides tools to create and enhance tables.

Word provides various ways for you to create a table. Insert a basic table quickly by clicking the Insert Table button 🎞 on the Standard toolbar and specifying the number of columns and rows you want (up to 4 rows in 5 columns). Click the Insert Table button 🎞 on the Tables and Borders toolbar or point to Insert on the Table menu and click Table then specify the number of rows and columns you want. The ready-made table grid appears in the document with the insertion point in the first **cell** (a box formed by the intersection of a column and a row).

You can *draw* a table by clicking the Draw Table button 🖉 on the Tables and Borders toolbar or by clicking Draw Table on the Table menu. When you draw a table, as when you insert one, Word switches automatically to Print Layout View.

HANDS on

Creating a Table

In this activity, you will create tables by inserting and drawing them.

1. Open a new, blank document and save it as *Three Tables* in the *Tutorial* folder in your *Word Data* folder. Close the task pane, if necessary.

NOTE *Make sure you are in Print Layout View as you work through the activities in this lesson that involve creating and formatting tables.*

2. Click the Insert Table button 🎞 on the Standard toolbar.

A drop-down grid appears allowing you to select the desired number of columns and rows.

3. Drag down four rows and across three columns of the grid (4 x 3 Table), then release the mouse button.

The 4 x 3 table displays, as shown in Figure 3.1. All cells are one size. The insertion point rests in the first cell.

4. Click below the table, then click Break on the Insert menu, click Page Break, and click OK.

5. Point to Toolbars on the View menu and click Tables and Borders to display the Tables and Borders toolbar.

NOTE *If the Tables and Borders toolbar is floating, drag it by the title bar so it docks above the status bar at the bottom of the document window.*

6. Click the Insert Table button 🎞 on the Tables and Borders toolbar.

The Insert Table dialog box appears.

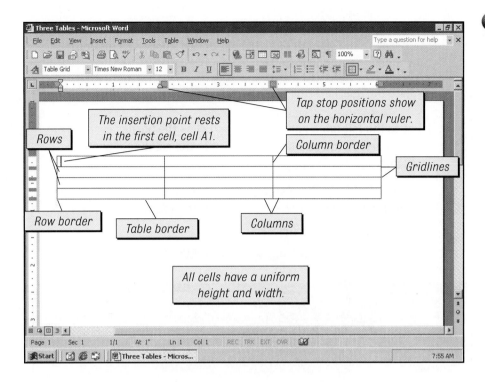

Figure 3.1
A 4 x 3 table

7. Click the **Number of columns up triangle button** until 8 appears in the box.

8. Click the **Number of rows up triangle button** until 20 appears.

9. In the *AutoFit behavior* section, select the **AutoFit to contents option**, and click **OK**.

The 20 x 8 table (20 rows x 8 columns) appears with the insertion point in cell A1 at the top of page 2. The small cells in this table will expand to the size of the entries you type since you chose the *AutoFit to Contents* option.

10. Click below the table on page 2. Click **Break** on the Insert menu, click **Next page** under *Section break types,* and click **OK**.

11. Click the **Draw Table button** on the Tables and Borders toolbar.

12. Move the pointer into the document area on page 3.

The pointer changes to a pencil, and a faint hairline appears on the vertical and horizontal rulers, indicating the location of the insertion point.

13. Move the pointer to align the hairline so it is even with the top of the white part of the vertical ruler and even with the left edge of the white part of the horizontal ruler. Click and drag the insertion point down to about 1.5″ on the vertical ruler and to the right about 2″ on the horizontal ruler. Release the mouse button.

NOTE *If you make a mistake, you can click the Undo button and try again. Or right-click the table and click Delete Rows.*

A rectangle representing the outside table border appears in the drawing area with the insertion point inside the border. The pencil pointer is still active and ready for you to draw the rows and columns of the table.

14. Point to the left table border at the 0.5″ mark on the vertical ruler then drag to the right until a straight dotted line snaps into position. Release the mouse button.

If you misplace the line, click the Undo button 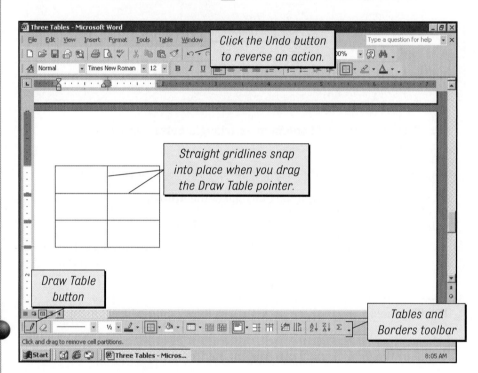.

15. Point to the left table border again and click the border even with the 1″ mark on the vertical ruler. Drag to the right until another line appears.

16. Click the top border even with the 1″ mark on the horizontal ruler and drag down until a line snaps into position forming two columns, as shown in Figure 3.2.

17. Click the **Draw Table button** to turn off the Drawing feature.

Figure 3.2
A 3 x 2 table created by drawing

18. Save your changes and close the document.

Entering Table Data

When you first create a table, the insertion point rests in the first cell—cell A1—ready for you to type information. The cell address, A1, is based on the convention of labeling columns with letters and rows with numbers. The text typed into a cell wraps around in that cell, instead of wrapping to the next row. Thus, a cell expands vertically (but not horizontally) for each line of text added. Press Tab or arrow keys to move from column to column, and press arrow keys to move from row to row. Pressing Enter inserts a blank line in the cell—it does *not* advance the insertion point to the next cell. To navigate within a table that is already filled in, click any cell or use the arrow keys.

To make a table fit more attractively on a page, use the Page Setup dialog box. If you want to print a wide table, you can change page orientation from the default portrait orientation to landscape orientation. With **portrait orientation,** data is printed across the shorter dimension of the page (the 8.5-inch dimension on standard 8.5 x 11-inch paper). With **landscape orientation,** data prints across the wider dimension of the page (the 11-inch dimension on standard 8.5 x 11-inch paper). (The page orientation, of course, can be changed to print on any size paper.)

HANDS on

Filling in a Table

In this activity, you will type entries in three tables. You will also change page orientation from portrait to landscape.

1. **Open** *Three Tables* **in the** *Tutorial* **folder in your** *Word Data* **folder and save it as** *Three Tables Revised* **in the** *Tutorial* **folder. Navigate to the top of page 3.**

2. **Type** Wednesday **in cell A1 and press** [Tab]. **In cell B1, type** Thursday **and press** [Tab] **again.**

When you press [Tab] in the last cell of a row, the insertion point automatically moves to the first cell in the next row.

3. **Type** Basic Indexing **and press** [Tab]; **type** Beyond the Basics **and press** [Tab]; **type** Indexing Online Help **and press** [Tab]; **and type** Web Indexing.

Your table should look similar to Figure 3.3.

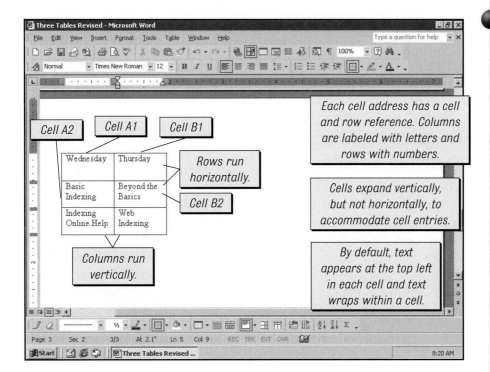

Figure 3.3
Completed table

Changing Page Orientation

1. Click Page Setup on the File menu.

2. Click Portrait or Landscape orientation, and click OK.

4. Scroll to the table on page 2, and click cell A1. Click **Print Preview** ▣. The table appears in Portrait Orientation (the default setting).

5. Click **Page Setup** on the File menu and click the **Margins tab**.

6. In the *Orientation* section, click **Landscape**, and click **OK**. Close Print Preview.

7. Type Workshop Registration Summary (in cell A1) watching the screen as you type.

Because you selected *AutoFit to contents* when you created this table, its cells expand horizontally to accommodate the text you type.

8. Type the following entries beginning in cell A2, pressing [Tab] after each entry: Workshop No.; Location; Date; Participant's Name; Telephone; Amount; Paid; T-M-X-E. **(T-M-X-E in the last column refers to the registration methods: telephone, mail, fax, e-mail.)**

NOTE *You may need to scroll or decrease the Zoom setting to see the entire table.*

9. Scroll to page 1 and type the data as indicated in Table 3.1. Then save your changes.

Table 3.1	Data for Table
Cell	**Data to Type**
A1	Conference Agenda
B2	Create Winners
C2	Inspire Teams
A3	9:30–10:30
A4	10:45–11:45

Text aligns at the top-left corner of the cells, and the uniform columns span from margin to margin.

10. Save your changes and close the document.

Modifying a Table

To improve readability and overall appearance, you can change the basic table structure by modifying column widths and row heights and **merging** cells. You can also change the table width, horizontal alignment, and text wrapping options. Some changes require that you first select the table or a cell, column, or row. The area above the top border is a selection bar for columns, while the area alongside the left border is a selection bar for rows. Selecting a cell is not the same as selecting the text in it. (You can select words, phrases, sentences, and paragraphs as usual.) Selecting an area includes the tab stop positions that define it. To work with tables and have access to all the tools for changing table structure, the Word window must be in Print Layout View. However, many table functions can also be performed in Normal View.

Did *you* **know?**

You can sort text, numbers, or dates in a table or list in ascending or descending order. Click anywhere in a table and click the Sort Ascending or Sort Descending button on the Tables and Borders toolbar. Type Sort Table in the *Ask a Question* box to learn more about sorting table data.

HANDS on

Changing the Table Structure

In this activity, you will merge cells and change row heights, column widths, and table width.

1. Open *Registration* in your *Word Data* folder and save it as *Registration Structure* in the *Tutorial* folder.

2. In the table on page 1, point to the right outside table border. When the two-way horizontal arrow appears, click and hold the mouse button. A faint vertical line displays on screen. Drag to the *left* about 0.5", noting marks on the horizontal ruler. Release the mouse button.

   NOTE *When the I-beam is in the table, you will notice small boxes at the top-left and bottom-right corners of the table. You will learn how to use these boxes later in this lesson.*

3. Point to the left border of column B. When the two-way horizontal arrow appears, click and drag to the *right* about 0.5", noting marks on the horizontal ruler.

You have changed the width of columns B and C.

4. Point to the area just above column A (the selection bar). Click when the pointer changes to the down arrow.

The entire column is selected.

5. Click **Table Properties** on the Table menu. On the Column tab, select the **Preferred width check box**, if necessary. Click the **down triangle button** in the Preferred width check box to change the preferred width to **1.5"**. Click **OK**, then deselect the column.

Notice on the horizontal ruler that column A is now precisely 1.5" wide.

6. Scroll to the table on page 2, and click the selection bar at the left of row 1.

The entire row is selected.

7. On the Tables and Borders toolbar, click the **Merge Cells button** ▦.

The column borders disappear from row 1, and the cell entry becomes one line.

8. Point to the bottom border of row 1. When the two-way vertical arrow appears, click and drag the border down about four marks on the vertical ruler then release the mouse button.

The row height increases, as shown in Figure 3.4.

WORD 2002

Word BASICS

Changing Table Structure
To change column width:

1. Point to a column border and click when the two-way horizontal arrow appears.

2. Drag the border to the desired width.

To change row height:

1. Point to a row border and click when the two-way vertical arrow appears.

2. Drag the border to the desired height.

To merge cells:

1. Select cells to be merged.

2. Click the Merge Cells button on the Tables and Borders toolbar.

To change table width:

1. Click anywhere in the table and click Table Properties on the Table menu.

2. On the Table tab, select Preferred width, and select or type the width. Click OK.

HINTS & TIPS

- To make all columns the same width, click the table and click the Distribute Columns Evenly button on the Tables and Borders toolbar.

- To make all rows the same height, click the table and click the Distribute Rows Evenly button on the Tables and Borders toolbar.

Figure 3.4

Merged cells and changed row height

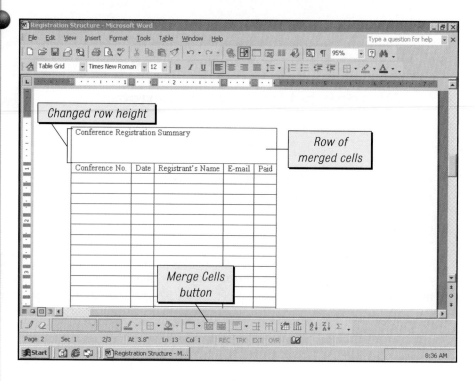

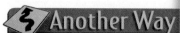
9. Scroll to the table on page 3, click in either cell of row 1, and click **Table Properties** on the Table menu.

10. On the Row tab, select the **Specify height check box**, if necessary, and type .25 as the height. Click **Exactly** in the *Row height is* box.

11. Click the **Table tab**. In the Size area, select the **Preferred width check box** and type 2.6. Click **OK**.

The table width and row height are changed to the exact settings you typed.

12. Save your changes and close the document.

Adding and Deleting a Column or Row

While entering data in a table, you may discover that you must insert or delete rows or columns. To insert one or more rows or columns, click the location where you want to insert the row or column. Then click the Insert Table triangle button ▦ on the Tables and Borders toolbar, and make the appropriate selection. You can add a row above or below or a column to the left or right of your insertion point. You can also add a row at the bottom of any table by clicking in the last column of the row and pressing [Tab].

To delete rows or columns, select the row(s) or column(s) to be deleted, then point to Delete on the Table menu and make the appropriate selection. Or you can right-click the selected cells to quickly delete rows or columns on the shortcut menu.

HANDS **on**

Inserting and Deleting Rows and Columns

In this activity, you will change the number of rows and columns in a table.

1. Open *Conference* in your *Word Data* folder and save it as *Conference Addition* in the *Tutorial* folder.

2. Navigate to the table on page 3. Click in row 1 and click the **Insert Table triangle button**  on the Tables and Borders toolbar.

The Insert Table menu appears, as shown in Figure 3.5.

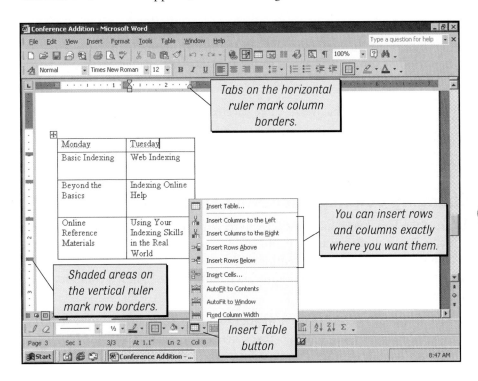

Tabs on the horizontal ruler mark column borders.

You can insert rows and columns exactly where you want them.

Shaded areas on the vertical ruler mark row borders.

Insert Table button

3. Click **Insert Rows Below**.

One row is inserted between the original rows 1 and 2. On the Tables and Borders toolbar, the icon and ScreenTip in the Insert Table button ▦ has changed to reflect your latest action: Insert Rows Below ▦.

4. Select the entire table, click the **Insert Rows Below triangle button** ▦, and click **Insert Columns to the Right**.

Two new columns appear in the table to the right of the first two columns, and the appearance of the Insert Rows Button changes again to reflect your latest action: Insert Columns to the Right ▦.

5. Click the table to deselect it. Right-click the third column and click **Delete Cells** on the shortcut menu. In the Delete Cells dialog box, click **Delete entire column**, and click **OK**.

Figure 3.5
Insert Table menu

The entire column is deleted. The table now consists of three columns.

6. With the insertion point in the third column, click **Repeat Delete Cells** on the Edit menu.

The last column is deleted.

7. Scroll to the table on page 2 and select the last four rows. Point to **Delete** on the Table menu and click **Rows**.

The last four rows are deleted.

8. Right-click in row 3 of the table and click **Delete Cells**. In the Delete Cells dialog box, click **Delete entire row** and click **OK**.

Another row is deleted from the table.

9. Scroll to the table on page 1 and select rows 2, 3, and 4. On the Tables and Borders toolbar, click the **Insert Columns to the Right triangle button** and click **Insert Rows Below**. Click the table to deselect it.

Three new rows appear below the three selected rows.

10. Save your changes and close the document.

Changing Cell Alignment and Enhancing Text

Tables often look better and are easier to read if you change the **cell alignment.** Initially, text is aligned at the top and left. Centering text horizontally and vertically in the heading cells is conventional. You may choose to center some column entries, too. You should align amounts in columns at the right if a column total is involved.

You can also rotate text to make it fit your table more evenly by simply selecting the text and clicking the Change Text Direction button ▦ on the Tables and Borders toolbar. This feature is most useful where a column heading is much longer than the column entries. Appearance and readability may also benefit from variation in font design, size, and styles.

HANDS on

Changing Cell Alignment

In this activity, you will change the vertical and horizontal alignment of table text. You will also change fonts and font sizes and apply special effects.

1. Open *Workshop* in your *Word Data* folder and save it as *Workshop Enhanced* in the *Tutorial* folder.

2. Select row 1 in the table on page 1. Click the **Cell Alignment triangle button** ▦ on the Tables and Borders toolbar.

Nine alignment options display as icons in the list box. The option name appears as a ScreenTip when you point to each icon.

3. Click the **Align Center icon**.

Text is centered both vertically and horizontally in the cell. The button name on the Tables and Borders toolbar changes to the Align Center icon.

4. While the text is still selected, click the **Font triangle button** Times New Roman and change the font to Arial. Click **Bold** B.

5. Select column A and change the cell alignment to Align Center.

All text in column A is now centered. The column heading has wrapped to two lines.

6. Type 1:00-2:00 in cell A5; type 2:15-3:15 in cell A6; and type 3:30-4:30 in cell A7.

Your table has a new look, as shown in Figure 3.6.

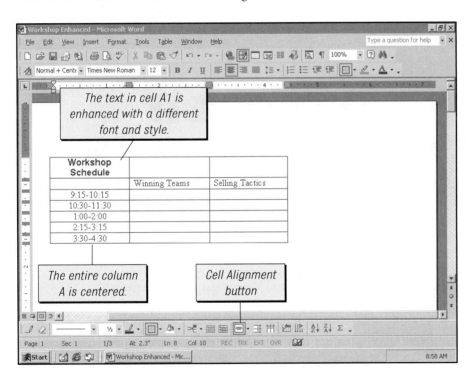

Figure 3.6
Table with changes in cell format

7. Scroll to the table on page 2. Change the cell alignment of row 1 to Align Center. Change the font to Arial, size 18, and bold.

8. Select row 2. Change the font to Arial, bold, and italic.

9. Make the last column slightly wider so that the column heading fits on one line.

10. Change the cell alignment of columns A, B, and C to Align Center.

11. Change the cell alignment of cell D2 to Align Center Right.

The *Telephone* heading is centered vertically and positioned at the right side of the cell.

Changing Cell Alignment
To change cell alignment:

1. Click a cell or select the cells to be aligned.

2. Click the Cell Alignment triangle button on the Tables and Borders toolbar.

3. Click an alignment option.

To enhance cell text:

1. Select the cell text to be enhanced.

2. Make the appropriate selections on the Formatting toolbar.

To rotate text:

1. Select the cell text to be rotated.

2. Click the Change Text Direction button on the Tables and Borders toolbar.

- Select entire adjoining columns and rows at once when you want the same alignment applied to them.

- Select only the column heading cells if you want to keep the default alignment for the column entries.

12. Change the cell alignment of cell E2 to Align Bottom Center.

The *E-mail* heading is centered horizontally and positioned at the bottom of the cell.

13. Save your changes and close the document.

Moving and Resizing Tables

When you point to a table, a **handle** appears in the upper-left and lower-right corner of the table. These handles help you to move and resize tables easily and quickly. The upper-left handle contains a four-way arrow. You can click this **move handle** and then move the table; this enables you to see the position on the rulers as you move the table. You can resize a table by using the resize handle at the lower-right corner of a table. When you point to the resize handle, the pointer becomes a diagonal two-way arrow; then, when you click, the pointer becomes the crosshair pointer.

You can align a table horizontally on the page through the Table tab of the Table Properties dialog box (Table menu). Centered is the usual alignment choice for a table on a page by itself. Aligning a table at the left or right leaves ample room for paragraph text alongside it.

HANDS on

Repositioning and Resizing Tables

In this activity, you will move, resize, and horizontally align tables.

1. Open *Resize* in your *Word Data* folder and save it as *Move* in the *Tutorial* folder.

2. Scroll to the table on page 2 and point to it.

Handles appear at the upper-left and lower-right corners of the table.

3. Click the table to activate the vertical ruler. Point to the move handle in the upper-left corner of the table.

The pointer changes to a four-way arrow.

4. Click outside the table to better view the 1.5″ mark on the vertical ruler. Click the move handle and drag the table slowly down the page until the outline of the top of the table reaches approximately 1.5″ on the vertical ruler. Release the mouse button.

The table moves to the new position.

5. Click the **Print Preview button** to check your document. Then close the Preview window.

6. Scroll to page 3 and click the table. Note where the table is on the rulers. Then point to the resize handle in the lower-right corner.

Word BASICS

Repositioning and Resizing Tables

To move a table:

1. Point to the table and point to the move handle.

2. When the pointer becomes a four-way arrow, drag the table to the desired position.

To resize a table:

1. Point to the table and point to the resize handle.

2. When the pointer becomes a two-way arrow, drag the table right and down to enlarge, or up and left to reduce the table size.

The pointer becomes a two-way diagonal arrow which will change to the crosshair pointer when you click.

7. Click the resize handle and drag the table slowly down and to the right until the right border is approximately at 5″ on the horizontal ruler and the bottom border is at 3″ on the vertical ruler.

Dragging diagonally changes both dimensions at once. Drag straight right or down (*not* diagonally) to change only one dimension. If you go beyond the ruler marks you are aiming for, drag up and to the left. If you should lose control of the crosshair pointer, click the Undo button and try again. Your table should be similar to Figure 3.7.

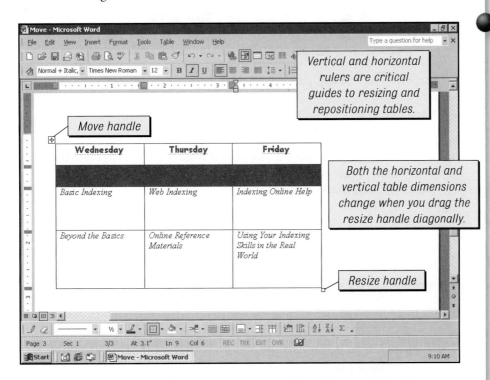

Figure 3.7
Resized table

8. Click the move handle in the table on page 3 and drag the table slowly down the page. Release the mouse button when the top border is approximately at 3″ on the vertical ruler.

NOTE *Click outside the table to view the vertical position of the table on the ruler. If the top of the table appears significantly short of the 3-inch mark, click the move handle again and drag it down.*

9. Click the table, click Table Properties on the Table menu, then click the Table tab.

10. In the *Alignment* section, click the Center icon. In the *Text wrapping section,* click the Around icon, and click OK.

The table is centered between the left and right page margins and any paragraph text entered in the document will wrap around the table.

11. Click the Print Preview button to view the table. Close the Preview window. Save your changes and close the document.

Adding Borders and Shading to Cells

You can enhance a table with a **border.** Thirteen border options are available including, for example, Outside Border (applied to outside edges only); All Borders (applied to every cell); Left Border (applied to left outside edge only); and Inside Vertical Border (applied to vertical lines except the outside edges). Shading is an attractive enhancement for tables. Shading can add emphasis or make parts of a table easier to read. Shading can be used to unify related entries while separating them from unshaded entries.

HANDS on

Adding Borders and Shading

In this activity, you will apply several border and shading treatments to tables.

1. Open *Conference* in your *Word Data* folder and save it as *Conference Shading* in the *Tutorial* folder.

2. Scroll to the table on page 3 and click the move handle to select the entire table. Then, click the **Line Style triangle button** on the Tables and Borders toolbar.

The Line Style list box displays various border options.

3. Point to the two-line border style as shown in Figure 3.8.

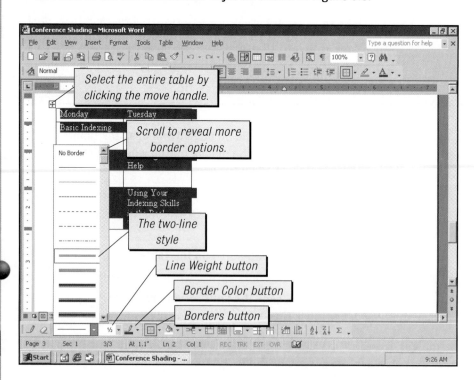

Figure 3.8
Line Style list box

4. Click the **two-line border style**.

Your pointer becomes the pencil pointer.

5. Click the **Line Weight triangle button**  and click **½ pt**, if necessary.

6. Click the **Border Color triangle button** and click **Lime** in the color palette.

7. Click the **Borders triangle button** and click the **Outside Border icon**. Deselect the table.

NOTE *By default, the Borders button shows the Outside Border option. After you select a different border option, the button will show your latest choice.*

The outside border of your table should have a new look: two green lines.

8. Select row 2, click the **Shading Color triangle button** , and click **Light Turquoise**. Deselect and view the table.

9. Scroll to the table on page 2. Select rows 1 and 2 and apply these border options: double line style, 1.5 line weight, black, All Borders. Then deselect the table to see your changes.

Two heavy black lines border every cell in the first two rows.

10. Apply these shadings: row 1—Gray-25%; row 2—Gray-15%; and column A below the heading—Gray-10%. Deselect and view the table.

11. Save your changes and close the document.

Using the Table AutoFormat Feature

Using Table AutoFormat is like applying styles to paragraph copy. When you choose a table format, you choose cell height and width, alignment of text in cells, bold and italic effects, and other appearance factors. You can use Table AutoFormat when you insert a table or you can apply a format later.

HANDS on

Using Table AutoFormat

In this activity, you will create two tables using Table AutoFormat.

1. Open a new, blank document and save it as *AutoFormat Tables* in the *Tutorial* folder in your *Word Data* folder.

2. Click the **Insert Table triangle button** on the Tables and Borders toolbar, then click **Insert Table**.

NOTE *Initially, the icon on the Insert Table button may appear dimmed as Insert Rows Below or another icon, depending upon how the button was last used.*

The Insert Table Dialog box appears.

3. In the *Table size* section, select 3 columns and 4 rows. Then click the **AutoFormat button**.

The Table AutoFormat dialog box appears. Table Grid is selected by default in the *Table styles* list box. A view of this format appears in the Preview window, as shown in Figure 3.9.

Figure 3.9
Table AutoFormat dialog box

Applying an AutoFormat

When inserting a table:

1. Click the Insert Table triangle button, then click Insert Table.

2. Click the AutoFormat button in the Insert Table dialog box.

3. Click an option in the Table styles list box and preview it.

4. Select appropriate special format options and click OK.

For an existing table:

1. Select the table and click the Table AutoFormat button on the Tables and Borders toolbar.

2. Click an option in the Table styles list box and preview it.

3. Select appropriate special format options and click Apply.

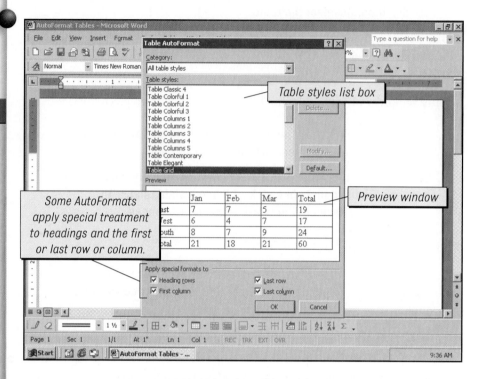

Some AutoFormats apply special treatment to headings and the first or last row or column.

4. Scroll the *Table styles* list box, click **Table List 8**, and preview the format.

5. Under *Apply special formats to,* select the *Heading rows* and *First column* check boxes. Clear the *Last row* and *Last column* check boxes, if necessary. Click **OK** and then click **OK** in the Insert Table dialog box.

A table with three columns and four rows appears in the specified format. Even though formats exist in the table, you can further customize the formats.

6. Select row 1 and click **Merge Cells** ▦. Type Main Heading in row 1.

7. Resize the table to align the right border at approximately 2″ on the horizontal ruler and approximately 1″ on the vertical ruler.

8. Click below the table, and press ⌷Enter↵⌷ repeatedly until the insertion point is about 2″ below the table.

9. Click the **Insert Table triangle button** ▦▾ and click **Insert Table**. Insert a table with four columns and three rows.

10. With the insertion point in the table, click the **Table AutoFormat button** ▦.

The Table AutoFormat dialog box appears.

11. Click the **Table Contemporary format** in the Table Styles list, and view the choice in the Preview window.

12. Clear all check boxes in the *Apply special formats* to section, then click **Apply**.

Notice the gray shadings and the white borders of the Table Contemporary format in your table.

13. Point to **Toolbars** on the View menu and click **Tables and Borders** to close the toolbar. Save and close the document.

Using Format Tools Table Window (Help)

Inserting a Watermark

In this activity, you will search Help for information about inserting a watermark in a document. Then using the search results, you will insert a text watermark.

1. Type Watermark in the *Ask a Question box* and press [Enter←]. Browse the search results for answers to these questions: (a) What is a watermark and how can a watermark be viewed? (b) How can you create custom text or use a picture as a watermark? (c) How can you insert a watermark into a document?

2. Open *Resize* in your *Word Data* folder and save it as *Resize Watermark* in the *Tutorial* folder. Click **Print Layout View** 🔲, if necessary.

3. Scroll to the end of the document, then point to **Background** on the Format menu and click **Printed Watermark**.

4. Click the **Text watermark option**.

5. Click **DRAFT** in the Text list box and click **Arial** in the Font box, as shown in Figure 3.10.

6. Click **OK** then scroll through the document.

The text watermark *DRAFT* appears on all three pages of the document.

7. Click the **Print Preview button** 🔍 to check your document. Then close the Preview window.

8. Save your changes and close the document.

Figure 3.10
Printed Watermark dialog box

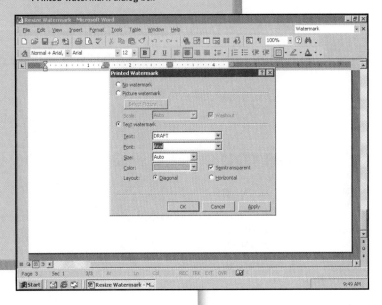

WORKING WITH CHARTS AND DIAGRAMS

Suppose that you want to present sales data at a company meeting. You could present the information as plain text or in table format, but the information might be displayed more effectively in a chart. A **chart** or **graph** is a picture that displays data from a datasheet in the form of circles, lines, bars, or other shapes. A **datasheet** is a grid of columns and rows for entering, viewing, and editing data to create charts or graphs. Perhaps you want to display a chart that shows the hierarchy (organization structure) in your department. You could use Word's Diagram feature to insert an organization chart diagram. Information presented in a chart or diagram format may help you get your point across more effectively than text alone.

A chart can be created from text already in your document, or you can enter new text once you create a chart. Once you create a chart in your document, you can modify it in the same way you modify text or graphics by resizing it, adding borders and shading, changing the way text wraps around it, and so on. You can work with a datasheet in much the same way you work with tables by adding and deleting information in cells or adding and deleting columns and rows.

When you insert an object such as a chart or diagram into a document it appears with a thick outer border. This border defines the perimeter of the **drawing canvas**—an area that contains one or more shapes or objects. The drawing canvas separates an object such as a chart from the rest of your document and allows you to move or resize multiple objects within it together all at once.

HANDS on

Creating and Modifying a Chart

In this activity, you will create a chart in a Word document, and then you will modify the chart. Finally, you will create a chart from information in a table.

1. Open *Sales Memo* in your *Word Data* folder and save it as *Sales Memo Chart* in the *Tutorial* folder. Click **Print Layout View** 🔲, if necessary.

2. Scroll to the bottom of the memo and click an insertion point below the last line. Click **Object** on the Insert menu.

The Object dialog box opens.

3. On the Create New tab, click **Microsoft Graph Chart** in the *Object type* box, and click **OK**.

A chart and the sample data associated with it display on your screen, as shown in Figure 3.11. Now you need to replace the sample data with data of your own.

> **NOTE** *If you accidentally close the datasheet and need to reopen it, click the document to ensure the chart is deselected. Right-click the chart, point to Chart Object on the shortcut menu, and click Edit. If necessary, right-click a blank area of the chart and click Datasheet on the shortcut menu.*

Word BASICS

Creating a New Blank Chart

1. Click Object on the Insert menu.

2. Click the Create New tab.

3. In the *Object type* box, click Microsoft Graph Chart and click OK.

NORTON ONLINE

Visit **www.glencoe.com/norton/online/** for more information on using tables, charts, and diagrams.

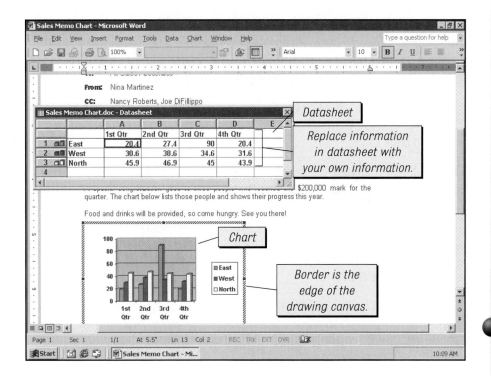

Creating a New Chart From a Table

1. Create a table with text in the top row and left column and numbers in the other cells.

2. Select the table.

3. Click Object on the Insert menu.

4. Click the Create New tab.

5. In the *Object type* box, click Microsoft Graph Chart and click OK.

Figure 3.11
Chart and datasheet

4. Click anywhere in Column D of the datasheet. Right-click the column then click **Delete** on the shortcut menu. In the Delete dialog box, click the **Entire column option** and click **OK**.

Column D is deleted in both the datasheet and the chart.

5. Select the data in the remaining columns below the column headings and press ⌨Delete⌨. Replace it with the information shown in Table 3.2. Enter text and navigate through the datasheet as you would through a table. To replace the sample data, click a cell on the datasheet and type the replacement text or numbers. Press ⌨Tab⌨ to advance to the next cell within a row. Press the arrow keys to advance up or down within the column. Use the horizontal and vertical scroll bars when necessary.

Table 3.2	Data for Table		
	1st Qtr	**2nd Qtr**	**3rd Qtr**
Juan	191,000	196,000	205,000
Sara	187,000	183,000	212,000
Keith	159,000	171,000	201,000

As you press ⌨Tab⌨, ⌨Enter↵⌨, or move otherwise between cells in the datasheet to enter data, the chart is automatically updated with the information you type.

6. Click the document (outside the chart) to close the datasheet and deselect the chart. Right-click the chart and click **Format Object** on the shortcut menu.

To identify an individual *chart object* (an element within a chart), first double-click the chart to select it. Then point to any object within the chart to identify it through a ScreenTip. (Example: The background area behind the bars is called *Walls*.)

The Format Object dialog box appears.

7. Click the **Colors and Lines tab**. Click the **Color triangle button** in the Fill section and click a light yellow as a fill color on the palette.

8. On the Layout tab, click the **Square icon** in the *Wrapping style* section. Click the **Center option** in the *Horizontal alignment* section and click **OK**.

The fill color of the chart is now the yellow shade you chose, and the chart is centered horizontally on the page.

9. Point to the middle of the chart. When the four-way arrow appears, click the chart and drag it so it appears about .5 inch below the last line of text in the memo. Text should not wrap around the chart.

Your screen should look similar to Figure 3.12.

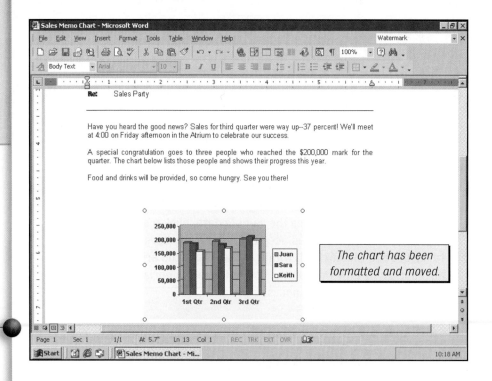

Figure 3.12
Modified chart

10. Save your changes and close the document.

NOTE *To change the default appearance of a chart, double-click the chart to select it, if necessary. Open the Chart Options dialog box (Chart Options on the Chart menu) to change the text or lines that appear in the chart. Click Chart Type (Chart Menu) to change the graphic depiction of the data (for example, to change it from a bar chart to a pie chart).*

Now you will create a chart from information in a table.

11. Open *Grades* in your *Word Data* folder and save it as *Grades Chart* in your *Tutorial* folder.

12. Click anywhere in the table, point to **Select** on the Table menu, and click **Table**.

13. With the table selected, click **Object** on the Insert menu.

14. On the Create New tab, click **Microsoft Graph Chart** in the *Object type* box, and click **OK**.

A chart with the data from the table displays on your screen along with a corresponding datasheet.

15. Click anywhere in the Word document to close the datasheet.

You decide that you don't want both the table and the chart in the document.

16. Select the table, point to **Delete** on the Table menu, and click **Table**.

17. Click the chart. Point to the resize handle in the lower-right corner of the chart and drag the chart slowly down and to the right until the right border is at 4″ on the horizontal ruler and the bottom border is at about 3.5″ on the vertical ruler, as shown in Figure 3.13.

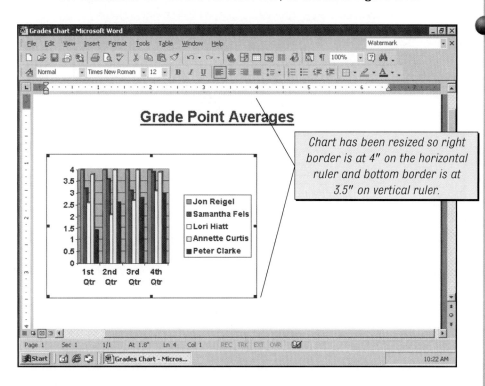

Figure 3.13
Chart created from table

Chart has been resized so right border is at 4″ on the horizontal ruler and bottom border is at 3.5″ on vertical ruler.

18. Save your changes and close the document.

Creating and Modifying a Diagram

You can use Word's Diagram feature to create several different types of diagrams in your document. Simply click the Insert Diagram or Organization Chart button  on the Drawing toolbar. The Diagram Gallery displays six different

types of diagrams. Click each one to see its name and description. Once you insert the diagram into your document, you can modify it by adding and deleting text, resizing it, moving it around on the page, and so on. When you insert a diagram, Word uses Print Layout View 🔲 as the default view.

In this activity, you will create and modify two different diagrams.

1. **Open a new, blank document and save it as *Organization Diagram* in the *Tutorial* folder in your *Word Data* folder.**

2. **Point to Toolbars on the View menu and click Drawing. Click the Insert Diagram or Organization Chart button 🔘 on the Drawing toolbar.**

The Diagram Gallery displays, as shown in Figure 3.14.

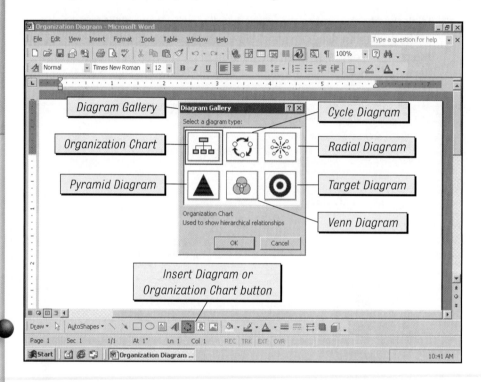

Figure 3.14
Diagram Gallery

3. **Click each diagram type and read its name and description.**

4. **Click the Organization Chart diagram, and click OK.**

An organization chart displays in your document along with the Organization Chart toolbar. Now you will add text to the diagram and modify its appearance.

5. **Click the top box in the chart and type President. Select the text and change the font to Arial. Click Bold B, then click Italic I.**

6. **With the top box still selected, click the Insert Shape triangle button 📐 Insert Shape ▾ on the Organization Chart toolbar, and click Subordinate.**

A fourth box is added to the second level of the organization chart. (If the insertion point had been in the second level when you clicked *Subordinate,* the new subordinate box would have been placed a level below that box.)

NOTE *When you add a box to the diagram, the font may be automatically adjusted to a smaller size so the text will fit in the chart.*

7. Click the **Insert Shape triangle button**  on the Organization Chart toolbar again, and click **Assistant**.

A new box is placed to the side and one level below the *President* box.

8. Click the new box and type *Assistant*. Select the text and change it to Arial, bold, italic.

9. Click each of the four boxes in the third level, type *Associate*, then make the font Arial, bold, and italic. (*Hint:* Use Format Painter.)

NOTE *If you unintentionally close the Organization Chart toolbar, click a box in the diagram to open it.*

10. Click the **Autoformat button** 🔣 on the Organization Chart toolbar.

11. In the *Select a Diagram Style list,* click and preview the various styles. When you find a style you like, click **Apply**.

12. Click in the right margin to deselect the diagram and close the Organization Chart toolbar. Save your changes and close the document.

13. Open a new, blank document and save it as *Sales Diagram* in the *Tutorial* folder in your *Word Data* folder.

14. Click the **Insert Diagram or Organization Chart button** 🔣 on the Drawing toolbar, click **Cycle Diagram** in the Diagram Gallery, and click **OK**.

A cycle diagram and the Diagram toolbar display on your screen, as shown in Figure 3.15. You can use the Diagram toolbar to make changes in the diagram.

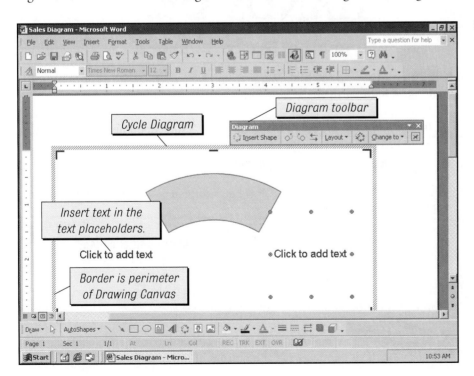

Another Way

To create an organization chart, point to Picture on the Insert menu and click Organization Chart.

Figure 3.15
Cycle diagram

HINTS & TIPS

To resize a diagram, click Layout on the Diagram toolbar then click Scale Diagram. Drag a corner handle to change the diagram size.

15. Click the **Click to add text placeholder** (at the upper left) and type *Advertise Product*. Select the text and change it to Arial Black (or another heavy, bold font). Click **Align Left**.

16. Working in a clockwise direction, click the next placeholder. Type *Create Product*; type *Sell Product* to replace the next placeholder. Change the font to Arial Black (or the similar font of your choice), then click **Align Left** in each instance.

17. Click within the right margin to deselect and view the diagram. Close the Drawing toolbar. Save your changes and close the document.

USING MAIL MERGE

One of the most powerful characteristics of a word processor is its ability to automate repetitive tasks, such as creating identical form letters that include personalized information. Creating each letter individually without Word's Mail Merge feature would be time-intensive and would increase the possibility of error. You can use Mail Merge to create letters, labels, e-mail messages, envelopes, faxes, and directories. The Mail Merge Wizard is the easiest way to create a document using the Mail Merge feature. A **wizard** is a tool that helps you create a document by offering content and organization choices.

In order to use Mail Merge, you need a **main document,** which is the document you want to personalize. Within the main document, you will have **fields,** or categories of information, such as Title, Name, or Address. You also need a **data source,** which is the origin of the personalized information.

HANDS on

Creating Form Letters

In this activity, you will use Mail Merge to combine a letter with a list of names and addresses in order to create form letters.

1. Open *Thank You* in your *Word Data* folder. (Your document should be in Print Layout View.) Click after *Sincerely yours* and press `Enter` four times. Type your name.

Notice that the letter does not yet have an addressee. The addressee will be added later.

2. Point to **Letters and Mailings** on the Tools menu and click **Mail Merge Wizard**.

The Mail Merge task pane opens, as shown in Figure 3.16. The wizard will guide you through the process of creating the mail merge.

3. Click **Letters** in the *Select document type* section, and then click **Next: Starting document** at the bottom of the task pane.

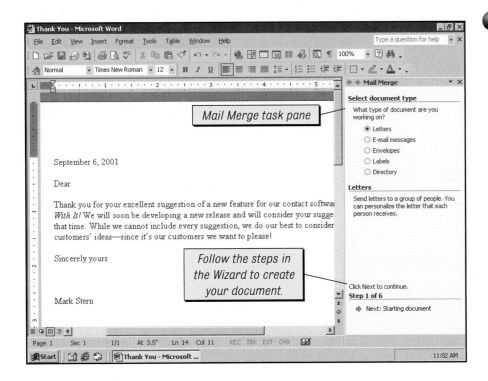

Figure 3.16
Mail Merge task pane

The Mail Merge Wizard task pane *Step 2 of 6* appears.

4. Click **Use the current document** in the *Select starting document* section, and then click **Next: Select recipients**, the next wizard step.

Now you will open the data source.

5. Click **Use an existing list** in the *Select recipients* section, if necessary, and then click **Browse** in the *Use an existing list* section.

The Select Data Source box opens.

6. Navigate to your *Word Data* folder within the Select Data Source box. Click *Address List* in your *Word Data* folder, then click **Open**.

The Mail Merge Recipients box opens.

> **NOTE** *You may need to expand the last column by dragging the last column header to the right in order to see all the information in the CSZ (City, State, Zip) column.*

7. Click **Select All**, if necessary, to place a check mark in the first column of each row and click **OK**.

8. Click **Next: Write your letter** to advance to *Step 4 of 6*.

9. Click an insertion point after the date in the letter and press [Enter⏎] four times. Click **More items** in the Mail Merge task pane.

The Insert Merge Field dialog box opens, as shown in Figure 3.17. The column headings from the *Address List* box display as fields that you can insert into your letter.

Visit **www.glencoe.com/norton/online/** for more information on Mail Merge.

Figure 3.17
Insert Merge Field dialog box

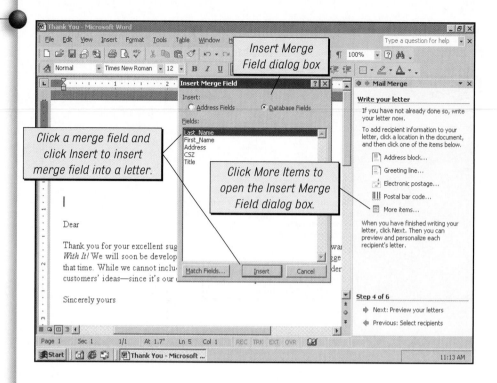

Click a merge field and click Insert to insert merge field into a letter.

Click More Items to open the Insert Merge Field dialog box.

10. Click **Title**, and then click **Insert**.

The title field is inserted into your document.

11. With your insertion point still on the same line, click **First Name** and click **Insert**, and then click **Last Name** and click **Insert**. Click **Close**.

12. Press [Enter⏎] to move to the next line. Click **More items** again, click the **Address field**, and then click **Insert**. Close the Insert Merge Field dialog box.

13. Press [Enter⏎] to move to the next line, then click **More items** in the task pane. Click **CSZ** in the Insert Merge Field dialog box, click **Insert**, and then click **Close**.

Now you will insert a greeting.

14. Click after *Dear* and press [Spacebar].

15. Click **More items** in the task pane. Click **Title** then click **Insert**; click **Last Name** then Insert. Click **Close**.

The merge fields are in the letter. Now you will merge the data source with your main document.

16. Insert a blank space between each of the three fields on the first line of the addressee section and between the two fields in the greeting section, and then click **Next: Preview your letters** to advance to *Step 5 of 6*.

The first merged letter displays on screen, as shown in Figure 3.18.

To format merged data, you must format the merge fields in the main document. You can't format text in the data source because the formatting will be lost when you merge the data into the main document.

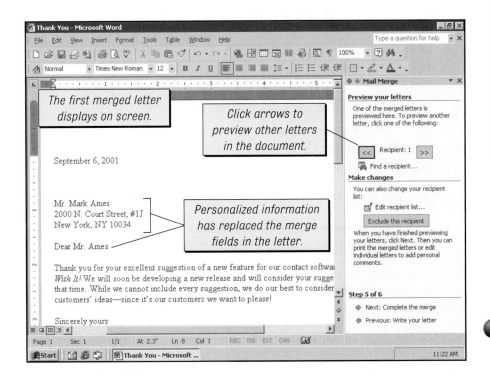

Figure 3.18
Completed letter with merge fields

17. Click the **right double arrow button** [>>] to preview the other three merged letters. Click **Next: Complete the merge**.

NOTE *If you can't see all options in the Mail Merge task pane, click the arrow at the bottom of the task pane.*

Now you are ready to either merge your letters to print them or merge them to a new document in case you want to edit them.

18. Click **Edit individual letters** in the Mail Merge task pane.

19. In the Merge to New Document dialog box, click **All** and click **OK**.

The Mail Merge task pane closes. All the letters have been merged.

20. Save your final merged letters as *Thank You Merged* in the *Tutorial* folder in your *Word Data* folder, and close the document.

The *Thank You* document reappears with the Mail Merge task pane.

21. Close the Mail Merge task pane and save the *Thank You* file as *Thank You Fields* in the *Tutorial* folder in your *Word Data* folder. Close the document.

HANDS on

Creating Labels

In this activity, you will use Mail Merge to create labels with the Mail Merge toolbar using the same data source you used in the previous activity.

Creating Labels Using the Mail Merge Toolbar

1. Create a data source document creating names and addresses, then open a new blank document.

2. Click the Main document setup button on the Mail Merge toolbar.

3. Click Labels in the Main Document Type box and click OK.

4. Choose a label product and product number in the Label Options dialog box and click OK.

5. Click the Open Data Source button on the Mail Merge toolbar.

6. Select your data source document, and click Open.

7. Click the Mail Merge Recipients button on the Mail Merge toolbar, click Select All, and click OK.

8. Click the Insert Merge Fields button on the Mail Merge toolbar, insert the appropriate fields, and click Close.

9. Click the Propagate Labels button on the Mail Merge toolbar.

10. Click the View Merged Data button on the Mail Merge toolbar to view the label text.

11. Click the Merge to New Document button on the Mail Merge toolbar, then click All and click OK.

---

1. Open a new, blank document.

2. Point to **Letters and Mailings** on the Tools menu and click **Show Mail Merge Toolbar**.

The Mail Merge toolbar displays at the top of the document window.

3. Click the **Main document setup button** 🖾 on the left side of the Mail Merge toolbar. Click the **Labels option** in the Main Document Type dialog box, and click **OK**.

The Label Options dialog box appears.

4. Click **Avery standard** in the *Label products* box, click **5160-Address** in the *Product number* box, and click **OK**.

Now you will open the data source.

5. Click the **Open Data Source button** 🔳 on the Mail Merge toolbar.

The Select Data Source box appears.

6. Navigate to your *Word Data* folder. Click *Address List* in your *Word Data* folder, then click **Open**.

7. Click the **Mail Merge Recipients button** 🖾 on the Mail Merge toolbar. In the Mail Merge Recipients box, click **Select All**, if necessary, to place a check mark in the first column of each row. Click **OK**.

8. Click the **Insert Merge Fields button** 🔳 on the Mail Merge toolbar.

9. In the Insert Merge Field dialog box, click **Title** then click **Insert**; click **First Name** and then **Insert**; and click **Last Name** then **Insert**. Click **Close**.

10. Press ⎆Enter↵ to move to the next line on the label and click the **Insert Merge Fields button** 🔳. Click **Address**, click **Insert**, then click **Close**.

11. Press ⎆Enter↵ to move to the next line and click the **Insert Merge Fields button** 🔳. Click **CSZ**, click **Insert**, then click **Close**.

12. Click between the fields in the first line and press ⎵Spacebar⎵.

Your document should now look like Figure 3.19.

13. Click the **Propagate Labels button** 🖾 on the Mail Merge toolbar.

The merge fields are copied to each label. The Next Record field appears at the beginning of each label. Now you will merge the data source with your main document.

14. Click the **View Merged Data button** 🖾 on the Mail Merge toolbar to view the labels, and then click the **Merge to New Document button** 🔳.

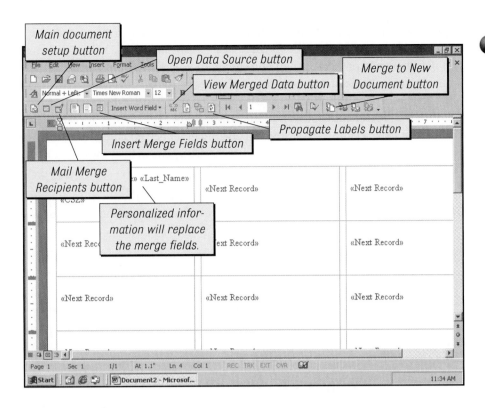

Figure 3.19
Label file with merge fields

WORD 2002

The following callouts appear on the figure:

Main document setup button

Open Data Source button

View Merged Data button

Merge to New Document button

Insert Merge Fields button

Propagate Labels button

Mail Merge Recipients button

Personalized information will replace the merge fields.

The Merge to New Document dialog box appears.

15. Click the **All option**, if necessary, and click **OK**.

The four labels appear in a new document.

16. Save your final merged labels as *Thank You Labels Merged* in the *Tutorial* folder in your *Word Data* folder, and close the document.

The unsaved document containing the data fields is still open.

17. Save the document as *Thank You Labels Fields* in the *Tutorial* folder in your *Word Data* folder, then close the document.

18. If necessary, point to **Toolbars** on the View menu and click **Mail Merge** to close the toolbar.

WORKING WITH MULTIPLE USERS

When working in teams or workgroups, you and other team members may need to work on the same document. Word provides several tools that allow multiple users to edit one document. Word allows users to easily track changes and make comments about a document while the document is displayed. Using the **Track Changes** feature, you and other reviewers can insert comments, insert and delete text, and make formatting changes. All of these changes are tracked so that you and others can view them and decide whether to accept or reject the proposed changes to your document.

Word allows multiple users to edit a document at one time by making copies of the document for each user and merging the documents back together. When you use the **Compare and Merge** feature, you can merge two or more documents

HINTS & TIPS

If you are comparing your original document with only one reviewer's changes, you can select the Legal blackline option. Word will compare the documents and display only what was changed between the two documents. Previous tracked changes will not display. Results will be shown in a new, third, document.

together and compare the changes made in each one. Imagine that you create a report and then send a copy file to three other team members. When the three team members return changes and comments to you, you can merge all of their comments into one document and then review each change, deciding whether to accept or reject the proposed change. If you decide that you need to make changes to the original document while it is in the process of being reviewed by team members, you can make changes to the original document. When you merge the reviewer documents, Word will show what the reviewers changed as well as the changes you made to the original document.

It is best if reviewers turn the Track Changes feature on as they edit documents, but Word will allow you to see their changes even if reviewers did not turn on the feature.

If you want to compare changes from several different reviewers, you can choose one of two different locations in which to display the comparison results. You can use the *Merge into current document* command to display the comparison results in the original document you currently have open or you can use the *Merge into new document* command to merge all comments and changes into a new, third document.

Displaying Changes in a Document

When viewing the changes that have been made or comments that have been added to a document, you can decide how you want the information displayed. You might choose to display only changes and comments made by a specific reviewer or you might choose to hide all comments and formatting changes so that you see only text insertions or deletions.

You can select one of Word's Display for Review settings by clicking the Show button on the Reviewing toolbar. You can also choose from a variety of options that allow you to choose how you want changes and comments to display in your document. Word's default (Print Layout View) is to show some changes in the body of the document and other changes in a balloon in the margin of your document. Showing changes in balloons in the margin helps to preserve the layout of your original document—giving you the feel of a marked up printout, with the ease of an electronic version. When you compare two documents using the Compare and Merge feature, Word shows the difference between the documents as tracked changes.

HANDS on

Comparing and Merging Documents and Editing Comments

In this activity you will view and edit changes and comments in a document, then you will use Word's Compare and Merge feature to compare two documents.

1. Open *Star Gazette Article Copy 1* in your *Word Data* folder. Click **Print Layout View** ▣, if necessary.

This is a copy of another document, *Star Gazette Article*, which has been reviewed by an editor.

2. Point to Toolbars on the View menu and click Reviewing to display the Reviewing toolbar.

Scroll to the right margin to view the comments shown in balloons. Now you will view all the comments and changes and edit the document appropriately.

3. With your insertion point at the top of the document, click the Next button ⏩ on the Reviewing toolbar.

The word *roman* is highlighted in the balloon in the right margin. The balloon indicates that the reviewer deleted the word and replaced it with *Roman* (with a capital *R*), as shown in Figure 3.20.

Word BASICS

Viewing Edits and Comments

1. Click the Next button on the Reviewing toolbar to move to the first edit or comment.

2. Click the Accept Change button or the Reject Change/Delete Comment button on the Reviewing toolbar.

3. Repeat steps 1 and 2 until you have viewed all edits and changes.

WORD 2002

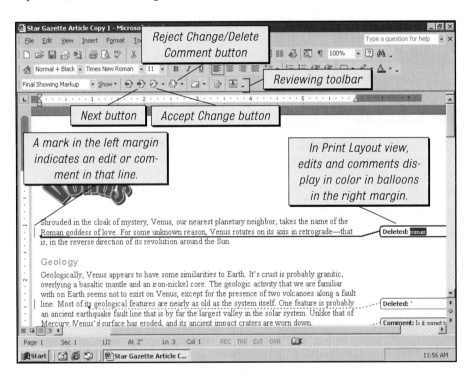

Figure 3.20
File with reviewer comments

4. Click the Accept Change button 🔲 on the Reviewing toolbar.

The comment balloon is deleted.

5. Click the Next button ⏩ to move to the next change or comment.

The word *Roman* is selected within the first paragraph.

6. Click the Accept Change button 🔲 to accept the capitalization, then click the Next button ⏩.

The reviewer has deleted an apostrophe to revise *it's* to *its*.

7. Click the Accept Change button 🔲 since you agree with this change, then click the Next button ⏩ to move to the next change or comment.

Compare and Merge Documents

1. Open the original document.

2. Click Compare and Merge Documents on the Tools menu.

3. Click the first file you want to compare and merge then click the Merge triangle button and click *Merge into current document.*

4. Repeat step 3 until you have merged all documents.

5. Click the Display for Review triangle button and click Original Showing Markup.

6. Click the Next button on the Reviewing toolbar.

7. Click the Accept Change button or the Reject Change/Delete Comment button on the Reviewing toolbar.

8. Read the grammar question the reviewer has entered as a comment. You decide to delete the second *s* in *Venus's.* Make the change in the document, then click the comment balloon and click the **RejectChange/Delete Comment button** ⬛▾ on the Reviewing toolbar.

The comment balloon is deleted.

9. Click the **Next button** ➡ to move to the next change or comment.

The reviewer has deleted the last heading, *Moons,* and has added a comment explaining the deletion.

10. Click the **RejectChange/Delete Comment button** ⬛▾ since you intend to add a paragraph after the heading.

The *Moons* heading is restored.

11. Click the comment balloon pointing to *Moons* and click the **RejectChange/Delete Comment button** ⬛▾ to delete the comment balloon.

12. Click the **Next button** ➡.

13. Click **OK** when a dialog box appears stating there are no remaining comments or tracked changes.

14. Save your changes as *Star Gazette Article Reviewed* in the *Tutorial* folder in your *Word Data* folder and close the document.

Now you will compare and merge two documents.

15. Open *Sandy Reef Island Tour* in your *Word Data* folder.

This is the original document into which you will merge the other documents.

16. Click **Compare and Merge Documents** on the Tools menu.

17. In the Compare and Merge Documents dialog box, click *Sandy Reef Island Tour-1* in your *Word Data* folder. Click the **Merge triangle button** in the lower-right corner of the dialog box, and click **Merge into current document**.

The reviewer's edits in *Sandy Reef Island Tour-1* are merged into your current document *Sandy Reef Island Tour.* The reviewer's edits appear in color on your screen. Now you will merge the second reviewer's comments into the current document.

18. Click **Compare and Merge Documents** on the Tools menu.

19. In the Compare and Merge Documents dialog box, click *Sandy Reef Island Tour-2* in your *Word Data* folder, click the **Merge triangle button**, and click **Merge into current document**.

The reviewer's edits and comments from *Sandy Reef Island Tour-2* are merged into *Sandy Reef Island Tour.* The comments and edits appear in a different color.

20. Click the **Display for Review triangle button**  and click **Original Showing Markup**.

The actual edits (the *markup*) appear in color in the document.

21. Click the **Next button** ➡️ on the Reviewing toolbar to move to the first edit. Click **Accept Change** ✅.

22. Click **Next** ➡️ to move through the rest of the document one comment at a time. Click **Accept Change** ✅ to accept each reviewer's change.

23. Save the revised document as *Sandy Reef Tour Compared* in the *Tutorial* folder in your *Word Data* folder and close the document.

HANDS on

Tracking Changes and Inserting a Comment

When the Track Changes feature is active, the status indicator button will display TRK in black letters. When the Track Changes feature is inactive, a dimmed or gray TRK button will display on the status bar. To turn on the Track Changes feature, you can either double-click the TRK button on the status bar or click Track Changes on the Tools menu.

In this activity, you will use the Track Changes feature to insert comments in and make changes to a Word document so that others can review the changes and comments.

1. Open *Sandy Reef Island Tour* in your *Word Data* folder and save it as *Tour Edited* in the *Tutorial* folder. Click **Print Layout View** 🔳, if necessary.

2. Click **Track Changes** on the Tools menu.

The TRK status bar button appears active.

3. Click the **Show button**  on the Reviewing toolbar and click **Options**.

The Track Changes dialog box displays, as shown in Figure 3.21.

4. Click **OK** to accept the default options.

5. In the first line of the document, select *about* and type why you'll want to visit.

The deletion you made *(about)* is displayed in a balloon in the margin. The new text you typed appears in color in the document.

6. Click **Normal View** 🔳.

Figure 3.21
Track Changes dialog box

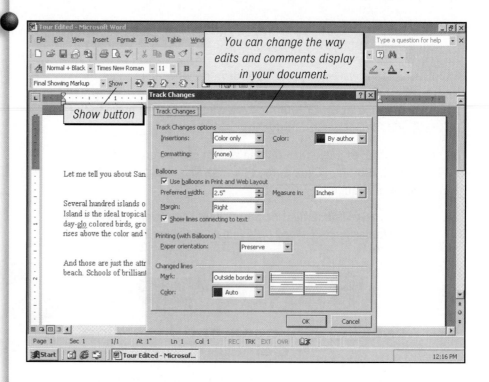

In Normal View the word you deleted is shown with a colored line through it. The new text you typed remains in color.

7. In the second paragraph, click immediately after the word *hundred* then click the **New Comment button** 🔲 on the Reviewing toolbar.

The Reviewing pane opens at the bottom of the document window. The first entry in the Reviewing pane displays the changes you made in the previous paragraph. The Reviewing pane also provides an area for comments. The insertion point is within the *Comment* section.

> **NOTE** *If you cannot see the Reviewing pane clearly, increase the zoom percentage.*

8. Type Should we give an exact number here? in the *Comment* section of the Reviewing pane as shown in Figure 3.22.

9. Click the **Reviewing Pane button** 🔳 on the Reviewing toolbar to close the Reviewing pane.

10. Click **Track Changes** 🔲 on the Reviewing toolbar to turn off the feature.

11. Click **Print Layout View** 🔳 to view your edits and comments in balloon format.

12. Point to **Toolbars** on the View menu and click **Reviewing** to close the Reviewing toolbar.

13. Save your changes and close the document.

You can enlarge the Reviewing pane by dragging the divider line at the top of the pane upward. You can navigate through the Reviewing pane by using the vertical scroll bar.

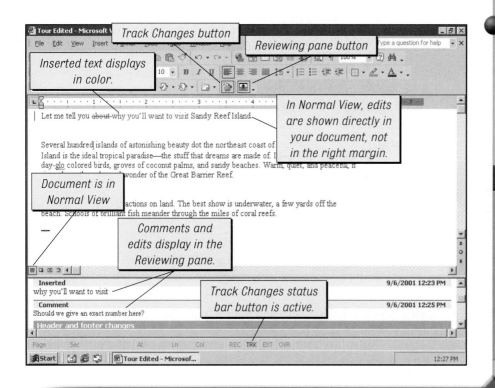

Figure 3.22
Reviewing pane (Normal View)

HANDWRITING IN WORD

Perhaps you want to sign your real handwritten signature on an e-mail message or at the bottom of a letter. Did you know that you can use Word's Handwriting Recognition feature to do this? You can write instead of type your information on screen, and it will appear in your Word document. You can use a handwriting input device, such as a tablet-PC or a graphics tablet used with 3-D drawing programs, but you can also use your mouse to write.

Access the Handwriting feature by using the Language bar that by default appears in the upper-right corner of the Word window. Click the Handwriting button Handwriting and select a writing area. Then move your mouse on your mouse pad to write. You can write as you normally would on a piece of paper. You can use printing or cursive writing—or a combination of both. Your handwriting is automatically inserted into your document wherever you last clicked the insertion point.

> **NOTE** *If the Language bar does not display, it may be minimized. If so, the language icon* **EN** *(EN for English) appears near the clock at the lower-right corner of the Word window. To display the minimized Language bar, click the language icon and click* Show the Language bar. *If the Language bar has* not *been minimized, click Start, point to Settings, then point to Control Panel. Click Text Services, click Language Bar, then select* Show the Language bar on the desktop. *If Text Services does not display on the Control Panel, the Handwriting feature was not installed when Word was loaded on your computer. If so, ask your instructor if you need a custom installation.*

Use the Options triangle button ▼ in the upper-left corner of the Writing Pad window to change the line color and width of your handwritten text on screen, to

turn off automatic recognition of your handwriting, and to change how fast or how slow Word recognizes your handwriting.

When you insert handwritten text, it appears in the font size, color, and style that are in place at the insertion point. After you insert handwritten text, you can select it and format it just as you do with regular text.

HANDS on

Using the Handwriting Feature

In this activity, you will practice using the Writing Pad option of the Handwriting feature in a blank document. Then you will use the Write Anywhere toolbar to write your name at the bottom of a letter and format it.

1. **Open a new blank document and save it as *Handwriting* in the *Tutorial* folder in your *Word Data* folder.**

2. **Click an insertion point at the top of the document, if necessary. Click the Font Size triangle button 12 ▾ and click 48.**

This large font size will allow you to see handwritten text very clearly on screen.

3. **Click the Handwriting button ✍ Handwriting on the Language bar and click Writing Pad.**

The Writing Pad window opens.

4. **Click the Ink button 🖋 in the Handwriting window so that the text you write will appear as handwritten text.**

5. **Point to the blank Writing Pad window.**

The pointer becomes a pen graphic.

6. **Press and hold the mouse button then write hello on the blue line in the Writing Pad window, as shown in Figure 3.23.**

7. **Release the mouse button.**

The handwritten word appears in the Writing Pad window as you are writing it; however, a few seconds after you release the mouse the word moves to the top of your document. (Drag the Writing Pad title bar to adjust the position of the window, if necessary.)

> **NOTE** *If you don't like the results of your first attempt at writing with the mouse, click the word, press* ⌈Delete⌋*, and try again.*

8. **Write the name Sue Smith in the Writing Pad window.**

The name appears in the document after *hello,* preceded by a space. Word automatically inserts a space between words that you add to your document.

Word BASICS

Using Handwriting
Writing Pad Option:

1. Click an insertion point where you want your handwritten text to appear.

2. Click the Handwriting button on the Language bar and click Writing Pad.

3. Click the Ink button in the Handwriting window.

4. Using your mouse, write on the line in the Writing Pad window.

5. Pause writing to have the text move into your document at the insertion point.

Write Anywhere Option:

1. Click your insertion point where you want your handwritten text to appear.

2. Click the Handwriting button on the Language bar and click Write Anywhere.

3. Click the Ink button on the Write Anywhere toolbar.

4. Use your mouse to write in the document.

5. Pause writing to have the text move to the insertion point.

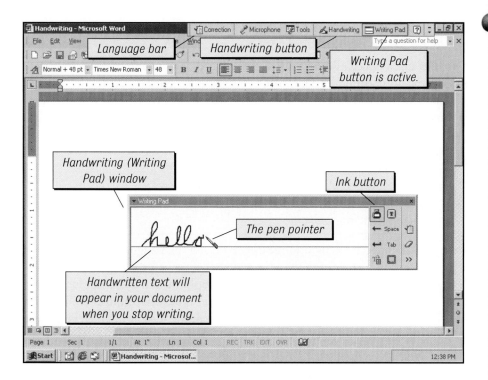

Figure 3.23
Writing Pad Handwriting window

HINTS & TIPS

You can convert handwritten text to typed text. Simply select the handwritten text, right-click, point to Ink Object, and then click Recognize.

WORD 2002

9. Close the Writing Pad window. Save your changes and close the document.

10. Open *Handwriting Letter* in your *Word Data* folder and save it as *Letter Signed* in the *Tutorial* folder.

11. Position the insertion point four lines below the word *Sincerely*. Click the **Handwriting button**  on the Language bar and click **Write Anywhere**.

The Write Anywhere Handwriting toolbar appears. The icons are the same as those that appear in the Writing Pad Handwriting window.

12. If necessary, click the title bar on the Write Anywhere toolbar and drag it to the right side of the document. Click the Ink button 🖊 on the Write Anywhere toolbar if it is not selected.

You are now ready to write text, even though a pen icon does not appear in the document as it did in the Writing Pad Handwriting window.

13. Move the mouse to sign your name anywhere in the blank part of the document.

Your name will initially appear on the screen wherever you happen to write it; however, once you pause a moment, it will be inserted at your insertion point.

14. Close the **Write Anywhere Handwriting window**, and then drag to select your handwritten name.

15. Change the font size to 18 and the font color to blue.

16. Save your changes and close the document.

Another Way

You can insert your handwritten text as typed text. Click the Text button in the Write Anywhere Handwriting toolbar and then write the text. Text will appear at the insertion point as if it were typed. If corrections are necessary, close the Write Anywhere toolbar and type your changes.

SPEECH RECOGNITION

Word has a new Speech Recognition feature that enables you to speak to your computer using a microphone. The words you speak are either accepted by Word as commands (such as *Print* or *Bold*) or they are translated into text in your Word document.

> **NOTE** *The minimum hardware requirements for Word's Speech Recognition feature include a 400 megahertz (MHz) or faster computer with 128 megabytes (MB) or more of memory, Windows 98 or later or Windows NT 4.0 or later. Ideally, you should also have a good quality close-talk headset microphone.*

Access Word's Speech Recognition feature by using the Language bar that appears in the upper-right corner of the Word window. Before you can begin using Speech Recognition, you will need to set up your microphone and then train your computer to recognize your voice. To train your voice, you will read text aloud in the Speech Recognition Training Wizard. The first training session will help you adjust your microphone and will take approximately 15 minutes to complete. Training the system to recognize your voice will result in fewer errors when you use Speech Recognition in your Word documents. Additional training will increase Speech Recognition accuracy. For best results, you should complete a minimum of two training sessions.

Speech Recognition works in two modes—**Dictation mode,** in which your voice is translated into text, and **Voice Command mode,** in which you can control menus. Speech is not designed to be completely hands free; you will still need to use your keyboard in conjunction with your microphone. To use Dictation mode, click the Dictation button [Dictation] on the Language bar. The words you speak will be added to your Word document as soon as the program recognizes them. (There may be a slight delay from the time you speak to the time you see your words on screen.) To use Voice Command mode, click the Voice Command button [Voice Command] on the Language bar. In this mode you can select toolbar, menu, and dialog box items simply by saying their names. For instance, say {Format} to pull down the Format menu; say {Font} to open the Font dialog box; and say {Bold} to format selected text in bold.

Until your system is completely trained to recognize your voice (and even after it is trained), you will likely need to make corrections. To save time, you should complete your dictation first and then go back and make changes. In this way, you will not have to switch back and forth between Dictation and Voice Command modes as often.

Setting Up Speech Recognition

To train your system, you will need a high-quality, close-talk microphone. For best results, you should use a headset microphone so that the microphone is always the same distance from your mouth—about an inch away from the corner of your mouth. However, you can also use hand-held and other types of microphones as long as you keep the distance between your mouth and the microphone consistent each time you use Speech Recognition.

When you use Speech Recognition, you need to work in a quiet environment so that the computer hears only your voice and not other sounds around you. You also need to speak in a consistent, level tone—not too quietly nor too loudly. In addition, you will need to speak at a consistent rate, and you should not pause between words. Word recognizes phrases more easily than it does individual words. For instance, you are better off saying, {My name is Jane} than saying {My} *(pause)* {name} *(pause)* {is} *(pause)* {Jane}.

HANDS on

Setting Up Your System and Training Your Voice

In this activity, you will create a new profile, set up your microphone, and train your system to recognize your voice.

1. Open a new, blank document. Close the New Document task pane, if necessary.

Your new, blank document appears in Print Layout View .

2. Click the Speech Tools button ⌨Tools **on the Language bar and click Options.**

The Speech Properties dialog box appears.

3. Click the Speech Recognition tab, if necessary.

NOTE *These instructions assume that multiple users will work on the same computer. In a multiple-user situation, each user must establish a separate speech profile by clicking the New button in the Recognition Profiles section.*

4. Click New in the Recognition Profiles section.

The Profile wizard opens.

5. Type your name in the Profile Wizard box, as shown in Figure 3.24.

6. Click Next to advance to the Microphone Wizard Welcome screen.

7. Read the instructions on the Welcome screen and then click Next.

The Microphone Wizard Test Microphone screen appears.

8. Read the instructions, read the sentence aloud, and click Next.

The Microphone Wizard Test Positioning screen appears.

9. Read the instructions then read the sentence aloud *even if you are not using a headset microphone.*

If you have speakers on your computer, you will hear your voice speaking back to you. Once your microphone is configured properly, you are ready to train the system to recognize your voice.

Creating a New Profile

1. Click Speech Tools on the Language bar.

2. Click Options to open the Speech Properties dialog box.

3. On the Speech Recognition tab, click New in the Recognition Profiles section.

4. Type your name in the Profile Wizard box.

5. Click Next and follow the steps in the wizard.

Setting Up Your Microphone

1. Click Speech Tools on the Language bar.

2. Click Options to open the Speech Properties dialog box.

3. On the Speech Recognition tab, click Configure Microphone in the Microphone section.

4. Follow the steps in the Microphone Wizard.

Figure 3.24
Profile Wizard

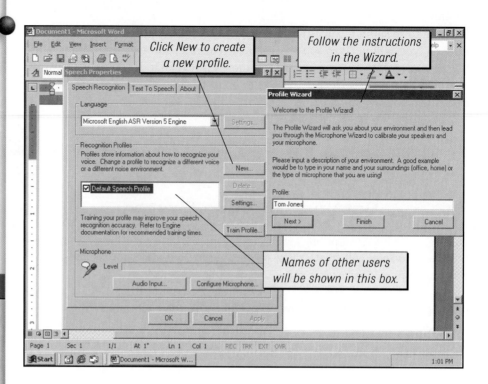

Training Your System

Initial Training:

1. Click Speech Tools on the Language bar, then click Options.

2. Click the Speech Recognition tab in the Speech Properties box.

3. Click New in the Recognition Profiles section and type your name in the Profile Wizard.

4. Click Next to proceed through the Microphone Wizard.

5. Follow the steps in the Voice Training Wizard.

Additional Training:

1. Click Speech Tools on the Language bar, then click Options.

2. Click the Speech Recognition tab in the Speech Properties box.

3. Click your name in the Recognition Profiles section.

4. Click Train Profile in the Recognition Profiles section.

5. Click a selected reading in the Voice Training Wizard, then click Next.

6. Follow the steps in the wizard.

NOTE *If you have speakers but cannot hear your voice speaking back to you, you may need to adjust the volume controls on your computer. Point to Settings on the Start menu, then point to Control Panel and click Sounds and Multimedia. On the Sounds tab, drag the Volume slider to adjust the sound.*

10. Click **Finish** to close the Microphone Wizard.

The Voice Training Wizard opens.

11. Proceed through each screen in the Voice Training wizard. Read and follow the instructions on each screen. If you make an error while reading aloud or the wizard doesn't recognize a word, the wizard will reset so you can speak the words again. Do not make corrections. If you get stuck on a word that the wizard does not recognize, click Skip Word.

NOTE *As you read the training text, the words will be highlighted on your screen, as shown in Figure 3.25. If you notice the words are no longer being highlighted, stop speaking and begin again with the first non-highlighted word. When you finish reading a selection, the wizard will automatically advance to the next selection. Click Pause, if necessary, if you are interrupted.*

12. At the end of the training session, click **Finish** if you are ready to end the training session or click **More Training** to train a second time. If you have time, go ahead and do a second training session now. You can read the same training text again or you can select a different session. If you don't have time now, you can go back later and train the system again.

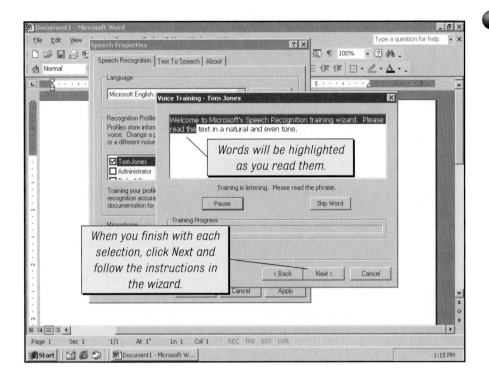

Figure 3.25
Training Wizard

NOTE *To complete a second training session at a later time, open the Speech Properties dialog box and click your profile in the Recognition Profiles section. Click the Train Profile button and follow the instructions.*

Using Speech Recognition

Now that you have set up your profile, adjusted your microphone, and trained your system, you are ready to use Speech Recognition. When you're ready to begin speaking, open a new blank document; then select your user profile on the Speech Tools button . Click the Microphone button on the Language bar. Then click either the Dictation button or the Voice Command button. To turn off the microphone, click the Microphone button again. Your microphone should be in the same position it was in during your training session, and you need to speak in the same tone of voice and at the same rate as you did during training. All punctuation needs to be spoken in Dictation mode, such as {period}. When you want to move to a new line, simply say {Enter} instead of pressing Enter. When you need to correct a word, you can select the word and type the correct word on your keyboard or you can select the word and a few words on either side of it and dictate over the error.

NORTON
ONLINE

Visit **www.glencoe.com/norton/online/** for more information on speech recognition.

Using Dictation and Voice Command Modes

In this activity, you will use Dictation mode and Voice Command mode to create and format a document.

1. Open a new, blank document.

2. Click **Speech Tools** 📖 Tools, point to **Current User**, and click your name (your Profile).

3. Click the **Options triangle button** ▼ and check that all the button icons are selected. (If an icon is not checked, it will not appear on the Language bar.)

4. Click the **Microphone button** 🎤 Microphone on the Language bar.

The Language bar expands to display the **Dictation button** 📖 Dictation and the **Voice Command button** 🎤 Voice Command.

> **NOTE** *After you click the Microphone button* 🎤 Microphone *for the first time, the Welcome to Office Speech Recognition dialog box may appear. If so, proceed again through the Microphone Wizard. When the Microphone Wizard is finished, close the dialog box. At this point, your browser may initiate the download of the Office Speech Training Video; if so, close your browser and continue with this activity.*

5. Click the **Dictation button** 📖 Dictation.

6. Speak the following sentences:

{My name is Mary} {period} {My dog is named John} {period} {My cat is named Tom} {period}

As shown in Figure 3.26, the words you speak will appear on screen. At this point, don't worry about errors—you'll correct them later.

Figure 3.26
Speech Recognition text

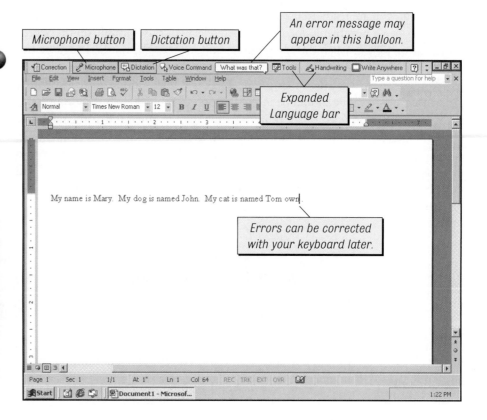

7. Move to a new paragraph and enter more speech by speaking the following:

{new paragraph} {Do you want to go to the movies tonight} {question mark} {The Sound of Music is playing at the Emerson Theater} {period}

Now you will format the text you've just entered.

8. Click the **Voice Command button**  on the Language bar.

9. Select the words *The sound of music,* using your mouse or keyboard.

10. Say {italics}.

The name of the movie becomes italicized.

11. With the name of the movie still selected, say {Font Color}.

The font color box opens.

12. Say {red} to apply the color to the movie title.

13. Select the *s* in *sound* and say {captialize}; select the *m* in *music* and say {captialize}; select the *t* in *theatre* and say {captialize}.

14. Select the word *Mary* and say {bold}.

15. Click the **Microphone button** to turn off the microphone.

16. Use the keyboard and mouse to make any necessary corrections.

17. Save your file as *First Speech* in the *Tutorial* folder in your *Word Data* folder, and close the file.

18. Click the **Minimize button** on the Language bar and click **OK** in the dialog box.

Word BASICS

Using Voice Command Mode

1. Click the Microphone button on the Language bar.

2. Click the Voice Command button on the Language bar.

3. Speak commands into your microphone.

4. Click the Microphone button on the Language bar to turn off the microphone.

WEB NOTE

Type **voice commands** into the *Ask a question* box, then click *Things you can do and say with speech recognition.* Click Show All and browse the information. Click Hide All then click the Microsoft Office Web site link for more information.

Self Check

Test your knowledge by answering the following questions. See Appendix B to check your answers.

1. The area of a table where text is typed is a _____ .

2. A _____ is a picture that displays data from a datasheet in the form of circles, lines, bars, or other shapes.

3. Categories of information, such as Title, Name, or Address, are referred to as _____ .

4. The _____ toolbar is used when viewing tracked changes in a document.

5. The _____ is used to access both Handwriting and Speech Recognition features.

SEARCHING THE INTERNET

Searching the Web for information is now a commonplace activity in most businesses. The information might be about a product or service or the search might be for current data for a project. In such cases, you can use a search page to locate relevant Web sites. Methods for searching the Web may vary, but most searches involve the basic steps of entering keywords to define the search; entering additional keywords to narrow the search; and exploring the search results.

A **search page** is a place to type the keywords for your search. A **search engine** is an Internet tool that looks for Web sites that contain your keywords and displays a list of those sites. Some popular search engines are Yahoo, AltaVista, Lycos, and Excite. Some search engines search every word of every document they find on the Internet; others search only portions of documents they find. Thus some search engines return many more sites than others do when searching for the same keywords. The results of a search appear in the form of links that you can click to navigate to the information. Many search engines let you use special symbols to narrow your search results.

> **NOTE** *For an excellent overview of most of the major search engines, point your browser to* www.101searchengine.com.

In this activity, you will use the Search the Web button ▣ in Word to navigate to the search page of your browser. Then you will search for Web sites published by companies that sell educational games.

1. **Open a new, blank document. Connect to the Internet, if necessary. Point to Toolbars on the View menu and click Web.**

2. **Click the Search the Web button ▣.**

Word launches your browser and your default search page appears.

3. **If necessary, click a search engine option. (You may use the default search engine if one is already selected; or you may not have a choice of search engines.)**

4. **When your Search Page appears, type games in the Search text box and press Enter⏎ or click the button to process your search request. (This button may be labeled *Search, Submit search, Find, Find It,* or *Go*.)**

> **NOTE** *A Security Alert dialog box may appear, warning you of security issues and asking if you want to continue. Click Yes to continue.*

In the search results (or matches), note the number of categories and sites. Instead of sifting through thousands of sites, you can read about ways to narrow your search. Many search engines let you use special symbols to narrow your search results. For instance, the AltaVista search engine allows you to use quotation marks around words that should always be found together, a plus symbol (+) to specify that the keyword must be found in the result, and a minus sign (−) to indicate a word that should not be found in the resulting pages. For instance, the keywords +*toy company "board game"* −*puzzle* will result in pages that all contain the word *toy*, may contain the word *company*, may contain the words *board game* together but will exclude those pages that contain just the word *board* and just the word *game*. The results will not include the word *puzzle*. (Other search engines let you use *AND* instead of a plus symbol, and *AND NOT* instead of a minus symbol.)

5. Look for a button or hypertext that offers search options, tips, or help. Explore for search guidelines to define or narrow a search.

6. Click the **Back button** [⇐ Back ▾] to return to the Search page, if necessary.

7. Type the keywords board games in the Search text box. (Remember to apply the search tips you just read, such as adding quotation marks around these words.) Process your search request.

Again, note the reported number of categories and sites containing both keywords.

8. Submit the search again, but exclude *puzzles* from the results and require all five of the following keywords: *order, preschool, educational, board,* and *games.* (*Hint:* You may be able to type + order + preschool + educational + board + games − puzzle in the Search text box.)

9. Scroll the page to view the search results.

Typically, search results are listed 10 links to a page, with the best links listed first. *Best* or *Top* in this case refers to sites that match keywords most precisely.

10. Click one of the links and explore the site.

The site should represent a vendor of educational board games for preschool children and should include information for ordering games.

11. Return to the list of search results and explore other sites as your time allows.

12. Close your browser, disconnect from the Internet, and return to the Word window. Close the Word Web toolbar.

> **WARNING** *You may proceed directly to the exercises for this lesson. If, however, you are finished with your computer session, follow the "shut down" procedures for your lab or school environment.*

SUMMARY AND EXERCISES

SUMMARY

Tables, charts, and diagrams convey some information more effectively than text alone, and they add interest to documents. Word provides users with tools for creating tables, charts, and diagrams that are both functional and attractive. Word also provides features such as Mail Merge, Tracking Changes, Comparing and Merging Documents, Handwriting, and Speech Recognition that make work easier and more efficient. Searching the Internet for information involves displaying the search page, choosing a search engine, entering keywords, and exploring the search results.

Now that you have completed this lesson, you should be able to do the following:

- Insert a table into a document. (page 164)
- Draw a table in a document. (page 164)
- Describe a cell, row, and column. (page 164)
- Explain the difference between portrait and landscape orientation. (page 167)
- Navigate through a table and enter data. (page 167)
- Modify a table by merging cells and changing column width and row height. (page 169)
- Insert and delete table rows and columns. (page 171)
- Change table cell alignment and enhance text. (page 172)
- Move and resize tables. (page 174)
- Describe the functions of a move handle and a resize handle. (page 174)
- Add borders and shading to table cells. (page 176)
- Use Table AutoFormat to change the appearance of tables. (page 177)
- Describe how to insert a Watermark into a document. (page 179)
- Explain the purpose of a datasheet. (page 180)
- Describe the significance of the drawing canvas. (page 180)
- Create and modify a chart. (page 180)
- Insert a diagram from the Diagram Gallery. (page 183)
- Use Mail Merge to create form letters and labels. (page 186)
- Track changes made by multiple reviewers; compare and merge edited documents. (page 192)
- Insert handwriting using Word's Handwriting Recognition feature. (page 198)
- Explain the difference between Dictation and Voice Command mode in the Speech Recognition feature. (page 200)
- Set up a voice recognition profile. (page 201)
- Use Speech Recognition to insert text into a document. (page 203)
- Describe the function of a search engine. (page 206)
- Perform an advanced Internet search using a search engine. (page 206)

CONCEPTS REVIEW

1 TRUE/FALSE

Circle T if the statement is true or F if the statement is false.

T F **1.** You can use tools on the Draw menu to create tables.

T F **2.** You can use `Tab` or `→` to move from cell to cell in a table.

T F **3.** You can change page orientation in the Page Setup dialog box.

T F **4.** A chart must be created from text that is already in your document.

T F **5.** The Mail Merge Wizard is the easiest way to create a document using the Mail Merge feature.

T F **6.** Comments inserted in Track Changes mode appear in either the reviewing pane or in a balloon in the margin.

T F **7.** When you write in Write Anywhere mode, the text appears exactly where you wrote it on your screen.

T F **8.** The move handle appears at the lower-right corner of an object such as a chart or diagram.

T F **9.** When you perform a search for a Web site, the search results appear as lengthy addresses that you must then type into a browser's address bar in order to visit the site.

T F **10.** Web searches based on several keywords yield better results than one-word searches.

2 MATCHING

Match each of the terms on the left with the definitions on the right.

TERMS	DEFINITIONS
1. landscape	**a.** To combine two or more cells into one cell
2. cell	**b.** Contains information used to create charts and graphs
3. datasheet	
4. data source	**c.** Feature that allows multiple users to work with the same document.
5. drawing canvas	**d.** A type of page orientation
6. merge	**e.** Contains personalized information for use in a mail merge
7. track changes	
8. Insert Diagram or Organization Chart	**f.** Smallest unit of a table
	g. A button on the Drawing toolbar
9. Dictation mode	**h.** Spoken words that control menus
10. Voice command mode	**i.** Area behind an object such as a chart
	j. Translates spoken words into text

SUMMARY AND EXERCISES

3 COMPLETION

Fill in the missing word or phrase for each of the following statements.

1. To combine two selected cells, click the _____ button on the Tables and Borders toolbar.

2. In a table, text is arranged in _____ and _____ .

3. You can align entries in cells _____ and _____ .

4. Use the _____ feature to create personalized form letters and labels.

5. Use the _____ feature to compare changes in two or more documents.

6. The two sources of information that are put together by Mail Merge are called the main document and the _____ .

7. Click the _____ button to turn off your microphone.

8. Use the _____ button in Word to navigate to your Search Page.

9. A(n) _____ looks for Web sites that contain information about your search topic.

10. You can add _____ to make a search more specific.

4 SHORT ANSWER

Write a brief answer to each of the following questions.

1. On a Word table, where is cell D5?

2. Name three ways to move around in a table.

3. Explain the difference between portrait and landscape orientation.

4. Explain how to format a table automatically.

5. How do you access the Diagram Gallery and what is in it?

6. Explain a way of using the Mail Merge feature other than the Mail Merge Wizard.

7. Explain two methods of using the Handwriting feature in Word.

8. Explain the steps involved in setting up your computer for Speech Recognition.

9. Name three popular search engines.

10. Describe the handles that appear when you point to a chart or table and explain the functions of these handles.

5 IDENTIFICATION

Label each of the elements in Figure 3.27.

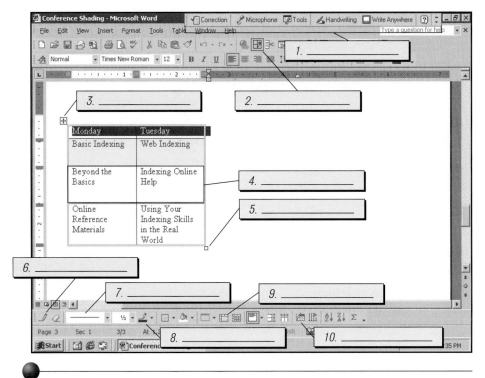

Figure 3.27

SKILLS REVIEW

Complete all of the Skills Review problems in sequential order to review your skills to create and format tables; change page orientation; move and resize a table; create and modify a chart and diagram; create form letters and labels; track changes and comments in a document; and use Handwriting and Speech Recognition.

1 Create a Table and Type Cell Entries

1. Open *Star Gazette Article* in your *Word Data* folder and save it as *Table in Report* in the *Skills Review* folder.

2. Find the phrase *are worn down,* click at the end of the sentence, and press `Enter ←` two times.

3. Click the **Insert Table button** 🔲 on the Standard toolbar and drag to create a 4 x 3 table.

4. In cell B1, type **Earth** and press `Tab` to move to cell C1. Type **Venus**.

5. Fill in the cells as shown in Table 3.3.

Table 3.3	Cell Entries
Cell	**Data to Type**
A2	Revolution period
B2	365.2 days
C2	224.7 days
A3	Rotation period
B3	23.9 hours
C3	243 days
A4	Source: *Information Please Almanac*, 2001

6. Save your changes and close the document.

2 Revise a Table and Change Page Orientation

1. Open *Table in Report* in the *Skills Review* folder in your *Word Data* folder and save it as *Table in Report Addition* in the *Skills Review* folder.

2. Click **Page Setup** on the File menu. On the Margins tab, click the **Landscape icon** and click **OK**.

3. Point to **Toolbars** on the View menu and click **Tables and Borders** to display the Tables and Borders toolbar. Click **Print Layout View** 🔲 if necessary.

4. In the table on page 1, select columns B and C and click the **Insert Table triangle button** 🔲▾ on the Tables and Borders toolbar. Click **Insert Columns to the Right**.

5. Select rows 1 and 2 and click the **Insert Columns to the Right triangle button** 🔳▾. Click **Insert Rows Below**.

6. Type the following entries starting in cell A3 (press Tab after the first two entries): **Miles from sun, 149.6 million, 108.2 million.**

7. Select columns D and E. Right-click the selected columns and click **Delete Columns** on the shortcut menu.

8. Point to the right table border. When the pointer becomes a two-way horizontal arrow, click and drag the border 0.25" to the left.

9. Click the table then click the **Distribute Columns Evenly button** 🔳.

10. Select row 6, right-click anywhere in the row, and click **Merge Cells** on the shortcut menu.

11. Select row 1 and click **Table Properties** on the Table menu. On the Row tab, select the **Specify height check box**, click **Exactly** in the *Row height is* box, and type **0.35** as the height. Click **OK**.

12. Deselect the row to view your changes.

13. Right-click in row 4 and click **Delete Cells** on the shortcut menu. Click **Delete entire row** and click **OK**.

14. Select the headings in cells B1 and C1. Click the **Cell Alignment triangle button** 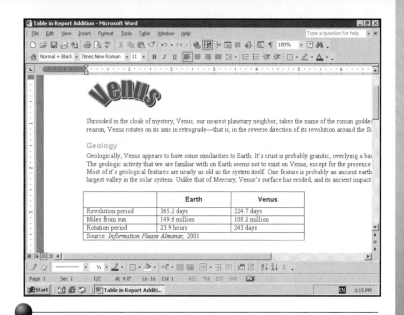. Then, click **Align Center**.

15. With cells B1 and C1 still selected, click the **Font triangle button** Times New Roman and click **Arial**. Click the **Bold button** B . Deselect the cells. Your document should look like Figure 3.28.

16. Save your changes and close the document.

3 Move and Resize a Table

1. Open *Star Gazette Table* in your *Word Data* folder and save it as *Star Gazette Table Moved* in the *Skills Review* folder.

2. Find the phrase *half a mile,* click at the end of the sentence, and press Enter← two times.

Figure 3.28

3. Scroll to the end of the document. Point to the table then point to the move handle when it appears in the upper-left corner of the table. When the pointer changes to the four-way arrow, click and drag the table upward. Release the table when the top of the table is about .5" below the paragraph that ends with *half a mile.*

4. With the insertion point in the table, right-click the table and click **Table Properties** on the shortcut menu. Click the **Table tab**.

5. In the *Alignment* section, click the **Center icon**; under *Text wrapping,* click **None** so the text will not wrap around the table. Click **OK**.

6. Point to the table, then point to the resize handle in the lower-right corner of the table. Click when the pointer becomes a diagonal arrow then drag down and to the right to make the table approximately .5" wider (horizontal ruler) and .25" deeper (vertical ruler).

7. Save your changes and close the document.

4 Add a Border and Shading to Cells and Apply an AutoFormat

1. Open *Star Gazette Table Moved* in the *Skills Review* folder in your *Word Data* folder and save it as *Star Gazette Table Format* in the *Skills Review* folder.

2. Scroll to the table on page 1 and click cell A1. Click the **Borders triangle button** on the Tables and Borders toolbar, then click the **Top Border icon**.

3. Click the **Borders triangle button** again and click the **Left Border icon**.

4. Select cells A2 through A4. Click the **Shading Color triangle button** and click **Gray-12.5%**.

5. Find the phrase *are worn down* in the document. Click at the end of the sentence and press Enter⏎ two times.

6. Click the **Insert Rows Below triangle button** ⊟ on the Tables and Borders toolbar, then click **Insert Table**. In the *Number of columns* box, click **3**; in the *Number of rows* box, click **9**; then click **OK**.

7. Click the selection bar at the left of row 1 to select the row then click the **Merge Cells button** ▦.

8. Type **Notable Venus Probes** in row 1.

9. Right-click row 1 and click **Table Properties**. On the Table tab, select the **Preferred width check box** then type 2.25 as the width. Click the **Left alignment icon**; click the **None text wrapping icon**; then click **OK**.

10. Click the **Table AutoFormat button** ▦ and click the **Table Columns 5 table style**. Select all options in the *Apply special formats* section *except* the Last row option, then click **Apply**.

11. Click **Print Preview** ▣ and view page 1 of the document. Notice the difference in the tables. Close Print Preview.

12. Save and close the document. Click the **Tables and Borders button** ▣ on the Standard toolbar to close the Tables and Borders toolbar.

5 Create and Modify a Chart

1. Open *Report Memo* in your *Word Data* folder and save it as *Report Memo Chart* in the *Skills Review* folder.

2. Click an insertion point about 1" below the last line of the report, then click **Object** on the Insert menu.

3. On the Create New tab, click **Microsoft Graph Chart** in the *Object type* box, then click **OK**.

4. Replace the data in the datasheet with the information shown in Table 3.4.

Table 3.4	Data for Tables			
	1st Qtr	**2nd Qtr**	**3rd Qtr**	**4th Qtr**
Midwest	201,000	172,000	155,000	183,000
North	193,000	168,000	147,000	162,000
South	187,000	173,000	138,000	174,000

5. Click anywhere in the document (away from the chart) to close the datasheet. Right-click the chart, and click **Format Object** on the shortcut menu.

6. On the Colors and Lines tab, click the **Fill Color triangle button** and click a pale green color as a fill color. On the Layout tab, click the **Square wrapping style icon**, click **Left** in the *Horizontal alignment* section, and click **OK**.

7. Save your changes and close the document.

8. Open *Scores* in your *Word Data* folder and save it as *Scores Chart* in your *Skills Review* folder.

9. Click the table, point to **Select** on the Table menu, and click **Table**.

10. Click **Object** on the Insert menu. Click the **Create New tab**, if necessary, in the Object dialog box.

11. Click **Microsoft Graph Chart** in the *Object type* box, and click **OK**.

12. Click the Word document (away from the chart) to close the datasheet.

13. Click the table then point to **Delete** on the Table menu and click **Table**.

14. Click the chart then point to the handle in the lower-right corner. When the pointer becomes a diagonal arrow, drag the chart slowly down and to the right until the right border is at about 4" on the horizontal ruler and the bottom border is at about 3.5" on the vertical ruler.

15. Save your changes and close the document.

6 Create and Modify a Diagram

1. Open a new, blank document and save it as *Sales Organization* in the *Skills Review* folder in your *Word Data* folder.

2. Point to **Toolbars** on the View menu and click **Drawing**. Click the **Insert Diagram or Organization Chart button** on the Drawing toolbar.

3. Click the **Organization Chart diagram icon**, and click **OK**.

4. Click the top box and type **Sales Leader**. Select **Sales Leader**, click the **Font button** Times New Roman, and click **Arial**. Click the **Bold button** B, then click the **Underline button** U.

5. Click the **Insert Shape triangle button** Insert Shape on the Organization Chart toolbar, and click **Assistant**.

6. Click the new second-level box and type **Assistant**. Select **Assistant**, click the **Font button** Times New Roman, and click **Arial**. Click the **Bold button** B then click the **Italic button** I. Click the **Align Right button**.

7. Click each of the three boxes in the third level, type **Sales Associate**, then make the font Arial, bold, and centered.

8. Click the **Autoformat button** on the Organization Chart toolbar.

9. Preview then select a pleasing diagram style in the Organization Chart Style Gallery. Click **Apply**.

10. Save your changes and close the document.

11. Open a new blank document and save it as *Cycle Diagram* in the *Skills Review* folder in your *Word Data* folder.

12. Click the **Insert Diagram or Organization Chart button** on the Drawing toolbar, click the **Cycle Diagram icon** in the Diagram Gallery, and click **OK**.

WORD 2002

13. Starting at the top left and working clockwise, type the following three titles in the text placeholders: **Stage 1: Discuss Ideas; Stage 2: Create Outline; Stage 3: Write and Edit.**

14. Select each of the titles and change the font and alignment. Format the titles attractively. Your completed Cycle diagram might look similar to Figure 3.29.

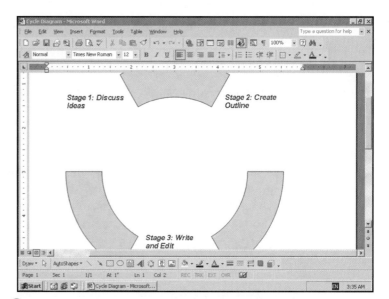

15. Close the Drawing toolbar. Save your changes and close the document.

7 Create Form Letters

1. Open *Form Letter* in your *Word Data* folder. Click after *Sincerely yours* and press ⟨Enter↵⟩ four times. Type your name.

2. Point to **Letters and Mailings** on the Tools menu and click **Mail Merge Wizard**.

Figure 3.29

3. Select **Letters** in the *Select document type* section of the Mail Merge task pane, then click **Next: Starting document** at the bottom of the task pane.

4. Select **Use the current document** in the *Select starting document* section, then click **Next: Select recipients**.

5. Select **Use an existing list** in the *Select recipients* section, then click **Browse**.

6. In the Select Data Source box, navigate to your *Word Data* folder. Click *Form Address* and click **Open**.

7. Click **Select All** in the Mail Merge Recipients box, if necessary, to place a check mark in the first column of each row, and click **OK**.

8. Click **Next: Write your letter** in the task pane.

9. Click after the date and press ⟨Enter↵⟩ four times. Click **More items** in the Mail Merge task pane.

10. In the Insert Merge Field box, click **Title** and click **Insert**; click **First Name** and click **Insert**; then click **Last Name** and click **Insert**. Click **Close**.

11. Press ⟨Enter↵⟩ to move to the next line, then click **More items** in the task pane. In the Insert Merge Field box, click **Address**, click **Insert**, then click **Close**.

12. Press ⟨Enter↵⟩ to move to the next line, then click **More items**. Click **CSZ**, click **Insert**, then click **Close**.

13. Click after *Dear* and press ⟨Spacebar⟩.

14. Click **More items** on the task pane; click **Title** then **Insert**; click **Last Name** then **Insert**. Click **Close**.

15. Click between each field in the first line of the addressee section and press [Spacebar]. Click between the two fields in the greeting section and press [Spacebar]. Click **Next: Preview your letters** in the task pane.

16. Click the **right double arrow button** [>>] in the *Preview your letters* section of the task pane to preview the other merged letters. Click **Next: Complete the merge**.

17. Click **Edit individual letters** in the Mail Merge task pane.

18. In the Merge to New Document dialog box, select **All** and click **OK**.

19. Scroll through the new document to view the letters. Save the document containing the merged letters as *Form Merged* in the *Skills Review* folder in your *Word Data* folder, and close the document.

20. Close the Mail Merge task pane. Save the *Form Letter* file as *Form Letter Fields* in the *Skills Review* folder in your *Word Data* folder, then close the document.

8 Create Labels

1. Open a new, blank document.

2. Point to **Letters and Mailings** on the Tools menu and click **Show Mail Merge Toolbar**.

3. Click the **Main document setup button** on the Mail Merge toolbar, click **Labels** in the Main Document Type box, and click **OK**.

4. In the Label Options dialog box, click **Avery standard** in the *Label products* box, click **5160-Address** in the *Product number* box, and click **OK**.

5. Click the **Open Data Source button** on the Mail Merge toolbar.

6. In the Select Data Source box, navigate to your *Word Data* folder and click *Form Address*, then click **Open**.

7. Click the **Mail Merge Recipients button** on the Mail Merge toolbar; click **Select All**, if necessary, to place a check mark in the first column of each row; and click **OK**.

8. Click the **Insert Merge Fields button** on the Mail Merge toolbar.

9. In the Insert Merge Field dialog box, click **Title** and then **Insert**; click **First Name** and then **Insert**; and click **Last Name** then **Insert**. Click **Close**, then click between each field and press [Spacebar].

10. Click at the end of the *Last Name* field and press [Enter] to move to the next line on the label. Click the **Insert Merge Fields button**, click **Address**, click **Insert**, then click **Close**.

11. Press [Enter] to move to the next line and click the **Insert Merge Fields button**. Click **CSZ**, click **Insert**, then click **Close**.

12. Click the **Propagate Labels button** on the Mail Merge toolbar.

13. Click the **View Merged Data button** on the Mail Merge toolbar, then click the **Merge to New Document button**.

14. In the Merge to New Document dialog box, select **All** and click **OK**.

15. Save your final merged labels as *Form Labels Merged* in the *Skills Review* folder in your *Word Data* folder, then close the document.

16. Save the open file as *Form Labels Fields* in the *Skills Review* folder in your *Word Data* folder, then close the document.

17. Close the Mail Merge toolbar.

9 Review Edits and Comments

1. Open *Australia Tour Pricing Copy 1* in your *Word Data* folder.

2. Point to **Toolbars** on the View menu and click **Reviewing** to display the Reviewing toolbar. Click **Print Layout View** ▣ if necessary.

3. With your insertion point at the top of the document, click the **Next button** ➡ on the Reviewing toolbar.

4. Click the **Accept Change button** ✅▾ on the Reviewing toolbar to accept the change, and then click the **Next button** ➡.

5. Repeat step 4 to accept each change until you reach the last comment in the document that reads *Are you sure this is correct?*.

6. Click the **RejectChange/Delete Comment button** ✖▾ on the Reviewing toolbar to delete the comment from the document.

7. Save your changes as *Australia Tour Pricing Reviewed* in the *Skills Review* folder in your *Word Data* folder. Close the document.

10 Compare and Merge Documents

1. Open *Australian Islands Article* in your *Word Data* folder.

2. Click **Compare and Merge Documents** on the Tools menu.

3. In the Compare and Merge Documents dialog box, click *Australian Islands Article-1* in your *Word Data* folder, click the **Merge triangle button**, and click **Merge into current document**.

4. Click **Compare and Merge Documents** on the Tools menu.

5. In the Compare and Merge Documents dialog box, click *Australian Islands Article-2* in your *Word Data* folder, click the **Merge triangle button**, and click **Merge into current document**.

6. Click the **Display for Review triangle button** [Final Showing Markup ▾] on the Reviewing toolbar and click **Original Showing Markup**.

7. Click the **Next button** ➡ on the Reviewing toolbar to move to the first edit. Click the **Accept Change button** ✅▾.

8. Proceed through the rest of the document following step 7 to accept each reviewer's change. When a dialog box tells you the document contains no further comments or changes, click **OK**.

9. Save the revised document as *Australian Article Compared* in the *Skills Review* folder in your *Word Data* folder. Close the document.

11 Track Changes and Insert a Comment

1. Open *Australian Islands Article* in your *Word Data* folder and save it as *Australian Article Edited* in the *Skills Review* folder.

2. Click **Track Changes** on the Tools menu. Click **Print Layout View** ▣, if necessary.

3. Find the word *northwest* and insert the word **corner** after it.

4. Click **Normal View** ▤.

5. Find the word *cows* and click immediately after the word.

6. Click the **New Comment button** ▣ on the Reviewing toolbar.

7. Type **Are there still cows on the island?** in the Reviewing pane.

8. Click the **Reviewing Pane button** ▣ on the Reviewing Toolbar to close the Reviewing Pane.

9. Click **Print Layout View** ▣ and scroll to view your new comment in balloon format.

10. Point to **Toolbars** on the View menu and click **Reviewing** to close the Reviewing toolbar.

11. Save your changes and close the document.

12 Use Handwriting Recognition

1. Open a new blank document and save it as *Writing Sample* in the *Skills Review* folder in your *Word Data* folder.

2. Click **Print Layout View** ▣, if necessary.

3. With your insertion point at the top of the document, click the **Font Size button** 12 ▾, then click **48**. Click the **Font Color triangle button** ▲▾ and click **Red**.

4. Click the **Language bar icon** EN near the clock, then click **Show the Language bar** on the shortcut menu to display the Language bar.

5. Click the **Handwriting button** ✍ Handwriting on the Language bar and click **Write Anywhere**.

6. Click the **Ink button** ▣, if necessary, on the Write Anywhere toolbar.

7. Use your mouse to write **Microsoft Word**, then pause and watch the text appear in 48 point, red type.

8. Press Enter↵ two times.

9. Click the **Handwriting button** ✍ Handwriting on the Language bar, and click **Writing Pad**.

10. Click the **Ink button** ▣ in the Writing Pad window, if necessary.

11. Use your mouse to write your name on the blue line, then watch it appear in your document.

12. Close the Writing Pad window.

13. Select all text in the document and change the font size to 36 and the font color to blue, as shown in Figure 3.30.

14. Save your changes and close the document.

13 Complete Additional Voice Training

1. Open a new blank document.

2. Click **Tools** on the Language bar, then click **Options**.

3. Click the **Speech Recognition tab** in the Speech Properties box.

4. Click your name in the Recognition Profiles section, then click **Train Profile**.

5. Click a selected reading for the Voice Training Wizard, then click **Next**.

6. Follow the steps in the wizard. When you complete the training session, close the Speech Properties dialog box.

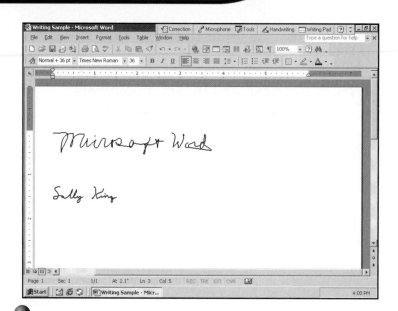

Figure 3.30

14 Use Speech Recognition

1. With a new blank document open, click the **Microphone button** [Microphone] on the Language bar. Click the **Dictation button** [Dictation].

2. Speak aloud as follows: {I am using my microphone to enter text into my Word document} {period} {Do you think additional training will help me to have fewer errors} {question mark}

3. Click the **Microphone button** [Microphone] to turn off your microphone. Then use the keyboard to correct errors and add capitalization.

4. Click the **Microphone button** [Microphone] then click the **Voice Command button** [Voice Command] on the Language bar.

5. Select *Word* using your mouse or keyboard and say {underline}.

6. With *Word* still selected, say {Font Color} and then say {blue}.

7. Select the word *fewer* and say {Italic}.

8. Select the entire paragraph and say {Font Size} then say {16}.

9. Click the **Microphone button** [Microphone] to turn off the microphone. Deselect the paragraph.

10. Save your document as *Sample Speech* in the *Skills Review* folder in your *Word Data* folder, then close the document.

11. Click the **Minimize button** ⬜ on the Language bar, then click **OK** in the dialog box to minimize the Language bar.

LESSON APPLICATIONS

1 Create a Table and Apply an AutoFormat

Create a table; add and delete rows and columns; apply and modify an AutoFormat; change the font, font size, and alignment; change borders and shading; and change page orientation.

1. Open a new blank document and save it as *Auto Table* in the *Lesson Applications* folder in your *Word Data* folder.

2. Display the Tables and Borders toolbar and use it to create a fixed-column width table with 3 rows and 3 columns.

3. Type the data in Table 3.5 into your table. When you need new columns and rows for the data, add them to the table.

Table 3.5	Table Data		
Item	**Estimate**	**Commercial Discount**	**Item Totals**
Excavation	4,700	470	4,230
Concrete	9,500	950	8,550
Finishing	3,550	355	3,195
Grading	650	None	650
Grand Total			16,625

4. Apply the *Table Columns 5* AutoFormat to the table. Keep all default special format options.

5. Delete the *Grading* row and change the Grand Total amount to 15,975. Delete the *Commercial Discount* column. Select the *Estimate* heading and type **Retail Price**. Select the *Item Totals* heading and type **Your Price**.

6. Select the column headings in row 1 and align them in the bottom center of the cells. Change the font in row 1 to Arial bold (no italic) and change the font size to 10. Change the height of row 1 to .3".

7. Add a new row to the top of the table and type **Newtown Custom Concrete** in any cell in the row. Merge the cells in row 1. Change the row 1 font to Times New Roman, size 14, bold, italic, blue. Align row 1 center left.

8. Select all cells with numbers and change the alignment to Align Center Right.

9. Select the cell containing 15,975 and add yellow shading. Select the gray shaded cell in the Grand Total row and remove the shading. Select the table and change the outside border to a two-line border style of ¼ point lines.

10. Reduce the width of columns B and C by approximately .5".

11. Change the page orientation to Landscape. Use Print Preview to view the document.

12. Close Print Preview. Close the Tables and Borders toolbar. Save your changes and close the document.

2 Create and Modify a Chart

Create a new chart and modify it; create a chart from a table and resize it.

1. Open a new blank document and save it as *New Chart* in the *Lesson Applications* folder in your *Word Data* folder.

2. Insert a new Microsoft Graph Chart. Replace the data in the datasheet with the information shown in Table 3.6.

Table 3.6	Data for Datasheet			
	1st Qtr	**2nd Qtr**	**3rd Qtr**	**4th Qtr**
Team A	25	35	45	70
Team B	40	30	40	60
Team C	80	70	65	85

3. Close the datasheet. Format the chart with a yellow fill color, square wrapping style, and right horizontal alignment.

4. Save your changes and close the document.

5. Open *Miles Run* in your *Word Data* folder and save it as *Miles Run Chart* in your *Lesson Applications* folder.

6. Select the table and insert a new Microsoft Graph Chart.

7. Close the datasheet and delete the table.

8. Resize the chart so it is approximately 5" in width.

9. Save your changes and close the document.

3 Create and Modify a Diagram

Create a diagram and modify it.

1. Open a new blank document and save it as *Modified Diagram* in the *Lesson Applications* folder in your *Word Data* folder.

2. Open the Diagram Gallery and insert *Target Diagram*. (The Drawing toolbar should automatically appear; if not, open it.)

3. In the top text placeholder, type **Family**; in the second placeholder, type **Social Structure**; in the third placeholder, type **National Policy**.

4. Change the font of each text item to Arial, size 10, bold, underline.

5. Select the outer segment of the graphic and change the Fill Color to Light Green and the line color to Plum.

6. Select the middle segment and change the Fill Color to Light Yellow and the line color to Plum.

7. Select the center of the graphic and change the Fill Color to Tan and the Line Color to Plum. Deselect the diagram. Your diagram should look like Figure 3.31.

8. Close the Drawing toolbar. Save your changes and close the document.

4 Create Form Letters and Labels

Use Mail Merge to create form letters and labels.

1. Open *Sample Letter* in your *Word Data* folder. Type your name four lines below *Sincerely yours.*

2. Use the Mail Merge Wizard to create form letters, using the *Sample Address* file in your *Word Data* folder as your data source. Enter the appropriate fields in the letter below the date and in the greeting line.

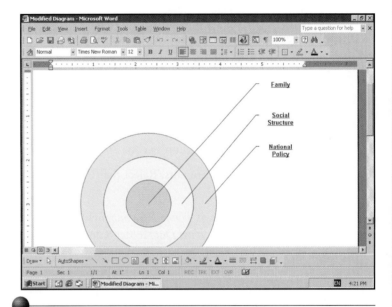

Figure 3.31

3. View the completed letters, and then complete the merge.

4. Merge the letters to a new document. (*Hint:* Click *Edit individual letters* in step 6 of the wizard.)

5. Save your final merged letters as *Sample Letters Merged* in the *Lesson Applications* folder in your *Word Data* folder, then close the document.

6. Close the Mail Merge task pane. Save the *Sample Letter* file as *Sample Letter Fields* in the *Lesson Applications* folder in your *Word Data* folder, then close the document.

7. Open a new blank document, then display the Mail Merge toolbar.

8. Use the Mail Merge toolbar to create labels, using *Sample Address* in your *Word Data* folder as your data source.

9. Insert the appropriate fields for a mailing label, view the labels, and then merge the labels to a new document.

SUMMARY AND EXERCISES

10. Save your final merged labels as *Sample Labels Merged* in the *Lesson Applications* folder in your *Word Data* folder, then close the document.

11. Save the open file as *Sample Labels Fields* in the *Lesson Applications* folder in your *Word Data* folder, and close the document. Close the Mail Merge toolbar.

5 Compare and Merge Documents

Merge two edited documents into the current document. View the Original Showing Markup and reject and accept changes.

1. Open *Home Page Support* in your *Word Data* folder.

2. Merge *Home Page Support-1* from your *Word Data* folder into the current document. (The Reviewing toolbar will automatically appear.)

3. Merge *Home Page Support-2* from your *Word Data* folder into the current document.

4. Choose Original Showing Markup as your Display for Review option.

5. Review the changes and comments. Reject the first change but accept all other changes.

6. Save the revised document as *Home Page Support Compared* in the *Lesson Applications* folder in your *Word Data* folder. Close the document.

6 Track Changes

Activate the Track Changes feature, edit a document, and add a comment.

1. Open *Changes* in your *Word Data* folder and save it as *Changes Edited* in the *Lesson Applications* folder.

2. Turn on the Track Changes feature.

3. Click at the end of the sentence in item 1 and add this comment: **Should we elaborate?**

4. In the paragraph following item number 2, select the word *organizing* and type **organizational.**

5. Turn off the Track Changes feature. Close the Reviewing toolbar.

6. Save your changes and close the document.

7 Use Handwriting

Display the Language bar and use the Handwriting feature to insert a handwritten signature into a letter. Change the size and color of the signature.

1. Open *AHS Workshop* in your *Word Data* folder, and save it as *Writing in Word* in the *Lesson Applications* folder in your *Word Data* folder.

2. Display the Language bar, and use the Writing Pad option to add a handwritten signature *(Mary Martinez)* to the letter.

3. Select the signature and change the font size to 26 and the Font Color to Blue.

4. Close the Writing Pad window. Save your changes and close the document.

8 Complete Additional Voice Training and Use Speech Recognition

Open your profile and complete additional voice training. Use Dictation Mode to enter information into a document, then correct errors using the keyboard. Use Voice Command mode to format your text.

1. Open a new blank document.

2. Select your Recognition Profile in the Speech Properties dialog box and click Train Profile.

3. Select an excerpt in the Voice Training wizard and proceed through the steps in the wizard.

4. After training has been completed, use Dictation mode to enter information about yourself in the open blank document. Dictate your name, age, and describe your street or neighborhood. Describe your favorite hobby.

5. Correct all errors in your document. Use Voice Command mode to format the text attractively with styles, special effects, and color.

6. Minimize the Language bar. Save your document as *Sample Speech* in the *Lesson Applications* folder in your *Word Data* folder, then close the document.

PROJECTS

1 Put It in a Table

You have been asked to prepare a list of names and addresses that may be used later in sending a mass mailing for your company. Create a table with the headings Title, First Name, Last Name, Address, and CSZ. Format the headings attractively. Use AutoFit to Contents, and change the page orientation so the entire table will display in Landscape orientation. Insert six rows of titles, names, addresses, and city/state/Zip information. Save the file as *Mailing Address* in the *Projects* folder in your *Word Data* folder. Close the document.

2 Back to the Table

Open *Mailing Address* (from Project 1) in the *Projects* folder in your *Word Data* folder. (If you have not completed Project 1, open *Mailing Address* in your *Word Data* folder.) Delete the Title column and the last two rows of the table. Increase the height of the heading row, and change the alignment in that row. Apply custom borders and add shading to the table. Save the file as *Mailing Address Revised* in the *Projects* folder in your *Word Data* folder. Insert a row above the first row. Merge the cells in that row, and insert the title **Mass Mailing Addresses**. Save these changes as *Mailing Address Enhanced* in the *Projects* folder of your *Word Data* folder, then close the document.

3 Charting Your Progress

Create a table that shows the numbers of hours you spend studying Monday–Friday, and create a chart from the information. Apply an AutoFormat to the table. Format the chart with a fill color, resize it, and move it. Add a chart title and delete the legend. (*Hint:* Double-click the chart and click Chart Options on the Chart menu.) Display both the table and the chart in your document. Save the document as *Study Chart* in the *Projects* folder in your *Word Data* folder, and close the document.

4 Diagrams, Diagrams

You have been asked to propose a new organization chart for the Sales Department. Create an organization chart. Include appropriate titles and number of positions needed. Format the titles attractively, and then format the entire organization chart. On the second page of the document, create a diagram that shows the Sales Department's relationship with at least three other departments in the company. (*Hint:* You may have to add a shape.) Format the diagram attractively. Save the document as *Organization Diagram* in the *Projects* folder in your *Word Data* folder, and close the document.

5 Caution—Merging Letters and Labels

You have been asked to prepare form letters for a mass mailing that will notify your customers of a change in your business hours. Your office will now be open two hours longer each day. Create a letter that will go to all customers. Use Speech Recognition to dictate and format the letter, and use Handwriting to sign your name at the bottom of the letter. Increase the font size if your signature appears too small. (If you are not able to access Handwriting and Speech Recognition, type the document.) Save the file as *Mailing Letter* in the *Projects* folder in your *Word Data* folder. This will be your main document. Use the Mail Merge Wizard and the Mail Merge toolbar to create form letters and mailing labels. Use *Mailing Address Revised* (from Project 2) in the *Projects* folder in your *Word Data* folder as your source data. (If you did not complete Project 2, use *Mailing Address Revised* in your *Word Data* folder.) Merge the letters and labels to a new document. Save the final merged letters as *Mailing Letter Merged* in the *Projects* folder in your *Word Data* folder. Save the letters showing fields as *Mailing Letter Fields* in the *Projects* folder in your *Word Data* folder. Save the final merged labels file as *Mailing Address Merged* in the *Projects* folder in your *Word Data* folder. Save the label file that shows fields as *Mailing Address Fields* in the *Projects* folder in your *Word Data* folder. Close all files, close the Mail Merge Wizard, and close the Mail Merge toolbar.

6 Track That Document

Open *Writing Workshop* in your *Word Data* folder. Merge both *Writing Workshop-1* and *Writing Workshop-2* into the current document. Review comments and edits and accept and reject changes and comments, as appropriate. Make changes to the document based on the comments, if necessary. Save your final document as *Writing Workshop Compared* in the *Projects* folder in your *Word Data* folder. Reopen *Writing Workshop* in your *Word Data* folder. Activate Track Changes and insert at least three edits and two comments into the document. Save your file as *Writing Workshop Tracked* in the *Projects* folder in your *Word Data* folder then close the document. Close the Reviewing toolbar.

7 Venus on the Web

Your paper about Venus is still in process. Today you've set aside some time to search the Web for information about the planet. Open *Star Gazette Article* in your *Word Data* folder and save it as *Venus Web* in the *Projects* folder in your *Word Data* folder. List keywords from the *Venus* document to define your search in the search engine. (Remember to list words to be excluded from the search.) Visit several of the sites in the search results and add one new site to your list of Favorites. On the basis of the information you read, add a paragraph anywhere in the *Venus* document. Include a footnote to document the information source. Save and close the document.

Project in Progress

8 Word Power

As the owner of Savvy Solutions, a business that provides writing, editing, and training services, you need to get to work creating documents that promote and organize your company.

◆ Create a document that describes your services to potential new customers. In the document, create a table that lists the services you provide in one column and gives information about those services in another column. Format and size the table attractively. Add and delete columns and rows as necessary. Apply an AutoFormat as a starting point, then change it as desired. Customize the borders and shading.

◆ In the same document, create a chart that shows the percentage of work you do in each area. (For instance, what percentage of your business is writing services?) On a new page in the document, create an organization chart for your company. Save the document as *Savvy Solutions Introduction* in the *Projects* folder in your *Word Data* folder.

◆ Use Speech Recognition and Handwriting to create and sign a form letter that you will send to potential new customers. (If you are not able to access Handwriting and Speech Recognition, type the document.) Save the letter as *Savvy Letter* in the *Projects* folder in your *Word Data* folder.

◆ Use Mail Merge to create form letters and mailing labels. Use *Form Address* in your *Word Data* folder as your data source. Merge both letters and labels into a new document. Save the final merged letters as *Savvy Letter Merged* in the *Projects* folder in your *Word Data* folder. Save the letters showing fields as *Savvy Letter Fields* in the *Projects* folder in your *Word Data* folder. Save the final merged labels as *Savvy Mailing Labels Merged* in the *Projects* folder in your *Word Data* folder. Save the label file that shows fields as *Savvy Mailing Labels Fields* in the *Projects* folder in your *Word Data* folder.

◆ When you are done, close all files. Have someone else review copies of both your letter and the document you created. Ask the person to track changes, then compare and merge documents with your originals. Review and accept or reject comments and edits. Make any necessary changes based on the feedback provided.

LESSON 4

Creating Web Pages

CONTENTS

OBJECTIVES

After you complete this lesson, you will be able to do the following:

- Save a Word document as a Web page.
- Plan the purpose and structure of your Web page.
- Create a Web page with a Word Web page template.
- Edit text and hypertext.
- Change text and background colors.
- Format a hyperlink.
- Insert a graphic and a graphic hyperlink.
- Apply a theme to a Web page.
- Work with smart tags.
- Create a multiple-page Web site using Word's Web Page Wizard.
- Work with frames pages.
- Preview a Web site in Internet Explorer.
- Explain how to publish a Web site to the Internet.

MOUS Objectives
In this lesson:
W2002-6-3
See Appendix D.

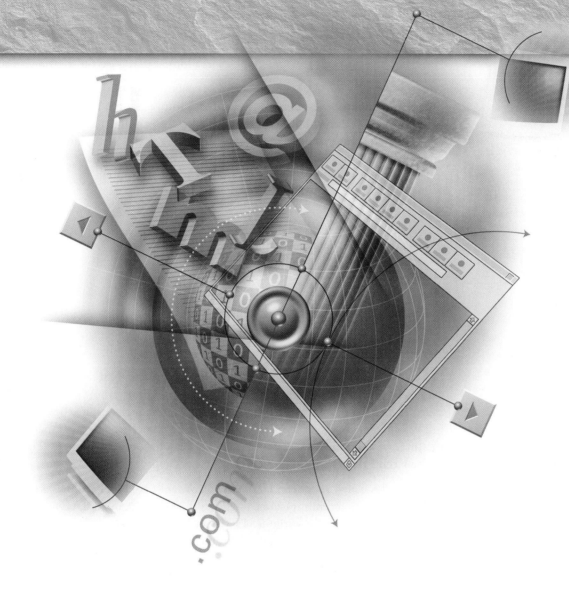

SAVING A WORD DOCUMENT AS A WEB PAGE

As you have seen by browsing the Web, people create and publish Web pages for a variety of reasons. Companies often publish Web pages to promote their products or services or to provide customer support. Other organizations provide general types of information, such as the weather, news, or flight schedules. Many individuals create Web pages to provide personal and professional information, to support a hobby, or to communicate ideas.

You already have some experience viewing Web sites and navigating over the Internet. The Internet is a worldwide network of computers that allows users to share information in the form of text, graphics, images, video, and audio. A **network** is a collection of computers that permits the transfer of data and programs between users. In a sense, the Internet is a *super network*. The World Wide Web is a part of the Internet that connects specially formatted documents called Web pages. A Web site or Web is a collection of individual Web pages that usually share a common theme and are connected by navigation links. Within the group of pages that make up a Web, the **home** or **start page** is the first page in the navigation structure and is usually given the file name *index.htm* or *default.htm*. Web pages are accessed by a Web browser, such as Internet Explorer or Netscape Navigator, that displays text and graphics in a format that is easy to view and read.

You can save any Word document as a Web page and publish it on an organization's intranet or on the Internet. (You'll recall from Lesson 2 that an *intranet* is a private, Web-like network for communicating within an organization.) Of course, you would not want to publish just any document to the Web. So what kinds of documents are good candidates? A Word document should have several of the following characteristics before you consider it to be appropriate for a Web page:

◆ A large potential readership or audience

◆ A significant volume of information

◆ Frequently changing information

◆ No secured or confidential information

◆ Hyperlinks

◆ Graphics files (pictures, sound clips, or motion clips)

◆ Cost and time savings to publish the information as a Web page (as opposed to producing a print version)

Before you publish a Web page, you must save your document in a form the Web can read. Web pages are written in a page description format or underlying code called **Hypertext Markup Language (HTML),** which includes the codes for linking Web documents to each other. A **Web server** has a permanent connection to the Internet and publishes documents so they can be viewed by others. The Web server accepts requests from browsers and returns appropriate HTML documents.

A set of rules called **Hypertext Transfer Protocol** (or **HTTP**) allows a browser and Web server to communicate and allows the exchange of all data on the Web. The Web would not exist without HTML and HTTP. A Word user, though, does not need to know HTML or HTTP to create a Web page. You can use simple Word commands to code an ordinary Word document with HTML and HTTP.

HANDS on

Enhancing and Saving a Document as a Web Page

In this activity, you will change the font attributes in a document and save the document as a Web page.

1. Open *Web Address List* in your *Word Data* folder. Point to **Toolbars** on the View menu and click **Web** to display the Web toolbar.

2. Select the heading (the first two lines in the document, including the bullet and lines). Change the font to Arial, the size to 18, and the font color to blue.

3. Select the next three lines (*Updated* through *Updated Web Addresses*) and change the text to Arial, size 14, plum.

4. Change the two-sentence paragraph to Times New Roman, bold, size 12, pink.

5. Deselect the text. Click **Save as Web Page** on the File menu.

The Save As dialog box opens. The file type automatically appears as *Web Page* in the *Save as type* box. Word will code the file as an HTML document.

6. Navigate to the *Tutorial* folder in your *Word Data* folder.

The *Tutorial* folder appears empty. No files are listed in the window because you have no Web Page file types in the *Tutorial* folder.

7. Save the document as *Textra Web Page* in the *Tutorial* folder.

Your document is now a Web page, as shown in Figure 4.1. Word has switched automatically to Web Layout View 📄. The New Blank Document button 📄 on the Standard toolbar becomes the New Web Page button 📄.

Saving a Document as a Web Page

1. Click Save as Web Page on the File menu.

2. In the Save As dialog box, navigate to the location where you wish to save your document.

3. Type a name in the File name box.

4. Click Save.

WORD 2002

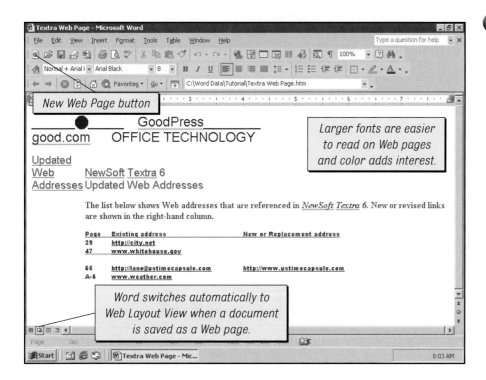

Figure 4.1
Word document saved as a Web page

8. Close the document.

9. Click the **Open button** 📄 and navigate to the *Tutorial* folder in your *Word Data* folder. Click the **Files of type triangle button** and click **All Files**, if necessary.

Scroll through the Open dialog box until you find the *Textra Web Page* file. A Web icon 📄 appears behind the Microsoft Word icon for the *Textra Web Page* file. From the icon you can tell that this file is a Web page.

10. Click **Cancel** to close the Open dialog box.

PLANNING AND CREATING A WEB PAGE

Before you create a Web page, you should plan the content and layout. Decide on the basic elements that you want to include in your Web page by answering the following questions:

◆ What is the purpose or focus of my Web page(s)?

◆ Do other sites exist that give the same information? If so, how can I make my Web page unique?

◆ Who is my audience? What can I include to make visitors want to return to my site?

◆ Do I want or need to include more than one page? If so, what information appears on each page? Should the pages be linked?

◆ Do I want or need to link to outside (external) Web sites? If so, what is the URL for each of those sites?

Remember that after you publish a Web page, anyone who has access to the Internet will be able to read your page. Therefore, do not include information that you would not want the public to know. For example, you may provide your e-mail address rather than your telephone number for readers who may want to contact you. (You might even consider using an e-mail address that doesn't include your full name.)

> **WARNING** *Even though activities in this lesson involve the creation of a personal Web page, you may decide it is a good idea to avoid publishing your actual name, address, and other personal information on the Internet. Seek professional advice in regard to this issue.*

Word simplifies the process of creating a Web page. You can create a Web page by using a Web page template. Most Web page templates involve one page and have a table of contents with links to various parts of the page. You can use the blank Web page template to add pages to your Web site. Then you can insert a hyperlink to link the new and existing pages.

HANDS on

Using a Web Page Template

Like the other templates you have used, the *Personal Web Page* template contains prompts (or placeholder text) that you replace. Thus, the placeholder text in the template reminds you to include the kinds of information visitors to your home page expect, such as biographical and contact information and information about your career and interests. In this activity, you will use the *Personal Web Page* template to create a Web page.

1. Click **New** on the File menu.

2. Click **General Templates** in the New Document task pane. Click the **Web Pages tab** in the Templates dialog box.

The Web Pages tab appears as shown in Figure 4.2.

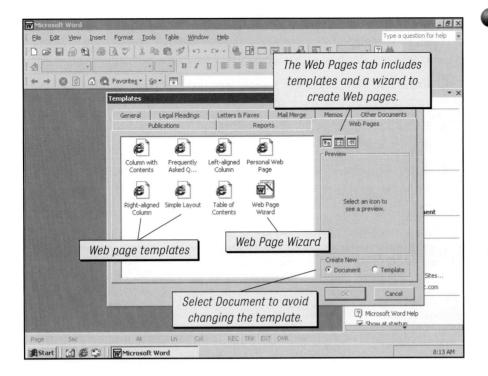

Figure 4.2
Web Pages tab of the
Templates dialog box

The Web Pages tab includes templates and a wizard to create Web pages.

Web page templates

Web Page Wizard

Select Document to avoid changing the template.

Word **BASICS**

Using a Web Page Template

1. Click New on the File menu.

2. Click General Templates in the New Document task pane.

3. Click the Web Pages tab in the Templates dialog box.

4. Click a Web Page template.

5. Under Create New, verify that Document is selected.

6. Click OK.

7. Replace the placeholder text.

3. **Click the Personal Web Page icon. In the *Create New* section of the dialog box, select Document, if necessary, and click OK.**

The document is already a Web page (see Figure 4.3). The template has different fonts and styles along with links. The document window is in Web Layout View 🖻 and the New Web Page button 🔲 appears on the Standard toolbar.

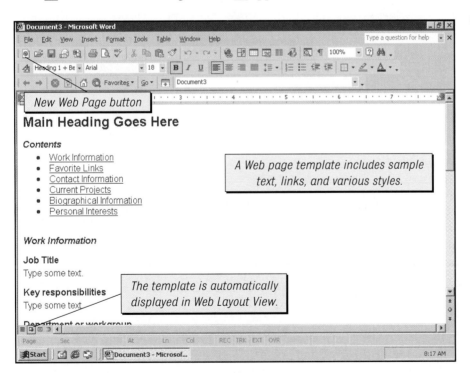

New Web Page button

Main Heading Goes Here

Contents

- Work Information
- Favorite Links
- Contact Information
- Current Projects
- Biographical Information
- Personal Interests

Work Information

Job Title
Type some text.

Key responsibilities
Type some text

A Web page template includes sample text, links, and various styles.

The template is automatically displayed in Web Layout View.

Figure 4.3
Personal Web Page template

4. **Scroll the page noting the various content areas, the styles, and the links that are included in the *Personal Web Page* template.**

NORTON
ONLINE

Visit **www.glencoe.com/norton/online/** for more information on creating a Web page.

5. Select **Main Heading Goes Here** at the top of the page and type a main heading in this style: Welcome to Dorinda's Home Page (replacing *Dorinda* with your name, of course).

6. Under *Job Title,* select the placeholder text and type the title of your current job or a job you plan to hold in the future.

7. Under *Key responsibilities,* replace the placeholder text with a list of your current (or future) job duties.

8. Under *Department or workgroup,* replace the placeholder text with your information.

Your document should resemble Figure 4.4.

Figure 4.4
Sample text replaced with your information

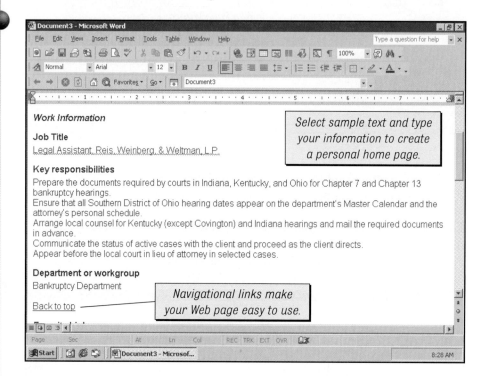

NOTE *If you want to include more than one job, copy all information for the current job and paste it below the information for the first job. Then edit the second entry appropriately.*

9. Save the document in this style: *Dorinda's Home Page* (replacing *Dorinda* with your name) in the *Tutorial* folder in your *Word Data* folder.

Word saves the document as a Web page automatically because you opened a Web page template. Now you will continue creating text on your Web page, including links to other Web sites.

10. Under *Favorite Links,* select **Insert a hyperlink here** and type www.glencoe.com and press Spacebar .

Word applies HTML to the Web addresses you typed and inserts hyperlinks automatically. You do not need to use the Insert Hyperlink button .

NOTE *If the hyperlink coding doesn't appear in your document, click AutoCorrect Options on the Tools menu. On the* AutoFormat As You Type *tab, verify that a check mark appears in the* Internet and network paths with hyperlinks *option. Click OK. Repeat step 10.*

11. Insert two additional URLs for your favorite sites.

12. Under *E-mail address*, replace the placeholder text with a real or fictitious e-mail address. Under *Web address*, replace the placeholder text with a fictitious URL. Under *Office phone*, replace the placeholder text with an area code and telephone number.

13. Under *Current Projects*, replace the placeholder text with the name of a project you are involved in at home, school, or work—for example, *Creating a personal Web page*.

14. Under *Biographical Information*, replace the placeholder text with a paragraph or more about your life. Under *Personal Interests*, replace each bulleted item with one of your interests.

15. Type the current date in the last line of the document, as shown in Figure 4.5.

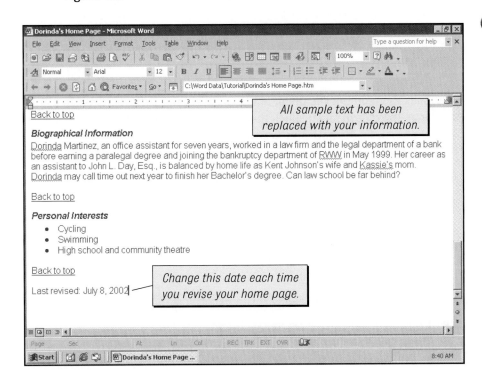

Figure 4.5
Sample Web page from the Personal Web Page template

NOTE *If you decide to use the Insert Date and Time command (Insert menu), deselect the Update automatically check box. Otherwise, individuals visiting your Web site will always see the current date instead of the date when you last updated the site.*

16. Save your changes and close the document.

DEVELOPING A PERSONAL WEB PAGE

After you develop the basic elements of your home page, you should get into the habit of editing the page to ensure quality and accuracy. You may also wish to make your text more appealing or easier to read by changing the font, font size, and/or color. Often you will need to insert links to navigate through your Web site. The addition of an image and a background color, texture, or pattern can also make your Web page more attractive.

HANDS on

Editing Text and Hypertext

If your document will be published on the Internet, remember that virtually anyone with access to a computer and a phone line may view it. The high visibility of a Web page suggests the need for very careful editing. You may also want to insert navigational links. A typical navigational link will jump from a table of contents to another area of the Web page. Word's **bookmark** feature allows you to mark a specific spot in the text then create a hyperlink to it so you can return to it quickly and easily.

In this activity, you will edit the home page you created in the last activity and insert a bookmark and a bookmark hyperlink.

1. Click **Open** on the File menu and navigate to the *Tutorial* folder in your *Word Data* folder. Click the **Files of type triangle button** then click **Web Pages and Web Archives** to view just the Web folders and files.

2. Open *Your Name's Home Page* and save it as *Your Name's Home Page Revised* (replacing *Your Name* with your name) in the same folder.

3. Under *Contents,* click immediately after Work Information and press Ctrl + ⇧ Shift + ←. Type over *Information* to change the link to Work Experience.

4. Edit Favorite Links to read Favorite Hyperlinks.

5. Press Ctrl and click **Work Experience**.

Word jumps to the bookmark—the *Work Information* heading.

6. Edit the heading to match the display text for the link (*Work Experience*).

7. Click the **Back button** ⇐ on the Web toolbar to return to the *Contents* section at the top of the page.

8. Press Ctrl and click **Favorite Hyperlinks**. Edit the bookmark to match the display for the link. Go back to *Contents*.

9. Point to the right of the bullet that precedes Work Experience. When the ScreenTip box appears, click. The insertion point will be

WEB NOTE

To learn more about Web page style and design, point your browser to the Yale Style Manual at **http://info.med.yale.edu/ caim/manual/**.

Word BASICS

Inserting a Bookmark

1. Select the text at the location where you want your bookmark.

2. Click Bookmark on the Insert menu then type a Bookmark name and click Add.

3. Select the hyperlink text and click the Insert Hyperlink button.

4. Click Place in This Document, then click the bookmark, and click OK.

set in front of <u>Work Experience</u>. Press $\boxed{\text{Enter}\leftarrow}$ to add a new bulleted line, press $\boxed{\uparrow}$, and type Educational Background after the new bullet.

10. Click after <u>Personal Interests</u>, press $\boxed{\text{Enter}\leftarrow}$ twice, and type Educational Background. Then, press $\boxed{\text{Enter}\leftarrow}$ and press $\boxed{\downarrow}$.

11. Below the *Educational Background* heading, type your education history. On one line, type the name of the school you are currently attending, followed by the city and state where it is located. On the next line, type the name of the degree you will receive and your anticipated graduation date. (If you do not plan to earn a degree, list another fact, such as courses you have taken.) On the following line(s), type the name(s) of schools attended previously, including high school, the city and state of each one, and the date you graduated or left. Add bold to the names of the schools.

At this point, your home page should resemble Figure 4.6.

HINTS & TIPS

You can add special symbols and characters to Web pages or any Word document. Click Symbol on the Insert menu. Click the Symbols tab or the Special Characters Tab. Click the character or symbol, click Insert, and then click Close.

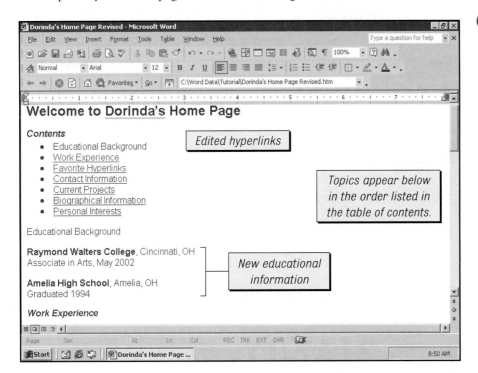

Figure 4.6
Educational Background section

Now you will add a bookmark hyperlink so visitors to your home page can jump directly to the *Educational Background* section from the *Contents*.

NOTE *Though a bookmark name may contain numbers, the name must begin with a letter. Do not include spaces in a bookmark name—instead press the Underline button* $\boxed{\text{U}}$ *between words.*

12. Click anywhere in the *Educational Background* heading (not the bulleted item). Click **Bookmark** on the Insert menu. In the Bookmark dialog box, type Educational_Background as the bookmark name, then click **Add**.

13. Select **Educational Background** in the bulleted Contents list and click the **Insert Hyperlink button** .

14. Under *Link to,* click **Place in This Document**. Under *Select a place in this document,* click the plus sign (+) to expand Bookmarks if necessary; then click **Educational_Background**, as shown in Figure 4.7. Click **OK**.

Figure 4.7
Linking to a bookmark

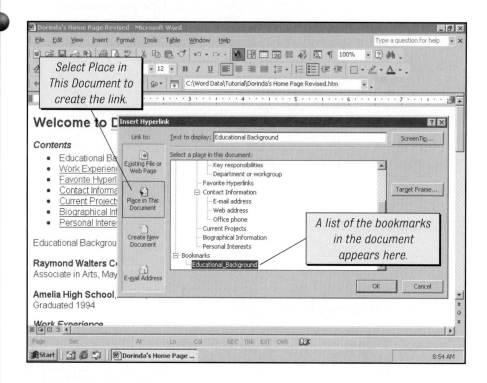

15. Test the new link by pressing Ctrl and clicking **Educational Background** in the bulleted Contents list.

Word jumps to the bookmark location and the text color of the hyperlink changes color to indicate you have followed the link.

16. Save your changes and close the document.

HANDS on

Changing Text and Background Colors

Since your home page represents you, its appearance should match your personality or the image you want to project. Colors, graphics, and font choices can depict you as easygoing or serious and practical. You can enhance a Web page by varying the alignment and the style, size, and color of text using the same commands you use for Word documents. You can also add a contrasting background color along with an interesting texture or a pattern. In working with colors, remember that too many colors can be distracting. You want to draw attention primarily to the content of your Web page, not the design of the page. As you change colors, make sure the text colors contrast with the

background. (**Contrast** is the difference in brightness between dark and light areas of a page.) If you choose a dark blue background, for example, choose a light color for the text. In this activity, you will enhance the appearance of your home page and add a background color.

1. Open *Your Name's Home Page Revised* in the *Tutorial* folder in your *Word Data* folder and save it as *Your Name's Home Page-Color* (replacing *Your Name* with your name) in the same folder.

NOTE *In the Open dialog box, click* Web Pages and Web Archives *in the* Files of type *list to view only the Web folders and files. This will make it easier to locate your Web page. When you want to view all your documents, click* All Files *in the* Files of type *list.*

2. Select the main heading at the top of the page. Change the text to font size 24 and the font color to bright green.

3. Select **Contents** and change the font size to 16 and font color to bright green. Select the bulleted items under *Contents* and change the font to Times New Roman, size 13, bold.

4. Select the **Educational Background heading**, change the font color to bright green, and add bold and italic styles. Change the text items under *Educational Background* to Times New Roman, size 13, white. Click the document.

NOTE *The white text disappears on the white background, as shown in Figure 4.8, but will be visible again when you change the background color.*

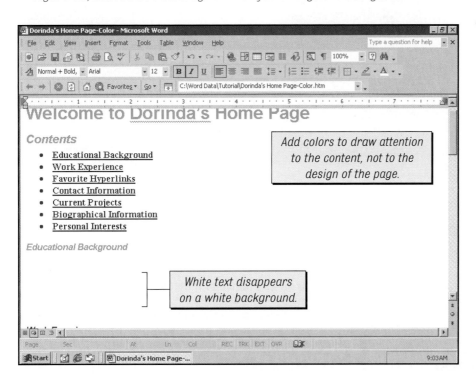

Figure 4.8
Enhancing text

5. Select the last line of text (including the date) and change the font to Times New Roman, size 10, white.

6. Change the font color of each remaining heading to bright green.

7. Change the bulleted items under *Current Projects* and *Personal Interests* to Times New Roman, yellow.

8. Under *Favorite Hyperlinks,* change the hyperlinks to Times New Roman, size 13, bold.

9. Change all body text to Times New Roman, size 13, and white.

10. Change the e-mail address and Web address to Times New Roman, size 13, bold.

Now you will change the background color.

11. Click the **Format menu** and point to **Background**.

The Background color menu (including a color palette) appears.

12. Click the **Blue-Gray** color on the palette.

The blue-gray background is applied, and the white and yellow text on your home page is now visible, as shown in Figure 4.9.

Figure 4.9
Color-enhanced home page

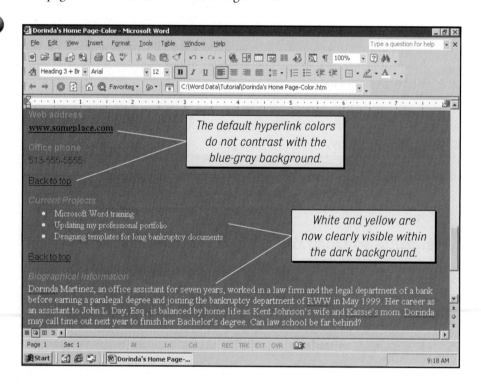

13. Save the updated home page and close the document.

HANDS on

Formatting a Hyperlink

Have you ever visited a Web site where you had trouble reading the text, especially the hypertext, because the text blended into the background? If so, you realize the importance of contrast, the difference in brightness between the light and dark areas of the Web page. In Word, the default color for hypertext is blue. After you follow a hyperlink, the color of the link changes to purple. You can change the default hyperlink colors, if necessary.

In this activity, you will change the hyperlink colors on your Web page.

1. Open *Your Name's Home Page-Color* in the *Tutorial* folder in your *Word Data* folder and save it as *Your Name's Home Page-Color Revised* (replacing *Your Name* with your name) in the same folder.

2. Click **Styles and Formatting** on the Format menu. Click the **Show triangle button** at the bottom of the Styles and Formatting task pane, then click **All styles**.

3. Scroll through the *Pick formatting to apply* box, then point to **Hyperlink**.

Both the character preview in the box and the description in the ScreenTip indicate that the hypertext is Times New Roman, underlined, blue.

4. Click the **Hyperlink triangle button** , and click **Modify**. In the Modify Style dialog box, click the **Format button**.

The Format menu appears, as shown in Figure 4.10.

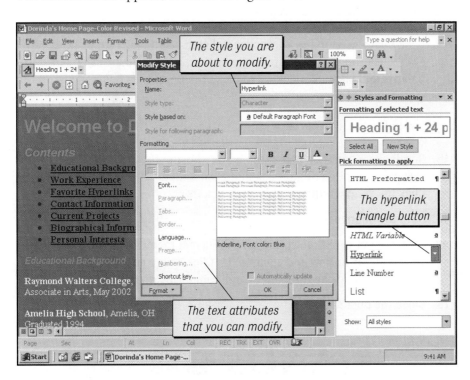

Word BASICS

Changing Hyperlink Colors

1. Click Styles and Formatting on the Format menu.

2. In the Styles and Formatting task pane, click All styles in the Show box.

3. In the *Pick formatting to apply* box, point to *Hyperlink* or *FollowedHyperlink* and click the triangle button.

4. Click Modify on the shortcut menu.

5. In the Modify Style dialog box, click the Format button and click Font.

6. Click the desired font color in the Font dialog box, then click OK.

7. Preview the color in the Modify Style dialog box and click OK.

Figure 4.10
Modify Style dialog box with Format menu displayed

5. Click **Font**. In the Font dialog box, change the font color to yellow. Click **OK**.

The preview window in the Modify Style dialog box shows yellow hyperlinks applied on a white background. Although this is not a clear contrast in the preview window, yellow will be visible on the dark background of your Web page.

6. Click **OK** in the Modify Style dialog box.

Did you know?

To insert picture bullets into your Web page, select the bulleted items and click Bullets and Numbering on the Format menu. Click Customize and then click Picture to find the picture bullet selections.

The Modify Style dialog box closes and the hyperlinks appear yellow in your Web page.

7. Scroll in the *Pick formatting to apply* box, then point to **FollowedHyperlink**. Click the **triangle button** , then click **Modify**.

8. In the Modify Style dialog box, click **Format** and then click **Font**.

9. Change the font color to Gray-25%. Click **OK**.

10. Click **OK** to close the Modify Style dialog box. Close the Styles and Formatting task pane.

11. Press Ctrl and click a yellow hyperlink in the Contents section.

12. Press Ctrl and click the nearest **Back to top** hyperlink.

The hyperlink that you followed in the Contents section appears light gray. You notice that the black bullets in the *Contents* section of the Web page are distracting.

13. Select all the bulleted items under *Contents,* and click **Bullets and Numbering** on the Format menu.

The Bullets and Numbering dialog box appears. The bullet style option used in the bullet list is automatically selected.

14. Click **Customize**. In the Customize Bulleted List dialog box, click **Font**. Click the **Font color triangle button**, click **yellow** on the palette, and click **OK**. Click **OK** to close the Customize Bulleted List dialog box.

The yellow bullets contrast nicely with the background.

15. Scroll down and then select the bulleted list in the *Favorite Hyperlinks* section. Right-click and click **Bullets and Numbering**. Click the **yellow bullet option** and click **OK**.

16. Save the changes.

17. Click **Bullets and Numbering** on the Format menu. Click the **yellow bullet option** and click **Reset**. Click **Yes** to reset the bullet options. Then, close the Bullets and Numbering dialog box.

18. Close the document.

NORTON ONLINE

Visit **www.glencoe.com/norton/online/** for more information on hyperlinks.

HANDS on

Inserting a Graphic and Graphic Hyperlink

Most Web pages have graphics incorporated into their designs. You can add graphics to your Web page to complement or replace text, or you can make a graphic into a hyperlink to lead to a bookmark or other Web resource. Sometimes after inserting a hyperlink, you may need to edit or remove the link. The Edit Hyperlink dialog box allows you to change the destination for an established hyperlink. You can also remove a hyperlink without removing the image that holds it. In this activity, you will insert an image at the top of your home page and then create and remove a graphic hyperlink.

1. Open *Your Name's Home Page-Color Revised* in the *Tutorial* folder in your *Word Data* folder and save it as *Your Name's Home Page-Image Link* (replacing *Your Name* with your name) in the same folder.

2. Click an insertion point in front of the *Contents* heading at the beginning of your Web page.

3. Point to **Picture** on the Insert menu and click **Clip Art**. Search for an appropriate image in the Insert Clip Art task pane or click **Clip Organizer** or **Clips Online** at the bottom of the task pane to browse for an image. Insert an image and arrange it attractively on your home page.

NOTE *You may also insert a drawing or a WordArt image. If you want to insert a personal photograph, ask your instructor for help with a digital camera or a scanner. You may also want to review the information on inserting clip art in Lesson 2 or explore Help for information on WordArt and drawings.*

4. Verify that the Web page heading and image complement each other. Edit the heading text and/or the image as desired.

5. Open *My Bio* in your *Word Data* folder. Using this document as a template, customize the text to be compatible with your Web page. Save the document in the *Tutorial* folder as *Your Name's Bio* (replacing *Your Name* with your name). Save and close the document.

Now you will insert a graphic hyperlink.

6. Click the image you just inserted in your Web page. Click the **Insert Hyperlink button** 📧 on the Standard toolbar.

The Insert Hyperlink dialog box opens.

7. In the *Link* to section, click **Existing File or Web Page**.

8. In the *Look in* box, navigate to the *Tutorial* folder in your *Word Data* folder and click *Your Name's Bio.*

9. Click the **ScreenTip button**, type Your Name's Bio, as shown in Figure 4.11, and click **OK**.

10. Click **OK** in the Insert Hyperlink dialog box, then save your changes.

11. Point to the image in your document to view the ScreenTip (*Your Name's Bio CTRL + click to follow link*).

12. Press ⌷Ctrl⌷ and click the image.

Word **BASICS**

Inserting a Clip Art Graphic and a Graphic Hyperlink

To insert a graphic:

1. Place the insertion point where you want the graphic to appear.

2. Point to Picture on the Insert menu and click Clip Art.

3. Search for an appropriate image in the Clip Art task pane.

To insert a graphic hyperlink:

1. Select the object.

2. Click the Insert Hyperlink button.

3. Click an appropriate *Link to* button in the Insert Hyperlink dialog box.

4. Type the URL in the Address box or select a file or page from the list.

5. Click the ScreenTip button, type the ScreenTip text, and click OK.

To edit a graphic hyperlink:

1. Click the graphic, then click Hyperlink on the Insert menu.

2. In the Edit Hyperlink dialog box, click Remove Link then type the link for the desired page, file, or Web site and click OK.

WORD 2002

Figure 4.11
Set Hyperlink ScreenTip box

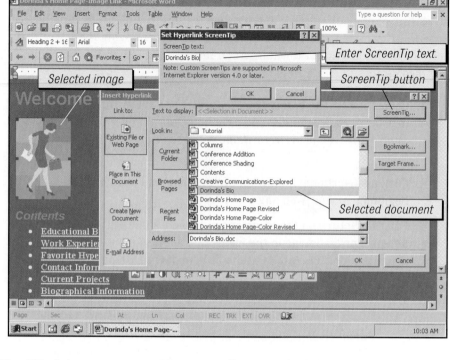

Your Word document opens. Now you will remove the link to this document.

13. Close *Your Name's Bio* without saving changes and save your Web page document as *Your Name's Home Page-Image Link Removed* (replacing *Your Name* with your name) in the *Tutorial* folder in your *Word Data* folder.

14. Right-click the image and click **Edit Hyperlink**.

15. In the Edit Hyperlink box, click the **Remove Link button**. Point to the image and note that the ScreenTip does not appear.

NOTE You can also change the hyperlink in the Edit Hyperlink dialog box if you want to link to a different page, file, or Web site.

16. Go to the top of your Web page. Check the overall appearance of the Web page and test all the links.

17. Save and close the document.

WEB NOTE

For free clip art and an online chat forum to answer your questions, visit the Clip Art Connection at **www.clipartconnection.com**.

HANDS on

Applying a Theme to a Web Page

You can enhance a Web page by applying a theme. A **theme** is a set of unified designs and colors for the background, bullets, fonts, and lines. A theme gives your document a finished look. When you apply a theme, Word customizes the background color or graphic, body text and heading styles, bullets, horizontal lines, hyperlink colors, and table border color. As you select a theme to apply, you can modify the colors, graphics, and background by selecting or deselecting three options: Vivid Colors, Active Graphics, and

Background Image. If you deselect all three options, you will use a few basic colors, flat bullets and lines, and a plain background. If you select all three options, your Web page will have more, brighter colors; 3-D bullets and lines; and a textured or figured background. In this activity, you will apply a theme to a Web page.

1. Open *Textra Web Page* in the *Tutorial* folder and save the file as *Theme* in the same folder.

2. Place your insertion point a few lines below the end of the document. Type Other Software Titles, then format this text as Times New Roman, size 12. Click at the end of this line and press ⌜Enter←⌟.

3. Type each of the following items on a separate line (in Times New Roman, size 12): Word Processing, Spreadsheet, Database, Internet, Operating System, E-mail, Presentations, Scheduling. Alphabetize the list of items and add bullets.

4. Click **Theme** on the Format menu.

The Theme dialog box appears.

5. In the *Choose a Theme* box, click and preview various themes, as shown in Figure 4.12, until you find one that you like.

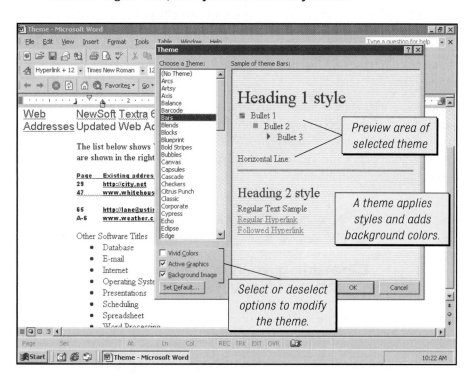

Figure 4.12
Theme dialog box

Your theme appears in the Preview window, showing font colors, bullet designs, and background.

6. Clear all three check boxes: Vivid Colors, Active Graphics, and Background Image. Then select all three options and note the changes in the preview as each option is selected. Click **OK**.

The theme is applied to the current document.

7. Select the column headings *Page, Existing Address,* and *New or Replacement address.* Change the font size to 12 so that all the text fits on one line.

8. Save and close the document.

USING THE WEB PAGE WIZARD

Word offers another tool to create a Web page: the Web Page Wizard. As you learned in Lesson 3, a *wizard* is a tool that helps you create a document by offering a series of step-by-step content and organization choices. Thus, the Web Page Wizard guides you through the process of creating a Web site. Through a series of dialog boxes, you answer questions by selecting options or typing a response. Questions include the title and location of the Web site; the type of navigation; the number and organization of pages; and the visual theme to be applied. Clicking the Finish button tells the wizard to generate your Web site and to display it in the Word window.

You have undoubtedly noticed that some Web page designs include a contents or navigation section with hyperlinks. This section often appears consistently on every page of the Web and allows you to navigate the site regardless of the page you are on. Such Web pages usually appear within frames. **Frames** are sections of a page separated by borders or scroll bars. Some framed Web pages allow you to adjust the size of each frame by dragging the frame border. A **frames page** contains two or more frames.

Through the Web Page Wizard, you can use a frame for navigation. You can use frames in your Web pages to organize information and to provide navigation links within your site. Even after you create a Web site with the Web Page Wizard, you can add frames pages and you can change the frame properties with the Frames command on the Format menu.

HANDS on

Creating a Web Page With the Wizard

In this activity, you will use the Web Page Wizard to create a multiple-page Web site.

1. Click **New** on the File menu, if necessary, to open the New Document task pane. Then click **General Templates**.

2. In the Templates dialog box, click the **Web Pages tab**, then click **Web Page Wizard**.

3. Under *Create New*, verify that **Document** is selected and click **OK**.

The opening window of the Web Page Wizard appears. The Web Page Wizard guides you through the steps necessary to create a multiple-page Web site. Each time you click the Next button, Word will display a new tip in the Wizard window. As you advance through each new step in the wizard, read the tip before you select options in the dialog box. It is also a good idea to activate Help and read the changing message in the Help balloon.

4. Click the Microsoft Word Help button ⟨?⟩ **in the dialog box and read the Office Assistant tip (see Figure 4.13).**

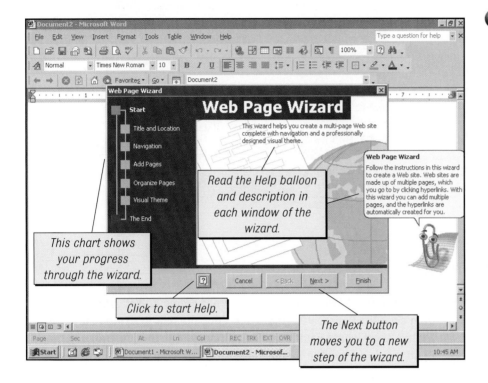

Figure 4.13
Web Page Wizard dialog box

Word BASICS

Using the Web Page Wizard

1. Click New on the File menu.

2. Click General Templates in the New Document task pane.

3. Click the Web Pages tab in the Templates dialog box.

4. Under Create New, verify that Document is selected.

5. Click Web Page Wizard and click OK.

6. Click Next and follow the prompts in each dialog box.

5. Click Next.

The Title and Location dialog box appears.

6. Type Anderson Village Association in the Web site title box.

As you type the Web site title, the wizard adds the same words to the *Web site location* box to create a folder for the Web site files.

7. Verify the path in the *Web site location* box.

NOTE *If the* Web site location *box does not show the correct path for your* Tutorial *folder, click the Browse button and navigate to the* Tutorial *folder in your* Word Data *folder. Click Open. Then after* Tutorial *in the* Web site location *box, type* **Anderson Village Association.**

8. Click Next.

The Navigation dialog box lets you choose where to place navigation hyperlinks: in a vertical frame at the left, on a horizontal frame at the top of the page, or on a separate page.

9. Click Vertical frame, if necessary, then click Next.

NORTON ONLINE

Visit **www.glencoe.com/norton/online/** for more information on using the Web Page Wizard.

· ·

The Add Pages dialog box lets you add pages to the Web site; remove pages from the site; and/or import a Word file into your Web page (see Figure 4.14).

Figure 4.14
Add Pages dialog box

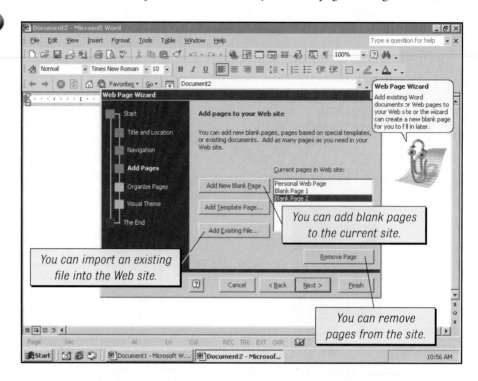

You can add blank pages
to the current site.

You can import an existing
file into the Web site.

You can remove
pages from the site.

10. Select **Personal Web Page** in the *Current pages in Web site* box, then click the **Remove Page button**. Click the **Add Existing File button**, then locate your *Word Data* folder in the Open dialog box. Open the *Anderson* file then click **Next** in the wizard.

In the Organize Pages dialog box, you will rearrange the three pages and change their names.

11. Click **Anderson**; then click the **Move Up button** twice. With *Anderson* still selected, click the **Rename button**. In the Rename Hyperlink dialog box, type Board of Trustees and click **OK**.

The name change appears in the list. You will now give the blank pages meaningful names.

12. Click **Blank Page 1**, click the **Rename button**, type Meetings, and click **OK**. Click **Blank Page 2**, click the **Rename button**, type Community Manager, and click **OK**.

The Web Page Wizard dialog box should resemble Figure 4.15.

13. Click **Next**.

In the Visual Theme dialog box, you will select a theme to apply to your Web site.

14. Click the **Browse Themes button**. In the Choose a Theme box, click **Nature** to preview the sample. Select all three check boxes if they

WEB NOTE

Many businesses use sophisticated programs to create and manage Web sites. Take a tour of Microsoft FrontPage at **www.microsoft.com/frontpage/**. Learn about Macromedia Dreamweaver at **macromedia.com/software/ dreamweaver/**.

are not already selected: **Vivid Colors**, **Active Graphics**, and **Background Image**. Click **OK**, then click **Next**.

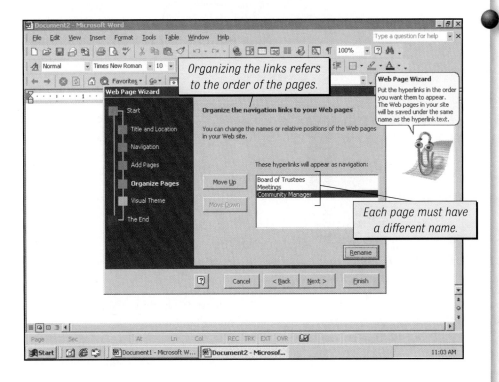

Figure 4.15
Organize Pages dialog box

You have supplied all the information that the Web Page Wizard needs to create your Web site.

15. Click Finish.

After a few moments, the pages appear in reverse order in rapid succession. Finally, the Web site and the Frames toolbar appear on your screen.

16. Click Open 📂 **and navigate to the *Tutorial* folder in your *Word Data* folder.**

The Web Page Wizard created a folder called *Anderson Village Association* in the *Tutorial* folder.

17. Double-click the *Anderson Village Association* folder then examine its contents.

The wizard saved each of the pages of the Web site you just created in the *Anderson Village Association* folder in the *Tutorial* folder. Also, each page has a folder that contains HTML files. You do not need to open these individual folders. You must keep them, however, for they contain the information that makes the hyperlinks work.

18. Click Cancel to close the Open dialog box then close your Web document.

Working With Smart Tags

You can save time by using smart tags to perform tasks in Word that would otherwise require you to minimize the Word window and open another program. **Smart tags** appear in a document when Word recognizes certain types of data. Purple dotted lines in a document are smart tag indicators. Point to these indicators to reveal an embedded icon leading to various options.

In this activity, you will explore Help to learn about smart tags and the actions you can perform with smart tags.

1. Type smart tags in the Ask a Question box, press [Enter←], and click the **About smart tags** topic. Scroll down, click *How to use smart tags* in the Help pane, and read the information.

2. Close the Help window, then open a new blank document.

3. Type today's date, press [Enter←] twice, type your street address, then press [Enter←].

Purple dotted lines (smart tag indicators) appear below both lines of text indicating the presence of a hidden smart tag.

4. Point to the date, and click the **Smart Tag Actions button** when it appears, to display the shortcut menu shown in Figure 4.16.

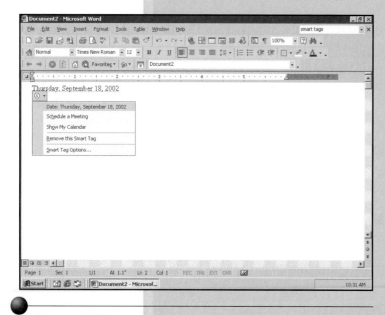

Notice that you can click to schedule a meeting or to view your calendar. You can perform these actions while in Word instead of having to open Microsoft Outlook.

Figure 4.16
Smart tag actions
shortcut menu

5. Click a blank area of the document to close the menu. Point to your address, click the **Smart Tag Actions button**, and view the options on the shortcut menu.

6. Click **Display Map**.

Your Web browser opens, and loads the *Expedia.com* Web site. You were able to perform this action in Word instead of having to open your Web browser and go to the maps site.

7. Close your browser. Close your document without saving the changes.

HANDS on

Editing Frames Pages

After you create a Web page using the Web Page Wizard, you should review the overall appearance of the site and edit as desired to achieve the look you want. In this activity, you will work with frames in the *Anderson Village Association* Web site you just created.

1. **Navigate to the *Tutorial* folder in your *Word Data* folder. Double-click the *Anderson Village Association* folder. Click the *Default* Web file then click Open.**

The page is divided into two frames—the navigation frame appears on the left (it appears the same on every page of the Web site). The *Board of Trustees* page (the current page) appears in the right frame.

2. **Click at the top of the right frame.**

You can see in the Address box on the Web toolbar that you are on the *Board of Trustees* page, as shown in Figure 4.17.

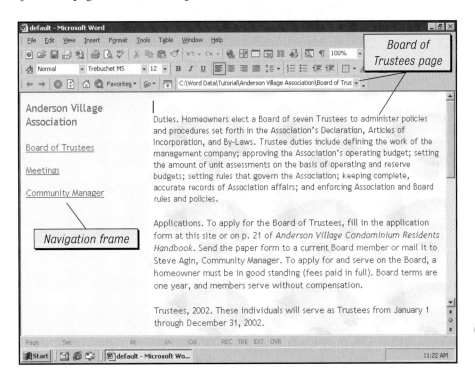

3. **Type Board of Trustees at the top of the right frame and press Enter↵. Change this heading to font size 16, bold, and centered.**

4. **Click the navigation frame, then press Ctrl and click the Meetings link.**

NOTE *If your insertion point is in the right frame, you must click inside the navigation frame before following another hyperlink.*

Word **BASICS**

Displaying Hidden Frame Borders

1. Point to Frames on the Format menu and click Frame Properties.

2. On the Borders tab in the Frame Properties dialog box, select *Show all frame borders.*

3. Change the border width and border color as desired.

4. Select *Frame is resizeable in browser* if you want to be able to resize the frame when viewing the page.

Figure 4.17
Board of Trustees page

5. At the top of the right frame, type Meetings and press ⌷Enter◄—⌷. Change the heading to font size 16, bold, and centered.

6. Click the navigation frame, then press ⌷Ctrl⌷ and click **Community Manager**. Type Community Manager as the heading in the right frame, then press ⌷Enter◄—⌷. Change the heading to font size 16, bold, and centered.

7. Click **Office Clipboard** on the Edit menu and clear all of its contents, if necessary.

8. Navigate to the *Board of Trustees* page. Scroll down and select the *Annual Meeting* and *Monthly Meetings* paragraphs. Right-click the paragraphs, then click **Cut**. Now cut the remainder of the page (from the insertion point to the end of the document) as a second item to the Office Clipboard.

You will paste the two Office Clipboard items on separate pages of your Web site.

9. Navigate to the *Meetings* page then delete the placeholder text. Click **Office Clipboard** on the Edit menu. Paste the Office Clipboard item that begins with *Annual Meeting*.

10. Navigate to the *Community Manager* page, delete the placeholder text, and click **Office Clipboard** on the Edit menu. Paste the Office Clipboard item that begins with *The managing agent*.

11. Click the navigation frame then follow each link. If you wish, edit the pages as desired, using styles to maintain consistency with the applied theme.

The Community Manager page of your Web site may resemble Figure 4.18.

Figure 4.18
Your edited Web site

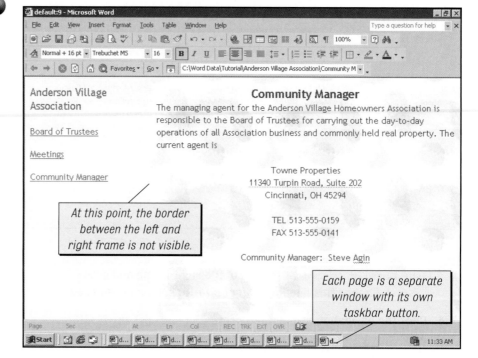

12. Point to **Frames** on the Format menu and click **Frame Properties**.

13. In the Frame Properties dialog box, click the **Borders tab**. Select **Show all frame borders**.

The preview now shows a border for the left frame that was previously hidden.

14. Change the width of the border to 5 pt and change the border color to dark blue. Verify that a check mark appears in *Frame is resizable in browser*. Click **OK**.

Your Web site now shows a frame border.

15. Resize the frames by pointing to the frame border and dragging to the left when the two-way horizontal arrow appears.

16. Point to **Frames** on the Format menu and click **Frame Properties**. On the Borders tab, select the **No borders option** and click **OK**.

17. Click **Save** 💾 then close the current page. On each page of your Web, click **Save** 💾 then **Close** 🗗.

VIEWING A WEB SITE IN EXPLORER

As you know, Word allows you to see all documents, including Web pages, in WYSIWYG view. Therefore, you already have a good idea how your Web pages will look in a Web browser. Still, most Web page authors want to see their creations exactly as their audience will see them. The Web Page Preview command on the File menu displays a Web page in the Explorer browser. You can also open a Web page in Explorer by clicking Open in Browser in the Open dialog box. Thus, before you publish a page on the Web or an intranet, you can see how it would look online. (Not all browsers support frames pages, however.)

WEB NOTE

Internet service providers (ISPs) offer different types of services. Some even allow members to publish their personal Web pages free of charge. To learn more, type **Internet service providers** into a search engine and browse the search results.

Previewing a Web Site in a Browser

In this activity, you will preview the Web site you created in the last activity. You will see what Web visitors would see if you published your pages. (The *On the Web* section for this lesson contains additional information about publishing a Web site.)

1. Open the *Default* Web file in the *Anderson Village Association* folder in the *Tutorial* folder in your *Word Data* folder.

2. Click **Web Page Preview** on the File menu.

Word BASICS

Previewing a Web Site in a Browser

1. With the *Default* file open in Word, click Web Page Preview on the File menu.
2. Click the navigation links to view the formatting.
3. Click the Edit with Microsoft Word button to make changes.

WORD 2002

The Web site opens within the Internet Explorer browser.

3. **Click the Maximize button, if necessary, on your browser window.**

Your Web site appears as shown in Figure 4.19.

NOTE *If a browser other than Internet Explorer is your default browser, the Web site will open in that browser instead of Internet Explorer.*

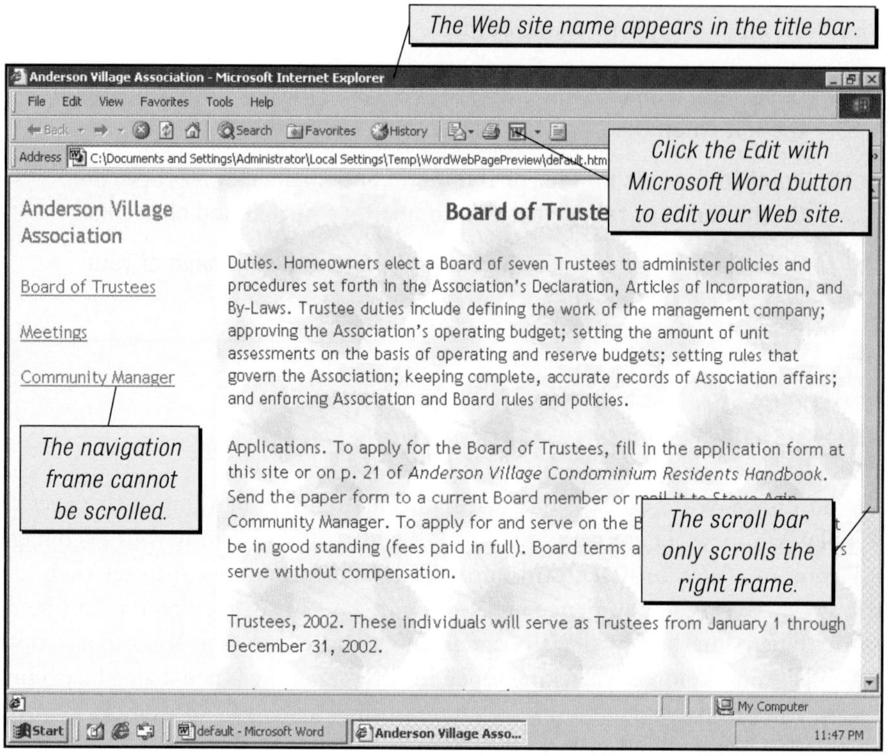

Figure 4.19
Your Web site in the Explorer window

4. **Point to the Meetings link in the navigation pane.**

The pointer becomes the shape of a hand (the Hyperlink Select pointer).

5. **Click the Meetings link and examine the formatting on that page. Then click the Community Manager link then the Board of Trustees link to view the formatting on those pages.**

NOTE *You cannot edit Web sites in the browser window; you must return to Word to use the editing features.*

6. **If you want to edit a page, click the Edit with Microsoft Word button on the Internet Explorer toolbar. Make the necessary changes and save and close the file. Close the browser window.**

Self Check

Test your knowledge by matching the terms on the left with definitions on the right. See Appendix B to check your answers.

TERMS

_____ **1.** HTML

_____ **2.** HTTP

_____ **3.** intranet

_____ **4.** frames

_____ **5.** wizard

DEFINITIONS

a. A private computer network within an organization

b. Separate sections or panels in a Web page

c. Allows a Web server and browser to communicate

d. The underlying code of Web documents

e. Creates documents to users' specifications

WORD 2002

PUBLISHING A WEB PAGE

After you create a Web page, you may want to share your page with others. If so, you need to publish your page to the Internet. To **publish** a Web page, you must store it on a server that has a permanent connection to the Web. (An alternative is to publish the page on your school's intranet.) As you learned at the beginning of this lesson, a Web server publishes documents on the Internet so they can be viewed by others.

Most people do not have their own Web server, so they choose to upload their page(s) to the Web server provided by their Internet service provider. An Internet service provider (ISP) is a company that provides Web access and various Web-based services (such as e-mail) usually for a monthly fee. Each Internet service provider charges a different fee (if any) and requires a different process to publish your page. With your instructor's approval, contact the system or network administrator at your school. This person will know how to upload Web documents to the server.

In order for a new site to get traffic, potential visitors must know the Web address and have a reason to visit the site. Web sites are typically publicized in several ways.

◆ Exchange links with others who own pages. They provide a link on their page that jumps to yours, and you include hyperlinks that jump to their pages. The more pages that contain links leading to your page, the more people will visit your site.

◆ Advertise in Web page banners or through traditional media such as television, print, or billboards. Of course, this type of advertising is most appropriate for commercial sites since it can be expensive.

◆ Register your page with search engines. In this way, a search on certain keywords will display your Web address in the search results.

◆ Announce a new page through a newsgroup or other online discussion group, forum, or chat group.

Whatever methods you choose to publicize your Web page, the key to obtaining readers who will return regularly is to provide interesting, informative, up-to-date information on your page.

In this activity, you will visit numerous Web sites. Some have the navigational links in a scrollable frame; others, in a borderless frame. Still other sites have the navigational links on a separate page. Some have elaborate themes and impressive graphics. You will develop a checklist to evaluate these sites then write a memo to your instructor to present your findings about the sites you visited.

1. **On Word's Web toolbar, click the Go button** Go ▾ **and click Open Hyperlink. Type** acwww.bloomu.edu **in the Address box and click OK.**

Your browser launches and connects to the Bloomsburg University *Center for Academic Computing* Web site.

2. **Click the Homepages link, and then click the Faculty and Staff Web pages link.**

3. **Scroll to see the alphabetic listing of faculty and staff members' names.**

4. **Explore at least five home pages on this Web site. Try to find pages whose authors use various different Web page design elements.**

As you navigate from one personal home page to another, you will notice differences in content as well as organization and general appearance. You will see various themes and backgrounds. Some pages will have graphics and frames pages with one or more frames containing scroll bars. Some pages may include numerous links allowing you to jump to information about the person or to other pages or Web sites.

5. In a Word document, develop a checklist to record comments about each of the personal home pages you visit at the Bloomsburg University site. Consider whether the Web page design elements have been used effectively or ineffectively. Note whether the overall appearance, structure, and organization effectively support the apparent content and purpose of the page. Consider these elements: frames; themes and backgrounds; graphics (animated objects, photographs, clip art, sound files, and so on); hyperlinks (text and graphics); content; and overall appearance.

6. When you are finished with your comments, save your Word document as *Home Pages* in the *Tutorial* folder in your *Word Data* folder, then close the document.

7. Now you will visit several different Web sites to see how other Web authors use a frames page. Table 4.1 lists several Web sites that include various Web page design elements. As your time allows, visit these sites. Note whether the navigational links at the visited sites are in a frame or on a separate page. If in a frame, is the frame scrollable? Does the frame have a border, or is it borderless?

Table 4.1	Sites to Visit
Web Site Name	**URL**
General Mills	www.youruleschool.com
Keating	www.keatingweb.com
Levenger	www.levenger.com
Mamie	www.mamie.com
OSRA	www.osra.org
White House	www.whitehouse.gov
Glencoe/McGraw-Hill Publishing	www.glencoe.com

8. Using a Word memo template, create a memo to your instructor. Assume that you are responding to your instructor's request for examples of frames pages. Include the name and URL of the Web sites you visited and provide a summary about the design of each Web site based on the checklist you developed in step 5.

9. Save the document as *Findings* in the *Tutorial* folder in your *Word Data* folder, then close the document.

10. When you are done, close your browser and disconnect from the Internet.

WARNING *You may proceed directly to the exercises for this lesson. If, however, you are finished with your computer session, follow the "shut down" procedures for your lab or school environment.*

SUMMARY AND EXERCISES

SUMMARY

WORD 2002

Web pages are created to accomplish many different goals including the communication of ideas, distribution of product information, and the sale of goods and services. It is important to think critically about the purpose of a Web site before you invest time in creating it. Any Word document can be saved as a Web page. Word users can create a Web site using a Word template or with the Web Page Wizard. Using frames throughout your Web site can provide convenient navigation links. Background colors and themes are available for enhancing appearance. You should choose colors to unify a Web site and ensure contrast between background and text.

You can view a Web page in your browser before it is published. To be shared with others, a Web page must be published on an intranet or the World Wide Web. Publication involves storing documents on a Web or intranet server. To publish a Web page, use the expertise of the system administrator in your organization or your particular Internet service provider.

Now that you have completed this lesson, you should be able to do the following:

■ Define Hypertext Markup Language (HTML) and Hypertext Transfer Protocol (HTTP). (page 230)

■ Explain the significance of a Web server. (page 230)

■ Save a Word document as a Web page. (page 230)

■ Plan the purpose and the structure of your Web page. (page 232)

■ Create a Web page with a Word Web page template. (page 232)

■ Edit text and hypertext in a Web page. (page 236)

■ Change text and background colors in a Web page. (page 238)

■ Explain the significance of *contrast*. (page 239)

■ Format a hyperlink. (page 240)

■ Insert a graphic and a graphic hyperlink. (page 242)

■ Apply a theme to a Web page. (page 244)

■ Explain the purpose of using *frames*. (page 246)

■ Create a multiple-page Web site using Word's Web Page Wizard. (page 246)

■ Work with smart tags. (page 250)

■ Work with frames pages. (page 251)

■ Preview a Web site in Internet Explorer. (page 253)

■ Explain how to publish a Web site to the Internet. (page 256)

CONCEPTS REVIEW

1 TRUE/FALSE

Circle T if the statement is true or F if the statement is false.

T F **1.** Before you can publish a page to the Web, you must save it in HTML format.

T F **2.** The last page in the navigation structure of a Web site is commonly called the home page.

T F **3.** Web pages are written in a page description format or underlying code called Hypertext Transfer Protocol (HTTP).

T F **4.** The Internet is a localized network of computers contained within an intranet.

T F **5.** You should draw attention primarily to the design of your Web page, not to the content of the page.

T F **6.** Blue and purple are the default colors of hyperlinks in Word.

T F **7.** You can create a Web page using a template or a wizard.

T F **8.** You can preview a Web site in your browser by using the Web Page Preview command on the File menu.

T F **9.** Word's bookmark feature allows you to mark a specific spot in the text.

T F **10.** An Internet service provider (ISP) is a company that provides Web access and various Web-based services.

2 MATCHING

Match each of the terms on the left with the definitions on the right.

TERMS	DEFINITIONS
1. frames page	**a.** The way that pages or frames link to each other
2. HTTP	**b.** Web page made up of two or more panels
3. home page	**c.** To make your Web page creation available to others
4. theme	**d.** Difference in brightness between dark and light areas of a page
5. intranet	
6. navigation frame	**e.** Computer permanently connected to the Web
7. wizard	**f.** Main page of a multiple-page Web site
8. contrast	**g.** A private Web-like network used within an organization
9. publish	**h.** A set of rules that allow a browser and Web server to communicate
10. Web server	**i.** A tool that creates documents based on user responses
	j. A set of unified designs and colors

SUMMARY AND EXERCISES

3 COMPLETION

Fill in the missing word or phrase for each of the following statements.

1. The _____ command on the File menu displays a Web page in the Explorer browser.

2. A company that provides Web access and various Web-based services is called a(n) _____ .

3. *Personal Web Page* is a _____ that allows you to create a Web page.

4. A(n) _____ is a collection of individual Web pages connected by navigation links.

5. The underlying code of a Web page is called _____ .

6. The _____ is a worldwide network of computers allowing users to share information in the form of text, graphics, images, video, and audio.

7. A _____ can easily coordinate all the design elements of a page, such as the background pattern and bullet shape, in one step.

8. The _____ dialog box allows you to change the destination for an established hyperlink.

9. To save a Word document in HTML, click _____ on the File menu.

10. Sections of a page separated by borders or scroll bars are called _____ .

4 SHORT ANSWER

Write a brief answer to each of the following questions.

1. Name four criteria a document should meet before it is published on the Web or an intranet.

2. Describe how a wizard works and saves time.

3. Describe the procedure for changing the color of hyperlinks from blue to yellow.

4. Name two ways to publicize a Web page.

5. What changes might be made to a document before saving it as a Web page?

6. Describe the purpose of bookmarks in a Web page.

7. Name five factors to be considered in planning a Web page.

8. Explain how using the *Personal Web Page* template differs from using the *Web Page Wizard*. How does the final product differ?

9. How is an intranet like the Internet? How are they different?

10. Briefly describe how to insert a bookmark hyperlink.

5 IDENTIFICATION

Label each of the elements in Figure 4.20.

Figure 4.20

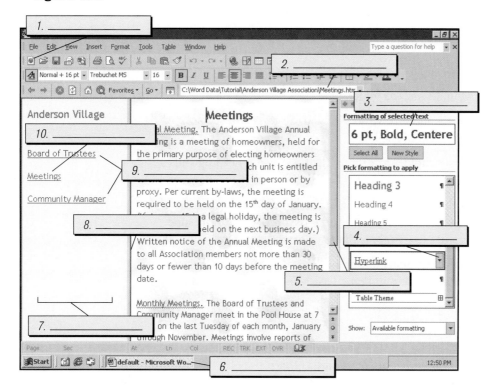

SKILLS REVIEW

Complete all of the Skills Review problems in sequential order to review your skills to save a Word document as a Web page; create a Web page with a template; add a background color; insert a bookmark; create and edit hyperlinks; apply styles to a Web page; insert a graphic and a graphic hyperlink; apply a theme; create a Web page with a wizard; and preview a Web site in a browser.

1 Save a Word Document as a Web Page

1. Navigate to your *Word Data* folder. Click **All Files** in the *Files of type* list, if necessary. Open *Woodsy View News.*

2. Change the *Summer Summary* heading to font size 20. Change the *Work, Work, Work* subheading to Palatino or other serif font, size 16. Change the text in the two paragraphs under the *Work, Work, Work* subheading (including the list) to Palatino (or similar font), size 13.

3. Select the *Pool Hours . . .* heading and all the remaining text material through the end of the document, and press ⌨Delete.

4. Click **Save as Web Page** on the File menu. Save the file as *WV News Web Page* in the *Skills Review* folder in your *Word Data* folder. Close the document.

2 Create a Web Page With a Template

1. If necessary, point to **Toolbars** on the View menu and click **Web** to display the Web toolbar.

2. Click **New** on the File menu. Click **General Templates** in the New Document task pane. Click the **Web Pages tab** in the Templates dialog box.

3. Click **Left-aligned Column**. Under *Create New*, verify that **Document** is selected, and click **OK**.

4. Click **Save as Web Page** on the File menu. Save the document as *Rita's Kitchen* in the *Skills Review* folder in your *Word Data* folder.

5. Select **Main Heading Goes Here** and type Rita's Kitchen. Select the **first Section Heading placeholder** and type Tip of the Day.

6. Select the two paragraphs of placeholder text under the first section heading and type the following paragraph:

   Extra virgin olive oil is from the first cold pressing of the olives and has the least amount of acid. It is a deep green color and has a fruity flavor. Because of its superior flavor and low acid content, extra virgin is the most expensive type of olive oil.

7. Select the **second Section Heading placeholder** and type Tex Mex Rice. Select the **third Section Heading placeholder** and type Last Minute Sandwich Filling.

8. Click the **Tip of the Day heading**. Click **Bookmark** on the Insert menu. Type **Tip** as the bookmark name, then click **Add**.

9. Insert a bookmark named *Rice* in the *Tex Mex Rice* heading. Insert a bookmark named *Sandwich* in the *Last Minute Sandwich Filling* heading.

10. Select *Caption goes here* under the photo, and type the following text:

    Contact Rita Nadler, a certified culinary professional, food consultant, and cooking teacher, at rnadler@dotnet.net.

11. Press [Enter←] 8 times. Type **Contents** and press [Enter←]. Type each of the three headings on this page, pressing [Enter←] after each heading.

12. Select **Tip of the Day** under **Contents**. Click the **Insert Hyperlink button** 🔗. Under *Link to*, click **Place in This Document**. Under *Select a place in this document*, expand **Bookmarks**, if necessary; then click **Tip**. Click **OK**.

13. Insert a hyperlink in the next two items under *Contents* set to the related bookmark.

14. Press [Ctrl] and click to follow each bookmark hyperlink in the Contents list. Click the **Back button** ⇐ on the Web toolbar to return to the Contents after following each link.

15. Click **Save** 💾 on the File menu, then close the document.

3 Add a Background Color

1. Click **Open** 📂 and navigate to the *Skills Review* folder in your *Word Data* folder. Click the **Files of type triangle button**, then click **Web Pages and Web Archives**. Open the *Rita's Kitchen* Word Web file and save it as *Rita's Kitchen-Color* in the same folder.

2. Select the main heading and change it to size 26, font color plum.

3. Change the three section headings to size 16, font color orange.

4. Change the body text in each section and the photo caption to font color green.

5. Point to **Background** on the Format menu. Click **Light Yellow**.

6. Point to **Background** on the Format menu. Click **Fill Effects**, then click the **Texture tab**. Click the fourth texture from the left in the top row (**Stationery**). Click **OK**.

7. Change *Contents* to bold and plum.

8. Save your changes and close the document.

4 Change Hyperlink Colors

1. Open *Rita's Kitchen-Color* in the *Skills Review* folder in your *Word Data* folder, then save it as *Rita's Kitchen-Hyperlink Color* in the same folder.

2. Click **Styles and Formatting** on the Format menu. In the Styles and Formatting task pane, click **All styles** in the Show box.

3. Scroll the *Pick formatting to apply* box, then point to **Hyperlink** and click the **Hyperlink triangle button** Hyperlink ⬚. Click **Modify**.

4. In the Modify Style dialog box, click the **Format button** and click **Font**.

5. In the Font dialog box, change the font color to pink and click **OK**. Click **OK** to close the Modify Style dialog box.

6. Scroll the *Pick formatting to apply* box, point to **FollowedHyperlink**, click the **triangle button** FollowedHyperlink ⬚, and then click **Modify**.

7. In the Modify Style dialog box, click the **Format button** and then click **Font**. Change the font color to red and click **OK**. Click **OK** to close the Modify Style dialog box.

8. Close the Styles and Formatting task pane.

9. Scroll down to the Contents hyperlinks, point to the **Tip of the Day link**, press Ctrl, and click. Scroll down again to view the appearance of the Contents hyperlinks (see Figure 4.21).

10. Save and close the document.

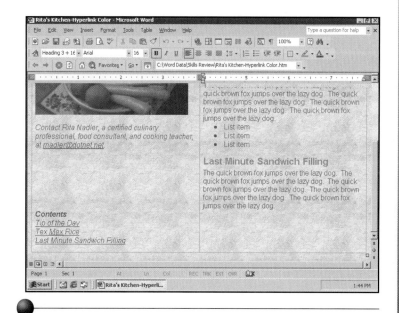

Figure 4.21

SUMMARY AND EXERCISES

WORD 2002

5 Insert a Graphic and a Graphic Hyperlink and Apply a Theme

1. Open *WV News Web Page* in the *Skills Review* folder in your *Word Data* folder. Save it as *WV News Theme* in the same folder.

2. Select the listed items, and click the **Bullets button** . Adjust the indentation of the bulleted list by clicking **Decrease Indent** or **Increase Indent** so the list is indented about .5 inch on the horizontal ruler.

3. Click at the end of the last line in the document and press Enter twice. Click **Borders and Shading** on the Format menu. On the Borders tab, click the **Horizontal Line button**. Click a line style and click **OK** to insert the horizontal line into your Web page.

4. Click **Theme** on the Format menu. In the Choose a Theme box, preview at least three themes, then click your choice. Verify that **Vivid Colors** and **Active Graphics** are selected; deselect **Background Image**. Click **OK**.

5. Change the main heading to size 18. Remove the italics from the subheading.

6. Click to the left of the main heading, press Enter, then click an insertion point above the heading. Point to **Picture** on the Insert menu and click **Clip Art**. Insert a Clip Art image of your choice. Close the Insert Clip Art task pane. Resize and position the image attractively.

7. Click the image and click the **Insert Hyperlink button** . In the *Link to* section, click **Existing File or Web Page**.

8. In the *Look in* box, navigate to your *Word Data* folder. Click the *Woodsy View News* document.

9. Click the **ScreenTip button**, type **Newsletter**, and click **OK**. Click **OK** to close the Insert Hyperlink dialog box. Save your changes.

10. Test the new link by pressing Ctrl and clicking the image. Close the *Woodsy View News* document; click **No** if asked to save changes.

11. Save *WV News Theme*, then close the document.

6 Remove a Graphic Hyperlink

1. Open *WV News Theme* in the *Skills Review* folder in your *Word Data* folder, and save it as *Hyperlink Removed* in the same folder.

2. Right-click the image and click **Edit Hyperlink**.

3. In the Edit Hyperlink box, click the **Remove Link button**.

4. Save and close the document.

7 Create a Web Page With the Web Page Wizard

1. Click **New** on the File menu. Click **General Templates** in the New Document task pane.

2. In the Templates dialog box, click the **Web Pages tab**, then click the **Web Page Wizard icon**.

3. Under *Create New,* verify that **Document** is selected and click **OK**.

4. Click **Next** in the wizard Start window.

5. In the Title and Location window, type **Tony Denier's Home Page** as the Web site title. If the Web site location box does not show the *Skills Review* folder, click **Browse** and click the *Skills Review* folder in your *Word Data* folder and click **Open**. Click **Next**.

6. In the Navigation window, select **Vertical frame** and then click **Next**.

7. In the Add Pages window, remove both blank pages. Click **Next**.

8. In the Organize Pages window, click **Rename**. Type **Tony Denier's Home Page** in the Rename Hyperlink dialog box. Click **OK** and click **Next**.

9. In the Visual Theme window, click **Browse Themes** and select the *Geared Up Factory* theme. (Select another theme with a dark background if the *Geared Up Factory* theme is not available.) Select **Vivid Colors**, **Active Graphics**, and **Background Image**. Click **OK**. Click **Next**.

10. In The End window, click **Finish** and click **No** in response to the prompt about navigation.

11. Select the main heading and type **Tony Denier's Home Page**. Press Ctrl and click the **Biographical Information hyperlink** under Contents.

12. Click the **Open button** 📂. Navigate to your *Word Data* folder. Click **All Files** in the *Files of type* list, then open *Tony Denier's Bio*.

13. Select all body text under the heading and click **Copy** on the Edit menu. Close the document. Select the placeholder text in the Biographical Information section then click **Paste** on the Edit menu.

14. Scroll up and select the placeholder text under the *Office phone* heading. Click **Styles and Formatting** on the Format menu. Scroll the *Pick formatting to apply* list to identify the style of the selected text (it is defined by a rectangle). Scroll down in the document, then select the Biographical Information text you just pasted into the page. Click the Style you identified in the *Pick formatting to apply* list.

15. Save and close the document. Close the Styles and Formatting task pane.

8 Work With Frames

1. Open the *Skills Review* folder in your *Word Data* folder. In the Open dialog box, click **Web Pages and Web Archives** in the *Files of type* list. Click *Tony Denier's Home Page* and click **Open**.

2. Point to **Frames** on the Format menu and click **Table of Contents** in Frame. In the right frame, select the *Contents* heading and the bulleted list below it and press Delete .

3. Click the left frame. Select the items under Contents in the left frame (drag to select them from the bottom up). Click the **Bullets button** ☰.

4. Click **Theme** on the Format menu. Click **Geared Up Factory** in the Choose a Theme list with all options selected, and click **OK**. Click the **Decrease Indent button** ☰ and drag the frame border to the right, if necessary, so that all Contents items are on one line.

5. Click the **Frame Properties button**  on the Frames toolbar. On the Borders tab, change the border width to 5 pt and the border color to Aqua. Deselect the **Frame is resizable in browser check box**. Click **OK**.

6. Save the file as *Home Page with Frame* in the *Skills Review* folder in your *Word Data* folder. Close the Frames toolbar. Your document should look similar to Figure 4.22.

7. Close the document.

9 Preview a Web Site in a Browser

1. Open *Home Page with Frame* in the *Skills Review* folder in your *Word Data* folder.

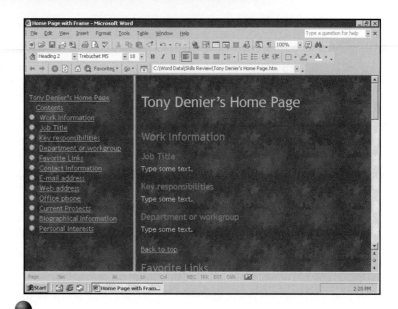

Figure 4.22

2. Click **Web Page Preview** on the File menu. Maximize the Internet Explorer window and scroll the page. Click at least two links in the navigation frame.

3. Close the browser and close the Word Web document.

4. Click the **Open button** 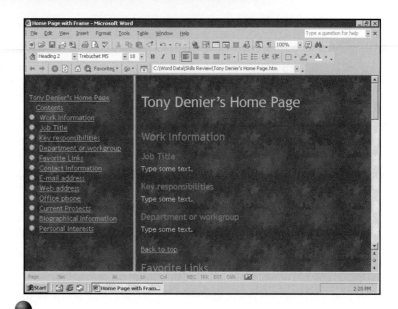 on the Standard toolbar. Click *Rita's Kitchen* in the *Skills Review* folder in your *Word Data* folder.

5. Click the **Open triangle button** and click **Open** in Browser.

6. Maximize the Explorer window, if necessary, and scroll the page. Close the browser.

LESSON APPLICATIONS

1 Going Online

Open a Word document. Insert bookmark hyperlinks and add text and a background color. Insert a graphic and a graphic hyperlink, then remove the graphic hyperlink. Save the document as a Web page.

1. Open *Writing* in your *Word Data* folder. Insert a bookmark named *Plan* in the *Plan* heading. Insert a bookmark in each of the other four paragraph headings with the bookmark names reflecting the heading titles. Change each of the paragraph headings to size 14.

2. Change the first two paragraphs of body text to font size 14. In the second paragraph, insert a hyperlink in each numbered word set to the corresponding bookmark. Follow each of the hyperlinks.

3. Below the last paragraph in the document, insert a Back to top hyperlink set to *Top of the document*. Below the link, type **Created by: Your Name** (insert your name).

On the next line, type **Last revised: 00/00/0000** (insert the current date). Follow the <u>Back to top</u> link.

4. Change the main heading to a sans serif font such as Arial, size 24, and white. Change the subtitle to the same sans serif font, size 20, and red. Add a pale blue background color.

5. Insert an image into your document. Resize and place the image attractively. Create a graphic hyperlink to an existing Web page. Type **http://www.bartleby.com/141** as the address. Connect to the Internet then follow the link. Remove the hyperlink, but leave the image in the document.

6. Save the document as a Web page named *Writing Web Page* in the *Lesson Applications* folder. Close the document. Close the task pane, if necessary.

2 Frequently Asked Questions

Open a Web page template. Add a theme and modify the hyperlink colors. Preview the page in your browser.

1. Open the Word Web page template named *Frequently Asked Questions.* Save it as *FAQ Page* in the *Lesson Applications* folder in your *Word Data* folder.

2. Apply the *Expedition* theme (substitute another theme if *Expedition* is unavailable). Select Vivid Colors, Active Graphics, and Background Image.

3. Modify the <u>Hyperlink</u> style so the color is orange. Modify the color of the <u>FollowedHyperlink</u> style to violet. (Choose alternative colors if these colors are not compatible with the background in the theme you have chosen.) Follow a Contents link then return to the top of the page. Your Web page may look similar to Figure 4.23.

4. Save the changes, then preview the document as a Web page in your browser. Close your browser. Close the document and the task pane.

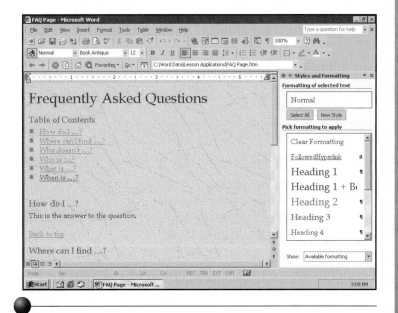

Figure 4.23

3 Web Page Wizardry

Create a Web site with the Web Page Wizard. Add a contents frame and a hyperlink.

1. Start the Web Page Wizard. Enter *Atlas Web Page* as the Web site title. The Web site location should be in the *Lesson Applications* folder in your *Word Data* folder.

2. Select Vertical frame as the navigation type. Remove all current pages and add the existing Word file *Atlas* in your *Word Data* folder. Rename the page as *Atlas Web Page*. Add the *Blends* visual theme (or choose another theme if *Blends* is unavailable). After you finish, respond No to the prompt about navigation.

3. Add a table of contents frame. (*Hint:* Point to Frames on the Format menu.)

4. Choose a visual theme for the contents frame. (*Hint:* Click Theme on the Format menu.) Choose a different theme than the theme shown in the right frame.

5. Follow the last link in the table of contents frame. Above the heading you jump to, insert a *Back to top* hyperlink, then follow the link.

6. Click Close on the File menu. Click Yes when prompted to save changes to the document. Save the document as *Atlas Web Page with Frame* in the *Atlas Web Page* folder in the *Lesson Applications* folder in your *Word Data* folder.

7. Close the Frames toolbar, if necessary. Close the document.

PROJECTS

1 Web Wizards

For about a year, you have been an office assistant at the fast-growing company called Web Wizards, Inc. Your organization offers professional design and consulting services for businesses that operate an intranet and/or do business on the Internet. Lately you have been creating pages for small clients as well as pages to promote Web site services on your company's own Web site.

New intranet users are often confused about the types of documents to publish on their network. Using a memo template, create a message to intranet users. Indicate four selection criteria for documents to be published to an intranet. Provide an e-mail address and a telephone number to contact your company. The page will be linked to your company's Web site, so apply a background color (or fill effect). Save the document as a Web page named *Intranet* in the *Projects* folder in your *Word Data* folder. Your Web page may look similar to Figure 4.24.

Figure 4.24

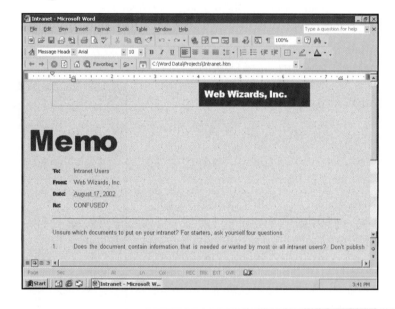

2 Woody's Tree Service

Forrest "Woody" Everett has hired Web Wizards, Inc. to design a home page for Woody's Tree Service. Use the *Simple Layout* Web page template to prepare the page. Include an address and telephone number. Using Table 4.2 as your source for information, incorporate one or more slogans; at least four tree services (in a bulleted list); at least three other services; and one or more memberships.

Insert a clip and apply an appropriate theme. Save the document as *Woody's Web Page* in the *Projects* folder in your *Word Data* folder. After you close the file, view it in your browser, since that is how the client will view the home page when it is finished.

Table 4.2	Items to Incorporate	
Category	**Items**	
Slogans	Serving the Tri-State Area Since 1963	We Focus on Saving Your Tree
	Trees Sick? We Can Help . . .	We Work on Your Trees, not Your Wallet!
	When Quality and Price Count, Call Our Experienced Pros	
	Competitive Rates	
Tree Services	Tree Removal	Tree Feeding
	Stump Grinding	Sap Injections
	Cavity Work	Topping
	Corrective Pruning	Storm Damage
Other Services	Accept Major Credit Cards	Certified Arborist on Duty
	Senior Citizen & Veteran Discounts	Fully Insured
	References Gladly Given	Free Estimates
	Emergency Service	
Memberships	International Society of Arboriculture	National Arborists Association

3 Computer Tutor

A department at Johnson & Joyner Career School uses this tutorial to teach word processing with Microsoft Word. The school's system administrator has consulted your company (Web Wizards, Inc.) for help in creating a Web document about the course for the school's intranet and the Web. She liked your idea: Give a brief description of course content and create links to actual documents that students have created in the course. (The instructor has permission from the publisher to show lesson headings from the tutorial to describe the course.)

◆ Use the *Table of Contents* Word Web template to create the course outline. Replace the main heading with a course title and change each section heading to match the lesson titles in Table 4.3. Include a one-sentence description of each lesson under the heading. Add a background and a border to the table.

Table 4.3	Lesson Titles and Hyperlinks	
Lesson	**Lesson Title**	**Link to**
1	Word Basics	Atlas Edited
2	Formatting Documents	Columns
3	Advanced Document Creation	Conference Shading
4	Creating Web Pages	Textra Web Page

◆ Create a folder in the *Projects* folder within your *Word Data* folder named *J & J Web Pages*. Save the Table of Contents document as *J & J TOC* in the *J & J Web Pages* folder in the *Projects* folder in your *Word Data* folder.

◆ Open the *Tutorial* folder in your *Word Data* folder. Save each of the documents listed in the *Link To* column (see Table 4.3) as a Web page in the *J & J Web Pages* folder. (When you save the documents, add *J & J* to the beginning of each file name.) Add a background to each document.

◆ Within the *J & J TOC* Web page, make each lesson title a hyperlink to the corresponding document indicated in Table 4.3. Test each link in the *J & J TOC* Web page. Edit the hyperlinks and modify background colors for contrast, if necessary. Save your changes.

4 Plan Ahead

Abby Steer, owner of Sharp Shots Photography, will be at Web Wizards, Inc. for a first consultation this afternoon. Abby uses digital cameras and, naturally, wants his new Web site to include examples of his work. Most of Sharp Shots business consists of portraits and weddings. Create a Word document listing questions to structure your Web site planning meeting with Abby. On paper, sketch a home page layout to use as a starting point. Show links to other pages at the site (if any) and to other sites that you propose. Draw circles, rectangles, squares, and so on, to represent photographs; and describe the photo in each case. On the back of your sketch, list five visual themes to show the client. Save your Word document as *Web Site Planner* in the *Projects* folder in your *Word Data* folder. Print your document and attach it to the sketch.

5 Web Page Directory

Coworkers asked you to catalog the Web pages designed at your company, Web Wizards, over the past three months. A list of client names and Web site addresses organized alphabetically by the type of business will work just fine—if the pages are linked for easy navigation. Create a folder named *Web Page Directory* in the *Projects* folder in your *Word Data* folder. Open the Web Page Wizard. Type the Web site title as **Web Work Completed** and browse to save your Web in the new *Web Page Directory* folder. Choose a vertical frame for your table of contents. Make sure the Web site has five blank pages. Rename the blank pages (the navigation hyperlinks) as follows and in this order: A-E; F-J; K-N; O-S; and T-Z. Apply no visual theme. When finished with the wizard, use the navigation hyperlinks to jump to each page, then type the page names (the hyperlink names) as headings. On each page, insert a table with these column headings: Type of Business, Name of Business, Web Address, Last Revised. Format the headings and tables attractively. Type the cell entries (see Table 4.4) on appropriate pages.

Table 4.4	Web Page Directory Information		
Type of Business	**Name of Business**	**Web Address**	**Last Revised**
Tree Service	Woody's Tree Service	www.woodytree.com	03/27/02
School	Johnson & Joyner Career School	www.jjcareerschool.edu	04/01/02
Photographer	Sharp Shots Photography	www.sharpshotsphoto.com	05/25/02

6 The Chocolate Page

A designer at Web Wizards, Inc. designed *Nadler's Kitchen,* a Web page in the *Web Files* folder in your *Word Data* folder. Now you will revise the site. Two innovations for this home page include a list of Web sites that will change daily and a page devoted to chocolate.

Add *Today's Hot Links* heading to the *Nadler's Kitchen* home page. Beneath the heading, add these links:

www.epicurious.com

www.ilovecheese.com

www.ilovepasta.org

Test each link. Save the revised Web page as *Nadler's Kitchen-Chocolate* in the *Projects* folder in your *Word Data* folder. Search the Web for sites that give recipes containing chocolate and record the URLs for at least two of them. Save a new, blank Web page as *Chocolate* in the *Projects* folder in your *Word Data* folder. Supply a heading and a background color. Add the URLs from your search. Explore Help to learn how to create a drawing object and a text box. Create a drawing object with text on *Nadler's Kitchen-Chocolate* home page and insert a graphic hyperlink set to *Chocolate*. View the home page in your browser. Save then close both pages.

Project in Progress

7 Savvy Solutions Online

As the owner-manager of Savvy Solutions, you have decided to create and publish a Web page promoting your business. You have already decided to let Web Wizards, Inc. create, publish, and maintain your site. You have organized the site content on paper and are preparing for a meeting with your Web Wizards, Inc. contact. At this point you are concerned that the look of the home page be just right. It would be a good idea to present some general design ideas to Web Wizards, Inc.

In a Word document, create the look you want on the home page. Insert a Savvy Solution logo containing your company name, the services you provide, and contact information. Insert Clip Art or explore Help to learn about drawings and AutoShapes for your logo. Apply a textured fill effect as a background. An example appears in Figure 4.25. Save the document as a Web page with the name S*avvy Solutions Home Page* in the *Projects* folder in your *Word Data* folder.

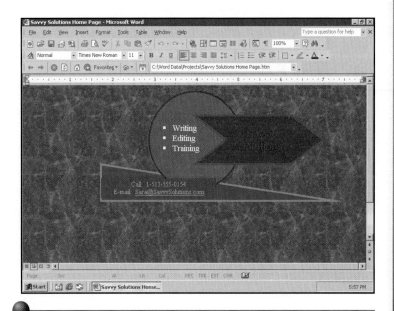

Figure 4.25

Overview: **Congratulations!** You have completed the lessons in the Word tutorial and now have the opportunity in this capstone project to apply the Word skills you have learned. Your biennial family reunion is set for next August in your hometown. You will be preparing the invitations, sign-up forms, family newsletter, and creating the family cookbook. As you create the case study documents, try to incorporate the following skills:

- Create and save various kinds of documents such as letters, forms, and graphics.
- Proofread and edit text. Use the Spelling and Grammar and Thesaurus features; use the Undo, Redo, Repeat, and Find and Replace commands.
- Ask the Office Assistant for help as needed.
- Navigate efficiently within and among documents.
- Use templates and wizards as desired to create documents.
- Search the Internet.
- Manage the files you create.
- Use the Office Clipboard to cut, copy, and paste text.
- Change page orientation, page and section breaks, margins, horizontal and vertical alignment, indentations, and character, line, and paragraph spacing; also set tabs.
- Add bullets and numbering to lists.
- Change font styles, sizes, attributes, and color.
- Create headers and footers, footnotes, and a table of contents.
- Add special effects to enhance document appearance, including highlighting, shading, and borders.
- Use the Format Painter and apply styles.
- Create hyperlinks to pages, documents, and Web sites.
- Insert, edit, and format graphics.
- Use Print Preview; print all documents.

Instructions: Read all directions and plan your work before you begin. You will be evaluated on these factors: (1) the number of skills involved in completing the case; (2) creativity; (3) practical applications for the task; (4) appropriate use of word processing features; (5) quality of the documents produced, including mechanical accuracy, format, and writing style; and (6) oral presentation of the case.

1. *Manage the Files and Research the Data.* Create a *Reunion* folder in the *Projects* folder in your *Word Data* folder in which to save all your Case Study documents. Search the Web, using keywords such as *reunions, genealogy, family ties,* and *entertaining* for family reunion ideas that you can use.

2. *Design a Family Graphic.* Design a family emblem to represent your family or this year's reunion. You may use this emblem on t-shirts, caps, sun visors, and so on. Using the family emblem, design a multi-purpose logo you can use (for example, as part of a letterhead or to incorporate into forms or a newsletter banner). (If necessary, search Help for information on how to draw an object.)

3. *Prepare the Invitation Letter.* Develop an invitation letter, incorporating the logo you just designed into your letterhead. Cover what, when, where, and whom to contact; announce the family Web page address; ask to have a sign-up form returned to you by a certain date; request favorite recipes for the family cookbook; request pictures of individuals and families; announce that an all-family picture will be taken at the reunion; announce that a donation will be collected (as usual) to cover expenses.

4. *Prepare Mailing Labels.* Create mailing labels for the whole family. If you are working alone, create a list of 15 fictional but realistic names and addresses. If you are a member of a team, contribute a list of five names and addresses to a combined list. Print the mailing labels.

5. *Create the Sign-up Form.* Use a table format to create a sign-up form to include with the invitation letter. Insert the letterhead at the top of the form. On the form, gather this information from family members: the number of persons who will attend the reunion; the full name, birth date, and birthplace of each; news items for the family newsletter; a list of general menu preferences for each person (for example, poultry, red meat, seafood, vegetarian).

6. *Create a Newsletter.* Create a newsletter sharing family reunion information. Limit the newsletter to two pages. Insert clip art, a poem, and a brainteaser. Secure feedback from others and edit as desired.

7. *Create the Cookbook.* Set up the sections of your cookbook. Type section headings on separate pages and apply a Headings style (for example, Desserts; Eggs & Cheese; Meat, Fish & Poultry; Pasta, Rice & Other Grains; Salads & Dressings; Soups & Stews; Vegetables). Type a recipe in any two sections, searching the Web for recipes, if necessary. Add a header and/or footer and a table of contents. Create a cover page for the cookbook. Add a border and shading to the cover.

Contents

WORD 2002

Portfolio Builder

WHAT IS A PORTFOLIO?

A **portfolio** is an organized collection of your work that demonstrates skills and knowledge acquired from one or more courses. The materials included in a portfolio should pertain to a specific educational or career goal. In addition to actual assignments, a portfolio should contain your self-reflection or comments on each piece of work as well as an overall statement introducing the portfolio.

Two types of portfolios exist. The first, which shows progress toward a goal over a period of time, is called the **developmental portfolio.** Developmental portfolios help you become more aware of your strengths and weaknesses and assist you in improving your abilities. The second type, called a **representational portfolio,** displays a variety of your best work. You can show a representational portfolio as evidence of your skills and knowledge. While you may use either type of portfolio when you are seeking employment, a representational portfolio is more effective.

WHY USE PORTFOLIOS?

Portfolios offer great advantages to you, your instructor, and potential employers. They allow you to reevaluate the work you have created, by determining which assignments should be included in the portfolio and analyzing how you can improve future assignments. If the goal of the portfolio is career related, portfolios also help you connect classroom activities with practical applications. A wide variety of genuine work is captured in a portfolio, rather than a snapshot of knowledge at a specific time under particular circumstances. Presenting a portfolio of your work to your instructor and potential employers gives them the opportunity to evaluate your overall skills and performance more accurately.

CREATING A PORTFOLIO

Creating a portfolio involves three steps—planning, selecting work to include, and providing comments about your work.

First, you should plan the overall purpose and organization of the portfolio. After you plan your portfolio, you can begin selecting pieces of work to include in it. Ideally, you should select the work as you complete each document; however, you can review prior work to include as well.

Table A.1 recommends Word documents from the Projects assignments that you may want to consider for inclusion in your Portfolio; however you may include additional documents, especially from the Projects section. If two documents demonstrate identical Word skills, choose only one for your portfolio. If you apply your Word skills in another course or elsewhere, include a sample in your portfolio.

Table A.1 **Possible Documents to Include in Your Portfolio**

Project	Document Name
Lesson 1, Project 7 (On the Web): Write This Way on the World Wide Web	*Web Link* (saved in *Projects* folder)
Lesson 2, Project 2: By Design	*Personal* (saved in *Projects* folder)
Lesson 3, Project 4: Diagrams, Diagrams	*Organization Diagram* (saved in *Projects* folder)
Lesson 4, Project 7 (Project in Progress): Savvy Solutions Online	*Savvy Solutions Home Page* (saved in *Projects* folder)

Create a list or log that provides a summary of the contents of your portfolio. (Your instructor may provide a preformatted log that you can complete.) The log can include columns in which you can list the file name, a description, when and by whom the document is reviewed, whether it was revised, and the grade you received on the assignment.

Lastly, you should prepare comments for each piece of work included in the portfolio. As you add work to your portfolio, generate comments about each piece. You may want to reflect on the skills used to create the document, or you can explain how it is applicable to a specific job for which you are interviewing. Your instructor may provide you with a preformatted comments form or you may type your comments.

Perform the steps listed in the following Hands On activity to build your portfolio.

HANDS on
Building Your Portfolio

In this activity, you will plan your portfolio, select the Word documents to include in the portfolio, and prepare written comments about each piece of work included in the portfolio.

1. **In a Word document, answer the following questions to help you plan your portfolio:**

   ◆ What is the purpose of your portfolio?

   ◆ What criteria will you use in selecting work to be included in the portfolio?

   ◆ What is the overall goal that your portfolio will meet?

   ◆ How will you organize your portfolio?

2. **Using Word, create a log that provides a summary of the contents of your portfolio. Follow the guidelines given by your instructor or provided in this appendix.**

3. Remember the purpose and goal of your portfolio and select and print one document that you have completed to include in your portfolio. Enter information about the document in your log.

4. Prepare comments about the selected document and attach them to the printout.

5. Repeat steps 3 and 4 and prepare comments for other documents to include in your portfolio.

6. Using Word, write a paragraph or two introducing your portfolio. Include some of the information considered in step 1.

7. Gather the documents to be included in your portfolio and place them in a binder, folder, or other container in an organized manner.

Self Check
Answers

Getting Started, page 31
1. T
2. T
3. T
4. F
5. F

Lesson 1, page 77
1. Word Count Statistics
2. OVR
3. Thesaurus
4. Office Clipboard
5. New

Lesson 2, page 142
1. d
2. e
3. c
4. a
5. b

Lesson 3, page 205
1. cell
2. chart
3. fields
4. Reviewing
5. Language bar

Lesson 4, page 255
1. d
2. c
3. a
4. b
5. e

APPENDIX C

COMMAND SUMMARY

Features	Button	Mouse	Keyboard Action
Entering and Editing Text			
Change case		Click Format, Change Case, choose option	[Alt] + [O], [E], then choose option or [⇧ Shift] + [F3]
Check grammar while typing		Right-click green, wavy underline; choose option	
Check spelling and grammar	ABC✓	Click Tools, Spelling & Grammar	[Alt] + [T], [S], then choose options or [F7]
Check spelling while typing		Right-click word with red, wavy underline; choose option	
Clear Office Clipboard	Clear All	Click Edit, Office Clipboard, select Clear All	[Alt] + [E], [B], [Tab] to Clear All, [Enter←]
Click and type		Double-click insertion point in the desired alignment zone	
Copy text to the Clipboard		Select text, click Edit, Copy	Select text, [Alt] + [E], [C] or [Ctrl] + [C] or [Ctrl] + [Insert]
Correct mistakes while typing		Click Tools, AutoCorrect Options, AutoCorrect tab, then choose options	[Alt] + [T], [A] then choose options
Correct repeated mistakes		Click Edit, Replace	[Alt] + [E], [E] or [Ctrl] + [H]
Create new blank document		Click File, New, Blank Document	[Ctrl] + [N]
Cut text to Clipboard		Select text, click Edit, Cut	Select text, [Alt] + [E], [T] or [Ctrl] + [X] or [⇧ Shift] + [Delete]
Delete text		Select text, click Edit, Clear, Contents Del	Select text, [Alt] + [E], [A], [C] or press [Delete]
Deselect text		Click anywhere in document	
Display nonprinting Characters	¶		

Entering and Editing Text (continued)

Features	Button	Mouse	Keyboard Action
Highlight text with color		Select text and click Highlight on the Formatting toolbar	
Insert AutoText		Click Insert, AutoText, choose option	`Alt` + `I`, `A`, then choose option
Insert date and time		Click Insert, Date and Time, choose option	`Alt` + `I`, `T`, then choose option
Insert text		Click I-beam at insertion point	
Open the thesaurus		Click Tools, Language, Thesaurus	`Alt` + `T`, `L`, `T` or `Shift` + `F7`
Paste all Clipboard contents	Paste All	Click Edit, Office Clipboard, Paste All	`Alt` + `E`, `B`, `Tab` to Paste All, `Enter`
Paste text from Clipboard		Click where you want to insert text, click Edit, Paste	Position insertion point in document, `Alt` + `E`, `P` or `Ctrl` + `V` or `Shift` + `Insert`
Repeat (Redo) action		Click Edit, Repeat	`Alt` + `E`, `R` or `Ctrl` + `Y` or `F4`
Replace specific text		Click Edit, Replace	`Alt` + `E`, `E` or `Ctrl` + `H`
Reverse (Undo) action		Click Edit, Undo	`Alt` + `E`, `U` or `Ctrl` + `Z` or `Alt` + `Backspace`
Select (highlight) text		Drag across text	
Select (highlight) a word		Double-click word	
Select a line of text		Click the selection bar	
Select a paragraph		Triple-click text or double-click selection bar	
Select a sentence		Press `Ctrl`, click in sentence	
Switch typing modes		Double-click OVR in status bar	Press `Insert`
Use AutoCorrect		Click Tools, AutoCorrect Options, AutoCorrect tab, choose options	`Alt` + `T`, `A`, `Ctrl` + `Tab` to AutoCorrect tab, then choose options

Formatting and Enhancing Documents

Features	Button	Mouse	Keyboard Action
Add a border (page or paragraph)		Select text, click Format, Borders and Shading, Borders tab or Page Borders tab, choose options	Select text, `Alt` + `O`, `B`, `B` (Paragraph) or `P` (Page), then choose options
Add shading (page, paragraph, or text)		Select text, click Format, Borders and Shading, Shading tab, choose options	Select text, `Alt` + `O`, `B`, `S`, then choose options
Align text horizontally		Click Format, Paragraph, Indents and Spacing tab, set options	`Alt` + `O`, `P`, `I`, then set options
Align text vertically		Click File, Page Setup, Layout tab, set Page options	`Alt` + `F`, `U`, `Ctrl` + `Tab` to Layout tab, `Alt` + `V`, then set Page options

Features	Button	Mouse	Keyboard Action
Formatting and Enhancing Documents (continued)			
Apply character effect		Select text, click Format, Font, Font tab, choose options	Select text, [Alt] + [O], [F], [Alt] + [N], then choose options
Apply styles	Normal ▾ or [A]	Select text, click Format, Styles and Formatting, choose options	Select text, [Alt] + [O], [S], then choose options
Apply Table AutoFormat	[▦]	Click in table, click Table, Table Auto Format, choose options	Click in table, [Alt] + [A], [F], then choose options
Bold text	**B**	Click Format, Font, Font tab, Bold font style	[Alt] + [O], [F], [Alt] + [N], [Alt] + [Y], choose Bold style or [Ctrl] + [B]
Change character to subscript	x₂	Select text, click Format, Font, Font tab, Subscript	Select text, [Alt] + [O], [F], [Alt] + [N], [Alt] + [B] or [Ctrl] + +
Change character to superscript	x²	Select text, click Format, Font, Font tab, Superscript	Select text, [Alt] + [O], [F], [Alt] + [N], [Alt] + [P] or [Ctrl] + =
Change font	Times New Roman ▾	Select text, click Format, Font, Font tab, choose font	Select text, [Alt] + [O], [F], [Alt] + [N], [Alt] + [F] or [Ctrl] + [⇧ Shift] + [F]; choose font
Change font color	[A ▾]	Select text, click Format, Font, Font tab, choose font color	Select text, [Alt] + [O], [F], [Alt] + [N], [Alt] + [C], then choose font color
Change font size	12 ▾	Select text, click Format, Font, Font tab, choose font size	Select text, [Alt] + [O], [F], [Alt] + [N], [Alt] + [S], then choose size
Change line spacing	[↕≡ ▾]	Select text, click Format, Paragraph, Indents and Spacing tab, choose line spacing	Select text, [Alt] + [O], [P], [Alt] + [I], [Alt] + [N], then choose option
Change margins		Click File, Page Setup or double-click end of horizontal ruler, Margins tab, set margins	[Alt] + [F], [U], [Ctrl] + [Tab] to Margins tab, then set margins
Change page orientation		Click File, Page Setup, Margin tab, choose orientation	[Alt] + [F], [U], [Ctrl] + [Tab] to Margin tab, [Alt] + [P] (Portrait) or [Alt] + [S] (Landscape)
Change paper size		Click File, Page Setup, Paper tab, choose paper size	[Alt] + [F], [U], [Ctrl] + [Tab] to Paper tab, [Alt] + [R], then choose option
Change paragraph spacing		Click Format, Paragraph, Indents and Spacing tab, set spacing	[Alt] + [O], [P], [Alt] + [I], [Alt] + [B] (Before) or [Alt] + [E] (After), then set options
Choose underline style		Click Format, Font, Font tab, choose underline style	[Alt] + [O], [F], [Alt] + [N], [Alt] + [U], then choose option
Copy text format and appearance	[🖌]	Select text to copy format from, click Format Painter, select text to copy format to	

Formatting and Enhancing Documents (continued)

Features	Button	Mouse	Keyboard Action
Create a table of contents		Click Insert, Reference, Index and Tables, Table of Contents tab, choose options	Alt + I, N, D, Alt + C, then choose options
Create an outline numbered list		Click Format, Bullets and Numbering, Outline Numbered tab, choose option	Alt + O, N, Alt + U, then choose option
Decrease paragraph indentation	![button]	Select text, click Format, Paragraph, Indents and Spacing tab, set indentation, or drag indent markers on ruler	Select text, Alt + O, P, Alt + I, Alt + L (Left) or Alt + R (Right), then set indentation
Format text automatically		Click Format, AutoFormat, choose options	Alt + O, A, O, then choose options
Increase paragraph indentation	![button]	Click Format, Paragraph, Indents and Spacing tab, set indentation, or drag indent markers on ruler	Select text, Alt + O, P, Alt + I, Alt + L (Left) or Alt + R (Right), then set indentation
Insert a column break		Click Insert, Break, Column break	Alt + I, B, C or Ctrl + Shift + Enter
Insert a page break		Click Insert, Break, Page break	Alt + I, B, P or Ctrl + Enter
Insert a section break		Click Insert, Break, choose option	Alt + I, B, then choose option
Insert bullets in list	![button]	Click Format, Bullets and Numbering, Bulleted tab, choose option	Alt + O, N, Alt + B, then choose option
Insert columns	![button]	Click Format, Columns, choose options	Alt + O, C, then choose options
Insert date and time in header or footer	![button] or ![button]	Click View, Header or Footer, position cursor in header or footer, then click Insert Date or Insert Time button on toolbar	Alt + V, H, position cursor in header or footer, Alt + S, → to select option, Enter
Insert footnote		Click Insert, Reference, Footnote, then choose options	Alt + I, N, N, then choose options
Insert headers and footers		Click View, Header and Footer, then choose options or type text	Alt + V, H, then choose options or type text
Insert number of pages in document in a header or footer	![button]	Click View, Header or Footer, position cursor in header or footer, then click Insert Number of Pages button on toolbar	Alt + V, H, position cursor in header or footer, Alt + S, → to select option, Enter
Insert numbering in a list	![button]	Click Format, Bullets and Numbering, Numbered tab, choose option	Alt + O, N, Alt + N, then choose option
Insert page numbers		Click Insert, Page Numbers, choose options	Alt + I, U, then choose options
Insert page numbers in a header or footer	![button]	Click View, Header or Footer, position cursor in header or footer, then click Insert Page Number button on toolbar	Alt + V, H, position cursor in header or footer, Alt + S, → to select option, Enter

WORD 2002

Features	Button	Mouse	Keyboard Action
Formatting and Enhancing Documents (continued)			
Italicize text	*I*	Click Format, Font, Font tab, Font style, choose Italic option	Ctrl + I or Alt + O, F, Alt + N to choose Font tab, Alt + Y, ↓ to choose option
Open Page Setup dialog box		Click File, Page Setup or double-click end of horizontal ruler	Alt + F, U
Select an entire document		Click Edit, Select All	Alt + E, L or Ctrl + A
Set tab stops		Click Format, Tabs, and set options or double-click ruler and set options	Alt + O, T, then set options
Sort a list in alphabetical or numerical order		Click Table, Sort, choose options	Alt + A, S, then choose options
Sort a list in reverse alphabetical or numerical order		Click Table, Sort, choose options	Alt + A, S, then choose options
Switch between header and footer		Click View, Header or Footer, click Switch Between Header and Footer button on toolbar	Alt + V, H, then use ↑ or ↓ to switch between header and footer
Underline text	U	Click Format, Font, choose underline style option	Ctrl + U or Alt + O, F, Alt + N, Alt + U, then choose option
Help			
Display a list of Help Topics		Click Show in the Help window and click Contents tab	
Display ScreenTips		Click Help, What's This?	Alt + H, T or Shift + F1
Hide additional Help tools in Help window		Click Hide in the Help window	
Hide the Office Assistant		Click Help, Hide the Office Assistant or right-click Office Assistant, click Hide	Alt + H, O
Print Help topic in Help window			
Search for Help by keyword		Click Show in the Help window and click Index tab	
Show additional help tools in Help window			
Use Ask a Question box	Type a question for help	Click the Ask a Question box; then type a question and press Enter	
Use Office Assistant		Click the Office Assistant character or click Help, Microsoft Word Help	F1
Use the Answer Wizard		Click Show in the Help window and click the Answer Wizard tab	

Features	Button	Mouse	Keyboard Action
Hyperlinks and the Web			
Add a frame to a frames page	New Frame Left / New Frame Right / New Frame Above / New Frame Below	Click Format, Frames, choose option	[Alt] + [O], [R], then choose option
Apply a background		Click Format, Background, choose option	[Alt] + [O], [K], then choose option
Apply a theme		Click Format, Theme, choose options	[Alt] + [O], [H], then choose options
Display Web toolbar		Click View, Toolbars, Web	[Alt] + [V], [T], [↓] to choose toolbar, press [Enter←]
E-mail a document		Click File, Send To, Mail Recipient or Mail Recipient (for Review) or Mail Recipient (as Attachment)	[Alt] + [F], [D], [M] or [Alt] + [F], [D], [C] or [Alt] + [F], [D], [A]
Enter Web address (URL)	Go ▾ / http://www.microsoft.com	Click Go, Open Hyperlink, and type address or click Address on Web toolbar and type address	[Alt] + [G], [O], type address
Go to a bookmark or favorite place	Favorites ▾	Click Favorites, name of favorite place on the Web toolbar	[Alt] + [S], [F], then choose option
Go to the Search Page		Click Go, Search the Web on the Web toolbar	[Alt] + [G], [W]
Go to the Start Page		Click Go, Start Page on the Web toolbar	[Alt] + [G], [S]
Insert a hyperlink		Click Insert, Hyperlink, type address	[Alt] + [I], [I], type address or [Ctrl] + [K], type address
Move forward one page or site		Click Go, Forward on the Web toolbar	[Alt] + [G], [F]
Preview a Web page		Click File, Web Page Preview	[Alt] + [F], [B]
Return to previous page or site		Click Go, Back on the Web toolbar	[Alt] + [G], [B]
Set a bookmark or favorite place	Favorites ▾	Click Favorites, Add to Favorites on Web toolbar	[Alt] + [S], [A]
Show Only Web toolbar		Click Show Only Web Toolbar	
Stop current connection		Click Stop	
Mail Merge			
Display Mail Merge toolbar		Click View, Toolbars, Mail Merge or click Tools, Letters and Mailings, Show Mail Merge Toolbar	[Alt] + [T], [E], [T] or [Alt] + [V], [T], [↓] to choose toolbar, [Enter←]
Use Mail Merge Wizard		Click Tools, Letters and Mailings, Mail Merge Wizard	[Alt] + [T], [E], [M]
Managing Files			
Close a document		Click File, Close	[Alt] + [F], [C] or [Ctrl] + [F4]

Features	Button	Mouse	Keyboard Action
Managing Files (continued)			
Create a folder		Click File, Open, Create New Folder, type folder name	[Ctrl] + [O] or [Alt] + [F], [O], then [Alt] + [I], [Tab], [→] to select Create New Folder button, [Enter←], type folder name
Open a document		Click File, Open, click file to be opened or click File, click file name shown at bottom of menu	[Ctrl] + [F12] or [Alt] + [F], [O] or [Ctrl] + [O], then choose file
Save a document		Click File, Save	[⇧Shift] + [F12] or [Alt] + [F], [S] or [Ctrl] + [S]
Save a document as a Web page		Click File, Save as Web Page	[Alt] + [F], [G]
Save a document in a different folder		Click File, Save As, navigate to location	[F12] or [Alt] + [F], [A], navigate to location
Save a document with a different name		Click File, Save As, navigate to location, type file name	[F12] or [Alt] + [F], [A], navigate to location, type file name
Managing the Word Window			
Display Formatting and Standard toolbars on one row		Click Tools, Customize, Options tab, deselect option	[Alt] + [T], [C], [O], then [Alt] + [S] to deselect option
Display Formatting and Standard toolbars on two rows		Click Tools, Customize, Options tab, select option	[Alt] + [T], [C], [O], then [Alt] + [S] to select option
Display more toolbar buttons	or		
Display Normal View		Click View, Normal	[Alt] + [V], [N]
Display Outline View		Click View, Outline	[Alt] + [V], [O]
Display Print Layout View		Click View, Print Layout	[Alt] + [V], [P]
Display Toolbars menu		Click View, Toolbars or right-click a displayed toolbar	[Alt] + [V], [T]
Display Web Layout View		Click View, Web Layout	[Alt] + [V], [W]
Display/hide ruler		Click View, Ruler	[Alt] + [V], [R]
Display/hide toolbars		Click View, Toolbars, select or deselect toolbar	[Alt] + [V], [T], [↓] to select or deselect toolbar, [Enter←]
Navigating Documents			
Display Document Map		Click View, Document Map	[Alt] + [V], [D]
Find specific text		Click Edit, Find, type text to find	[Alt] + [E], [F] or [Ctrl] + [F], then type text to find

Navigating Documents (continued)

Features	Button	Mouse	Keyboard Action
Go to beginning of document		Drag scroll box on vertical scroll bar to top of page or click Edit, Go To, Page, type page number 1	[Ctrl] + [Home]
Go to bookmark	🔍	Click Edit, Go To, Bookmark, choose bookmark name	[Alt] + [E], [G] or [F5] or [Ctrl] + [G], then [Alt] + [O], [↓] to highlight Bookmark, [Alt] + [E], choose bookmark name
Go to specific page	🔍	Click Edit, Go To, Page, type page number	[Alt] + [E], [G] or [F5] or [Ctrl] + [G], then [Alt] + [O], [↓] to highlight Page, [Alt] + [E], type page number
Go to end of document		Drag scroll box on vertical scroll bar to bottom of page	[Ctrl] + [End]
Insert Bookmark		Click Insert, Bookmark, type bookmark name	[Alt] + [I], [K], type bookmark name
Scroll gradually (one screen at a time)		Click vertical or horizontal scroll bars	[PgUp] or [PgDn]
Scroll rapidly		Drag scroll box on vertical or horizontal scroll bar	[Ctrl] + [PgUp] or [Ctrl] + [PgDn]
Scroll slowly (one line at a time)		Click scroll arrows	[↓] or [↑]

Objects

Features	Button	Mouse	Keyboard Action
Add a shadow effect	▣	Select object and click Shadow Style on Drawing toolbar	
Change fill color	🎨	Double-click object, click Colors and Lines, choose fill color	
Change line color	✏	Double-click object, click Colors and Lines, choose line color	
Change line style	≡	Double-click object, click Colors and Lines, choose line style	
Change wrapping style of text around AutoShapes		Double-click AutoShape, click Layout, choose options or select AutoShape, click Format, AutoShape, Layout, then choose options	Select AutoShape, [Alt] + [O], [O], [→] or [←] to select Layout, then choose options
Change wrapping style of text around Drawing Canvas		Double-click Drawing Canvas, click Layout, choose options or Select Drawing Canvas, click Format, Drawing Canvas, then choose options	Select Drawing Canvas, [Alt] + [O], [D], [→] or [←] to select Layout, then choose options
Change wrapping style of text around objects	🖼	Double-click object, click Layout, then choose options or Select object, click Format, Object, then choose options	Select object, [Alt] + [O], [O], [→] or [←] to select Layout, then choose options
Change wrapping style of text around pictures	🖼	Double-click picture, click Layout, then choose options or Select picture, click Format, Picture, then choose options	Select picture, [Alt] + [O], [I], [→] or [←] to select Layout, then choose options

Features	Button	Mouse	Keyboard Action
Objects (continued)			
Display Drawing toolbar		Click View, Toolbars, Drawing	`Alt` + `V`, `T`, then use `↓` to choose toolbar, press `Enter←`
Draw a freeform shape	AutoShapes ▾	Click AutoShapes, Lines, Freeform or click AutoShapes, Lines, Scribble	`Alt` + `U`, `L`, then use `←` and `↓` to choose shape, press `Enter←`
Draw a line		Click Line tool or click AutoShapes, Lines, choose option; drag crosshair pointer	`Alt` + `U`, `L`, `Enter←`, draw line
Draw a rectangle		Click Rectangle tool or click AutoShapes, Basic Shapes, choose option; drag crosshair pointer	`Alt` + `U`, `B`, `Enter←`, draw rectangle
Draw a text box		Click Text Box tool, drag crosshair pointer	
Draw an arrow		Click Arrow tool or click AutoShapes, Lines, Arrow; drag crosshair pointer	`Alt` + `U`, `L`, then use `←` to choose arrow, press `Enter←`, draw arrow
Draw an oval		Click Oval tool or click AutoShapes, Basic Shapes, Oval; drag crosshair pointer	`Alt` + `U`, `B` then use `↓` to choose oval, press `Enter←`, draw oval
Embed an object		Click Edit, Paste Special	`Alt` + `E`, `S`
Format an object		Double-click or select picture or object, click Format, Object or Picture	Select picture or object, `Alt` + `O`, `I` (picture) or `O` (object), choose tab
Group objects	Draw ▾	Select objects, click Draw, Group	Select objects, `Alt` + `R`, `G`
Insert a picture		Click Insert, Picture, click location/type	`Alt` + `I`, `P`, click location/type
Insert Clip Art		Click Insert, Picture, Clip Art, then choose options	`Alt` + `I`, `P`, `C`, then choose options
Insert horizontal line		Click Format, Borders and Shading, Horizontal Line, then choose option	`Alt` + `O`, `B`, `Alt` + `H`, then choose option
Insert WordArt		Click Insert, Picture, WordArt	`Alt` + `I`, `P`, `W`, choose option
Move an object		Drag object with four-way pointer	Select object, then use `←`, `→`, `↑`, or `↓` to position object
Preview a clip		Click Clip Organizer in Insert Clip Art task pane, click clip name	
Resize an object		Select the object, drag resizing handle with two-way pointer	
Select an object		Click object	

WORD 2002

Features	Button	Mouse	Keyboard Action
Previewing and Printing			
Increase magnification in Print Preview	100%	Click View, Zoom, click option	Alt + V, Z, choose option
Preview a document	[icon]	Click File, Print Preview	Alt + F, V or Ctrl + F2
Preview multi-page document	[icon] then [icon]	Click File, Print Preview, Multiple Pages	Alt + F, V or Ctrl + F2, then click Multiple Pages
Preview single-page document	[icon] then [icon]	Click File, Print Preview, One Page	Alt + F, V or Ctrl + F2, then click One Page
Print a document	[icon]	Click File, Print, click options	Ctrl + Shift + F12 or Alt + F, P or Ctrl + P; choose options
Print envelopes	[icon]	Click Tools, Letters and Mailings, Envelopes and Labels, Envelopes tab, type text, click Print	Alt + T, E, E, Alt + E, type text, Alt + P
Print labels	[icon]	Click Tools, Letters and Mailings, Envelopes and Labels, Labels tab, type text, click Print	Alt + T, E, E, Alt + L, type text, Alt + P
Reviewing Documents			
Compare and Merge Documents		Click Tools, Compare and Merge Documents, file name, Merge or choose Merge options	Alt + T, D, choose file, then Alt + M or choose Merge options
Display Reviewing Toolbar		Click View, Toolbars, Reviewing	Alt + V, T, then use ↓ to choose toolbar, Enter↵
Starting and Exiting Word			
Exit Word	[icon]	Click File, Exit	Alt + F, X or Alt + F4
Start Word	[Start]	Click Start, Programs, Microsoft Word	⊞, P, then ↑ or ↓ to select Microsoft Word, Enter↵
Tables			
Add borders	[icon]	Right-click selected cells, click Borders and Shading, Borders tab, click options or select cells, click Format, Borders and Shading, Borders tab, click options	Select cells, Alt + O, B, B, then choose options
Add shading in cells	[icon]	Right-click selected cells, click Borders and Shading, Shading tab, click option or select cells, click Format, Borders and Shading, Shading tab, click options	Select cells, Alt + O, B, S, then choose options
Align table horizontally		Right-click table, click Table Properties, Table tab, click option or with insertion point in table, click Table, Table Properties, Table tab, click option	With insertion point in table, Alt + A, R, T, then Alt + L (Left), Alt + C (Center), or Alt + H (Right)

Features	Button	Mouse	Keyboard Action
Tables (continued)			
Align text in multiple cells		Right-click selected cells, Cell Alignment, click option	Select cells, [Alt] + [A], [R], [E], then [Alt] + [P] (Top), [Alt] + [C] (Center), or [Alt] + [B] (Bottom)
Align text in single cell		Right-click selected cell, Cell Alignment, click option	With insertion point in cell, [Alt] + [A], [R], [E], then [Alt] + [P] (Top), [Alt] + [C] (Center), or [Alt] + [B] (Bottom)
Change color of borders		Right-click selected cells, click Borders and Shading, Borders tab, choose color or select cells, click Format, Borders and Shading, Borders tab, choose color	Select cells, [Alt] + [O], [B], [B], [Alt] + [C], then use [↑], [↓], [←], or [→] to choose color, [Enter←]
Change direction of text in cells		Select cell, click Format, Text Direction, then choose option or right-click cell, click Text Direction, choose option	Select cell, [Alt] + [O], [X], then use [←] or [→] to choose option, [Enter←]
Change style of borders		Right-click selected cells, click Borders and Shading, Borders tab, choose Style options or select cells, click Format, Borders and Shading, Borders tab, choose Style options	Select cells, [Alt] + [O], [B], [B], [Alt] + [Y], then use [↑] or [↓] to choose style, [Enter←]
Change weight (thickness) of borders	½	Right-click selected cells, click Borders and Shading, Borders tab, choose Width options or select cells, click Format, Borders and Shading, Borders tab, choose Width options	Select cells, [Alt] + [O], [B], [B], [Alt] + [W], then use [↑] or [↓] to choose Width, [Enter←]
Delete a row or column	or	Select row or column, click Table, Delete, choose Rows or Columns or select row or column, right-click, click Delete Cells, then choose option	Select row or column, [Alt], [A], [D], then [R] or [C]
Distribute columns evenly		Select columns, click Table, AutoFit, Distribute Columns Evenly	Select columns, [Alt] + [A], [A], [Y]
Distribute rows evenly		Select columns, click Table, AutoFit, Distribute Rows Evenly	Select columns, [Alt] + [A], [A], [N]
Draw a table		Click Table, Draw Table, drag pencil pointer	[Alt] + [A], [W], drag pencil pointer
Format a table automatically		Click Table, Table AutoFormat, then choose options	With insertion point in table, [Alt] + [A], [F], then choose options
Insert a table	or	Click Table, Insert, Table or click Table, Draw Table, then drag pencil pointer	[Alt] + [A], [I], [T], then set options

Features	Button	Mouse	Keyboard Action
Tables (continued)			
Insert a row or column		With insertion point in table, click Table, Insert, choose option or with insertion point in table, click the drop-down arrow next to the Insert Table button on the Drawing toolbar, click option	With insertion point in table, [Alt] + [A], [I], then choose option
Merge cells	⊞	Select cells, click Table, Merge Cells	Select cells, [Alt] + [A], [M]
Navigate a table		Click the desired cell	Press [Tab] or use [↑], [↓], [←], or [→]
Set column width		Click column to be changed, click Table, Table Properties, Column tab, set width or drag column border	With insertion point in column, [Alt] + [A], [R], [U], set width
Set row height		Click row to be changed, click Table, Table Properties, Row tab, set height or drag row border	With insertion point in row, [Alt] + [A], [R], [R], set height
Set table width		Click table, click Table, Table Properties, Table tab, set width or drag table borders	With insertion point in table, [Alt] + [A], [R], [T], [Alt] + [W], set width
Split cells in a table	⊞	Select cells, click Table, Split Cells, set options	Select cells, [Alt] + [A], [P], set options
Templates			
Open a Web page template		Click File, New, General Templates, Web Pages tab, choose template	[Alt] + [F], [N], use [↓] to choose General Templates, [Enter←], [Ctrl] + [Tab] to Web Pages tab, then [→] and [↓] to choose template
Open a template		Click File, New, General Templates, choose option	[Alt] + [F], [N], use [↓] to choose General Templates, [Enter←], [Ctrl] + [Tab] to choose template tab, then [→] and [↓] to choose template
Open Web Page Wizard		Click File, New, General Templates, Web Pages tab, Web Page Wizard	[Alt] + [F], [N], use [↓] to choose General Templates, [Enter←], [Ctrl] + [Tab] to Web Pages tab, then use [→] and [↓] to choose Web Page Wizard

APPENDIX D

MOUS CERTIFICATION REQUIREMENTS

Use the following tables to identify and locate the Core MOUS objectives found in this text.

Table D.1	Core MOUS Objectives Related to Lessons	
Code	**Activity**	**Lesson**
W2002-1-0	**Inserting and Modifying Text**	
W2002-1-1	Insert, modify and move text and symbols	1
W2002-1-2	Apply and modify text formats	2
W2002-1-3	Correct spelling and grammar usage	1
W2002-1-4	Apply font and text effects	2
W2002-1-5	Enter and format Date and Time	1
W2002-1-6	Apply character styles	2
W2002-2-0	**Creating and Modifying Paragraphs**	
W2002-2-1	Modify paragraph formats	2
W2002-2-2	Set and modify tabs	2
W2002-2-3	Apply bullet, outline, and numbering format to paragraphs	2
W2002-2-4	Apply paragraph styles	2
W2002-3-0	**Formatting Documents**	
W2002-3-1	Create and modify a header and footer	2
W2002-3-2	Apply and modify column settings	2
W2002-3-3	Modify document layout and Page Setup options	2,3
W2002-3-4	Create and modify tables	3
W2002-3-5	Preview and print documents, envelopes, and labels	1
W2002-4-0	**Managing Documents**	
W2002-4-1	Manage files and folders for documents	1
W2002-4-2	Create documents using templates	1
W2002-4-3	Save documents using different names and formats	Getting Started, 1
W2002-5-0	**Working With Graphics**	
W2002-5-1	Insert images and graphics	2
W2002-5-2	Create and modify diagrams and charts	3
W2002-6-0	**Workgroup Collaboration**	
W2002-6-1	Compare and Merge documents	3
W2002-6-2	Insert, view and edit comments	3
W2002-6-3	Convert documents into Web pages	4

Table D.2	Lessons Related to MOUS Objectives
Getting Started	W2002 4-3
1 Word Basics	W2002 1-1, 1-3, 1-5, 3-5, 4-1, 4-2, 4-3
2 Formatting Documents	W2002 1-2, 1-4, 1-6, 2-1, 2-2, 2-3, 2-4, 3-1, 3-2, 3-3, 5-1
3 Advanced Document Creation	W2002 3-3, 3-4, 5-2, 6-1, 6-2
4 Creating Web Pages	W2002 6-3

GLOSSARY

WORD 2002

A

active application The application that is currently running, as indicated by the highlighted button on the Windows taskbar.

active window The window in which the cursor is located and where the program will accept your input, as indicated by the darkened title bar.

animation Motion effects that make text or objects move on the screen.

Answer Wizard One of the three tabs in the expanded Help window, this tool is similar to the Office Assistant but provides many more topics from which to choose for further exploration. See also *Contents* and *Index*.

application program Specialized software program used to create or process data, such as creating text in a word processing document, manipulating financial information in a worksheet, tracking records in a database management file, or creating a presentation with a presentation or graphics program. Also called *application*. See also *program* and *software*.

application window A rectangle on the desktop containing the menus and files for an application. See also *document window*.

archive (attribute) A property setting that lets users modify or delete a file. Compare with *read-only*. See also *attribute*.

Arial A common font for headings; a sans serif font.

ascending sort A sort that arranges letters from A to Z, numbers from smallest to largest, and dates from earliest to most recent. Also called *ascending*. See also *sort*. Compare with *descending sort*.

Ask a Question A box at the right end of the menu bar in which you type a word, phrase, or question to quickly access Help information.

aspect ratio The width-to-height ratio of an image.

attribute A property that controls the use of a file or folder. See *archive* and *read-only*.

automatic page break Break inserted automatically by Word where one page ends and another begins.

B

bold A thick, heavy effect applied to text for emphasis.

bookmark (1) A specified location in text marked for quick navigation to it. (2) A tool used with Netscape's browser to provide a shortcut to the location of a specific file, folder, or Web site so a user can return to it later without typing the address. See also *favorites*.

booting the system Another expression for starting up which the computer often accomplishes by loading a small program which then reads a larger program into memory. Also called *system boot*.

border An edging, such as a rule or color bar, around a paragraph, page, graphic, or table.

bottom aligned Page alignment in which text is even with the bottom margin regardless of the amount of text on the page.

browser A software package that lets the user access and navigate the major components of the Internet, such as the World Wide Web, e-mail, and so on. Also called *Web browser*.

bullet A character, typographical symbol, or graphic used as a special effect.

button A box labeled with words or pictures that you can click to select a setting or put a command into effect.

C

CD drive A specialized type of disk drive which enables a computer to read data from a compact disc. See also *compact disk read-only memory*.

cell A box formed by the intersection of a column and a row. Each cell can hold a single value or text entry.

cell alignment The combined vertical and horizontal placement of text in cells; for example, Top Left, Center, or Bottom Right.

center aligned Paragraph alignment in which each line of text (or an image) is midway between the left and right margins. Also, page alignment in which text or an image is midway between the top and bottom margins.

character effects Special effects (for example, shadow, subscript, superscript, or small caps) you can add to selected text.

character spacing The amount of space between characters.

character style Formatting style (for example, strong or emphasis) that affects selected text such as the font and size of text or bold and italic formats.

chart A picture that displays data in the form of circles, lines, bars, or other shapes.

check box A square box in a dialog box that contains a check mark ✓ when an option is selected or appears empty when the option is not selected.

choose See *select*.

clear To designate (typically by clicking an item with the mouse) which option will be disabled or turned off. Formerly called *deselect*. Compare with *select*.

click The technique of quickly pressing and releasing the left button on a mouse or trackball. See also *double-click* and *right-click*.

Click and Type Word feature that allows the user to double-click a document anywhere and then insert text or an image where the insertion point is located.

clip See *clip art*.

clip art A collection of ready-to-use graphic images that you can insert into a document and then resize, move, and modify as desired. Also called *clips*.

Clipboard An area in memory used by all Windows applications for temporarily storing text or graphics to be placed in a new location. Also a task pane (in Word, Excel, and PowerPoint) for controlling and clearing items from Clipboard memory.

Clip Organizer A folder containing clip art that can be inserted into a document. See also *clip art*.

close To remove a file, a dialog box, or a window from the screen or desktop and the computer's memory.

collapsed A state of an item in which details or subordinate items are hidden from view. A plus sign (+) in the box to the left of the item indicates the item is collapsed. Compare with *expanded*.

command An instruction that you issue to a computer by clicking a menu option, clicking a button, or pressing a combination of keys on the keyboard.

command buttons Small, labeled rectangles in a dialog box and window that perform actions such as accepting or canceling changes.

compact disc read-only memory (CD-ROM) The most common type of optical storage medium. On a CD-ROM, data is written in a series of lands and pits on the surface of a compact disc (CD), which can be read by a laser in a CD drive. A standard CD stores approximately 650 MB (about 450 times as much as a diskette), but data on a CD-ROM cannot be altered. See also *CD drive*.

Compare and Merge Word feature that allows you to merge two or more documents together and compare the changes made in each document.

Contents One of the three tabs in the expanded Help window, this tool provides a list of general Help topics that is useful if you don't know the name of a feature. See also *Answer Wizard* and *Index*.

context-sensitive Help Tips and Help topics related specifically to tasks underway in the application window.

contrast The difference in brightness between dark and light areas of a page.

copy To place a copy of text or graphics on the Clipboard.

crop To trim an image.

customize (1) To make or alter to individual or personal specifications; (2) to add a button, menu, or toolbar to an application window because it is used frequently. Also called *personalize*.

cut To remove text or a graphic and to place it on the Clipboard.

D

data Raw facts, numbers, letters, or symbols that the computer processes into meaningful information.

data source The origin of the personalized information in the Mail Merge process.

datasheet A grid of columns and rows used for entering, viewing, and editing data to create charts or graphs.

default A preset value or setting that an application program uses automatically unless you specify a different value or setting.

delete To remove text or graphics from a file.

descending sort A sort that arranges letters from Z to A, numbers from largest to smallest, and dates from most recent to the earliest. Also called *descending*. See also *sort*. Compare with *ascending sort*.

deselect See *clear*.

desktop (1) The working area of the screen that displays many Windows tools and is the background for computer work; (2) the most common PC model, sized to fit on a desk, with separate units for the CPU and the monitor.

developmental portfolio An organized collection of your work that demonstrates your progress toward a goal over a period of time. Developmental portfolios help you become more aware of your strengths and weaknesses and assist you in improving your abilities. See also *portfolio* and *representational portfolio.*

dialog box A rectangle containing a set of options that appears when the application requires more information from the user to perform a requested operation.

Dictation mode Speech recognition feature that translates spoken words into text. See also *Voice Command mode.*

disk drive A storage device that reads data from and writes to disks.

docked toolbar A toolbar that is attached to the edge of the application window. Compare with *floating toolbar.*

document A computer file consisting of a compilation of one or more kinds of data; a file that stores the work you have created with the computer. File types include documents, worksheets, presentations, databases, graphic files, HTML files, and so on. A file, which a user can open and use, is different from a program file, which is required by a software program to operate. Also called *file.*

document window A rectangle within an application window for viewing and working on a file. See also *application window.*

double-click The technique of rapidly pressing and releasing the left button on a mouse or trackball twice when the pointer is pointing to an object. See also *click* and *right-click.*

drag To move an object on screen by pointing to the object, pressing and holding the mouse button, moving the mouse to a new location, and then releasing the mouse button. Also called *drag-and-drop.*

drag-and-drop See *drag.*

drawing canvas An area that contains one or more shapes or objects and that separates the objects from the rest of the document.

drop-down list A list of options displayed when you click a triangle button.

E

ellipsis A series of three dots that indicates a dialog box will display when you click this option.

e-mail The exchange of messages and computer files through the Internet and other electronic data networks; electronic mail.

embed To paste text or an object from the Clipboard.

end mark The short horizontal line within a document that moves downward each time you begin a new line.

endnote Supporting or additional information that appears on a separate page at the end of a document. Compare with *footnote.*

expanded A state of an item in which details or subordinate items are visible. A minus sign (−) in the box to the left of the item indicates the item is expanded. Compare with *collapsed.*

expanded menu A list of all commands available on a menu that displays when a user clicks the arrows at the bottom of a short menu. Compare with *short menu.*

extension A one-to-three character file name component at the end of a file name that an operating system uses to identify the type of data stored in the file.

F

favorites Tool used with Microsoft's browser to provide a shortcut to the location of a specific file, folder, or Web site so a user can return to it later without typing the address. See also *bookmark.*

field In Word, a category of information, such as a name or address, used in the Mail Merge process.

field code An underlying hidden code inserted into a document (for example, in a date/time format). These codes may be edited in the Field dialog box to create custom formats.

file A named, ordered collection of information stored on a disk. See also *document* and *application program.*

file format The patterns and standards that a program uses to store data on a disk. Also called *file type.*

file name The characters used to identify a file, limited to 215 characters in Windows 2000.

file type See *file format.*

fill color A color used to fill the interior of an enclosed space, such as a cell in a table.

first-line indentation The conventional paragraph indentation style in which the first line is indented from the left margin.

floating toolbar A toolbar that is not attached to the edge of the application window. Compare with *docked toolbar.*

folder A named location on a removable or nonremovable disk for storing and organizing files, folders, and programs. See also *subfolder.*

font The design of a set of characters. Also called *typeface.*

font size The size of text characters, measured in points. Also called *point size*.

footer Information that appears at the bottom of each printed page.

footnote Supporting or additional information that appears at the bottom of a page. Compare with *endnote*.

format A conventional arrangement of text on a page; also, the act of arranging and enhancing text (aligning, indenting, spacing, and so on).

formatting Changing the alignment, indentations, line spacing, margins, and/or paragraph spacing of text.

frames Panels in the window of a Web page that are separated by borders or scroll bars. Frames can be scrolled or resized without affecting other frames in the window.

frames page A Web page consisting of two or more frames that divides the browser window into different areas or frames.

G

glossary term A word or phrase appearing in colored text on a Help screen that you can click to display or hide the definition of the word or phrase.

graph See *chart*.

graphic A picture, drawing, photograph, or WordArt that can be inserted into a file. Also called *image* and *object*.

H

handles Squares or circles that surround an object or placeholder in a document and allow you to move or resize it. Also called *selection handles* or *sizing handles*. See also *move handle* and *resize handle*.

hanging indentation A paragraph indentation style in which the first line of text is flush with the left margin and succeeding lines are indented.

hard return Pressing the Enter key to end a short line of text and force the insertion point to the next line.

header Text that appears at the top of each printed page.

Help An electronic manual that provides assistance with the features and operations of an application program (for example, Word, PowerPoint, or Access). Also called *online Help system*.

highlight An enhancing Word tool that allows you to place color over text to appear much like a highlighter. Can be used to emphasize important text or to mark text to be reviewed.

home page The main page of a Web site which usually includes links to other Web pages at that site. Also called *start page*.

horizontal alignment The arrangement of text in relation to the left and right margins.

horizontal scroll bar A rectangular bar that appears along the bottom side of a window or dialog box that is too narrow to display all of its contents; clicking or dragging in the scroll bar brings additional contents into view and allows the user to scroll information from side to side. Compare with *vertical scroll bar*.

hyperlink Text or a graphic inserted in a Help frame, a file, or a Web page that links to additional related information, another frame, a file, an Internet address, a page on the World Wide Web, or an HTML page on an intranet. Also called *link* or *jump*.

Hypertext Markup Language (HTML) The language that serves as the basis for Web pages and the World Wide Web.

Hypertext Transfer Protocol (HTTP) The set of rules that defines the way hypertext links display Web pages. HTTP allows a browser and Web server to communicate and allows the exchange of all data on the Web.

I

I-beam pointer Pointer in the shape of the capital letter "I" when moved over text.

icon A small image that represents a device, program, file, or folder.

image See *graphic*.

import To insert or add into a file; for example, inserting a graphic file into a document.

indentation Distance of text from the left or right page margins.

Index One of the three tabs in the expanded Help window, this tool allows you to search an alphabetical listing of Help topics. See also *Answer Wizard* and *Contents*.

Insert mode Mode in which typed text is inserted into existing text, pushing the characters after it to the right. See also *Overtype mode*.

insertion point The blinking, vertical bar within a document that indicates where text will appear when typing begins.

Internet A worldwide system of interconnected computer networks allowing users to exchange digital information in the form of text, graphics, and other media.

Internet Service Providers (ISPs) Companies that provide Internet access to users for a monthly or an annual fee.

intranet A network within an organization allowing users to exchange messages and data with other users in the organization. Intranets are configured to look and function like the World Wide Web, enabling users to interact with the network by using a Web browser.

italic Thin, right-slanted effect applied to text for emphasis.

J

joystick An input device used to control the on-screen pointer; a small joystick is often found in the middle of the keyboard on a laptop computer.

jump Also called *link*. See *hyperlink*.

justified Paragraph alignment in which both the left and right edges of text are perfectly even. Also, page alignment in which paragraphs are distributed among the top, middle, and bottom sections of a page.

K

keyword A word or phrase that defines or narrows the topic for which you are searching in Help or on the World Wide Web.

L

language bar A toolbar that appears in the upper-right corner of the screen in Office XP programs, the language bar is used to activate handwriting and speech recognition programs for data input.

landscape orientation Layout that prints data across the wider dimension of the page (for example the 11-inch dimension on 8.5 by 11-inch paper). Compare with *portrait orientation*.

launch To enter a command that runs an application program.

layout The arrangement and spacing of text and graphics on a page.

left aligned Paragraph alignment in which text is perfectly even at the left margin; the standard (default) paragraph alignment.

line spacing The amount of white space between text lines.

link Also called *jump*. See *hyperlink*.

list style Formatting style that applies similar alignment, numbering, or bullet characters and fonts to lists of text.

log on To type a user name and a password when starting up a computer. See also *password* and *user name*.

M

main document The document you want to personalize in a Mail Merge operation in which you place the necessary fields such as a name or address.

manual page break Forced page break you can insert in a document.

margins Blank areas bordering text on a page.

maximize A Windows sizing feature in which an open window is enlarged to fill the screen; also, the name of the button which performs this function. Compare with *minimize*.

Media Gallery A Microsoft Office folder that contains professionally designed images (pictures, photographs, sound, and video clips) from which you can choose to complement many different subjects.

menu A list of commands or options displayed in an application window from which you can choose.

menu bar An area below the title bar of all application windows containing menu names that, when clicked, display a list of commands.

merging The process of making two or more cells in a table into one cell.

minimize A Windows sizing feature which reduces an open window to a button on the taskbar; also, the name of the button which performs this function. Compare with *maximize*.

mouse A hand-held, button-activated input device that when rolled along a flat surface directs an indicator to move correspondingly around a computer screen. Allows the operator to move the indicator freely to select operations or to manipulate data or graphics.

mouse pointer See *pointer*.

move handle A square containing a four-way arrow (at the top-left corner of a table) used to drag an object.

N

navigate To move about on the Windows desktop or in an application window in a planned or preset course.

network A group of connected computers that permits the transfer of data and programs between users.

newsletter columns Side-by-side column layout in which one column fills with text before text flows into the next column.

Normal style The default paragraph style in Word.

object An element in a document, a chart, or a worksheet that you can manipulate independently, such as clip art, photos, sound files, or video clips. See also *graphic*.

Office Assistant An animated character that can answer specific questions, offer tips, and provide help with the program's features.

Office Clipboard See *Clipboard*.

online Help system See *Help*.

open (1) To copy a file from disk into the computer memory and display it on screen; (2) to start an application program; (3) to access the contents of an icon in a window.

operating system A collection of programs that allows you to work with a computer by managing the flow of data between input devices, the computer's memory, storage devices, and output devices. Also called *operating system software*.

option button A small circle filled with a solid dot when selected; you can select only one in a set of option buttons at one time. Formerly called *radio button*.

organization chart A diagram that depicts the structure of an organization, such as the hierarchy of managers and employees. In an organization chart, each worker's position is represented by a box; the relationships between positions are indicated by the connections between the boxes.

orientation Position of text and/or graphics on a printed page. See also *landscape orientation* and *portrait orientation*.

orphan The first line of a paragraph printed by itself at the bottom of a page.

Overtype mode Mode in which text replaces existing text as it is typed. See also *Insert mode*.

page (1) An area equivalent to dimensions and text capacity of standard-sized paper (8.5″ x 11″); (2) another name for *Web page*.

page break The point at which a page ends and another begins. Can be inserted automatically or manually.

pane A bordered area within a window.

paragraph mark In Word, an on-screen symbol (¶) marking the end of a paragraph. Also a proofreading symbol indicating the location to begin a new paragraph.

paragraph spacing The amount of white space above and below paragraphs; measured in points.

paragraph style Formatting style that controls all aspects of a paragraph's appearance, such as text alignment, tab stops, line spacing, and so on.

password A string of characters known only to the user which the user must enter before accessing a computer system. See also *log on* and *user name*.

paste To insert cut or copied text or a graphic from the Clipboard.

path The sequence of disk, folder, and subfolders that leads from the disk drive to the location of a particular folder or file.

personalize See *customize*.

point A unit of measure (1/72 of an inch) used for text and white space. Twelve points equal a *pica* which is approximately 1/6 of an inch.

point size See *font size*.

pointer An arrow or other on-screen image that moves in relation to the movement of a mouse or trackball. Also called *mouse pointer*.

pointing Moving the pointer to position it over an on-screen object.

portfolio An organized collection of your work that demonstrates skills and knowledge acquired from one or more courses. The materials included in a portfolio pertain to a specific educational or career goal. See also *developmental portfolio* and *representational portfolio*.

portrait orientation Layout that prints data across the shorter dimension of the page (for example, the 8.5-inch dimension on 8.5 by 11-inch paper). Portrait is the default orientation.

Power On Self Test (POST) A program that checks a computer system's memory, keyboard, display, and disk drives.

print preview An accurate image of the printed output displayed on the screen. Print preview lets you view exactly what you will be printing before you send the output to the printer.

printout A paper copy of your document.

program Instructions written in programming code that direct the computer to execute certain functions based on additional user input. See also *application program*.

publish To place a Web page or Web site on a Web server to make it available to others through the World Wide Web or an intranet.

R

random access memory (RAM) A computer's volatile or temporary memory which exists as chips on the motherboard near the CPU. RAM stores data and programs while they are being used and requires a power source to maintain its integrity.

read-only (attribute) A property setting that lets users view and use an object, such as a file, but not modify or delete it. Compare with *archive*. See also *attribute*.

read-only memory (ROM) A permanent, or non-volatile, memory chip used to store instructions and data, including the computer's startup instructions. ROM's contents cannot be altered.

Redo A command that reverses the effect of the previous Undo command.

representational portfolio An organized collection of your work that displays a variety of your best work. You can present a representational portfolio as evidence of your skills and knowledge. See also *developmental portfolio* and *portfolio*.

resize To change the height and/or width of a graphic.

resize handle A square at each corner and along the sides of a selected clip or object (or a square in the lower-left corner of a table) that may be used for expanding or contracting the object (or table). See also *handles* and *move handle*.

Restore Down To return a maximized window to its previous size; also the name of the button that performs this function.

right aligned Text alignment in which all lines are flush with the right margin.

right-click The technique of quickly pressing and releasing the right button on a mouse or trackball. See also *click* and *double-click*.

ruler A display of numbered tick marks and indent markers that indicate measurements across a document. The ruler is used to format paragraphs and to position objects.

S

sans serif A font without serifs (for example, Arial). See also *serif*.

save To transfer a file from computer memory to a storage disk (for example, a removable disk or a hard disk).

ScreenTip A note that appears on the screen to provide information about a toolbar button or other window element, a comment, a footnote or endnote, or a date or AutoText entry.

scroll arrows Buttons at each end of a scroll bar that let you scroll information in small increments when clicked—for example, when scrolling text line by line.

scroll bar A rectangular bar that appears along the right or bottom side of a window or dialog box when not all the contents are visible; used to bring hidden contents into view. See also *horizontal scroll bar* and *vertical scroll bar*.

scroll box A rectangle in a scroll bar that you can drag to display information; its location represents the location of the visible information in relation to the entire contents of the window or dialog box.

scrolling Using a scroll bar, scroll box, or scroll arrows to move around in a window or in a dialog box.

search engine An Internet tool that allows a user to search for information on a particular topic. See also *search page*.

search page The Web page used as a starting point for an Internet search or a Web page that uses a search engine or subject directories to hunt for information on the Web. See also *search engine*.

section break In Word, a way to subdivide a document (next page break) or page (continuous break) so that each defined section may have distinctive formatting.

select (1) To designate or highlight (typically by clicking an item with the mouse) where the next action will take place, which command will be executed next, or which option will be put into effect; (2) to extract specified subsets of data based on criteria that you define. Also called *choose*. Compare with *clear*.

selection bar The invisible column between the left edge of the Word document window and left margin of the page. Responds to the pointer by selecting the line of text.

selection handles Black boxes that surround a selected area, such as a chart, a portion of a chart, or an object. You can drag a selection handle to resize the selected area. Also called *handles*.

serif Finishing strokes on the characters of some fonts (for example, Times New Roman) that form a fine line.

shading Color or gradations of gray applied to cells, paragraphs, and pages, often in combination with a border.

short menu A list of the most basic commands that appears when you click a menu name on the menu bar. Compare with *expanded menu*.

shortcut menu A context-sensitive menu that appears when you right-click certain screen elements.

size (1) To change the dimensions of a window or dialog box so that its contents remain visible, but the window occupies only a portion of the desktop; (2) to change the dimensions of an object.

smart tags An icon embedded within data that leads to various options.

software A collective term for programs or instructions that are stored in electronic format and tell the computer what to do. See *application program*.

sort To rearrange records, text, or table data into alphabetical, numerical, or chronological order. See *descending sort* and *ascending sort*.

start page See *home page*.

status bar A bar at the bottom of the application window that indicates information about a selected command, an operation in progress, or other information about the program.

style A named set of character and paragraph attributes.

subfolder A folder nested within another folder. See also *folder*.

submenu A second list of commands or options indicated by an arrow on an initial menu.

system boot See *booting the system*.

system software A computer program that controls the system hardware and interacts with application software; includes the operating system and the network operating system.

T

tab A control at the top of some dialog boxes and windows that displays different screens within the dialog box or window.

tab stop A preset (default) or user-set position on the horizontal ruler that defines the beginning of text columns and the size of paragraph indentations.

table of contents Chapter and heading listings usually with their corresponding page numbers. Also called *TOC*.

table style Formatting style that provides a consistent look to borders, shading, alignment, and fonts in tables.

taskbar An area on the Windows 2000 desktop that displays a button for the Start menu, icons for commonly used Windows 2000 features, a button for each application running, and a button for the clock.

task pane A window within an Office XP application that provides quick access to commonly used commands and features while you are still working on a file.

template Master copy of a type of document. A model document that includes standard and variable text and formatting and may include graphics.

text box (1) In Office XP applications, a box used to hold text (or a graphic). (2) In Windows 2000, a rectangular control that displays the name or value of a current setting and in which you can type a different name or value to change the setting.

theme A set of unified design elements and color schemes for enhancing documents, including Web pages.

Thesaurus A Word reference tool containing synonyms and antonyms.

Times New Roman The standard or default font in Word 2000 for paragraph copy (a serif font).

title bar A bar at the top of the window that displays the name of the application, file, or device that the window represents.

toggle key A command or an option that you can turn on and off by repeatedly clicking the command or option.

toolbar A row of buttons representing frequently used commands that is used to execute commands quickly. Toolbars can also contain menus. See also *button*.

top aligned Page alignment in which text is even with the top margin regardless of the amount of text on the page. The default vertical alignment in Word.

touch-sensitive pad An input device used to control the on-screen pointer by pressing a flat surface with a finger; usually found on laptop computers.

Track Changes Word feature that allows you to track all edits made and comments inserted into a document.

trackball An input device that functions like an upside-down mouse, containing a ball that is rolled by the thumb or fingers to move the on-screen pointer; used frequently with laptop computers and video games.

triangle button A button in the shape of a small downward-pointing triangle which displays a menu of options when clicked.

U

underline A line under text characters that is used for emphasis.

Undo A command that restores your file to the condition it was in before the previous action.

Uniform Resource Locator (URL) The address of a Web site; can be made up of letters, numbers, and special symbols that are understood by the Internet.

unnamed file A new file before it is saved. The file name is represented by *Document#* in Word.

user The person who inputs and analyzes data using a computer.

user name A name by which you are identified on a computer. You enter a user name as part of the log-on procedure. See also *log on* and *password*.

V

variable information n a Word template, placeholder text that you replace with your own information.

vertical alignment The arrangement of text in relation to the top and bottom margins.

vertical scroll bar A rectangular bar that appears along the right side of a window or dialog box that is too short to display all of its contents. Clicking or dragging in the scroll bar brings additional contents into view and allows the user to scroll information from beginning to end. Compare with *horizontal scroll bar*.

Voice Command mode Speech recognition feature that allows you to control menu functions through voice commands. See also *Dictation mode*.

W

Web See *World Wide Web (WWW)*.

Web browser See *browser*.

Web page A parcel of information located on the World Wide Web that may contain text, graphics, animation, sound, and video. The terms *Web page* and *Web site* are often used interchangeably. Also called *page*. See also *Web site*.

Web server A computer that publishes Web pages on the Internet so others can view them. The Web server accepts requests from browsers and returns appropriate HTML documents. A Web server has a continuous connection to the Internet or an intranet.

Web site Specific location on the World Wide Web accessible by means of a unique address or URL. See also *Uniform Resource Locator* and *Web page*.

wheel On a mouse, a button in the shape of a wheel between the left and right buttons; used for scrolling to view text above or below the information on the screen.

widow The last line of a paragraph printed by itself at the top of a page.

window A rectangular area that displays information, such as the content of a file or the controls of an application; you can open, close, move, size, maximize, and minimize a window.

window borders The edges of a window. Frequently, you can drag the borders to resize a window.

window corners The point at which two window borders meet. Dragging the corner lets you change the height and width of a window simultaneously.

wizard A tool that helps create a document or perform some other type of task by offering step-by-step content and organization choices.

word processing program Computer program for creating word-based documents that are changed and stored easily.

word wrap Word processing feature that automatically moves the insertion point to the next line as you type when text reaches the right margin.

WordArt Decorative text that you can stretch, skew, or rotate to fit a particular shape. See also *graphic*.

World Wide Web (WWW) An Internet service that allows users to view documents containing hyperlinks to other documents anywhere on the Internet. The graphical documents are controlled by companies, organizations, and individuals with a special interest to share. Also called the *Web*.

wrapping style In Word, the way in which lines of text break in relation to an object on the same page.

WYSIWYG An acronym for *What you see is what you get*, a GUI characteristic in which documents appear on screen much as they will appear on a printed page or on a Web page.

INDEX

WORD 2002

WORD 2002

WORD 2002

Z

WORD 2002